This radical and trail-blazing  minded scientists and academics who seek an expansion of our understanding of consciousness and are dissatisfied with the limitations and restrictions imposed by a materialist mindset in academia. The primacy of consciousness rather than of matter provides a fresh philosophical point of departure that enables us to explain so-called anomalous experiences in a coherent manner rather than having to explain them away because they are inconsistent with the assumption that the brain gives rise to consciousness. The authors draw on both personal and professional experience, building bridges between science, philosophy and spirituality, in first- and third-person perspectives.

David Lorimer
Programme Director
The Scientific and Medical Network
Editor, Paradigm Explorer

A provocative discussion by many of the leading scholarly proponents of the view that consciousness extends in the universe in ways typically dismissed by most scientists. Although skeptics can reasonably disagree with the perspectives offered here, they should be cautious in doing so without first familiarizing themselves with the range of evidence presented.

Jonathan Schooler
Professor,
Department of Psychological and Brain Sciences
University of California, Santa Barbara

These essays, representing a range of disciplines and points of view, by authors whose academic bona fides confirm that they are "real scientists" not so easily dismissed by materialist skeptics, set out the cogent arguments offering a road map toward the remarkable possibilities inherent in non-materialist views, and suggest where they may take us in the coming decades.

Neil Theise, MD
Professor of Pathology
New York University Grossman School of Medicine

IS CONSCIOUSNESS PRIMARY?

*Perspectives from Founding Members of
the Academy for the Advancement of
Postmaterialist Sciences*

*Volume I
Postmaterialist Sciences Series*

Edited by
Stephan A. Schwartz
Marjorie H. Woollacott, PhD
Gary E. Schwartz, PhD

AAPS
Press
Battle Ground, Washington

© copyright 2020 by The Academy for the Advancement of Postmaterialist Sciences

AAPS Press
P.O. Box 156
Battle Ground, WA 98604

All rights reserved. No part of this book may be reproduced or utilized in any form of by any means, electronic or mechanical, including photocopying, recording, or by any information storage and retrieval system, without permission in writing from the publisher.

L.C. Cat. No.: 1-9013070081

ISBN-13: 978-1-7354491-0-4 print edition

ISBN-13: 978-1-7354491-1-1 e-book editions

This book was typeset in Baskerville.

The cover image is the Cat's Eye Nebula (NGC 6543), as captured by the Hubble Space Telescope in 2004.

To send correspondence: info@aapsglobal.com

All matter originates and exists only by virtue of a force...
We must assume behind this force the existence of a conscious and intelligent Mind.
This Mind is the matrix of all matter.

Max Planck

Table of Contents

The Academy for the Advancement of Postmaterialist Sciences.........i

Preface to Advances in Postmaterialist Sciences Series..................iii

PART ONE
Math, Physics, and Consciousness

CHAPTER ONE 1
   How Do Scientists Change Their Minds? The Example of
   Survival of Consciousness Research, Gary E. Schwartz, PhD

CHAPTER TWO 31
   Journey to Idealism, Dean Radin, PhD

CHAPTER THREE 50
   Mathematical Unification of Space, Time, Mass, Energy &
   Consciousness, Edward R. Close, PhD

CHAPTER FOUR 112
   Bridging the Perceived Gap Between Science and Metaphysics:
   The Primacy of Consciousness and Experience, Menas C. Kafatos,
   PhD

PART TWO
Neuroscience and Consciousness

CHAPTER FIVE 157
   The Elementary Mind, Mario Beauregard, PhD

CHAPTER SIX 183
   What do Near-Death and Meditation Experiences Tell Us
   About the Primacy of Consciousness?, Marjorie Woollacott, PhD

CHAPTER SEVEN..221
A History of Postmaterialism With a Mild Warning to Not Completely Dismiss Matter, Circa 2072, Julia Mossbridge, PhD

PART THREE
Psychology, Psychiatry, and Consciousness

CHAPTER EIGHT 233
   Mind Rover: Exploration With Nonlocal Consciousness,
   Stephan A. Schwartz

CHAPTER NINE..281
   Beyond Materialism and Madness:
   A Neuropsychiatrist's Perspective on Anomalous Experiences,
   Diane Hennacy Powell, MD

CHAPTER TEN 337
   Postmaterial Medicine, Health, and Healing, Larry Dossey, MD

CHAPTER ELEVEN...384
   Supersynchronicity and Primacy of Consciousness:
   Bridging Science, Metaphysics and Spirituality, Gary E. Schwartz, PhD

CHAPTER TWELVE..434
   Scientism and Religion: Essential Science and Essential Spirituality,
   Charles T. Tart, PhD

About the Authors...456

Acknowledgments 478

Bibliography..479

Index 522

The Academy for the Advancement of Postmaterialist Sciences

The Academy for the Advancement of Postmaterialist Sciences (www.AAPSglobal.com) is a non-profit membership and education organization whose mission is to promote open-minded, rigorous and evidence-based enquiry into postmaterialist consciousness research. Our vision is to inspire scientists to investigate mind and consciousness as core elements of reality.

To achieve this paradigm changing mission, AAPS embraces the following values:

    Support rigorous applications of the scientific method
    Nurture curiosity and creativity in research
    Encourage open-minded exploratory and confirmatory investigations
    Model integrity and honesty in communication and education
    Value experimental and empirical data over dogma
    Create safe settings for sharing theories, evidence, and experiences
    Promote evidence-based innovation and positive societal change
    Expand awareness of the interconnectedness of all things
    Share postmaterialist evidence and understanding with the public

With these values in mind, AAPS is publishing an *Advances in Postmaterialist Sciences* book series to educate scientists, students, and science-minded readers about postmaterialist consciousness research and its applications. Our intent is that each volume combines rigor and creativity, expresses first person (inner experiences) as well as third person (external observations), and facilitates the betterment of humanity and the planet. Some volumes will address specific topics or themes, others will be wide ranging and diverse collections of research topics. Collectively they will help define and advance the evolution of postmaterialist theory, research and applications. The editors and contributors donate their time to APPS to prepare these volumes; all royalties are used to support AAPS' s mission to advance postmaterial consciousness science.

Preface

This volume is part of the AAPS book series Advances in Postmaterialist Sciences, created with the intent to educate scientists, students, and science-minded readers about postmaterialist consciousness research and its applications. Our intent is that each volume combines rigor and creativity, expresses first person (inner experiences) as well as third person (external observations), and facilitates the betterment of humanity and the planet. Some volumes will address specific topics or themes, others will be wide ranging and diverse collections of research topics. Collectively they will help define and advance the evolution of postmaterialist theory, research and applications.

The inspiration for the theme of this first volume, "Is Consciousness Primary?," came about at the end of the first meeting of the Founding Board of Directors of the Academy for the Advancement of Postmaterialist Science in August of 2017 in Tucson, Arizona.

During the last session of the meeting, each presenter shared the evolution of the thinking and research that led them to accept the idea that nonlocal consciousness, not physical or biological matter, is causal and fundamental. The group was intrigued by the overlapping themes they heard from their co-presenters, spread across the group's varied research in neuroscience, psychology, physics, and clinical medicine.

It was suggested that each presenter at the meeting share their research and conclusions in chapters to be published in this volume, in which they each respond to the question "Is Consciousness Primary?" through examples from their own life experience and research. We believe this volume is unique in sharing both the contributing authors' first-person experiences that transformed their understanding of the primacy of consciousness, and the research that supports this perspective.

PART ONE

MATH, PHYSICS, AND CONSCIOUSNESS

Chapter One

How Do Scientists Change Their Minds? The Example Of Survival Of Consciousness Research*

Gary E. Schwartz, PhD

Accordingly the cases in which inductions from classes of facts altogether different have thus jumped together belong only to the best established theories which the history of science contains.

William Whewell
The Philosophy of Inductive Sciences, 1840

Introduction

How do we decide when it is time to change our minds, especially concerning deeply ingrained beliefs? This is not simply an academic question; it is a personal one as well.

For example, let's consider the controversial belief (or disbelief) in survival of consciousness after physical death. This belief is

---

* *Portions of this chapter dealing with FACT were published previously in* The Beacon of Mind *(Blackie and Spencer, 2015). I include the FACT portions here because they are foundational to developing a more rigorous synergistic approach for integrating complex converging information spanning (1) theory, (2) research, (3) expert opinions, (4) personal experiences, and (5) responsible skepticism.*

strongly held by some individuals and firmly rejected by others; for the first fifty years of my life, I was in the latter camp. I was raised in an atheist reform Jewish home, and I was educated by mainstream Western materialist professors at prestigious institutions (Cornell University, BA, and Harvard University, MA, PhD). I was taught that death was "ashes to ashes, dust to dust," case closed. At that time I accepted this definitive materialist conclusion unquestionably as being (1) required by established scientific theory, and (2) verified by controlled laboratory research.

However, over the past two decades I have (1) conducted controlled laboratory research, as well as (2) witnessed or heard many replicable "anecdotes" that together have required a radical shift in my core beliefs about the continuity and essence of consciousness (reviewed in Schwartz, 2002; 2005; 2011; 2016). For example, I have examined numerous credible accounts provided by laboratory tested mediums (evidential psychics who claim to be able to communicate with the deceased) that these mediums unexpectedly experience the presence of specific deceased persons coming to them prior to the scheduled readings with the loved ones of the deceased.

During these unanticipated pre-reading communications, the seemingly motivated spirits provide highly specific information that becomes important during their subsequent readings. Moreover, they may even request that the medium bring a specific present for a loved one that proves to be highly meaningful to the recipient (e.g. Schwartz, 2002).

Let's assume that potential fraud has been ruled out (it has), and that the particular mediums and the sitters / loved ones are both credible and responsible (they are). How do we decide whether such evidence deserves the interpretation that survival of consciousness is real, and that the hypothesized deceased people are actually engaging in purposeful, intentional, and creative interactions with these mediums?

For example, consider the following specific question: how many times would you need to see accurate pre-reading evidence replicated, in how many different credible mediums, before you would believe that the mediums' conclusions of active spirit involvement were probably correct?

Or, consider the novel phenomenon where one deceased person brings another deceased person to a medium under double-blind conditions (see Schwartz, 2011; 2018). As difficult as this may be to imagine for some readers, the fact is that my colleagues and I have witnessed more than fifty verified instances of this phenomenon, including in controlled double-blinded laboratory experiments. Again, how do we decide whether such evidence deserves the interpretation that survival of consciousness is real, and that the hypothesized deceased people are actually engaging in purposeful, intentional, and collaborative interactions (1) with each other, as well as (2) with these mediums? The human capacity to form and hold beliefs is one of our greatest gifts as well as dangerous curses.

On the one hand, we can be highly creative; we can be inventive and innovative, and we can pursue visionary and even beautiful hypotheses in the face of incomplete or even contradictory information. On the other hand, we can sometimes adopt and hold erroneous and even pathological beliefs, which can foster horrific actions, both individually and collectively.

I have pondered the challenge of attempting to understand the nature of truth seeking and the process of scientific discovery, especially concerning those instances in our professional and personal lives when circumstances require that we reconsider certain key beliefs that we hold dear (e.g. Bourey & Schwartz, 2019).

This is especially the case when considering something as fundamental—and as far reaching—as the emerging shift from the philosophies of materialist to postmaterialist science (Beauregard et al., 2014). The question arises, how do we responsibly make the decision to radically change our core beliefs about the centrality of mind and consciousness in the cosmos and the nature of reality? Carl Sagan, PhD, the distinguished professor of astronomy at Cornell University and acclaimed skeptic, illustrated the challenge this way: When Kepler found his long-cherished belief [geocentric view of the universe] did not agree with the most precise observation, he accepted the uncomfortable fact. He preferred the hard truth to his dearest illusions; that is the heart of science. Sagan does not mince words here, and I appreciate his candor. I would propose that Sagan's quoting Kepler "preferring the hard truth to our dearest illusions" is not only "the heart of science"; it is also the heart of living a responsible (and compassionate) life.

The Importance of Convergence of Information

Can we derive an effective, unbiased, formal, and mutually agreed upon information processing system for reaching decisions as important as these – especially when the information is complex and converges from multiple sources? The key term here is "converges"? In the December, 2015 issue of *Scientific American*, the skeptic Michael Shermer published an article about the importance of the 'consilience of inductions' and the 'convergence of evidence' in advancing science. He wrote: *An answer may be found in what 19th-century philosopher of science William Whewell called a "consilience of inductions." For a theory to be accepted, Whewell argued, it must be based on more than one induction—or a single generalization drawn from specific facts. It must have multiple inductions that converge on one another, independently but in conjunction. 'Accordingly, the cases in which inductions from classes of facts altogether different have thus jumped together,' he wrote in his 1840 book The Philosophy of the Inductive Sciences, 'belong only to the best-established theories which the history of science contains.' Call it a 'convergence of evidence.* The controversial area addressed by Shermer was the importance of the convergence of evidence in the development of theories of apparent climate change.

The same logic can be applied to the controversial areas of

apparent survival of consciousness and the primacy of consciousness hypothesis. The approach taken in this chapter is that it is the consilience of inductions and the convergence of evidence which justifies our adopting a postmaterialist approach to understanding mind and consciousness, including survival of consciousness research and the primacy of consciousness hypothesis.

For the past twenty years, my academic research has taken me into ever more controversial areas—from the role of energy in health and healing (Schwartz, 2007), through the possibility of survival of consciousness after physical death (Schwartz, 2002, 2005, 2011a), to the existence of some sort of a universal "Guiding-Organizing-Designing (G.O.D.) Process" (Schwartz, 2006) and what Dossey, 2013 calls the "One Mind," expressing itself through the process of super synchronicities in contemporary life (Schwartz, 2014, 2015a-b; 2016a,b; 2017).

In the process of my facing the challenge of questioning—and eventually giving up—some of my own long-cherished materialist beliefs about nature and the cosmos, I ended up formalizing a five additive criteria test (FACT) for fostering the process of truth seeking and the development of accurate and responsible beliefs (Schwartz, 2015c). As you will see, FACT can be useful framework for helping us change our minds about concepts that are (1) paradigm changing and (2) fit the criteria of being revolutionary. This is especially the case as applied to the challenge of the emerging postmaterialist paradigm in science and society.

The five essential additive criteria are listed in Table I.

Criteria	Description
Criterion 1:	Reason and Scientific Theory
Criterion 2:	Scientific Evidence

Table I: The five additive criteria comprising FACT

Is Consciousness Primary?

Criteria	Description
Criterion 3:	Community of Credible and Trustworthy Believers
Criterion 4:	Direct Personal Experiences
Criterion 5:	Responsible Consideration of Skepticism about Criteria 1-4

Though FACT can become quite complex, the framework can also be taught in a relatively simple fashion. Criteria 1-5 in FACT can be associated with our five fingers, as shown in Figure I below. I use this figure with students and lay persons. I will first provide a brief overview to FACT, followed by a demonstration of how FACT can be applied to understanding one of humanity's most challenging and extraordinary ideas: FACT, followed by a demonstration of how FACT can be applied to understanding one of humanity's most challenging and extraordinary ideas: the belief that mind is not only separate from the brain and survives physical death, but that it may be more primary than matter itself (e.g. termed a Type III postmaterialist theory in Schwartz, 2016c, described below).

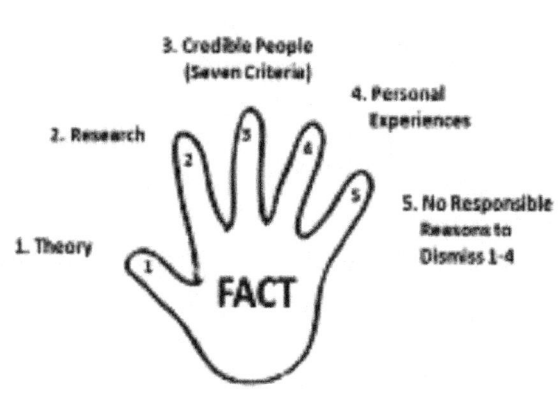

What is FACT?

FACT integrates five essential criteria for forming and holding accurate and responsible beliefs. What is novel about FACT are not the individual criteria themselves, but rather their additive and integrative cohesion as a whole – i.e. their essential convergence.

Note that convergence here refers not only to convergence of scientific evidence per se (Category 2), but the additional convergence of logic and theory (Category 1), community of responsible believers (Category 3), direct personal experiences (Category 4), and responsible skeptical review (Category 5). We are speaking about the convergence of information both within and across domains of knowledge.

In my numerous queries of both creative scientists and conservative skeptics alike, the consensus is that (1) *each* of these five criteria is fundamental for their synergistic convergence, and (2)*each* factor contributes to the process of valid and responsible truth seeking. Moreover, thus far no one has proposed that a sixth criterion needs to be added to the framework to justify it being a valid and responsible system for fostering accurate understanding.

What is innovative about FACT are its implications for formalizing the process of our coming to believe something—especially something that is new and challenging—*when all five criteria have been met and synergistically converge.* This is the key take home message of the chapter.

Here is the logical sequence of the FACT convergence of information:

IF:

Logic and scientific theory both support a given belief (Criterion 1),

AND, IF

Extensive scientific evidence confirms a given belief (Criterion 2),

AND, IF

There exists a community of highly credible and trustworthy people who hold the belief is true (Criterion 3),

AND, IF

You have had direct personal experience which supports the belief (Criterion 4),

AND, IF

There are *no* good, reasonable, and responsible reasons for rejecting (i.e. *no* good reasons to be skeptical) of Criteria 1-4 (Criterion 5),

THEN,

It is prudent and responsible to adopt this new belief as probably true, and to do so with honesty and integrity.

In other words, when all five criteria have been simultaneously met / converge concerning a new belief, it follows that we should feel compelled to rationally accept this belief as being probably accurate and most likely true—even if this means that we are "forced" to give up, as Sagan put it, a "long-cherished belief."

Conversely, if we *reject* a new belief when all five criteria have been met / converge, in order for us to hold onto a long-cherished belief, it follows that this will reflect a state of dishonesty and disinformation. In extreme instances this state can have disastrous consequences for our wellbeing and evolution.

The question arises: must all five criteria be met / converge in order for us to hold an accurate and responsible belief?

My understanding is that they do not. It can be rationally argued that if Criteria 1 + 2 + 3 + 5 have been clearly met, but Criteria 4 (direct personal experience) has not (or cannot) be met, then the combination of the four criteria which have been met is often sufficient to justify our accepting a given belief as probably being true (i.e. accurate). For example, most of us alive today believe that twelve astronauts have actually set foot on the moon, even though we have not done so ourselves (and likely never will).

However, in those special instances where all five criteria have been met/converge, logic requires (i.e. it becomes essential) that we accept those beliefs as likely being true—whether we happen to prefer those beliefs or not.

This is ultimately how science advances, increasing our understanding and evolving our beliefs accordingly.

Now that you have been introduced to the big picture of FACT, I will systematically take you through each of the five criteria illustrating how collectively they provide a useful structure for our deciding to adopt and hold a novel and challenging belief—in this instance, the belief in the separation of mind and matter, and probably the primacy of mind over matter as well.

But first, let us briefly consider a heuristic metaphor about seeing the big picture, and examine the distinction between what can be termed "ostrich" science versus "eagle" science.

Ostrich versus Eagle Science: A Call for Integrative Big Picture Thinking

The ostrich and the eagle are both magnificent birds. Each is large and powerful, and each has unique attributes and skills. It is possible to contrast these two species in terms of their cognitive experiences, and by extension, their thinking styles. The differences are both illuminating and enlightening.

Metaphorically, we often say that the ostrich "puts its head in the sand." The implication is that when ostriches are frightened or do not wish to confront challenging situations, they avoid seeing what is unfolding by hiding their heads in the ground. The premise is that ostriches often confront challenges via avoidance, if not denial.

Despite these widely held beliefs about ostriches, the facts do not support them. Apparently, ostriches have been observed putting their heads in the sand primarily when they are caring for their eggs or baby chicks, and secondarily when they are eating. Hence their behavior is not avoidant; rather, it is nurturing. Despite this meaningful discrepancy with the metaphor, the fact remains that ostriches do not fly and their perceptions are limited accordingly. Ostriches are lucky if they can see six feet off the ground (obviously they can look up). Their perception experience is limited to a relatively micro, "flat earth view" of reality.

The ostrich's limited experience stands in stark contrast to the eagle's experiences. The eagle is known to be among the highest-flying birds; they have been observed flying 10,000 to 15,000 feet in the air. As a result, eagles naturally see the "big picture"—they have an extensive and expansive "macro-view" of their surroundings.

Moreover, besides seeing the big picture, eagles can see small details as well. The eagle has a so-called "eagle's eye" that can see a tiny rabbit on the ground while it is soaring thousands of feet in the sky.

In sum, eagles can see both the "whole" and the "parts." Moreover, we can say that eagles can see both the whole and the "holes" (i.e. see what is missing).

Extending the ostrich-eagle metaphor to the philosophy of science, we can say that conventional reductionist and materialist science (i.e. bottoms-up science) encourages ostrich-like vision, whereas postmaterialist science (i.e. top-down science) encourages eagle-like vision.

Although we will discuss the FACT process from a simple bottoms-up, ostrich's point of view, the deeper value of FACT is its emphasis on a top-down, eagle's point of view. This enables us to see and understand the big picture (the whole) of adopting and holding responsible beliefs. Together, this enables us to honor both ostrich and eagle cognition.

The First Criterion: Reason and Theory

The first criterion refers to reason and theory. Does a theory, or a system of logic, exist which supports the possibility that a given belief may be valid?

Before specifically addressing the primacy of mind versus matter hypothesis, it is valuable to briefly consider three types of postmaterialist theories envisioned by a postmaterialist paradigm (Schwartz, 2016c):

Type I Postmaterialist Theories: Neo-physical theories which are derived from materialist theories, where the materialist theories are still seen as primary and are viewed as being fundamentally necessary to create "non-material" (yet physical) phenomena such as consciousness. These are a subclass of physicalist theories.

Type II Postmaterialist Theories: Postmaterialist theories of consciousness existing alongside materialist theories, where each class of theories are seen as primary and are viewed as not being derivable from (i.e. are not reducible to) the other. These are types of dualist theories as well as panpsychic theories, and

Type III Postmaterialist Theories: Where materialist theories are derived from, and are a subset of, more inclusive postmaterialist theories of consciousness; here postmaterialist theories are seen as primary and are viewed as the ultimate origin of material systems. Such theories have historically been called Idealist Theories. And recently some investigators have been considering "nondualist' theories as well (e.g., see Chapter 5 by Kafatos). The present volume focuses on the plausibility of Type III postmaterialist theories.

Understandably, Type I theories are the least controversial, and Type III theories are the most controversial. Also, understandably, different kinds of reasoning and evidence may support one or more Types of postmaterialist theories.

The materialist reader may wonder whether established findings from neuroscience even *allow* for a postmaterialist paradigm. It turns out that the answer is a definitive yes. A seminal illustration concerns the relationship between mind and matter, and whether consciousness requires a brain.

Though relatively few biomedical scientists and neuroscientists recognize this important fact, it turns out that the three core methods used by neuroscience to come to the conclusion that the brain "creates consciousness" are the *identical core methods used by electrical engineers and computer scientists* to come to the conclusion that radios, televisions, and smart phones are "antennae/receivers/ transceivers" for external signals. The logic is explained in Schwartz (2012).

	Methods in Neuroscience	Methods in Electrical Engineering
Type I	Correlation	Correlation
Type II	Stimulation	Stimulation
Type III	Ablation	Ablation
Conclusion	The brain "creates" Consciousness; it is not a "transceiver" for the Information (i.e. it does not receive it from an External Mind)	The television is a "transceiver" for Information; it does not "create" the programming (i.e. instead it receives the content from external sources)

Table II: The identical methods used in neuroscience (left) and electrical engineering (right)

As Table II indicates, there are three types of experimental evidence that together "seem" to point to the conclusion that consciousness is created by the brain. The word "seem" is put in quotes here because careful examination of the totality of evidence, when viewed from the perspective of electronics and electrical engineering, reveals how the totality of this evidence is actually *as consistent with the explanation that (1) the mind is separate from the brain as it is with the explanation that (2) the mind is created by the brain.*

Unfortunately, it is not widely appreciated by mainstream scientists that the three experimental approaches used to investigate mind–brain relationships *do not, by themselves, require a materialistic conclusion—and they are wholly consistent with a non-materialistic (postmaterialist) explanation.*

The three kinds of evidence are as follows:

Evidence from recordings: Neuroscientists record brain waves (via electroencephalograms [EEGs]) using sensitive electronic devices. For example, it is well known that occipital alpha waves decrease when people see visual objects or imagine them.

Evidence from stimulation: Various areas of the brain can be stimulated using electrodes placed inside the head or magnetic coils placed outside the head. For example, stimulation of the occipital cortex is typically associated with people experiencing visual sensations and images.

Evidence from ablation / removal: Various areas of the brain can be removed with surgical techniques (or areas can be damaged through injury or disease). For example, when areas of the occipital cortex are damaged, people and lower animals lose aspects of vision.

The generally accepted and seemingly commonsense —neuroscience interpretation of this set of findings is that visual experience is created by the brain.

However, the critical question is whether this *creation of consciousness* explanation is the *only* possible interpretation of this set of findings.

The answer is actually no. The three kinds of evidence are *also consistent* with the brain as being a *receiver of external consciousness information*.

The reasoning is straightforward and is illustrated in electronics and electrical engineering (the same logic applies to computer science). Consider the television (be it analog or digital). It is well known—and generally accepted—that televisions work as *receivers* for processing information carried by *external* electromagnetic fields oscillating in specific frequency bands. Television receivers *do not create* the visual information (i.e., they are *not the source* of the information)—they *detect* the information, *amplify* it, *process* it, and *display* it.

Moreover, today's "smart" televisions (as well as smart phones) can actually function as "transceivers," both receiving and transmitting information.

As mentioned above, it is not generally appreciated that electrical engineers conduct the same three kinds of experiments as neuroscientists do. The parallel between the brain and the television is essentially perfect.

Evidence from recordings: Electrical engineers can monitor signals inside the television set using sensitive electronic devices. For example, electrodes can be placed on particular components in circuits that correlate with the visual images seen on the screen.

Evidence from stimulation: Electrical engineers can stimulate various components of the television using electrodes placed inside the television set or magnetic coils placed outside the set. For example, particular circuits can be stimulated with specific patterns of information, and replicable patterns can be observed on the TV screen.

Evidence from ablation: Electrical engineers can remove various components from the television (or areas can be damaged or wear out). For example, key components can be removed and the visual images on the screen will disappear.

However, do these three kinds of evidence imply that the *source* or *origin* of the TV signals is *inside* the television—that is, that the television *created* the signals? The answer is obviously no. Televisions (or smart phones) require antennas (or cables) to receive signals that are external to the devices/systems.

It should be clear how this basic logic—as applied to television receivers—can equally be applied to neural network (brain) receivers. The three kinds of evidence (correlation, stimulation, and ablation) only allow us to conclude that television sets—as well as brains—play some sort of *role* in visual experience. The truth is that the three kinds of evidence, by themselves, do *not* tell us whether either television sets or brains: "self-create" the information internally—the materialist assumption, or function as complex receivers of external information—which allows for both survival of consciousness after death and a larger spiritual reality.

In other words, the three kinds of evidence, by themselves, do not speak to (and do not enable us to determine) whether the signals—the information fields—are: Coming from *inside* the system (the materialistic interpretation applied to brains), *or* coming from *outside* the system (the interpretation routinely applied to televisions).

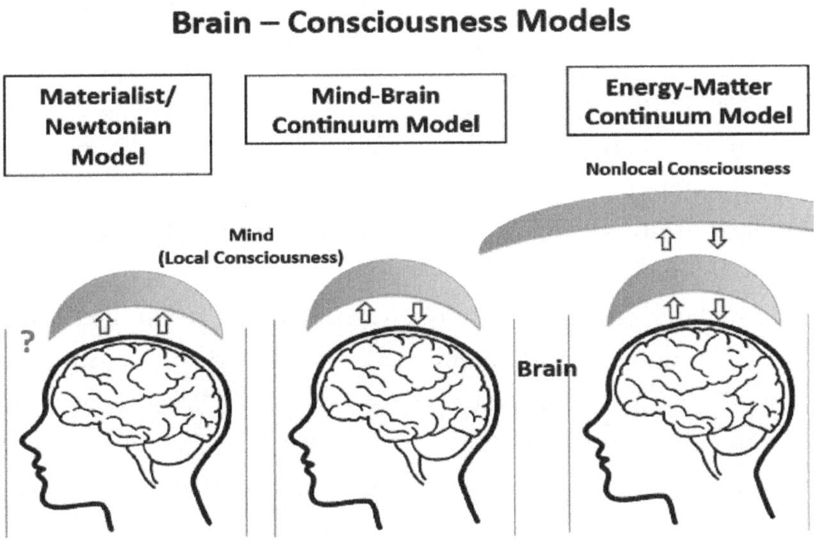

Brain – Consciousness Models

Figure 2: Three models of the relationship between brain and mind (adapted from Woollacott, 2015)

It follows that *additional kinds of experiments* are required to distinguish between the "self-creation" versus "receiver" hypotheses. Experiments on life after death with skilled research mediums (e.g. Beischel & Schwartz, 2007) provide an important fourth kind of evidence that can neither be predicted nor explained by the self-creation (i.e., materialism) hypothesis, but it can be predicted and explained by the receiver/transceiver hypothesis (explained more in the second criterion below).

It should be noted that in physics, external electromagnetic fields are not labeled as being "material" per se. These fields do not have mass (e.g., they do not have weight) and they are invisible; they are described by a set of equations that characterize an as-yet-unexplained property of the "vacuum" of space (which may be empty of "mass" but is actually full of energy and information).

A visual representation of these alternative models is depicted in Figure 2 (from Woollacott, 2015).

The Second Criterion: Scientific Evidence

Concerning the specific question of the existence of mind separate from brain, there are at least five areas of scientific research that strongly support postmaterialist theories of mind and consciousness (i.e. they are predicted by Types I, II, and/or III theories). These five areas of evidence are:

Research Area 1: There is extensive survey research concerning the frequency of different kinds of "after-death communications" (ADCs) experienced by people worldwide. Probably the most famous of these is the ADC Project (http://www.after-death.com/) of Bill and Judy Guggenheim as summarized in their 1997 book *Hello from Heaven*. The types of experiences Davids and Schwartz report in their 2016 book *An Atheist in Heaven* associated with Forrest J Ackermann are prototypic of the types of experiences reported in the ADC Project. The totality of this evidence cannot be explained (away) as due to conventional materialist mechanisms such as (1) fraud, (2) misperception (e.g. confirmation bias), and/or (3) faulty memory.

Research Area 2: There is extensive clinical research supporting the occurrence of profound spiritual experiences that people occasionally have during periods of time that they were near physical death (e.g. when their hearts have stopped beating and their brain waves have flat lined). These are called Near Death Experiences (NDEs). The father of NDE research, Raymond Moody, MD, first classified these experiences in his 1976 book *Life After Life*. One of the most comprehensive medical studies of NDEs was performed by cardiologist Dr. Pim van Lommel, as reported in his 2010 book *Consciousness Beyond Life*.

Research Area 3: There is extensive field research for validated reincarnation evidence in adults and children. The hypothesis of reincarnation requires that consciousness continues beyond physical death in order for it potentially to reincarnate. The most distinguished of this research was performed by the late Ian Stephenson, MD, and his colleagues in the Department of Psychiatry at the University of Virginia. This work has been continued by James Tucker, MD as described in his 2013 book *Return to Life*. (http://www.medicine.virginia.edu/clinical/departments/psychia-try/sections/cspp/dops/home-page)

Research Area 4: There is extensive laboratory research documenting how some mediums can obtain accurate information about people who have died. These controlled experiments rule out: (1) fraud, (2) cold reading (and other magician tricks), (3) possible rater bias (for example, people's beliefs, expectations, interpretations), and (4) potential experimenter bias as plausible explanations of the findings. I have summarized my team's research in *The Afterlife Experiments* (Schwartz, 2002), *The Truth about Medium*

(Schwartz, 2005), and *The Sacred Promise* (Schwartz, 2011). Other research teams who have independently replicated our findings include Emily Kelly and her colleagues at the University of Virginia (e.g. Kelly and Archangel, 2011), Julie Beischel and her colleagues at the Windbridge Institute (e.g. Beischel Boccuzzi, Biuso & Rock, 2015), and the late Archie Roy and his colleagues at the University of Glasgow in Scotland (Roy & Robertson, 2001).

Research Area 5: There is a growing body of both field and laboratory research documenting how contemporary electronic technology can be used to detect the presence of spirit and even serve as potential spirit communication technology. Sometimes called by the acronym ITC (or Instrumental Trans-Communication) as illustrated by the exploratory work of Mark Macy (http://www.itcbridge.com/index.html) and described in his 2001 book *Miracles in the Storm*. ITC is the least well-developed of the five areas. Nonetheless, state-of-the-art controlled research published in my laboratory clearly illustrates the promise of this research (e.g. Schwartz 2010, 2011b). Applications of these technologies are included in the Davids and Schwartz 2016 book *An Atheist in Heaven*.

Returning to the metaphor of eagle science, it takes the combination / convergence of all five of these research areas to "see the big picture" of life after death and place this grand painting on the wall of scientific understanding.

The Third Criterion: Community of Credible and Trustworthy Believers

The third criterion requires a community of credible and trustworthy people who support the possibility that a given belief is probably valid.

When it comes to novel beliefs, and especially highly controversial beliefs, discovering a community of credible and trustworthy people who have formed and adopted the belief provides additional justification for seriously considering the possibility that the belief

may be accurate and responsible. I have found that discovering such people has played an important role in my coming to accept the conclusions provided by Criteria 1 and 2. This is especially the case when the required change in belief is as fundamental and as far reaching as the shift from materialism to post-materialism.

I have developed a simple yet comprehensive set of parameters for determining whether someone fits Criterion 3. For ease of learning and remembering, I call this set of seven parameters the "Seven S's." They are:

Successful
Smart
Skeptical
Sophisticated
Savvy
Sane
Straight (as in, honest and trustworthy)

Though we could debate the precise definitions of each of these seven S's, the fact is that it is relatively easy to find individuals who clearly meet all of these seven S's:

People who are highly *successful* in their chosen professions (CEOs and executives in major companies, senior professors at major universities, directors of distinguished institutions and centers, winners of esteemed prizes and awards, etc.),

AND

They are very *smart* (they may have high IQ scores, have received high grades in college and graduate schools, are established problem solvers, etc.),

AND

They are demonstrably and genuinely *skeptical*, as in they are questioning, thoughtful, challenging of information and ideas, cautious about drawing conclusions, etc.,

AND

They show strong evidence of being *sophisticated* in complex thinking, are careful to consider multiple viewpoints and alternative sources of information and interpretation, are able to analyze and integrate divergent and even conflicting information and interpretations, etc.,

AND

They have a history of being *savvy*, as in they are experienced, knowledgeable, balanced, mature, clever, not easily fooled, etc.,

AND

They are described by their peers (as well as reliable health care professionals) as being *sane* (e.g. they do not show any evidence of neurosis, psychosis, delusions, psychopathy, personality disorder, cognitive impairments of information processing and memory, etc.),

AND, MOST IMPORTANTLY

They are *straight*, as in they are trustworthy, honest, ethical, focused on accuracy/truthfulness, humble, and aware of limitations or absence of important information or knowledge in a given circumstance, etc.

Now, when these types of "Seven S" people hold a belief in something, it is wise (i.e. rational and responsible) for us to give them the "benefit of the doubt" regarding the probable validity of the belief in question.

In the case of postmaterialist science, I have probably met over 100 "Seven S" people who have formed and now hold this core belief. They include scientists, professors, CEOs, lawyers, creative artists, physicians, and therapists. The contributors to this volume are illustrative of the qualities of Seven S people.

Note that I am not proposing that we accept Seven S peoples' beliefs about postmaterialist science without reflection, but that we give their beliefs serious consideration, and not let our "emotional doubt" get in the way. Also, I am not proposing that Criterion 3, by itself, is sufficient to justify adopting and holding a belief.

What I am saying is that when Criteria 1 and 2 have been met/ converge, the *addition* of Criterion 3 adds further reason to support the idea that adopting and holding a given belief may be accurate and responsible (i.e. remembering the "A" in FACT).

The Fourth Criterion: Direct Personal Experiences

The fourth criterion refers to direct personal experience. For many people, the "sine qua non" of adopting and holding a belief is direct personal experience. In the case of the specific question of the survival of mind separate from the brain, I have been blessed to have had a wealth of direct personal experiences whose veracity is highly justified (e.g. Schwartz, 2006; 2011; 2015 a-b; 2016).

In these instances, possible confounding factors such as misperception, confirmation bias, and self-deception have been carefully considered and justifiably and responsibly ruled out. This is especially the case because many were witnessed and confirmed by one or more Seven S persons.

My experience with potential spirit communication technology is a case in point. I shared some of my earliest experiences with a specific hypothesized spirit named Harry (herein called HH, for Hypothesized Harry) in *The Sacred Promise*. I will briefly review some of this history, and then share some of my more recent experiences with HH (reported in Davids and Schwartz, 2016).

It was a Wednesday afternoon in 2010, and I was having a private meeting with Jerry Cohen, at that time the CEO of Canyon

Ranch, about the current progress of our spirit communication technology research. I left the silicon photomultiplier system (see Schwartz, 2010) at home with the TV monitor running and informed "them," our friendly hypothesized spirit collaborators, that this was a "free play period"—where they could practice using the system in any way they wanted. These "play time" periods were made available at various times (morning, noon, and night). Though in those days I videotaped the TV monitor using time-lapse recording equipment, since the data were completely uncontrolled, I did not analyze the data.

At this meeting, I had prepared a short "show and tell" video plus a PowerPoint presentation for Jerry about the possible use of the photomultiplier system for spirit communication technology, and I briefly mentioned the possibility that HH was using the equipment. It turned that Jerry was an HH fan, and he asked the following question, which I paraphrase: "If Harry is that good, can he hit a home run? Can he make larger spikes than just 25 or 30 unit bursts?" In those days, I simply counted the number of photon bursts that were greater than 25 units.

I told Jerry that every now and again, a larger spike would be observed—50, or even 75 units large. But I had never asked "them" to try and make larger ones, or smaller ones, for that matter.

As I drove home, I recalled the movie *Field of Dreams*. I remembered the comment that a secret sitter once made about the gifted medium Mary Occhino. He said, and I paraphrase, "Mary not only hit the ball out of the park. She hit it out of New York City."

I wondered, could HH hit a home run when requested, and could he hit it out of the park, if not the city of Tucson? I happened to have a meeting at my home scheduled with a then postdoctoral research fellow, Dr. Jolie Haun, and I was ten minutes late. I raced in, and quickly looked at the TV monitor in my study. To my amazement, the sporadic photon bursts on the screen were tiny, less than one/fifth their normal size. I had never seen such tiny bursts before.

Normally the silicon photomultiplier computer program displayed 25-unit high bursts in such a way that they reached the full height of the Y-axis. Only if a 50 or 75 units spike occurred would the Y axis be adjusted, reducing the size of the 25 unit spikes accordingly. Why did the spikes now look so tiny? Had the software automatically adjusted the Y-axis scale because an anomalously large burst had appeared?

When I looked at the Y-axis, I noticed that the scale was not displaying 0 to 25; it was not displaying 0 to 50, or even 0 to 75, it was now displaying 0 to 175! In other words, the new 0 – 175-range implied that at least one photon burst had occurred that was possibly as large as 175 photons. It is important to understand that under the conditions of this research, that most of the bursts in the pitch-black chamber were just 25 units or less. A burst of 175 photons would be 700% greater than a typical burst of 25 photons.

I thought to myself "Wow . . . I need to check this out." Since Dr. Haun was not aware that I was conducting this research, and since our meeting was not about life after death or spirits, I simply noted the time. Later I would review the digital time-lapse photography and see when the super-large photon burst occurred—presuming it was a burst.

After our meeting, I replayed the time-lapse video and discovered that a 173-unit burst had actually occurred just around the time that I was driving into my garage. I wondered, could this be an intentional response by HH?

If something happens once, it could be a chance event, an artifact or accident, something unimportant. But if this phenomenon was real and was somehow attached to HH, he should theoretically be able to duplicate it.

I decided to restart the Free Play period, and carefully watched what was unfolding. The time-lapse camera was taking snapshots of the screens. As I was watching the screen, I specifically asked HH, in my mind, could he make a large spike?

What happened next I witnessed with my own two eyes. I actually saw a burst occur that was 173-units, *and it occurred shortly after I had asked HH if he could make a big one!*

In watching hundreds of hours of outputs, I rarely saw bursts above 50 – 75 units. I was now seeing a 173-unit burst. Was this just another accident? Or could it be something more? I did not know. Unfortunately, I had to give a lecture at Canyon Ranch that evening, so I left the system running in "Play Time". When I returned around 10:00 p.m., I noticed that the Y-axis was back to normal: 25 units. I was really tired, but I wanted to watch a little more.

Around 10:15, I decided to ask HH if he could make another "big one." This time I invited Rhonda to be present. *To my and Rhonda's utter amazement, another huge 173-unit burst appeared on the screen.*

One big spike occurring after Jerry had spontaneously asked about HH possibly producing home runs out of the park, and me wondering about hypothesized spirits playing baseball and a medium metaphorically hitting the ball out of New York City—yes, this could have been "accidental".

A second big spike, occurring within a minute of me asking in my head whether HH, if he was here, could he hit another home run—and we can begin to wonder if this was "too coincidental to be accidental".

However, a third big spike, again occurring within a minute of me asking in my head, in Ronda's presence, whether HH could hit the ball out of the park. Did it make sense to label this simply a third accident, or was this "the third time is the charm"? In fact, I began to wonder if HH had metaphorically hit the ball out of the city of Tucson.

As you can probably guess, it was only a matter of time before I would attempt to see if HH could learn to make spikes of different amplitudes under more controlled experimental conditions. The graph below displays the findings of an experiment where I asked

HH (1) to simply increase the number of photon bursts without trying to make a large one (called "Spirit Intention" or "SI"), (2) to actively try and make a "Big" one, and (3) to attempt to make a "Huge" one, as compared to a resting baseline trial. To my surprise and delight, HH appears to have been successful. In Figure III you can see that the largest amplitude spike during the baseline condition was 75 units (left bar). During the Spirit Intention trial, the largest amplitude spike increased slightly to 100. However, when I asked HH to try and make a "Big" one, the largest amplitude during the trial reach 152. And when I asked him to attempt to make a "Huge" one, one of the spikes reached 327 units (right bar)!

It is one thing to read about such occurrences and view the graphs of the data; it is another thing to experience them *as they occur*. Moreover, I have tried to produce such changes with my own mind, and the truth be known, using the metaphor of baseball, HH can hit the ball out of the city, and I rarely make it to first base!

Since I am not a medium, and I do not see or hear spirit under virtually all circumstances (Dr. Robert Stek once referred to me as the Helen Keller of survival of consciousness research), I still find it extraordinarily challenging to accept the obvious conclusion – that HH is not only here, but he is doing his darn best to earn Jerry's title of the photomultiplier home run king. You may be experiencing a similar challenge in accepting these data. However, the evidence is the evidence. And for the record, at the time I wrote these words, the evidence clearly indicates that HH remains at the top of his game.

However, as discussed previously, in many instances it is not possible for us to have a direct personal experience, and therefore we may not be able to include this criterion in our decision-making process.

The Fifth Criterion: Responsible Consideration of

Skepticism about Criteria 1-4

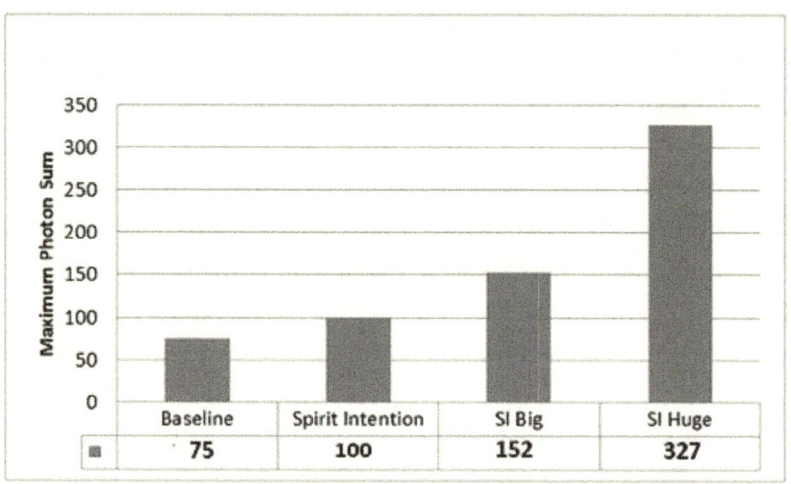

The fifth criterion refers to responsible consideration of skepticism about Criteria 1-4. Does responsible skepticism about Criteria 1-4 still support the possibility that a given belief is valid? The key word here is "responsible."

By "responsible" I mean:

honest

fair

comprehensive

unbiased

open-minded

critical

discerning

flexible

accountable

This kind of skepticism is not only valid; it is essential. It is my conviction that the process of responsibly questioning everything for the purpose of seeking truth, whatever it may be, is not only a core quality of (1) science, but of (2) personal integrity in general. True/genuine skeptics are *skeptical about everything, including the process of skepticism itself*. If they are not, then they are pseudo-skeptics.

It has been said that we should act with "moderation in everything, including moderation."†

The same can be said for skepticism, and this applies to a philosophy of being *skeptical about everything, including professional skepticism.*

The key here is discernment, i.e. knowing when to continue questioning a belief versus reaching a decision about the probable veracity of the belief.

Carl Sagan believed in responsible skepticism, and he attempted to practice it in his own life and career. Moreover, he firmly believed that "it is the tension between creativity and skepticism that has produced the stunning and unexpected findings of science"‡.

I added Criterion 5 to this evolving framework to remind me personally (and by extension, my scientist colleagues collectively) that the formal process of "taking stock" and "doing due diligence" concerning Criteria 1-4 is an essential fifth step in the truth seeking process.

Taking the time to step back and carefully re-evaluate (1) theory, (2) evidence, (3) people, and (4) experiences to ensure that they *all* pass muster increases the probability that a conclusion about a given belief is accurate and responsible.

I regularly include Criterion 5 in my research activities, and have illustrated how it can be applied to controversial topics, such as the belief in the survival of consciousness after death (discussed in detail in Davids & Schwartz, 2016).

In the process of working through Criterion 5, I regularly consider the four most extreme skeptical criticisms that speak directly to Criteria 1-4:

Criticism 1: "The professed belief is scientifically

---

†*Source unknown*

impossible." (Criterion 1)

Criticism 2: "There is no credible research for the belief, and what research exists can be explained by conventional theories." (Criterion 2)§

Criticism 3: "Anyone who holds this belief is not credible and cannot be trusted, e.g. the person is uneducated, or not very intelligent, or they are irrational, etc." (Criterion 3)

Criticism 4: "All personal experiences that support the belief are invalid, e.g. the experiences reflect misperceptions, misinterpretations, delusions, etc." (Criterion 4)

All four of these criticisms can be responsibly rejected concerning the emergence of the totality of postmaterialist science.

Is Passing FACT Foolproof?

If a given belief addresses all five criteria successfully and passes FACT, does this convergence of information necessarily imply that the given belief is therefore accurate and true? The answer is no.

Just because we have engaged in a responsible process of truth seeking (e.g. Bourey & Schwartz, 2019) and have comprehensively addressed a belief using a formal framework such as FACT, this does not guarantee that the belief in question is accurate. Logic, as well as history, reminds us that new theories (Criterion 1), discoveries (Criterion 2), people (Criterion 3), and/or direct personal experiences (Criterion 4) may appear in the future which justify our re-engagement of the FACT process. *The process of implementing FACT is a forever-open process; FACT encourages re-evaluation and evolution as a function of new evidence.*

§ *Carl Sagan (2011). "Broca's Brain:Reflections on the Romance of Science", p.73, Ballantine Books*

This is especially important when evaluating and accepting our direct personal experiences. Even if we cannot attribute a given direct personal experience to erroneous factors such as a misperception, confirmation bias, and/or self-deception, this does not necessarily mean that a given specific belief is accurate.

For example, there was a time when virtually all human beings believed that the sun revolved around the earth. Moreover: Our theories and reasoning at the time predicted it (Criterion 1). The available scientific evidence at the time (e.g. before the invention of the telescope) supported it (Criterion 2). Highly trustworthy and credible people believed it at the time (Criteria 3), and we had direct personal experiences (Criterion 4), which we interpreted as supporting the belief at the time (i.e. we witnessed on a repeated basis what we interpreted as the sun rising in the East and setting in the West).

However, what became known as the Copernican Revolution led humanity to a different belief, i.e. that the earth actually revolves around the sun, and moreover, it rotates on its axis, creating the "false" impression that the sun revolved around the earth.

Employing the five steps laid out in FACT, Copernicus engaged in Criterion 5, and using logic (Criterion 1) and evidence (Criterion 2, e.g. seeming complexities and "anomalies" in the evidence which had either been ignored or dismissed by the mainstream scientists of his day), Copernicus (1) developed an alternative theory which (2) made new predictions, which were (3) subsequently confirmed with the development of the telescope (as revealed through discoveries made by Galileo).

Simply stated, Copernicus used Criterion 5 of FACT in the service of formulating a *new theory* that turned out to be supported by all five criteria comprising the FACT process.

Once we understand this historical and logical fact (no pun intended) and honor this lesson, we can become more effective and responsible truth seekers concerning the process of our adopting and holding beliefs.

By itself, the emerging area of research encompassing survival of consciousness – as strong as it is when viewed in terms of the convergence of evidence across domains of knowledge (e.g. ADCs, near-death experiences, evidence of reincarnation, laboratory studies with evidential mediums, laboratory research with technology), is only consistent with the primacy of consciousness hypothesis (i.e., Type III). Logic tells us that this evidence is also consistent with Type I and II postmaterialist theories.

However, when we take a broader, bigger picture (eagle's) approach to viewing all of the postmaterialist evidence, the convergence of the information supports the viability of the primacy of consciousness hypothesis.

FACT can be thought of as a "work in progress": though the future may reveal that we need to add additional criteria to the framework (and give up the acronym in the process), learning and using some version of the current FACT paradigm holds the potential to improve our personal and species-wide ability to engage in responsible and accurate truth seeking.

Doing so has the potential to provide a common path to reaching accurate and responsible beliefs, and in the process enhance the evolution of peace and well-being personally, institutionally, and globally.

Chapter Two

Journey to Idealism[**]

Dean Radin, PhD

After decades of inculcation into the standard Western worldview, by the time I was in graduate school I naturally assumed that all mental processes were ultimately reducible to brain activity. As part of my master's degree in electrical engineering, I focused on cybernetics, which includes topics like biological control systems, feedback mechanisms, homeostatis, self-organization, and computation in neural networks. Later, in my psychology doctoral program, I developed computer simulations of cognitive processes. These topics all conformed with my way of understanding reality at the time, known as *reductive materialism*. This is a philosophical position, but I never thought of it as such at the time. It proposes that reality can ultimately be understood as a fancy clockwork mechanism made out of matter (or, from a relativistic perspective, energy). This idea remains the dominant worldview within science today.

With my background in engineering and psychology, I was fascinated by the idea of developing thinking machines, robots, and human-like androids, and I could have easily followed that as a career path. But I had a nagging suspicion that something was missing, because I was more interested in a topic that was nowhere to be found within academia – psychic phenomena, like telepathy and clairvoyance. My interest was not because of personal psychic experiences, but rather from curiosity stimulated by the many fairy tales

---

[**] *Portions of this chapter are from Radin, D. (2018). Real Magic. New York: Penguin Random House.*

and science fiction I had read as a teenager. In such tales, strange mental powers were taken for granted, and I intuitively felt that these stories were more than just amusing fantasies.

In school I did not find much formal support for my interests in psychic phenomena. But I was delighted to learn that the university library had an extensive collection in parapsychology, the scientific discipline that studies psychic phenomena, and I ended up reading most of that literature. I also found several faculty members who had a quiet interest in the topic, and we informally conducted a number of experiments.

For practical purposes, my doctoral work followed a more conventional path, as did my first job after gaining my degree. But I never forgot my interest in "powers of the mind," especially after I learned that such effects were amenable to being studied using rigorous scientific methods. And so, during my working career, I have always studied these phenomena either as an avocation or as my vocation.

For nearly 40 years (as I write this), I've spent the majority of my post-doctoral profession engaged in the scientific study of psychic phenomena. Researchers in this field use the term *psi* as a shorthand way to refer to these phenomena, where psi is simply the Greek letter ψ, the first letter in the word *psyche*. My interest in psi phenomena increased over the years because I had witnessed these effects first-hand in experiments I conducted, and I saw that the same effects had been reported in thousands of scientific experiments published over the last century by researchers around the world.

Psi as observed in the laboratory tends to be much weaker than what is typically reported spontaneously in the everyday world, and of course it is much less impressive than the fictional embellishments of fairy tales and movies. Laboratory effects are weaker because of the on-demand nature and artificial context of controlled experiments. Still, what we observe in the lab tells us with high confidence that humans (and animals) have the capacity to gain information that is unconstrained by the everyday limitations of space or time, and that mental intention can affect properties of physical systems outside the body, also unbound by limitations of space or time.

I have described the evidence for psi in many journal articles and four popular books. The first book focused on how science studies subtle human experiences like psi (*The Conscious Universe*, 1997), the second book explained why psi is compatible with a modern physical understanding of reality (*Entangled Minds*, 2006), the third discussed ancient yogic technique for training psi (*Supernormal*, 2013), and the fourth considered these phenomena from the perspective of the esoteric traditions (*Real Magic*, 2018). In the process of my studies and writing, my original assumption that materialsm would be adequate to explain psi slowly eroded. It eventually evolved into *idealism* – the philosophical position that the only thing that exists is consciousness.

To appreciate how my journey ended up with a worldview that was completely opposite from the one I was educated in, we need to briefly review what is meant by today's scientific worldview.

The Scientific Worldview

The scientific worldview rests on three key assumptions: reality, locality, and causality.

Reality: The physical world consists of objects with real properties that are completely independent of observation. In the vernacular, the moon is still there even when you're not looking at it.

Locality: Objects are completely separate, or put in another way, "action at a distance" is impossible. For object A to affect object B, A must directly interact with B.

Causality: The arrow of time is uniformly in one direction, a consequence of the Second Law of Thermodynamics.

Based on these three assumptions, four principles can be found at the core of the scientific worldview: *mechanism, physicalism, materialism,* and *reductionism.*

Mechanism says that everything can ultimately be understood like the gears of a clock. Events unfold forward in time in a strictly orderly, cause and effect, fashion.

Physicalism says that everything can be described with real properties that exist in ordinary space and time.

Materialism says that everything consists of matter and energy.

Reductionism says that everything is made up of a hierarchy of ever-smaller objects, with subatomic particles at the bottom. Causation flows strictly "upward" in this hierarchy, from the microscopic to the macroscopic.

These principles and assumptions are very powerful. After adopting them, it only took a few hundred years to advance from log cabins to skyscrapers, and from wagon trains to rockets. So it does not make sense to throw away what demonstrably works. But the reigning worldview does not account for everything, and in particular it fails to explain psi experiences. Of greater concern, it fails to explain why consciousness – our personal sense of awareness – exists. What then is missing from the otherwise extremely powerful scientific worldview?

One hint is provided by the fact that the assumptions of reality, causality, and locality *do not hold in all circumstances.* From quantum mechanics, and verified by experimental tests, we know that elementary objects like electrons and photons do not have fully determined properties before they are observed. So the common sense understanding of *reality* is a special case of a more comprehensive worldview. From Einstein's Theory of General Relativity, and empirical tests thereof, we know that a fixed arrow of time is an illusion. So the everyday experience of *causality* is a special case of a more comprehensive worldview. From quantum theory, again verified by experimental results, we also know that entanglement, labeled "spooky action at a distance" by Einstein, exists, so the common sense meaning of *locality* is again a special case of a more comprehensive worldview.

The Perennial Philosophy

Given that our fundamental assumptions turned out to not be so fundamental after all, then what is the more comprehensive worldview we are looking for? A clue is provided by a repeated theme found in the *esoteric* literature, which consists of cosmologies, lore, and practices found throughout history and across all cultures; such information was declared unacceptable or heretical by the status quo, and thus forced to go underground (the terms esoteric and occult simply mean hidden or secret). The opposite was *exoteric* knowledge, which was supported and promoted by the status quo, and thus made widely available.

Many scholars have attempted to synthesize similarities among the esoteric traditions. One such crystallization is known as the *perennial philosophy*. A book by this title was popularized in modern times by British novelist Aldus Huxley (Huxley, 1945). The idea is that there is a single, underlying mystical cosmology from which all of the tremendously diverse religious traditions of the world emerged. The same idea has been found by other scholars, who used terms like the primordial tradition, the secret wisdom, the forgotten truth, the ancient theology, the *prisca theologia*, and so on (Levin, 2008).

There are, of course, many nuances among the esoteric traditions due to idiosyncratic differences in cultural, historical, sociopolitical and linguistic factors. But when we focus on the similarities, we repeatedly find three commonalities:

Consciousness is fundamental.
Everything is interconnected.
There is only one Consciousness.

These same interrelated ideas are also expounded in the various philosophies that assume there's ultimately just one "substance" underlying reality. Historically that substance has been called Spirit, Advaita, Brahman, Tao, Nirvana, Source, Yahweh, God, and many other names. In recent times, to avoid religious connotations, the more neutral term *consciousness* is often used.

By consciousness, I mean *awareness* – that which allows us to enjoy subjective experience. We know the taste of a lemon. But when we attempt to trace *how* we know, based on signals produced by electrochemical sensors on the tongue or neural pathways carrying other signals to the brain, then nowhere do we find what the *taste* of a lemon is actually like. The experience we are seeking is inside the brain-body machinery in a way that cannot be observed from the outside. Science is exceptionally adept at studying features of the external world by taking things apart, but so far it has just barely scratched the surface at developing ways to study the "inner world."

But reductionism only works for objects that can be cleanly separated, and that does not include the set of all possible things. We have no idea how to take awareness apart, or even if stating the problem in that way makes sense. Recognition of this problem has sparked a revival of interest among scientists and scholars toward the philosophical notion of *idealism* – the idea that reality is fundamentally of, and in, the mind. Related concepts include *panpsychism* – the idea that matter at all levels, including fundamental particles, have an inherent property of sentience, or mind, and *neutral monism* – the idea that mind and matter are actually complementary aspects of the same "stuff," like two sides of the same coin.

Bernardo Kastrup provides a clear explanation of idealism in his book, *Why Materialism Is Baloney* (Kastrup, 2014). His claim is that the neuroscience assumption that the physical brain gives rise to subjective experience is full of holes (or perhaps, baloney), and he takes great pains to explain why. Kastrup cites a 2007 article in the journal

Nature which showed that the common sense assumption of realism is incompatible with quantum theory and with experimental results that confirm the theory. The authors of that article concluded their discussion with the following statement: "We believe that our results lend strong support to the view that any future extension of quantum theory that is in agreement with experiments must abandon certain features of realistic descriptions" (Groblacher, Paterek, & Kaltenbaek, 2007).

What this means is that insisting on naïve realism as a basic assumption about reality is a serious mistake. In simpler terms, it appears that reality is not "out there," nor completely independent of you, but instead *reality depends on observation* (Stapp, 2007). If that is the case, then who or what is the observer? This was addressed in a 2005 article published in *Nature*, by Johns Hopkins University physicist, Richard Henry. In an essay entitled "The mental universe," Henry wrote:

Physicists shy from the truth because the truth is so alien to everyday physics. A common way to evade the mental Universe is to invoke "decoherence" — the notion that "the physical environment" is sufficient to create reality, independent of the human mind. Yet the idea that any irreversible act of amplification is necessary to collapse the wave function is known to be wrong.... The Universe is entirely mental (Henry, 2005).

A Sketch of Reality

The universe as entirely mental is another way of saying that consciousness is fundamental. The reality suggested by this notion is sketched in Figure 1. Above the horizontal line is ordinary conscious awareness and the everyday world of large, stable objects. This "high" reality is the domain of common sense and where the majority of science has focused upon. Note that there's a parallel between consciousness, physics, and different categories of numbers.

Is Consciousness Primary?

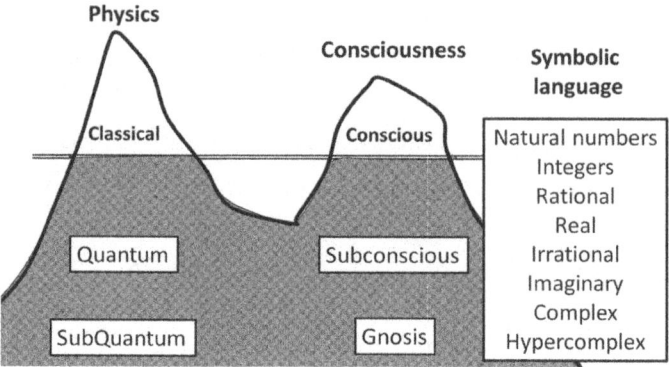

Figure 1. A cartoon model of reality.

Just below the horizontal line in Figure 1 is the human subconscious, quantum reality, and a list of increasingly abstract numbers. To describe physical reality below everyday awareness requires the use of mathematics that are more abstract than simple integers. We also know that a deeper mental domain exists from research in psychotherapy, psychology, the neurosciences, and meditation. Our conscious life emerges from the subconscious, and likewise, the classical physical world emerges from the quantum domain.

From our advantage point "above" this sketch we see that what appears to be two separate islands is actually two peaks of the same mountain, most of which resides under the surface. The separations experienced in the everyday world are similarly an illusion, based on our limited perspectives. The esoteric traditions can be understood as attempting to describe this mountain from the bottom up.

Until the beginning of the 20th century, scientists studying the physical world did not realize that there was anything below the "surface." Nor did scientists, psychiatrists, and psychologists studying the mind realize that the mind too existed in layers below the surface. As science continues to advance, it probes progressively deeper levels of reality. At some point, a threshold may be reached where further dives may not be possible without a tighter integration of consciousness and physics, because the differences in those two domains may be illusory. As neuroscientist Christof Koch, has said, "Consciousness is really physics from the inside. Seen from the inside, it's experience. Seen from the outside, it's what we know as physics, chemistry, and biology" (Paulson, April 6, 2017).

Hierarchies of Knowledge

Sketches of reality can be instructive as metaphors, but how do we actually move from today's halting understanding of deep reality to a scientifically testable understanding? Consider Figure 2 as a model of today's hierarchy of knowledge. It assumes that the foundations of reality are physical: matter and energy. From that domain elementary particles and energies combine in complex ways and emerge into the realms we call chemistry. From there biology emerges, and then psychology.

In each of these hierarchical stages, higher levels emerge from lower levels. The higher levels often contain new properties that the lower levels do not share, and that could not be predicted from the lower levels.

For example, the atomic elements hydrogen and oxygen can be combined to form H_2O, the water molecule. But neither hydrogen nor oxygen exhibit properties of water.

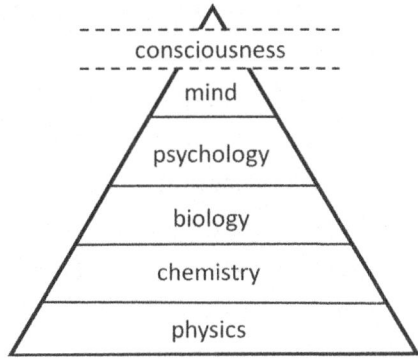

Figure 2. Today's hierarchy of scientific disciplines.

Somehow at the top of this hierarchy a new property is said to emerge
— it is called consciousness. But that property is radically different from all of the others because consciousness does not have physical properties. Philosophers refer to subjective experience as *qualia*, because experience is an internal *quality* rather than a measurable external *quantity*.

Confusion over this inside-mind vs. outside-matter relationship has persisted for millennia without a clear resolution. The impasse has led to a growing sense that radically new approaches to understanding consciousness may be required. We increasingly find such proposals in philosophy, physics, the neurosciences, and psychology.

Some propose that reality literally is information, like a cosmic "conscious hologram" (Currivan, 2017). Others talk about reality as a mathematical or supercomputer-based simulation. A 2016 article in the online magazine, *BBC Earth*, cites technology entrepreneur Elon Musk, MIT cosmologist Alan Guth, MIT physicist Seth Lloyd, Oxford University philosopher Nick Bostrom, Nobel Laureate astrophysicist George Smoot, and others, as fans of the idea that we're living inside a simulation (Ball, September 5, 2016). These themes have been extensively explored since the 1940s in science fiction literature, television programs, and movies, perhaps most famously as the central theme in the movie trilogy, *The Matrix*.

In 2013, the Foundational Questions Institute held an essay contest on John Wheeler's famous quip, "It From Bit or Bit From It?" The contest attracted 170 entries. The Institute's 2015 contest was on the topic, "The mysterious connection between physics and mathematics." In 2017, the theme was "How can mindless mathematical laws give rise to aims and intention?" The director of the Foundational Questions Institute, MIT physicist Max Tegmark, described the burgeoning interest in these questions in his 2014 book, *Our Mathematical Universe*:

"There's something very mathematical about our Universe, and ... the more carefully we look, the more math we seem to find. So what do we make of all these hints of mathematics in our physical world? Most of my physics colleagues take them to mean that nature is for some reason described by mathematics, at least approximately, and leave it at that. But I'm convinced that there's more to it." (Tegmark, 2014)

Tegmark proposes that "there exists an external physical reality completely independent of us humans." But as we've already discussed, there are good reasons to believe that reality is actually *not* completely independent of observation. What Tegmark is getting at is that the abstract structures provided by mathematics seem to have a life of their own. They don't just describe it, but in some sense he believes that mathematics, a purely symbolic language, literally *is* the universe.

This resonates with an earlier consideration by Nobel Laureate physicist Eugene Wigner, who marveled over the astonishing ability of mathematics to accurately describe the behavior of the physical world. He noted that in spite of the baffling complexities of the world some features are stable enough, and we've been clever or lucky enough, to identify them as "laws of nature." Without those regularities science would never have developed. Wigner believed it was neither natural nor expected that such laws of nature should exist, much less that we've been able to discover some of them.

Like Wigner, mathematician Sir Roger Penrose also noted that "some of the basic physical laws are precise to an extraordinary degree, far beyond the precision of our direct sense experiences or the combined calculational powers of all conscious individuals within the ken of mankind" (Penrose, September 1, 2009). As an example, Penrose cited Newton's gravitational theory as applied to the movements of the solar system. The theory is precise to one part in 10 million. Einstein's theory of relativity improved on Newton's by another factor of 10 million, and it also predicted bizarre new effects like black holes and gravitational lenses. When astrophysicists went looking for these unexpected phenomena, to everyone's astonishment (except maybe Einstein's), they were found.

Penrose suggested that the amazing accuracy of these mathematical predictions "was not the result of a new theory being introduced only to make sense of vast amounts of new data. The extra precision was seen only *after* each theory had been produced" (Penrose, September 1, 2009). One way to interpret these astounding coincidences is that pure math is in contact with Plato's concept of primordial Forms or Ideas. This again implies that we live within a *symbolic reality*.

For those who insist that mind is nothing more than active circuits in the brain, then mathematics too must be nothing more than the brain's representation of a pre-existing, independent, external physical world. That seems reasonable enough until we realize that the symbols generated by three pounds of neural tissue somehow describe not only vast swatches of the physical universe to an unbelievably precise degree, but they also predict phenomena that strongly contradict common sense, such as quantum entanglement and black holes.

How then is it possible for a hunk of warm, wet tissue to not only describe itself but also describe exotic realms that the human body and brain cannot access through its ordinary senses, and that must have been around for billions of years before we developed methods of detecting them with mindboggling accuracy? That question suggests that maybe the brain didn't dream up these ideas after all. Rather, maybe *the ideas dreamt up the brain.*

A Symbolic Reality

Mathematics has been called the language of physics. Max Tegmark thinks that mathematics literally *is* the universe. But despite the appeal of symbolic and informational models of reality, there's a problem: Gödel's Incompleteness Theorem. Mathematician Kurt Gödel *proved* – that's a word not to be taken lightly – that no system of mathematics can be considered complete. Any non-trivial mathematical or logic system must either be incomplete or inconsistent.

And that in turn means the universe cannot be completely modeled with mathematics. Said another way, a symbolic language *by itself* can describe physical reality amazingly well, but something is always being left out. Is that something "outside" the physical world, meaning *nonphysical*? Could the missing element be consciousness? As physicists Sara Walker and Paul Davies explained:

"We propose that the hard problem of life is the problem of how "information" can affect the world.... We suspect that a full resolution of the hard problem*will not ultimately be reducible to known physical principles*.... If we are so lucky as to stumble on new fundamental understanding of life, it could be such a radical departure from what we know now that it might be left to the next generation of physicists to reconcile the unification of life with other domains of physics." (Walker & Davies, 23 Jun 2016) [emphasis added]

What the trend in information physics suggests is illustrated in Figure 3. The hierarchical structure of science remains exactly the same as before, except now the bottom of the hierarchy is a form of primordial consciousness that permeates all of reality. The physical world emerges from this universal consciousness, and the top of the pyramid is the mind, meaning the brain's machinery involved in information processing, cognition, and perception. From this perspective we enjoy consciousness that permeates all of reality. What the trend in information physics suggests is illustrated in Figure 3. The hierarchical structure of science remains exactly the same as before, except now the bottom of the hierarchy is a form of primordial. The physical world emerges from this universal consciousness, and the top of the pyramid is the mind, meaning the brain's machinery involved in information processing, cognition, and perception. From

43

this perspective we enjoy conscious awareness not because the brain generates it, but because consciousness already permeates every layer of the physical world, just like electrons permeate every layer "above" the discipline of physics. Based on this hierarchy, which importantly *maintains everything currently known in science*, we don't have to throw away any of our textbooks. In addition, suddenly psi phenomena, which reflect the capacities of consciousness, are no longer impossible or even anomalous.

Scholarly interest in consciousness as a fundamental property of reality has always existed among some philosophers. But now it's increasingly appearing within science, and unlike times past, scientists today are becoming less shy about admitting this possibility. This trend can be seen in a 2015 article in the orthodox *Philosophical Transactions of the Royal Society*. Giulio Tononi of the University of Wisconsin and Christof Koch of the Allen Institute for Brain Science, both influential thought-leaders in mainstream neuroscience, wrote:

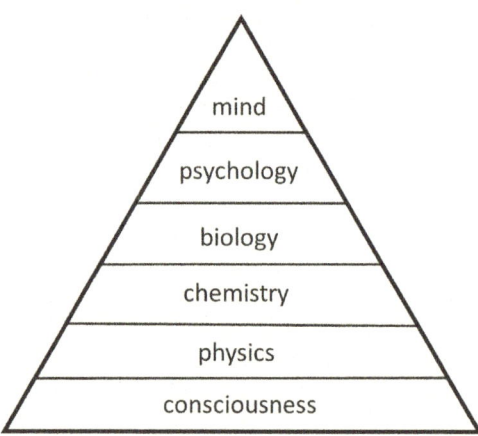

A more comprehensive scientific knowledge hierarchy. Consciousness as fundamental
Figure 3.

"Is consciousness – subjective experience – ...not only in other people's heads, but also in the head of animals? And perhaps everywhere, pervading the cosmos, as in old panpsychist traditions and in the Beatles' song? While these kinds of questions may seem scientifically inappropriate, we argue below that they can be approached in a principled and testable manner." (Tononi & Koch, 2015)

The long-held taboo that once prohibited scientists from even mentioning the word *consciousness*, especially the heretical idea that consciousness might "pervade the cosmos," required that Tononi and Koch add an apology along with their proposal. But in a less formal publication, Koch was more forthcoming. In a 2014 article in *Scientific American*, entitled "Is consciousness universal?", he wrote:

"The mental is too radically different for it to arise gradually from the physical. This emergence of subjective feelings from physical stuff appears inconceivable and is at odds with a basic precept of physical thinking, the Ur-conservation law—*ex nihilo nihil fit* [out of nothing comes nothing].... *The phenomenal hails from a kingdom other than the physical* and is subject to different laws." (Koch, January 1, 2014) [emphasis added]

I have already mentioned Max Tegmark's ideas and the essay contest of the Foundational Questions Institute. But we also find statements like the following offered in 2005 by the quantum physicist, Anton Zeilinger, of the University of Vienna: "Reality and information are the same. We need a new concept which encompasses both. In a sense, reality and information are the two sides of the same coin. I feel that this is the message of the quantum" (Zeilinger, no date). Or this by New York University science writer, Charles Siefe, in his 2007 book, *Decoding the Universe*: "Information appears, quite literally, to shape our universe" (Seife, 2007). Or an idea by physicist Vlatko Vedral, in his similarly titled 2012 book, *Decoding Reality*:

"Information (and not matter or energy or love) is the building block on which everything is constructed. Information is far more fundamental than matter or energy .... Information can also be used to explain the origin and behaviour of microscopic interactions such as energy and matter... Information, in contrast to matter and energy, is the only concept that we currently have that can explain its own origin." (Vedral, 2012)

Entire journal issues are now devoted to the mathematics and physics of consciousness and post-materialistic ideas are appearing in new journals dedicated to consciousness studies, including *Psychology of Consciousness*, published by the voice of mainstream academic psychology, the American Psychological Association (APA). In 2016, the APA also published a book entitled *Transcendent Mind*, by psychologist Imants Baruss of Kings University College in Canada and neuroscientist Julia Mossbridge of the Institute of Noetic Sciences. Baruss and Mossbridge emphasized this growing movement in the following paragraph:

"We are in the midst of a sea change. Receding from view is materialism, whereby physical phenomena are assumed to be primary and consciousness is regarded as secondary. Approaching our sights is a complete reversal of perspective. According to this alternative view, consciousness is primary and the physical is secondary. In other words, materialism is receding and giving way to ideas about reality in which consciousness plays a key role." (Barušs & Mossbridge, 2016)

The trend is also visible in biology. Physician Neil Theise and physicist Menas Kafatos proposed in an article in *Communicative & Integrative Biology* that "Non-dual awareness is foundational to the universe, not arising from the interactions or structures of higher level phenomena.... The cosmos ... can be understood to derive *from* awareness rather than being suffused by it or giving rise to it" (Theise & Kafatos, 2016).

Medical researchers too are sensing a shift from solely materialistic models of health and healing. This can be seen as an exponential rise of publications on the role of spirituality in health and healing. Based on a search on PubMed, the US government's online National Library of Medicine, we find that from 1940 to 2016 some 2,645 articles were published on the topic of "spirituality in medicine." Nearly all of those articles were published since 2000. Before

1980, a grand total of two articles were published, indicating that until the 21st century mainstream medicine had little interest in non-material concepts like spirituality.

The same trend is evident in complexity theory. Stuart A. Kauffman, one of the principals at the famed Santa Fe Institute and a pioneer in the study of complex systems, writes in his 2016 book, *Humanity in a Creative Universe*:

"From Newton we achieved and are now trapped by the view that there is a "theory of everything," reductive materialism, whose laws will "govern" and logically "entail" all that can or does become since the Big Bang, but are themselves somehow "outside of the universe." This is the Pythagorean dream of a mathematizable world. I aim to show that this view is surely false for the living world and perhaps aspects of the abiotic world." (Kauffman, 2016)

In philosophy, the discipline that has struggled to understand reality thousands of years before science appeared, we increasingly find opinions like those of Philip Goff, of the Central European University in Budapest. As Goff bluntly put it in a 2017 essay, "Panpsychism is crazy, but it's also most probably true" (Goff, March 1, 2017). Similarly, as philosophers Robert Koons of the University of Texas at Austin, and George Bealer of Yale University, wrote in *The Waning of Materialism*:

"Materialism is waning in a number of significant respects—one of which is the ever-growing number of major philosophers who reject materialism or at least have strong sympathies with anti-materialist views. It is of course commonly thought that over the course of the last sixty or so years materialism achieved hegemony in academic philosophy…. It is therefore surprising that an examination of the major philosophers active in this period reveals that a majority, or something approaching a majority, either rejected materialism or had serious and specific doubts about its ultimate viability." (Koons & Bealer, 2010)

One of those "major philosophers" was Jerry Fodor from Rutgers University, who put it this way: "I think it's strictly true that we can't, as things stand now, so much as imagine the solution of the hard problem [of explaining subjective awareness].... I would prefer that the hard problem should turn out to be unsolvable if the alternative is that we're all too dumb to solve it" (Koons & Bealer, 2010). In case Fodor's position was not clear enough, he later emphasized that "nobody has the slightest idea how anything material could be conscious. Nobody even knows what it would be like to have the slightest idea about how anything could be conscious" (Laszlo, 2006). In a similar vein, the distinguished philosopher Thomas Nagel from New York University wrote the following in his 2012 book, *Mind and Cosmos:*

"It is prima facie highly implausible that life as we know it is the result of a sequence of physical accidents together with the mechanism of natural selection... My skepticism is not based on religious belief, or on a belief in any definite alternative... I realize that such doubts will strike many people as outrageous, but that is because almost everyone in our secular culture has been browbeaten into regarding the reductive research program as sacrosanct." (Nagel, 2012)

Here's the bottom line: Throughout science and scholarship a basic principle of the perennial philosophy – that consciousness is fundamental – is slowly becoming acceptable to talk about. Within science this notion tends to be cast into the more conventional language of information and mathematics, but the connection with consciousness is undeniable. After centuries of life-threatening suppression, the move toward what is now possible for scientists and scholars to talk about in public might seem like a trifling matter. But it's a major shift in our understanding of reality.

Chapter Three

Mathematical Unification of Space, Time, Mass, Energy and Consciousness

Edward R. Close, PhD

"The day science begins to study non-physical phenomena, it will make more progress in one decade than in all the previous centuries of its existence". -
Nikola Tesla, 1856

I am honored to be among the group of scientists invited by the founding members of the Academy to write a chapter for this volume. We were asked to focus on the primacy of consciousness hypothesis and explain, based on our individual experiences, both professional and personal, how and why we came to consider it as a valid scientific hypothesis. In this chapter you will find a brief account of a double life: By day, I have earned a living by applying sound mathematical and scientific methods as a US Government systems analyst, mathematical modeler and professional engineer, while by night and on weekends, single-mindedly seeking to understand the meaning of existence and the true nature of reality by practicing time-honored consciousness expansion techniques and pursuing independent research in several major universities.

As someone who has spent most of his life passionately seeking to understand the nature of reality at its deepest level, I can tell you this much: I am quite certain that there is no reality without consciousness. Consciousness is fundamental, and I have no hesitation in saying that *consciousness is primary*, because I have proved it to my satisfaction using hard evidence, including experimental data and rigorous mathematical logic. In this chapter, I will present an outline of this proof, along with disclosure of a significant discovery that provides answers to, and explanations of issues that have puzzled mainstream scientists for decades.

Much of what you will find in this chapter was discovered by applying a primary system of mathematical logic developed over a period of nearly forty years. It is a system that combines number theory, geometry, algebra and calculus, and it is specifically designed for application at the quantum scale of physical reality. I understand that not many people have the time or inclination to learn a whole new system of mathematical logic, so I have invested a great deal of time and energy over the past ten years with the help of Dr. Vernon Neppe, to build a bridge translating this system into conventional math and physical concepts that can be expressed verbally. So that the reader might understand that this work is not trivial, I will outline the basic concepts in this chapter, and I will start by providing a little about my background.

Background

I was fourteen years old in the summer of 1951, when I found a little book on analytical geometry among some old books. Reading it, I had the very distinct awareness that I already knew this. It was as if I were remembering it, not learning it for the first time. About the same time, opened a whole new world for me. One evening, in the twilight just after sunset, I walked out of the little house on my parents' farm in the Southern Missouri Ozarks, past a line of catalpa trees, to the bank of a pond. I had been thinking about the "electrodynamics of moving objects" described in Einstein's Special Theory of Relativity, and I had reached a point beyond which I could not go. Frustrated, I looked up at the darkening sky and complained: "God, I want to know *everything*!"

The response was startling: Suddenly, I could 'hear' the silence around me. My surroundings took on a glow, as if *everything* were *alive*. My consciousness seemed to melt, and the distinctions between my physical body and the surrounding landscape began to fade. I was filled with an all-pervading feeling of well-being. Over-joyed, I knew I had received an answer! I decided then and there that I would follow in the footsteps of Albert Einstein. This was the beginning of a passion that would be the driving force throughout the rest of my life. A few years later, the high school counselor told me that my scores on aptitude and IQ tests indicated that I could be successful in science, engineering, or pretty much any field I might choose. I vowed that I would become a theoretical physicist!

I received solid academic training in mathematics and physics at Central Methodist College (now Central Methodist University) and the University of Missouri. As an undergraduate student, in 1957 while at Central, my roommate and I carried out some experiments with psi phenomena that produced some remarkable results. Our work was monitored by two of our professors. One of the most successful experiments, in which we obtained meaningful information that we could not have known through normal means, was reported to Dr. J.B. Rhine at the Duke University Department of Parapsychology in 1958. Dr. Rhine encouraged us to continue our research but advised us to get training for a day job because there was little demand for parapsychologists! Because I was a member of Kappa Mu Epsilon, the National Honorary Mathematics Society, in 1959 I was privileged to meet Dr. Norbert Wiener, the father of cybernetics, who was lecturing at the University of Missouri in Columbia. His mathematical analysis of human brain waves suggested to me a non-material aspect of brain function, and I thought this might be an avenue to describing and explaining psi phenomena scientifically.

Interests in mind/matter interaction and psi phenomena, propelled me on a personal search of comparative religions, linguistics, symbolic logic and philosophy. And my interest in these subjects was such that when I took the graduate record exam (GRE), even though I was completing a degree in mathematics and physics, I did the specific-field part of the exam in philosophy. Based on the results of the GRE, I was accepted into a PhD program in symbolic logic at Tulane University. However, due to poor planning and personal circumstances, I never attended Tulane, but instead, enrolled in a graduate program in theoretical physics in a school close to home, the University of Missouri at Rolla, where I focused on mathematics, electronics, and quantum mechanics. My interests in mind/matter interaction and psi phenomena research were generally rejected by my professors in physics and mathematics. This was disheartening, but I encountered a charismatic professor who sparked my interest in geology and geophysics, and I took a summer job as a seismology technician in Texas. Because there was no academic interest in mind/matter research at the time, after teaching mathematics for a few years, I took a job with the Water Resources Division of the US Geological Survey (USGS-WRD).

I spent twelve (12) years with the USGS, working my way up from hydraulic engineering technician to research hydrologist. During my career, I was often transferred to special projects because of my background in math and physics, and I received additional training in systems analysis and mathematical modeling at the University of Arizona, Flagstaff, Case Western Reserve, and UCLA. As Project Engineer for a cooperative USGS/US Army Corps of Engineers research project with the Hydrologic Engineering Center in Sacramento, in 1967, I took graduate courses in environmental engineering and hydrology at the University of California, Davis.

When the project in Sacramento was completed, I was transferred to Washington, DC, where I became one of the seven charter members of the Department of Interior Systems Analysis Group, working under the direction of Dr. Nicholas C. Matalas, a Harvard

PhD, along with leaders in state-of-the-art environmental modeling, including Walter Langbein, USGS senior scientist, and IBM mathematician, Benoit Mandelbrot, the inventor of fractals. While a member of the Systems Group, I also completed one year of my PhD program in environmental science and engineering in residence at Johns Hopkins University in Baltimore MD, after which I was transferred to an Island-wide water resources modeling project in Puerto Rico.

You may be wondering why would a scientist educated in mathematics, physics and engineering, who has taught and applied mathematics for years, and who has been successful as a systems analyst, modeling environmental problems and solving real problems as a professional engineer, believe that science must be expanded beyond the current materialistic paradigm. The answer is simple: Even though I love mathematics and science and have spent most of the last fifty-plus years pursuing a career in environmental engineering, I have always known that there is more to reality than matter and energy interacting in time and space. I will include a few brief examples of personal experiences that shaped, and ultimately formed the basis of my core beliefs, after which I will present scientific arguments and mathematical proofs supporting my conviction that science *must* move beyond materialism. Even though I turned to engineering and mathematics to address the demands of daily life, I also pursued personal studies in theoretical physics and focused all available free time on my passionate purpose: I still wanted to understand *everything*.

As a young child, I had experiences that could be called expanded awareness, with unusually heightened senses. For example, while sitting in a fifth-grade classroom one afternoon, I looked up at the teacher in the front of the room, and her face seemed to fill all space. I could see the smallest details, as if they were magnified by some invisible lens: the pores of her skin, fine hairs on her upper lip, a faint birthmark on her neck ... then, very suddenly, her face zoomed away from me until it looked the size of a pea, somewhere in the distance. And often, when I went to bed at night, just before sleep, my sense of hearing would be enhanced to the point that I could hear even the slightest sound. Any movement in the house sounded like an avalanche. I found that by focusing my attention internally, I could hear music that would drown out the outer sounds. I could 'tune in' to the sounds of a marching band, or I could hear beautiful orchestral music, hearing every note of each individual instrument with incredible clarity. I would drift off to sleep enjoying soothing and uplifting harmonies. I told my father about these experiences, and he said not to worry, that they were normal for a growing boy, and that I would outgrow them. While I never completely outgrew such experiences, their nature did change over time.

While I was a young physics student, like most physicists, I believed that mathematical physics was the only *real* science, and that all other science was physics without the clarity. Engineering and technology were simply applied physics, and in my opinion, the truly great physicists, the paradigm shifters like Einstein, Planck and Schrödinger, did not see physics as an end in and of itself, but rather as a doorway into the true nature of reality, a way to understand *everything*.

Some of the psi experiments performed with a classmate under the control of two of our professors during my early college years, bore out this growing hypothesis. We had some sessions that resulted in discovering the mathematics of Pierre de Fermat. And during one of our experiments we obtained advanced concepts and mathematical notations that were beyond our training at the time but were verified and explained to us by one of my physics professors, Dr. Harley Rutledge.

In looking for answers that might help me integrate these two parts of my personal experience, science and spirituality, I took lessons from the Rosicrucian Order by mail, and attended a few meetings in Kansas City Missouri, but decided that their rituals would not hold my interest in the long-term. Then, in 1959, my former college roommate sent me a book called *The Holy Science*, written by Swami Sri Yukteswar Giri of India. After reading this book, I became a lessons student of Self-Realization Fellowship and took Kriya Yoga Initiation in 1960 in Los Angeles, California. I have practiced the SRF yoga and meditation techniques ever since, and have taught meditation classes in Florida, California, Missouri, Puerto Rico, and Colorado. I have also served as a group leader for SRF Meditation Groups in several states and in Washington DC. I believe that all scientists, if they are interested in understanding the nature of reality, should learn to expand their consciousness through effective meditation techniques.

Even though I was not raised in a particularly religious home, and I pursued education in theoretical physics and mathematics, as well as a career in engineering, and often associated with people who were either agnostic or atheistic, I continued to have experiences that would qualify as paranormal, spiritual, or even mystical. Yet, it has been science and mathematics that has convinced me beyond any doubt that materialism is a dead end, an unscientific point of view that is stuck in the fears of the middle ages. Science must take off the blinders of materialistic dogma in order to progress. We must move beyond the simplistic belief in materialism, and accept the mounting scientific evidence that consciousness is primary and should be included as part of the scientific basis for the science of the future. That can only be done, in my opinion, with new mathematics. Unlike theories that change over time, mathematical theorems, once proved, are true forever. Plato's solids, Euclid's Elements, the Pythagorean Theorem, Fermat's Last Theorem, Gödel's Incompleteness Theorems, …do not change. They were true when they were first proved, and they remain true forever.

The Deeper Meaning of Reality

Himmel und Erde müssen vergeh'n,
Aber die Müsici, aber die Müsici, aber die Müsici,
bleiben besteh'n!

A German folksong. Translation: The heavens and the Earth must pass away, but the music will ever remain!

Under the right circumstances, music can touch the soul. Such a magical personal experience is possible because real, *spiritually inspired* music can express in sound, with mathematical precision, the logical structure behind all forms.

The truth is that all things physical must change and thus must eventually pass away, but the *music*, i.e. the *spiritual essence behind all things* is mathematical and eternal.

The deep beauty of pure mathematical truth elegantly reflects the logical structure of the universe. But the full beauty and elegance of reality can only be experienced when conscious awareness is expanded beyond the material body and the physical senses and aligned with the elegant logical structure underlying reality.

The science of the 20th Century, especially work by Einstein and Bohr, Planck, Schrödinger, and Bohm, has shown the way to a new understanding that includes consciousness. It is time to develop the mathematics required to take their discoveries forward and re-examine everything we know in light of those discoveries. But we cannot try to force them to fit into the antiquated materialistic Standard Model paradigm. We must question the assumptions and determine how to explain things in a simpler, more comprehensive way. If we make one major but simple adjustment, and instead of thinking of consciousness as emergent, see it as fundamental, then everything changes. This is where pursuit of my passionate purpose has led me.

I first proposed primacy of consciousness as a scientific hypothesis in Infinite Continuity, (Close, 1990), and again in Transcendental Physics (Close, 1997). The basics of the mathematical system I developed, which I call the Calculus of Dimensional Distinctions (CoDD) are in an appendix to my 1997 book. Discussions of the CoDD have been published in Infinite Continuity, Transcendental Physics and subsequent work with Vladimir Brandin and with Dr. Vernon Neppe, in Reality Begins with Consciousness (Neppe & Close, 2011).

Beyond Matter-Energy, and Space-Time

Enhanced states of consciousness and higher dimensional domains have been written about in the mystical traditions of every culture. Seers and sages have, through deep concentration, and through advanced techniques for consciousness expansion, gone beyond the physical, and even beyond thought and mind. They have experienced a state of Pure Consciousness, and returned to tell us that Pure Consciousness is bliss, and that it depends upon nothing physical.

Today, many documented near-death experiences (NDEs) are providing verifiable evidence that is telling us the same thing in a slightly different way. And scientifically rigorous studies by researchers at the Princeton Engineering Anomalies Research Lab (Jahn & Dunne, 2005) the Institute of Noetic Sciences (Radin, et al, 2015), and the University of Arizona (Schwartz, 2002), are providing hard evidence of the reality of a variety of psi phenomena. A growing number of researchers around the world are conducting studies that show us that there is something real beyond the physical. These studies are producing solid evidence demonstrating direct effects of individual consciousness, group consciousness, and even global consciousness on physical reality. And some are producing evidence of the persistence of consciousness after death (Stevenson, 1987; Schwartz, 2002). Those who say there is no way to prove that consciousness exists outside the physical brain and body, have either ignored, or are unaware of the evidence. Increasingly repeatable scientific evidence points consistently in a direction that mainstream science stubbornly does not want to go. Thankfully, that is slowly changing. Truth will eventually triumph over academic reticence and doubt.

Echoing the teachings of the major spiritual traditions, all of this new evidence from scientists outside the mainstream is telling us something quite profound: Besides matter, energy, space and time, the salient aspects of physical reality, there is also Pure Consciousness, which is pervasive, undifferentiated and unlimited.

I'll have more to say about this later, but for now, the point I want to make is this: Our only direct knowledge of reality is through the experience of consciousness. Therefore, consciousness must be included in any truly scientific analysis of reality. More than 85 years ago, Max Planck said: "I regard consciousness as fundamental. I regard matter as a derivative of consciousness" (Planck, 1931).

If Planck was right, then we must include consciousness in our scientific descriptions of reality. My intention here is to present a glimpse into a new scientific paradigm, expanded beyond materialism, with supporting data and mathematical proof, providing the basis for a new, more comprehensive understanding of reality. This new paradigm begins with the assumption that consciousness is fundamental, as Planck said so long ago. It is an ambitious task, but I believe it is crucial. Reality cannot be governed by one set of rules on the macro-scale and another set of strange, incompatible rules at the quantum scale. There is only one reality, and we should not confuse the current scientific paradigm with reality. It is not reality that is paradoxical and incomplete. It is our map of reality, the Standard

Model, that is a patchwork of paradoxical and incomplete theories. In this short essay, I will discuss what is missing from the current paradigm, and show how we can incorporate the new evidence mentioned above to produce a much more comprehensive paradigm. To begin, let's take a look at the last major paradigm shifts: Relativity and quantum physics.

What Was Missing Before Einstein and Planck?

Consider the equation $E = mc^2$ which can be derived from the kinetic energy of an electron moving in a magnetic field as shown by Albert Einstein in his 1905 paper entitled "The Electrodynamics of Moving Bodies." This equation is directly derivable from Newton's laws of motion, and had already been derived by physicists before Einstein, including Sir Isaac Newton himself, Friedrich Hasenöhrl and Henri Poincare. And the equations in Einstein's paper describing the measurable space and time distortions, that occur as the velocity of a moving object approaches the speed of light, were also known before Einstein. In the late 1800s both Henri Poincare and Hendrik Lorentz derived them from Maxwell's wave equations. They were known as the Lorentz Transformation Equations. Lorentz saw that they made the calculated orbit of the electron of a Hydrogen atom fit experimental data, but failed to think of them as affecting the physical measurement of space and time. Albert Einstein simply looked a little deeper.

Einstein knew that the Lorentz Transformation corrections were only necessary when velocities approached very near the speed of light relative to the observer's frame of reference. In an intuitive leap, he realized that c must always have the same value for all observers, regardless of their motion relative to each other and the light source. This conclusion, while certainly consistent with Maxwell's wave equations, was an astonishing contradiction of the law of the addition of velocity vectors that was assumed to be true for all moving objects. A very important consequence of this discovery is that no object can be accelerated past the speed of light. Almost no one in the scientific community at the time believed Einstein's theory could possibly be correct. Notable exceptions were Max Planck and Sir Arthur Eddington.

In Planck units, $E = mc^2$ is *a unitary equivalence equation*. As a unitary equivalence equation, it expresses the mathematical equivalence between mass and energy. Also note that this simple equation incorporates mass, energy, space, and time, all four of the basic parameters of physical science. The mathematical equivalence of mass and energy was unknown before Einstein, and the fact that energy is *quantized* was unknown before Planck. Both these discoveries came as major surprises to mainstream physicists. Planck's discovery that energy is meted out by nature in multiples of a basic unit revolutionized our understanding of the nature of reality as much, and probably even more than Einstein's relativity did, but the implications of this discovery have not yet been fully realized by mainstream science even today. Something is still missing.

Relativity and Quantum Mechanics

When quantum physics was first being formulated, it was expected that the equivalence of mass and energy, defined by the equation $E = mc^2$, would establish a solid link between relativity and quantum physics. It was widely predicted that the picture of reality would be complete when both were fully incorporated into the Standard Model. Physicist Erwin Schrödinger incorporated mass/energy quantization with de Broglie's particle/wave duality in a probabilistic wave equation, while Niels Bohr and Werner Heisenberg developed the nuts and bolts of quantum mechanics with statistics and matrix algebra, and it looked as if the paradigm shift from classical mechanics to a relativistic quantum mechanics paradigm was accomplished. However, quantum physics concepts proved to be a little too strange. Einstein objected to quantum uncertainty, and declared that quantum mechanics was at best incomplete (Einstein et al, 1935). Bohr and Heisenberg defended quantum mechanics with probability theory and statistics; and Schrödinger, finding the whole thing distasteful, turned his considerable skills to thinking about biology.

The Einstein – Bohr Debate

Einstein famously said: "God does not play dice!" and he and two colleagues, physicists Boris Podolsky and Nathan Rosen, devised what became known as the EPR Paradox, a thought experiment that appeared to disprove Heisenberg's Uncertainty Principle. The Uncertainty Principle declared that both the momentum and the location of an elementary particle could not be known precisely at the same time; that there would always be an inherent uncertainty in one parameter or the other. This uncertainty was a central concept of quantum mechanics. If it was wrong, then quantum physics was in trouble.

Based on the known fact that certain pairs of particles created in subatomic processes have complementary properties, the EPR thought experiment revealed a way that Einstein, *et al*, believed the so-called inherent uncertainty could be circumvented by measuring the momentum of one particle and the location of the other. Their complementarity would allow both properties to be known precisely at the same time, contradicting Heisenberg's Uncertainty Principle. Bohr and Heisenberg were stumped for a while, but finally replied that there was no way to claim that the two particles measured at a distance from their originating point were the same two particles, because the particles did not exist as localized objects until their impacts were registered. This became known as the Copenhagen Interpretation of quantum mechanics.

Einstein did not accept this explanation as valid because it implied what he termed "spooky action at a distance." If the particles had no localized existence until they registered on a receptor, then somehow, when the measurements were made, at considerable distances apart in space and time, one particle would immediately manifest the complementary opposite feature of the other, transferring information faster than the speed of light. This would violate the relativity principle that nothing can accelerate past the speed of light. Quantum physics and relativity appeared to be so incompatible that they could not be integrated.

Mathematician John Bell, believing Einstein was correct, devised a way to prove who was right, with a probabilistic inequality that became known as Bell's Theorem (Bell, 1964). The technology was not available to perform the deciding experiment until after Einstein's death, and when it was performed by a team of French physicists led by Alain Aspect, Bohr's answer to the EPR Paradox was vindicated. This left physicists with some very difficult choices: either elementary particles were something quite different than they thought, or the space-time continuum was something different than it was assumed to be, or both. None of the choices were very palatable. The physical reality we thought we knew and loved seemed to be slipping away!

The Double-Slit Experiment and the Measurement Problem

Long before the Einstein-Bohr debate, physicists were already in deep trouble; they just didn't know it. In 1801, an English physician named Thomas Young devised a simple experiment that appeared to invalidate Newton's theory that light is propagated through space as particles that he called "corpuscles" (now called photons). Shining light through two very thin slits, onto a screen or photographic plate,

Dr. Young showed that interference patterns like those formed by waves moving through water were formed. His conclusion was that light is waves of energy moving through a universal substance that physicists called the luminiferous aether. However, before very long, physicists came to Newton's defense, showing that the same beam of light could also behave as particles when one of the two slits was closed. This created a big problem for classical physics. It meant that light could behave as either wave or particle, depending upon a choice made by an observer. Prior to this, objective physical reality was assumed to be completely independent of the observer. The double-slit experiment was the first hint that consciousness might be directly involved in shaping objective reality.

The Delayed-Choice Experiment

John Wheeler, a student of Einstein's, put the results of the double-slit experiment and the Aspect experiment together, and reasoned that, if the Copenhagen Interpretation were correct, i.e. elementary particles are not localized waves or particles until they impact upon a receptor, then one could open or close one of the slits at any time, *even after the light had passed the slits, any* time before impact on the screen, and produce the desired results (Wheeler, 1978)! He had hoped to disprove Quantum theory, but when two teams of experimental physicists, one in the US and one in Germany, refined the technology to the point where they could actually perform the delayed-choice experiment, they confirmed Wheeler's conjecture (Wheeler, 1994)! This put physics right back where John Bell said we were: either space and time are not what we think they are, or reality is not independent of the observer - or both.

Few physicists have been able to accept the evidence of direct observer involvement and move forward toward a future that accepts consciousness as fundamental. They include David Bohm,

Eugene Wigner, and more recently, Amit Goswami, Vernon Neppe, some members of this Academy, and a few others. It seems that incorporating consciousness as fundamental to physical reality is offensive and perhaps a little threatening to most physicists. Why do physicists have so much trouble with this? Because it's not what they think physics is supposed to be! The options are so unpalatable that, in the years since the Einstein-Bohr debate and the delayed-choice experiment, physicists have devised an ever-growing number of unnecessarily complex and largely untestable theories trying to avoid the implication that physical reality is not independent of the consciousness of the observer.

What is Physics?

Physics is the simplest of the sciences, involving only four primary *a priori* variables: mass, energy, space and time. The word "physics" is taken from Ancient Greek: φυσική, defined as "knowledge of natural things." The dictionaries say: "Physics is the study of matter (that which has weight and occupies space) and its motion and behavior through space and time." Therefore, by definition, physics excludes the study of the non-physical. Because of this, most mainstream scientists have not accepted what Planck and Einstein, the founders of modern physics said:

Planck: "*As a man who has devoted his whole life to the most clearheaded science, to the study of matter, I can tell you, as a result of my research about the atoms, this much: There is no matter as such! All matter originates and exists only by virtue of a force which brings the particles of an atom to vibration and holds ... the atom together. ... We must assume behind this force the existence of a conscious and intelligent Spirit. This Spirit is the matrix of all matter.* - The Nature of Matter, a 1944 speech, delivered in Florence, Italy.

And Einstein said: "*There is no such thing as an empty space, i.e. a space without a field (involving mass and energy). Space-time does not claim existence of its own, but only as a structural quality of the field."* – Relativity, the Special and General Theory, page 155 of Appendix V. (Einstein,1952)

If you accept these statements by Einstein and Planck, then you must suspect that mainstream science has been on the wrong track for some time now. Matter, energy and space-time cannot exist by themselves, and something major is still missing from the mainstream Standard Model.

What is Still Missing with Planck and Einstein

Separately, the principles of relativity and quantum physics have enjoyed tremendous success in engineering and technology, producing a plethora of electronic devices, gadgets, games and toys, and relieving us of much of the manual labor and drudgery of centuries past. Science, however, has languished without a major paradigm shift since 1935. And worse, mainstream scientists have sought to ignore or explain away the unpalatable involvement of consciousness, because it contradicts the belief that materialism is the metaphysical basis of reality.

Mainstream physicists have busied themselves with working out details within the Standard Model, looking for traces of particles predicted by the model. They continue to try to explain puzzling discoveries, like missing mass, dark matter and dark energy, within the particle zoo. Science simply cannot explain everything using existing mathematical tools, and there are paradoxes and conflicts still existing within the uncomfortable mix of relativity and quantum physics. This situation has led mainstream physicists to say things like: "The more we learn about reality, the more meaningless it becomes!" And: "Quantum physics is counter-intuitive" or: "Quantum physics is weird, don't try to understand it, just accept it and do the calculations!"

All of this is calling out loudly for us to consider another possibility: Could it be that something is still missing from the mainstream map of reality?

We already have the answer to what is missing. Einstein, Planck and others pointed us in the right direction long ago. That which is missing is *consciousness*. We must bring consciousness into science. But the question is: how? Incorporating consciousness into the mathematics of science has been my passion and focus for nearly 50 years. I have spent a lot of effort promoting the need to change the theoretical basis of our scientific paradigm by putting consciousness into the equations of science; but, for the most part, it has fallen on deaf ears. An exception is Dr. Vernon Neppe, who has encouraged me and worked very hard for ten years to get the word out.

Much work is needed for the birthing of a new paradigm. The focus must be on developing a realistic theoretical basis, a workable scientific framework for the next step in the effort to understand the nature of reality. Without creating a solid, empirically supported theoretical basis with the premise that consciousness is fundamental, as Planck and others have suggested, and as the double-slit and delayed-choice experiments have demonstrated, then all the effort will be for naught. Materialists will continue to ignore and/or ridicule the idea that consciousness is primary. We must have a solid scientific basis to support a science that incorporates the actions and effects of the conscious observer, and of Pure Consciousness itself, in objective reality. In the pages that follow, I will endeavor to present an unambiguous way that science can be expanded beyond the confines of materialistic dogma and the current mainstream paradigm.

Gödel's Incompleteness Theorems

The importance of Gödel's Incompleteness Theorems (Gödel, 1931) lies in the fact that they prove that in any finite logical system, there will always be legitimate questions that cannot be answered within that system. And there are questions arising from contradictions and paradoxes existing within the mainstream paradigm today that cannot be answered within the mainstream paradigm. This means that we cannot find answers to these questions unless we expand the paradigm, and expanding the paradigm will require making significant changes in the way we think about reality. It is clear to me that the way to answer those questions and resolve the contradictions and paradoxes, is to expand science to include consciousness so that the next, and most important paradigm shift of all, can occur. The way to do this is to put consciousness directly into the equations of science, and that will require a fundamentally new mathematical approach such as the one proposed in this essay.

What is Missing from the Standard Model?

The methods of particle physicists are clearly prime examples of destructive testing and reductive reasoning. Ernest Rutherford started it all at the University of Manchester in 1899, by firing alpha particles (Helium atoms stripped of their electrons) through a thin gold foil to probe matter and learn how atoms are structured. (Rutherford, 1911) He found that atoms appeared to be made up of tiny dense centers surrounded by a swarm of even tinier negatively charged electrons in a lot of apparently otherwise empty space. This led to the practice of smashing atoms and parts of atoms together with great force in carefully engineered collisions to study the pieces produced. Bigger and better atom-smashers were built over the years, from the cyclotron to the Large Hadron Collider (LHC) to break atoms, protons and neutrons down into smaller and smaller pieces.

The Standard Model of particle physics has been constructed from terabytes of data obtained from destructive testing in particle colliders, and the mathematics used to describe it reflect that approach. In the practical manner of engineering, mathematical concepts have been borrowed from the body of mathematical logic as needed to solve problems, largely without regard for the axiomatic assumptions underlying the mathematics. Understandably, the focus is on results, not overall logical coherence. As a result, some applications, while yielding useful results, may be producing an incorrect and misleading picture of the underlying reality.

A prime example of how this happens is the application of the differential and integral calculus of Leibniz and Newton to quantum phenomena. Newton's calculus depends on the assumptions that equations describing physical processes are continuous functions with variables that can approach zero infinitely closely. Quantum reality, on the other hand, is not continuous, and the variables describing it are not infinitely divisible. Put as simply as possible: There is a bottom to physical reality. The structures of physical reality cannot be divided indefinitely. This means that the calculus of Newton and Leibniz, while very useful at the mid-scale of reality, is inappropriate for application at the quantum level.

This problem with Newtonian calculus has no effect on most macro-scale computations because it lies below the threshold of direct observation and measurement. It is, however, a major problem when investigating reality at the quantum scale. More than a century after Planck's discovery that physical reality is quantized, science still has not fully realized the implications of this discovery. Mainstream scientists remain unaware of the need to replace or refine the calculus they are using to investigate the quantum world. And while all the data identifying the multitude of particles of the "particle zoo" has been very useful, it has produced a picture of reality, which is a sign that something is wrong, and that changes must be made in the way we are investigating quantum phenomena.

When physicists discovered that the elementary particles that make up atoms were spinning with incredible angular velocities, and Einstein's equation $E = mc^2$, called their attention to how much energy is locked up in even the smallest atom, (One unit of mass is equivalent to approximately 90,000,000,000,000,000 units of energy.) they realized that if they could release even part of this energy in an atomic explosion, it would make one hell of a bomb! With the focus on getting funding for producing results for government and the industrial-military complex, it is not surprising that scientific advancement of the understanding of the nature of reality has been at a virtual standstill since 1935.

Beyond the utility of atomic energy as a source of enormous power, the useful knowledge derived from reducing atomic structure to its various parts has been immense: Radio, television, computers, and all the electronic devices that have impacted our lives so profoundly, both positively and negatively. The benefits gained from reductive reasoning are huge. But, is the whole no more than the sum of the parts? Are we missing something by not putting more effort into trying to understand the whole rather than the fragmented parts? What are we missing?

Fortunately, we can now answer that question. We can use the data from destructive testing to reconstruct the language of the quantum world and shed some much-needed light on the way elementary particles combine to form the structure of physical reality.

Language, Mathematics and Units of Measurement

We must re-examine the basics, and language is basic. Language is constructed of individual words and phrases, organized into logical structures that are used to communicate. Just as the average person uses language to describe and think about things, scientists use mathematics to describe the real world. Traditionally, the units of quantification have been chosen for practical purposes and convenience of computation. Since funding for research is predominantly driven by the problem-solving requirements of government and military concerns, the mathematical language being used in the Standard Model is tailored primarily for reductive reasoning, not the integrative reasoning that is required for investigating the nature of reality.

What the Standard Model particle physicists do, by blowing atoms apart and applying reductive reasoning, is to conclude that atomic structure is simpler than it really is. I think another quote attributed to my hero, Albert Einstein, is appropriate here. He said: *"Everything should be made as simple as possible, but not simpler"* (Einstein, 1953).

Scientists have tried throughout history to identify the basic building blocks of physical reality, starting with cells and molecules, proceeding downward to atoms and smaller and smaller particles, all the way to electrons and quarks that combine to form atoms. However, the process of breaking atoms and subatomic particles apart to see what they're made of has its limitations. Is an atom really just the sum of the parts flying away from a collision? Or is the whole more than the sum of the parts? The unfounded belief that reality is no more than physical structures built up of the random combination of lifeless particles is the fallacy of materialism in a nutshell.

If what particle physicists have assumed was true, then by reductive reasoning it follows that all the mass and energy of the parts added up should equal the mass and energy of the whole. In fact, terabytes of experimental data indicate otherwise. The mass of the proton, e.g., is much more than the sum of the masses of their particle constituents consisting of two up quarks and one down quark. Something else is going on. The current paradigm proposes the existence of "gluons" or a "gluon plasma" as the answer. Gluons are said to be "force carriers." But, individual gluons are said to be massless, and thus have only been detected by statistical analysis of jets seen shooting from certain types of collisions in particle colliders. The data appear to be statistically significant; however, statistical analysis is used when physical detail is lacking, and it doesn't seem to bother particle physicists that a massless particle is a physical oxymoron! As we proceed with our analysis, we will see that gluons were just an *ad hoc* invention needed to make the Standard Model work.

Bohr's resolution of the EPR paradox and the Aspect experiment tell us that elementary particles do not exist until irreversibly registered in some way. Gluons are teased into existence in high energy particle colliders, but do not actually exist inside protons and neutrons. A much more reasonable hypothesis is the possibility that particles inside the atom merge volumetrically, like drops of a fluid, until forced apart by collision and measurement. If this is true, then our picture of the stable atom as particles held together by massless force-carrying "particles" and physical bonds is wrong. While the tinker-toy models in our physics and chemistry textbooks may help us imagine what a molecule is thought to be made of, they are probably almost completely wrong.

How do we change it? Planck's discovery told us that there is an end to the descent into the building blocks of reality. Smaller than the smallest particle, there is a smallest unit of measurement beyond which nothing in physical reality can be quantified. Unfortunately, the Standard Model does not tell us what that measurement unit is. Planck attempted to provide such a unit (Planck, 1899), but he did not have the information and terabytes of data from particle colliders that we do today. Our first task in defining a new truly quantum math is to establish a minimum quantum equivalence unit to which all measurements can be mathematically related. This unit must be tied directly to data like that provided by the LHC and other particle colliders. This newly defined quantum unit will give us the basis for the quantum math needed to replace Newtonian calculus. Doing this will allow us to describe quantum reality within the atom more accurately.

Conclusion

We must develop appropriate natural units, and an appropriate calculus for the proper description of quantum reality, a description that accommodates and incorporates the principles of quantum physics and relativity and includes consciousness.

The Calculus of Dimensional Distinctions

Rigorous derivations of the mathematical concepts of the CoDD are too lengthy for inclusion in this chapter. Nevertheless, a brief discussion of some of the basic concepts should be helpful because many of the key concepts being presented were discovered by applying the CoDD to questions and paradoxes in the current mainstream paradigm (Close, 1990). The CoDD is a proto-type system of mathematical logic developed from an adaptation of G. Spencer Brown's calculus of indications found in his major work, Laws of Form. (Brown, 1977) It retains the simplicity and logical precedence of Brown's calculus, while expanding the conceptual basis and notation to describe multi-dimensional distinctions. It also highlights the importance of existence, which is crucial in mathematical physics, but was considered unnecessary in the symbolic logic of Brown's calculus. The CoDD also goes beyond Brown's work to include consciousness.

Because of the importance of dimensionality in mathematical physics, movement from an n-dimensional domain to an n+1-dimensional domain, warrants mention here. Called Dimensional Extrapolation, it involves rotation in a plane within an n-dimensional domain and projection out of that domain into an n+1-dimensional domain. When applied, it reveals the relationship of the geometry of dimensional domains with the imaginary and complex numbers of number theory. An important advantage is gained over the conventional Newtonian calculus with the CoDD because the basic existential units of the CoDD are 3-dimensional, allowing the operations of the CoDD to start where Newtonian calculus becomes difficult and often intractable, i.e., dealing with phenomena existing in more than three dimensions. As noted before, an in-depth understanding of the CoDD is not required for the reader to understand the material presented here. These facts about the CoDD are included to help the reader who might be interested in knowing how this new understanding of multi-dimensional reality was obtained.

The Nature and Role of Consciousness

Consciousness is involved at the quantum level in the drawing of distinctions, as shown by the resolution of the EPR Paradox and the double slit, delayed choice experiments. Therefore, as stated previously, we must also include consciousness in any calculus designed to deal with quantum reality, starting with the Axiomatic assumptions of the calculus.

The axiomatic Basis for a Quantum Calculus that includes consciousness:

Consciousness is *a priori*: it Depends on Nothing.

The First Distinction is the Distinction of Self from Other.

The Logic of the Calculus of Dimensional Distinctions is Triadic, not Binary.

We exist in a reality that is currently defined by three dimensions of space (3S), and a single point in time (1t). In this dimensional domain (3S-1t), the three functions of consciousness in making a physical observation are:

The primary function of consciousness is to draw the distinction of self from other. This is the basis of all cognition.

The secondary function of consciousness is to *draw* distinctions in self and other and *organize* them into *meaningful* patterns.

The tertiary function of consciousness is to create negative entropy for the purpose of spiritual evolution, which is the motive behind all mental and physical change.

Consciousness has been incorporated in the CoDD from the beginning. In this discussion, however, we will use conventional mathematical concepts, introducing the physical aspects of the quantum equivalence unit first, allowing consciousness to make its appearance in the natural course of the logical development of the quantum equivalence units.

The Basis of the Quantum Equivalence Unit

The mass, energy and volume of the smallest object among the natural components that make up the subatomic structure of the observable universe are the *logical* basic units for use as the unitary distinctions of the CoDD. Therefore, the basic parametric values of the quantum equivalence unit are the rest mass, energy and volume of the free electron. Particle physicists define one unit of energy as the energy required to move an electron across an electrical potential difference of one volt. This basic unit of energy is defined as one electron volt (1eV), which is about 1.602×10^{-19} joule in standard international (SI) units. A reference frame is established in the LHC, so that mass and energy are directly related by $E = mc^2 \rightarrow m = E/c^2$, allowing mass to be measured as MeV/c^2. Since the number of eV units is very, very large for most measurements of mass, the notation mega (million) electron volts (MeV) is commonly used. We will also follow the practice established in the system of Planck units, where the speed of light is normalized, by defining one unit of distance as the distance traveled by light in one unit of time. In this way, both mass and energy are measured in equivalence units of mega electron volts.

Next, to complete the definition of the basic equivalence unit of the quantum calculus (CoDD), we need to determine the volume of the rest mass of the electron, which is usually assumed to be a point, i.e., *zero*, in contemporary particle physics. We know, however, that this cannot be literally true, because in a quantized reality, mass and energy are quantized in finite units greater than zero; but what about space? The concept of "empty" space implies that space can be divided indefinitely. But recall that Einstein said, based on the findings of general relativity: *"There is no such thing as an empty space"* (Einstein, 1952). If he was correct, then the calculus of Newton and Leibniz, the mathematical procedure used today to analyze physical reality, is inappropriate for application to quantum phenomena because it is based on the axiomatic assumption that space is indefinitely divisible.

Planck units (Planck, 1899) are derived by normalization of the five "universal" constants, which besides the speed of light, c, are the gravitational constant, G^0, the Coulomb constant, C, the Boltzmann constant, K, and the reduced Planck constant, which is the Planck constant, h, divided by 2π. Normalization means that these constants become units of measurement. In the CoDD quantum calculus system, we have normalized the minimal quantum of mass, the electron, and by normalizing space-time units, we also normalize the speed of light, as is done in the Planck system of units and other "natural" unit systems, but that is where the similarity ends. In the Planck unit system and other natural unit systems, normalization is done at the macro-scale to simplify computations in SI or English units of measurement, whereas in the CoDD we have normalized the basic units of measurement of mass, energy, space and time at the quantum scale. With this difference in mind, let's look again at the equation $E = mc^2$, which expresses the mathematical equivalence of mass and energy.

$E = mc^2$, → $c = \sqrt{(E/m)}$. In the CoDD, the speed of light is defined as the movement of radiant energy over one unit of distance in one unit of time ($c = \Delta x/\Delta t = \sqrt{(E)}/\sqrt{(m)}$). The current materialistic paradigm has not incorporated Einstein's declaration that *"Space-time does not claim existence of its own"* (Einstein, 1952) by assuming that space-time is something that can be divided indefinitely. That means that Δx and Δt can approach zero, but then $c = \Delta x/\Delta t \to 0/0$ which is undefined, and cannot be true if c is constant. On the other hand, if we recognize that, as we descend to the quantum scale, Δx approaches a non-zero quantum limit, and if we can normalize the quanta of space and time as we did the mass of the electron, then $\Delta x \to 1$. and $\Delta t \to 1$, and $c = \Delta x/\Delta t = 1/1 = 1$, which is the normalized value of c, presenting no contradiction. For applications of Newton's calculus to be valid at the quantum scale, Δx must be infinitely divisible. But, if that were true, then, the de Broglie wave length, λ could approach zero, which means that $h = p\lambda$ can approach 0, which cannot be true, because h is Planck's constant and p is momentum, which, as a function of energy, is quantized. By allowing Δx to approach zero, as it must do in Newtonian calculus applications, self-contradictory concepts of dimensionless and massless quantum particles like gluons and bosons are needed to make the Standard Model work.

Max Planck said; *"Heretofore we cannot speak of matter or energy alone"* (Planck, 1914). And Albert Einstein said: *"There is no such thing as an empty space"* (Einstein, 1952).

These two brilliant scientists were telling us that the world we perceive through the filters of our physical senses, and which we think of as solid matter existing in empty space, is an illusion. If we take Planck seriously, there is no such thing as solid matter, and the measurement we call mass is simply a measure of inertia. But what is inertia? Why do elementary particles have inertia?

How is it generated? We know that elementary particles spin, and spin creates inertia. Could they be spinning fast enough to create the inertia we detect as mass?

We usually think of mass and weight as the same thing, but this is not true. *Mass and weight are demonstrably not the same thing.* Weight is a relative measure that is meaningless if taken out of environmental context. A person who weighs 180 pounds on Earth only weighs about 30 pounds on the moon, and becomes weightless in outer space. However, the mass of any object, the measure of the inertial resistance to motion, remains the same if the object is at rest relative to the reference frame of measurement. So, the real measure of mass is inertia, not weight. This is an important distinction, and a key concept in relating mass-energy to space-time in natural quantum equivalence units.

The mathematical relationships between finite mass, motion, momentum, and inertia are well known, so let's see how they apply to the electron. If there is a minimum volume of space that can be occupied by the electron, then that volume is the quantum unit of space in our quantum calculus. Once developed, a fully quantized mathematical system will help us to see beyond the illusion of matter and empty space.

Normalization of the light-speed constant c, and the use of the mass/energy equivalence expressed by $E = mc^2$, ensure that Planck and Einstein's injunctions are included in the unitary equivalence of mass, energy, space, and time, but the natural quantum equivalence unit must also include the unitary equivalence of a measure of consciousness if it is to function as the basic unit of our new calculus. To date, mainstream science has not accepted the direct involvement of consciousness in physical reality, and has no real definition of consciousness, and has so far developed no way to measure consciousness. So, how do we do this? First, we restate and expand Planck's axiomatic statement that "*…we cannot speak of matter or energy alone…*" (Planck, 1914) to include space, time and consciousness as follows:

"Henceforth, we cannot speak of mass, energy, space, time or consciousness alone. Any observed distinction, i.e. any existential phenomenon, must involve all five of the basic parameters: mass, energy, space, time, and consciousness."

The application of this axiom to the stable phenomena of quarks and electrons, will allow us to determine the quantum equivalence units of any one of the measurement parameters, if we have the empirical values of the other four translated into quantum equivalence units. We have taken the rest mass of the electron as the quantum unit of mass to which all other measures of mass are normalized because, among the primary particles that make up the natural elements, it has the smallest mass. And with $E = mc^2$ and the normalization of c, we can calculate quantum equivalence units for any subatomic particle detected in the LHC. Then, by writing the equation for the combination of the up-quarks and down-quarks that form a proton, using normalized LHC data, we can determine the total number of quantum equivalence units needed to form a stable proton. Since mass, energy, space and time are included in the normalization of $E = mc^2$, if any additional units are needed for symmetrical stability, they will have to be units of the fifth variable, and the fifth variable, after mass, energy, space and time, is consciousness.

The Derivation of Quantum Equivalence

Warning: The discussions that follow contain mathematical physics with derivations and proofs. They are needed to make this presentation complete, and to demonstrate the ability of the new paradigm to explain quantum phenomena. There are three steps involving mathematics and physics needed to derive and apply the quantum equivalence unit. They are:

The application of relativistic adjustments to the dynamic spin of the electron when it is stripped from a Hydrogen atom in the process of ionization. This must be done to determine the minimum volume occupied by the free electron. The minimum volume and rest mass of the free electron are critical components in the definition of the quantum equivalence unit.

The second step involves applying the quantum equivalence unit to the symmetric combinations of the quarks that form protons and neutrons. This results in the discovery that a third form of the content of reality is required for atomic structure to be stable. Since this third form of content cannot be measured as mass or energy, it is by definition, *non-physical*. We have chosen *gimmel*, the third character of the Hebrew alphabet to represent it.

The third step is the determination of the proportions of gimmel to mass and energy in the atoms of the Periodic Table of Elements, illustrating the role of the non-physical in the forming of the mathematical structure of the physical universe.

I have tried to make the mathematical physics as self-explanatory as possible, but some readers may find the math too much to wade through. Those readers may want to read the text, skipping over the equations and calculations, and come back to them later, if necessary for clarity. Some of the calculations that follow were performed by the Austrian-born, Swiss Physicist Wolfgang Pauli in the 1930s when he was exploring extra dimensions and symmetry (Guilini, 2008). It is probable that others have made similar calculations, but perhaps failed to recognize their significance.

In quantum reality, by definition, there is no such thing as a dimensionless particle, so we can relate de Broglie's wave length for the electron, $\lambda_e = \Delta x$, to the quantum volume of the free spinning electron, and we shall find that Einstein's relativity provides us with a way to do this. To determine the relativistic effects of the spinning of the free electron that affect its spatial volume, we begin by determining the angular momentum of the electron in orbit around a Hydrogen atom. To do that, we need to know the rest mass of the electron, the velocity, v_o, of the electron in orbit, and r_o, the radius of the orbit.

De Broglie's equation for the quantum matter-wave applied to an electron in orbit around a Hydrogen atom is: $\lambda_o = h/m_e v_o \sqrt{[1 - (v_o/c)^2]}$, where λ_o is wave length associated with the electron, which is also the circumference of the orbit; h is Planck's constant, m_e is the mass of the electron, v_o is the velocity of rotation around the atom's nucleus, c is the speed of light, and $\sqrt{[1 - v_o^2/c^2]}$, often represented by the Greek letter γ, is the Lorentz contraction factor of wave length due to velocity relative to the observer.

To calculate v_o, the velocity of the orbiting electron, we will assume that it is a small fraction of the speed of light, making the relativistic adjustment at this point negligible, so that λ_o is approximately equal to $h/m_e v_o$. This is expressed symbolically by $\lambda_o \approx h/m_e v_o$. We can also make use of four other well-known equations:

1. $F_o = m_e v_o^2/r_o$, the outward Centrifugal Force equation (v_o = tangential orbital velocity, r_o = orbital radius)
2. $\lambda_o = 2\pi r_o$, the wave length of the electron in orbit
3. F_i (inward force) = $(K q_1 q_2)/r_o^2$, Coulomb's equation for the attractive force due to electrical charge, where K is Coulomb's constant, q_1 is the electron charge and q_2 is the charge on the nucleus of the hydrogen atom.
4. $E = \frac{1}{2} m_e v_o^2$, the classical equation for kinetic energy

Note: In these calculations, we are using SI units rather than the natural units we are developing, for two reasons: 1) We haven't yet defined all five of the basic quantum equivalence units, and 2) we'll be able to directly compare our results with known empirical results that are expressed in SI units, as we go through the calculations.

The SI parameters used in these calculations are defined as follows:

F = Force in joules, m_e = the mass of the electron = 9.1094×10^{-31} kg, r_o = radius of the electron's orbit in meters, v_o = orbital velocity in meters per second (m/s), $\pi = 3.14159$, E = energy in electron volts (Ev), $q_1 = -q_2 = 1.6021 \times 10^{-19}$ coulomb, h = Planck's constant = 6.6261×10^{-34} joule sec (J·s), K = Coulomb constant = 8.9876×10^9, and $c = 2.99792 \times 10^8$ m/sec.

Note: $q_1 = -q_2$ because the charge of the electron, generally considered to be negative, is equal and opposite to the charge of the proton.

In the calculations below, the units of measurement will be applied as defined above, but they will not appear in most of the equations for brevity. Using the first three equations above, Planck's constant, the Coulomb constant, the mass and charge of the electron, all measured and validated empirically by generations of experimental physicists, we can test our assumption that the orbital velocity of the electron encircling the Hydrogen atom is a relatively small fraction of the speed of light as follows:

Solving equations (1) and (2) for r_o, we have $r_o = m_e v_o^2 / F_o$ and $r_o = \lambda_o / 2\pi$. Then, equating the two expressions for r_o, we have:

$\lambda_o / 2\pi = m v_o^2 / F_o \rightarrow F_o = (2\pi m_e v_o^2) / \lambda_o$ and $\lambda_o = h / m_e v_o \rightarrow F_o = (2\pi m e^2 v_o^3$ (5.)

Also, substituting $r_o^2 = (\lambda_o / 2\pi)^2$ into equation (3.), we have:
$F_i = (4\pi 2 \, K q_1 \, q_2) / \lambda_o^2$, and $\lambda_o = h / m c v_o \rightarrow F_i = (4\pi^2 \, K q_1 \, q_2 \, m e^2 \, v_o^2) / h^2$ (6.)

We can equate the two expressions (5) and (6) for force, because, if the outward centripetal force, F_o, were not exactly equal to the inward attractive force of electrical charge, F_i, the electron would either fly away from the hy-drogen atom, or spiral into the nucleus. Setting the expressions for the two forces equal, we have: $(2\pi m e^2 v_o^3)/h = (4\pi^2 \, K q_1 \, q_2 \, m e^2 \, v_o^2)/h^2$. Cancelling like terms on both sides of the equation, we have $v_0 = 2\pi K|q_1 q_2|/h = 2\pi K q_1^2/h = [2\times(3.14159)\times(8.9876\times10^9)\times(1.6021\times10^{-19})^2]/6.6261\times10^{-34}$, which simplifies to:

$v_0 = 2.1874\times10^6$ m/s

This is a tremendous velocity relative to our everyday experience of velocities of objects like automobiles or jet planes (it is approximately five thou-sand times the speed of the fastest commercial jet), but it is only a small fraction of the speed of light (about 0.0073 c). The relativistic effect at this velocity is determined by applying the factor $\sqrt{[1 - v^2/c^2]} = 0.9997$ to Louis de Broglie's matter-wave equation. But we see that the resulting value of vo will be changed by less than the rounding error.

This demonstrates the fact that our beginning assumption, λ_0 h/mevo was valid. We can also check this result against empiri-cal measurement data as follows: The energy required to free an electron from a hydrogen atom, is measured in high-energy particle physics experiments as 13.6 Ev. If we calculate the orbital energy of the electron using our result for vo and the equation relating energy to mass and velocity, we get: $E = 1/2(m_e v_0^2) = 1/2(9.1094\times10^{31})(2.1874\times10^6)^2 = 2.1793\times10^{-18}$ joules, and $(2.1793\times10^{-18}$ joules$)/1.6021\times10^{-19}$ joules per Ev $= 13.603$ Ev, in very close agreement with the experimental value of 13.6 Ev.

Definition #1: The quantum unit of mass is the rest mass of the electron, and its equivalence in energy is the quantum unit of energy. The next step is to see how the angular momentum of the electron in orbit translates to the angular momentum of the free electron, and determine the minimum possible volume of space occupied by the free electron. This is the volume of space that we will use as the quantum equivalent measure of space in our quantum calculus.

Conservation of Angular Momentum and Electron Spin

The effects of conservation of angular momentum is impressively demonstrated by a spinning figure skater. If the skater starts to spin with arms out-stretched laterally, and then slowly pulls her arms in close to her body, the velocity of the spin increases dramatically. In a Hydrogen atom, a negatively charged electron spins around the nucleus, a positively charged proton, in a hollow spherical volume capable of containing two electrons, trying to neutralize the positive charge of the proton to reach equilibrium. The electron can be separated from the hydrogen atom by an external force equal to or greater than its attraction to the nucleus. When that happens, the electron stripped from the atom no longer occupies the volume of the orbit around the atom. It contracts, falling into its center, occupying less and less volume and, just as with the skater, conservation of angular momentum causes its angular velocity to increase dramatically.

The angular momentum of an electron in orbit around a Hydrogen atom is:

$$L_o = I_o \omega_o$$

Where I_o is the moment of inertia in kg·m^2, and ω_o is angular velocity in radians per second. In accordance with Newton's second law, the mass of an object rotating about a center is thrown outward toward a maximum circumference in the plane of rotation until the centrifugal force is equaled by the electrical force attracting the electron back toward the center. This process yields $I_o = m_e r_o^2$, where m_e is the mass of the electron and r_o is the radius of the orbit. The tangential velocity of the electron at any point in orbit around the Hydrogen atom is $v_o = r_o \omega_o \rightarrow \omega_o = v_o/r_o$, and the momentum of the electron is $L_o = I_o \omega_o = m_e r_o^2 (v_o/r_o) = m_e r_o v_o$.

Conservation of momentum requires that when the electron is

freed from the hydrogen atom, all the momentum of its orbital motion is transferred to the angular momentum of spin as the volume it occupies contracts from the geometry of the outer shell of the atom toward the minimum localized quantum volume of the free electron, and the resulting angular momentum is $L_e = I_e\omega_e = m_e r_e^2(v_e/r_e) = m_e r_e v_e$. Since momentum is always conserved, *and the rest mass of the electron is known*, we can equate the angular momentum before and after ionization:

$$L = m_e r_o v_o = r_e m_e v_e \rightarrow r_o v_o = r_e v_e \quad (7.)$$

Where r_e is the radius of the free electron and v_e is the spin velocity of the free electron. Solving equation (7.) for v_e, we have:

$$v_e = r_o v_o / r_e \quad (8.)$$

The radii of the hydrogen atom and the electron are well known from experimental data. The radius of the hydrogen atom is $r_o = 5.290 \times 10^{-11}$m and the radius of a free electron is $r_e = 2.8179 \times 10^{-15}$m. We calculated the velocity of the electron in orbit as $v_o = 2.1874 \times 10^6$ m/s. Substituting in these known values, we have:

$$v_e = 5.290 \times 10^{-11} \times 2.1874 \times 10^6 / 2.8179 \times 10^{-15} = 4.106 \times 10^{10} \text{ m/s}$$

The velocity of the electron in orbit was a very small fraction of the speed of light, but we have calculated the angular velocity of the free electron, as more than 100x c! ($c = 2.99792 \times 10^8$ m/s). But this is impossible. The electron cannot be spinning with an angular velocity faster than light speed.

A basic axiom of the theory of relativity is that nothing can be accelerated past the speed of light. Even if the angular velocity of the spinning electron reaches light speed, the volume of the electron must still be finite in quantized reality. This volume is the smallest possible space that can be occupied by the electron, and is thus our CoDD quantum of space, corresponding with the mass of the spinning free electron. i.e., 0.511 MeV/c^2 = 1 quantum equivalence unit.

Definition #2: The quantum unit of extent is the minimum

volume of the free electron.

Just as it made sense to make the rest mass of the free electron the CoDD quantum unit of mass, it makes sense to take the minimum volume of the free electron as the quantum unit of space. That volume is $4/3\pi r_e^3 = 4/3\pi(2.8179 \times 10^{-15}\text{m})^3 = 2.6411 \times 10^{-43}$ m³. This ultimately small distinction of extent has this finite value because of the limit placed on the rotational velocity of any physical object by relativity. We make it our *normalized* unit of space-time volume in the CoDD by assigning it the numerical value of 1, and we now have a vortical unit of mass-energy-space equivalence to use as the basic unit of the CoDD.

To complete the set of quantum equivalence units for the basic measures of physical reality, we need to determine the magnitude of the appropriate quantum unit of time. We can do this using the quantum nature of the electron, and the normalized speed of light. The speed of any physical object moving in the reference frame of an observer is defined as the distance traveled in one unit of time. Considering light as a physical object, a particle, i.e. a photon, $c = \Delta x/\Delta t \rightarrow \Delta t = \Delta x/c = 2\pi r_e/c = 2\pi(2.8179 \times 10^{-15}\text{m})$ divided by $(2.99792 \times 10^8 \text{m/s}) = 5.5059 \times 10^{-23}$ second. In normalized quantum equivalent units, c and $\Delta x = 1$. Therefore, because $c = \Delta x/\Delta t$, it follows that $\Delta t = 1$ in quantum equivalent units.

Definition #3: The quantum unit of time is the time for light to travel one unit of space.

And we have all five quantum equivalence units normalized to the measurements of the electron as the unitary distinction of the CoDD.

> *All measurements described in these quantum equivalence units will always be integers. And all equations describing the combinations of subatomic particles will be Diophantine equations (equations requiring integer solutions). This proves to be very useful for describing the*

combinations of elementary particles to form the atom, providing powerful insights into atomic structure, producing unambiguous results.

The next step is to determine the exact number of CoDD quantum equivalence units contained in each of the elementary particles that make up the natural atoms of the Periodic Table.

The Building Blocks of the Universe

Within the theoretical framework of the Standard Model of particle physics, terabytes of particle collider data are analyzed statistically to yield numerical values for the masses of sub-atomic particles in units of MeV/c^2. The masses that are of particular interest to us are the up-quarks, down-quarks, electrons, neutrons and protons. We will convert the LHC data for these particles into true quantum equivalence units, which will provide us with a way to analyze sub-atomic structure. Using CoDD Diophantine equations with the true quantum equivalent unit as the basic unit of measurement, we can explore the relationships between the elementary particles within the Hydrogen atom, and see how each of the stable elements of the Periodic Table are formed.

The empirically determined inertial masses of the three most basic elementary entities that make up the atoms of the elements of the periodic table, i.e. electrons, up-quarks and down-quarks are 0.511, 2.01 and 4.8 MeV/c^2, respectively. The values for up and down quarks are derived statistically from millions of terabytes of data. We can see from these data that the conventional mass-energy unit, MeV/c^2, is not a completely quantum unit, because the data contain fractions of one MeV/c^2. In the basic quantum equivalence system of units, we defined above, the masses of the electron, up-quark and down-quark are integer multiples of the basic quantum unit. Our task now is to determine what the actual integer values of the electron and up- and down-quarks are in quantum equivalence units.

Except for the electron, the data for the mass/energy equivalence of the elementary particles, up and down quarks, in Table One below, are given in *ranges* of values because the masses of these elementary particles are determined as energy equivalents in the particle collider. Even with the advances in technological precision from the first atom smasher, the Cockcroft-Walton particle accelerator, in 1932, to the LHC today, some measurement error is unavoidable due to the extremely small size of the phenomena and the indirect methods required to collect and interpret the data. However, because the electron mass is one of the most fundamental constants of physics, and is very important in physical chemistry and electronics, great pain has been taken to determine its rest mass very accurately. The rest mass of the electron is 0.511 MeV/c^2. The integer values in Table One are obtained by setting the electron mass equal to unity and determining the average masses of the up- and down-quarks as multiples of that unit. This gives us the normalized (integer) masses of the electron, up- and down-quarks.

Using the latest available data, the masses of the up- and down-quarks to three significant figures are 2.01 MeV/c^2 and 4.79

Table One: The Stable Elementary Objects

particle	Symbol	Spin	Charge	Mass in MEv LHC Data	Normalized Mass	Naturalized Mass
Electron	e	½	-1	0.511	0.511	1
Up-quark	u	1/2	+2/3	1.87 - 2.15	2.05*	4
Down-quark	d	1/2	-1/3	4.60 - 4.95	4.63*	9
Proton	p⁺	1/2	+1	740 - 1140	938.1	1836
Neutron	N⁰	1/2	none	939.6	939.6	1839

MeV/c^2 respectively. Dividing by 0.511 and rounding, we have the normalized mass/energy equivalence for the electron, up- and down- quarks, as 1, 4 and 9 respectively. Using these values, we can determine how the finite distinctions they represent can combine to form protons and neutrons

These estimates fall within the current most mathematically precise ranges of quark mass

determined by Lattice QCD calculations: Up-quark mass = 2.01±0.14 MeV/c2; Down-quark mass = 4.79±0.16 MeV/c2. - Cho, Adrian (April 2010). "Mass of the Common Quark Finally Nailed Down" . Science Magazine

** *"Normalized" means converting to quantum equivalence units. This is justified because in a quantized reality, the actual values must be integer multiples of the basic quantum unit.*

Elementary Particles and Units of Measurement

To see how the minimal quantum extent and content of our smallest CoDD distinction relates to known elementary particles, we must write equations describing the combination of up- and down-quarks to form the proton and neutron of the Hydrogen atom. Since all measurable parameters are quantized in the CoDD, for quarks to combine in stable structures, they must satisfy the Diophantine (integer) equations describing the combination. The family of Diophantine equations describing the combination of particles is represented mathematically by the Conveyance Expression:

$$\Sigma^n_{i=1} (X_n)^m = Z^m$$

Because the various forms of this expression, as m varies from 3 to 4 and more, convey the geometry of multi-dimensional reality to our observational domain of 3S-1t, we call this expression the "Conveyance Expression", and individual equations of the expression, *Conveyance Equations*. When $n = m = 2$, the expression yields the Conveyance Equation:

$$(X_1)^2 + (X_2)^2 = Z^2$$

which, when related to areas, describes the addition of two square areas, A_1 and A_2 with sides equal to X_1 and X_2 respectively, to form a third square area, A_3, with sides equal to Z. When these squares are arranged in a plane with two corners of each square coinciding with corners of the other squares to form a right triangle, as shown below, we have a geometric representation of the familiar Pythagorean Theorem, demonstrating that the sum of the squares of the sides of any right triangle is equal to the square of the third side (the hypotenuse) of that triangle.

$$(AB)^2 + (BC)^2 = (AC)^2$$

The Pythagorean Theorem

We use the Pythagorean Theorem in Dimensional Extrapolation to define the rotation in, and orthogonal projection from one dimensional domain into another. There are an infinite number of solutions for this equation, one for every conceivable right triangle, but in a quantized reality, we are only concerned with integer solutions.

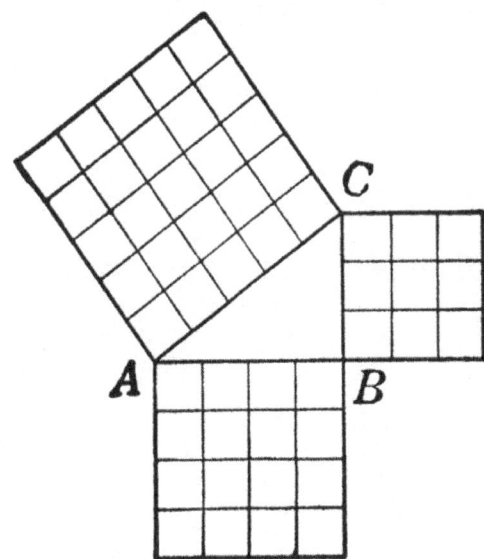

So, considering the Pythagorean equation as Diophantine, we find that there exists an infinite subset of solutions with AB = X_1, BC = X_2 and AC = Z all equal to integers. Members of this subset, e.g. (3,4,5), (5,12,13), (8,15,17), etc., satisfy the equation: ($3^2 + 4^2 = 5^2$, $5^2 + 12^2 = 13^2$, $8^2 + 15^2 = 17^2$, ...) these solutions are called "Pythagorean triples."

It should not be surprising that the Pythagorean Theorem equation, the equations of Fermat's Last Theorem and other important equations are generated by the Conveyance Expression. These theorems play key roles in the geometry and mathematics of the CoDD and the combination of elementary particles to form stable physical structures. When n = 2 and m = 3, the expression yields the equation:

$$(X^1)^3 + (X^2)^3 = Z^3$$

And when we define X^1, X^2 and Z as measures of volumes, just as we defined them as measures of areas when n = m = 2, we can apply this equation to volumes in a three-dimensional domain.

Using the minimal electron volume as the quantum unit of measurement, we have a Diophantine equation with X^1 and X^2 equal to whole-number multiples of our quantum equivalence unit. If these particles are spherical, the combination of their volumes would be described by the expression $4/3\pi(r_1)^3 + 4/3\pi(r_2)^3$, and if their combination produces a third spherical object, then we would have:

$$4/3\pi(r_1)^3 + 4/3\pi(r_2)^3 = 4/3\pi(r_2)^3,$$

where r^3 is the radius of the new particle. Dividing through by the common factor $4/3\pi$, we have:

$$(r_1)^3 + (r_2)^3 = (r_3)^3,$$

which we can treat as a Diophantine equation of the form:

$$X^m + Y^m = Z^m, \text{ with } m = 3$$

Notice that the factor $4/3\pi$ cancels out, indicating that this form of the equation is obtained regardless of the shape of the particles, *so long as all three particles have the same shape*. In a quantized reality, the radii will be integer multiples of the minimum quantum length. Fermat's Last Theorem (Singh, 2002) tells us that if X and Y are integers, Z *cannot be an integer*. This means that the right-hand side of this equation, representing the result of combining two symmetric quantum particles, cannot be a symmetric quantum particle. The Diophantine equation, $X^m + Y^m = Z^m$, becomes an inequality, and as a physical object, the result will be asymmetric, and the combined high-velocity angular momentum transferred into the new particle will cause it to fly apart.

This may lead one to wonder why there are *any* stable particles, and why there is a physical universe at all. Suddenly, we are confronted with Leibniz's "most important" question: *why is there something instead of nothing* (Leibniz, 1697)? The answer is relatively simple, but has been hidden from us by the limitations of our methods of observation and calculation. Depending upon physical observations, the most perfectly symmetrical object appears to be a sphere; but this is not true in a quantized reality.

Symmetrical spherical objects *would* exist if we were in a Newton-Leibniz non-quantized world, but we exist in a Planck-Einstein quantized world. In this world, the simplest 3-dimensional symmetrical objects are the regular convex polyhedrons, known as the Platonic solids. (*A regular* convex *polyhedron is a multi-sided, three-dimensional convex form with all sides of equal length.*) There are only five Platonic solids. This fact is closely related to the geometrical restrictions of Fermat's Last Theorem and the integral solutions of Conveyance Equations. The question of how the 5 Platonic solids relate to elementary particles is an interesting one; it is, however, beyond the scope of this discussion.

An easily visualized regular convex polyhedron is the six-sided one, the cube. In a Newtonian world, the number of sides of a two-dimensional regular polygon could increase indefinitely, approaching the symmetrical form of a circle. Similarly, if we imagine the number of sides of a regular convex polyhedron increasing without limit, while the total volume approaches a finite limit, the object would become a sphere. But in the real world of quantized distinctions, the number of sides possible is limited because of the finite size of the unit of measurement, the quantum equivalence unit. And, because the shape factor cancels out for m = 3, Fermat's Last Theorem tells us that, regardless of the number of sides, two regular convex symmetric solids composed of unitary quantum volumes cannot combine to form a third regular convex symmetric solid composed of unitary quantum equivalence volumes.

To help understand the physical reality of this, we can visualize the quantum unit in the shape of a cube. Using it as a building block, we can investigate particle symmetry by constructing perfect cubes as follows: a cube with 2 blocks on each side will contain 8 blocks; a cube with 3 blocks on each side, 27 blocks; a cube with 4 blocks on each side, 64 blocks, etc. Fermat's Last Theorem tells us that if we stack the blocks of any two cubes together, the resulting stack of blocks will always be at least 1 block short, or 1 block or more over the number needed to form a cube.

Elementary particles spin with a lot of *angular momentum*, and combining *two* of them composed of quantum units will never produce a symmetric result, and the combined angular momentum will cause it to fly apart. This requirement of symmetry for maximum physical stability creates the intrinsic structure of reality and is reflected throughout universe. It turns out that there *can* be symmetrically stable structures in the universe because when n = m = 3, the Conveyance Expression yields the equation:

$$(X^1)^3 + (X^2)^3 + (X^3)^3 = Z^3,$$

which *does* have integer solutions. The first one (with the smallest integer values) is:

$$3^3 + 4^3 + 5^3 = 6^3$$

The Diophantine equations produced by the Conveyance Expression, $\Sigma^{ni=1} (X^n)^m = Z^m$ when n, m, X_i and Z are *integers* yields Diophantine equations describing the only symmetrical structures *possible* in the 3S-1t domain of physical observation. Thus, they convey the logical structure of the conscious drawing of distinctions. The equations yielded when n = m = 3 describe all the possible combinations of unitary quantum distinctions. When the equations have *integer* solutions, they represent symmetrically stable combinations, and when they do not have integer solutions, they are inequalities representing asymmetric, *unstable* combinations that will not be capable of supporting and sustaining life, and acting as suitable vehicles for consciousness.

The table below shows the first five equations generated by the Conveyance Expression.

As we saw, when n = 3 and m = 2, Fermat's Last Theorem proves that the Diophantine Conveyance Expression yields only inequalities, excluding three-dimensional binomial combinations from the stable structures that elementary particles may form.

On the other hand, the Expression when n = m = 3, yields an equation which has integer solutions, producing trinomial combinations of elementary particles that *do* form stable structures. *This explains why there is something rather than nothing, and why quarks forming stable protons and neutrons are only found in combinations of three.*

Table Two: Combinations of Quantum Equivalence Distinctions

n	m	$\sum_{i=1}^{n} (X_n)^m = Z^m$	The Conveyance Expression
1	1	$(X_1)^1 \equiv Z^1$	Identity
2	1	$(X_1)^1 + (X_2)^1 = Z^1$	Closure of Integers
2	2	$(X_1)^2 + (X_2)^2 = Z^2$	Pythagorean Triples
2	3	$(X_1)^3 + (X_2)^3 = Z^3$	No Integer Solutions Exist (Fermat)
3	3	$(X_1)_3 + (X_2)_3 + (X_3)_3 = Z_3$	Integer Solutions Exist

Table One lists the fermions that make up the Hydrogen atom, with their spin, charge and mass. Using the volume of the mass/energy equivalence unit as the unitary volumetric distinction, allows us to apply the logic of the CoDD to 3-D quantum phenomena. With this approach, the paradoxical dimensionless points and singularities of conventional mathematical physics are replaced by more realistic 3-D quantum objects.

The fundamental operations of mathematics must be redefined in the CoDD, but that is beyond the scope of this presentation. Fortunately, some important discoveries and explanations can be revealed by looking at the combination of elementary particles as distinctions expressed in quantum equivalence units. We can proceed with two reasonable assumptions: 1) Reality is parsimonious; i.e., natural processes prefer the simplest paths that work, and 2) Stable spinning objects are geometrically similar and symmetric.

Next, we need to identify the Conveyance Equations with integer solutions that can describe combinations of elementary particles. Equations with m < 3 can be eliminated because they cannot contain three-dimensional distinctions of mass and/or energy, and those with n = 2 and m ≥ 3 cannot have integer solutions, because they are eliminated by Fermat's Last Theorem. So, n = m = 3 yields the first set of equations that can represent the combination of distinctions representing subatomic particles in three dimensions. The first 27 are displayed in Table Three.

Table Three: Integer Solutions for $(X^1)^3 + (X^2)^3 = Z^3$
(Primitives in Bold)

$3^3 + 4^3 + 5^3 = 6^3$	$1^3 + 6^3 + 8^3 = 9^3$	$6^3 + 8^3 + 10^3 = 12^3$
$2^3 + 12^3 + 16^3 = 18^3$	$9^3 + 12^3 + 15^3 = 18^3$	**$3^3 + 10^3 + 18^3 = 19^3$**
$7^3 + 14^3 + 17^3 = 20^3$	$12^3 + 16^3 + 20^3 = 24^3$	**$4^3 + 17^3 + 22^3 = 25^3$**
$3^3 + 18^3 + 24^3 = 27^3$	**$18^3 + 19^3 + 21^3 = 28^3$**	**$11^3 + 15^3 + 27^3 = 29^3$**
$15^3 + 20^3 + 25^3 = 30^3$	$4^3 + 24^3 + 32^3 = 36^3$	$18^3 + 24^3 + 30^3 = 36^3$
$6^3 + 20^3 + 36^3 = 38^3$	$14^3 + 28^3 + 34^3 = 40^3$	**$2^3 + 17^3 + 40^3 = 41^3$**
$6^3 + 32^3 + 33^3 = 41^3$	$16^3 + 23^3 + 41^3 = 44^3$	$5^3 + 30^3 + 40^3 = 45^3$
$3^3 + 36^3 + 37^3 = 46^3$	$27^3 + 30^3 + 37^3 = 46^3$	$24^3 + 32^3 + 40^3 = 48^3$
$8^3 + 34^3 + 44^3 = 50^3$	**$29^3 + 34^3 + 44^3 = 53^3$**	**$12^3 + 19^3 + 53^3 = 54^3$**

Substituting the normalized masses for up- and down-quarks from Table One into the Conveyance Equation $(X_1)^3 + (X_2)^3 + (X_3)^3 = Z^3$, we have:

$$(4)^3 + (4)^3 + (9)^3 = Z^3, \rightarrow Z^3 = 64 + 64 + 729 = 857.$$

But this is not an integer solution of $(X^1)^3 + (X^2)^3 + (X^3)^3 = Z^3$, because 857 is not an integer cubed. 857 lies between $9^3 = 729$ and $10^3 = 1,000$. This means that these integer multiples of quantum equivalence units cannot form a symmetrically stable object. Protons are very stable, and if our extension of Planck's statement is correct, then units of mass and energy cannot exist alone, and the elementary particles will have to have additional quantum equivalence units of the other parameters to combine to form a stable proton. To determine what the minimum necessary additional quantum equivalence units may be, we must find a solution with a combination of units that will include the masses of two up-quarks and one down-quark and as few additional quantum units as possible in Table Three.

One of the things that makes science interesting and challenging is that much of reality is hidden from us because of the limitations of our physical senses. I never tire of quoting Albert Einstein, and here's another of my favorite Einstein quotes: *Rafinert ist der Herr Gott, aber Bohaft ist er nicht!* (Einstein, 1953) Which translates to "The Lord God is very clever, but he is not malicious!" As Einstein suggested, there is no reason to believe that reality, whatever its ultimate nature, is maliciously hiding things from us.

In cases where the answer to a problem is not immediately obvious, scientists and mathematicians are guided by the principle of *Occam's razor* which says: "Among competing hypotheses, the one with the fewest assumptions should be selected." This is known as the law of parsimony. With this in mind, let's look at the solutions in Table Three. The first solution that will work for the proton, is the third one in the table: $6^3 + 8^3 + 10^3 = 12^3$. Using this to calculate the additional quantum equivalence units required for a spinning proton to be symmetrically stable, we have:

Table Four: The Symmetrically Stable Proton

Particles (Quarks)	Quantal Mass	Additional Required Units	Total Quantum Equivalence Units	Volume
$u1*$	4	2	6	216
$u2$	4	4	8	512

d^1	9	1	10	1,000
Total	17	7	24	1728 $=12^3$

* u^1 and u^2 have 4 quantum equivalence units of mass, and d^1 has 9 quantum equivalence units of mass, and therefore register as up-quarks and down-quarks in collider data. But they must also have additional units to produce a symmetric, and therefore stable proton, but these units cannot be quantum equivalence units of mass or energy, because, if they were, the resulting particle would not be a proton.

They are, therefore, quantum equivalence units of something else, a third form of the stuff of reality, occupying space-time, but not registering as mass or energy.

The neutron has within it, one up-quark and two down-quarks, so what does the neutron look like in quantum equivalence units? From the list of solutions (Table Two), we find that the smallest solution that works for the neutron, with one up-quark and two down-quarks, is the fourth primitive solution: $7^3 + 14^3 + 17^3 = 20^3$. Using this we can determine the additional required quantum equivalence units needed to produce a stable neutron:

Table Five: The Neutron

Particle	Mass	Required Additional Units	Total Units	Volume
u^3	4	3	7	343
d^2	9	5	14	2,744
d^3	9	8	17	4,913
Totals	22	16	38	$8,000=20^3$

The simplest stable compound structure containing all three elementary particles: electrons, protons and neutrons, is Deuterium. Using the quantum equivalence unit totals for the proton and neutron, i.e., 24 and 38, the smallest integer solution in Table Two containing the values $X^1 = 24$ and $X^2 = 38$ is obtained by multiplying the solution $12^3 + 19^3 + 53^3 = 54^3$ by 2, yielding the integer solution $24^3 + 38^3 + 106^3 = 108^3$. One electron combined with one proton and one neutron is the stable combination known as Hydrogen 2, or Deuterium. For this combination to be symmetrically stable, the electron requires a total of 106 additional units:

Table Six: The Deuterium Atom (H2)

Particle	Mass	Additional Units	Total Units	Volume
e^-	1	105	106	1,191,016
P^+	17	7	24	13,824
N^0	22	16	38	54,872
Totals	40	128	168	$(108)^3$

By inspecting these tables, we see that the stability of these spinning objects, and therefore, the stability of the universe as we know it, depends on the existence of additional units that are not detectable as mass or energy. Mass and energy are the measurable parameters by which we identify elementary particles. If the additional units could be detected as mass and/or energy, the resulting particles would not be identifiable as electrons and quarks. But, if the additional units required for stability are neither mass nor energy, what are they? Since they have not been identified before, we have chosen gimmel, the third letter of the Hebrew alphabet, to represent this new, third form of reality, and we propose that they represent the logic of consciousness.

Triadic Rotational Units of Equivalence (True)

Focusing on three of the most abundant elementary particles (electrons, up-quarks and down-quarks), we have developed the basics of a system of mathematical logic operating on quantum mass-energy-space-time volumetric equivalence units. In our published works, Dr. Neppe and I call this the Triadic Rotational Unit of Equivalence (TRUE, or true quantum unit). The TRUE is derived from the basic principles of quantum mechanics, relativity and particle-wave complementarity. Introduction of these true quantum equivalence units enabled us to revise the calculus of Newton and Leibniz to produce a calculus (the CoDD) that is appropriate for application to the phenomena of relativistic quantum reality.

Applying this new understanding to elementary particles and combinations of elementary particles, we obtain a clearer picture of sub-atomic and atomic structure, and of the interchange of mass, energy and the third form of reality we have called gimmel. The use of this system of quantized mathematical logic clears up much of the "quantum weirdness," yields additional information about the multi-dimensional nature of reality, and makes the scientific description and analysis of quantum phenomena more comprehensible. With this new quantum unit, and the CoDD, some experimental data and observations that have puzzled scientists for decades, and/or that are inexplicable within the Standard Model of the current paradigm, such as the $\frac{1}{2}$ intrinsic spin of fermions, the masses of protons and neutrons, and the exact value of the Cabibbo angle (the quark mixing angle) are relatively easily explained.

In the Standard Model, describing the geometry of these elementary particles is a complex task requiring advanced mathematical tools, including Group Theory and geometric algebras such as those developed by Grassmann and Lie (Doran & Lasenby, 2003; Hestenes & Sobczyk, 1984), quantifying the geometry of elementary particles with Lagrangian matrices invariant under local rotational transformations, leading to the localized symmetries of Gauge Theories. We have eliminated the necessity of this kind of complexity by assuming that elementary particles are spinning symmetrically and occupying volumes that are measurable in quantum equivalence units. This assumption is justified by the results it has produced including the explanations listed above, and it is also justified by the following:

> Experimental evidence: All elementary particles behave the same way in experiments such as the double-slit and delayed-choice experiments. This could not be the case if they had differing geometries, or were spinning asymmetrically.
>
> Einstein concluded that space-time has no separate existence apart from being an extension of mass and energy. This implies that *space and time are not fundamental*, and justifies the assumption of volumetric equivalence of mass, energy, space, time and gimmel as represented in the tables above.

The Hydrogen Atom

Hydrogen makes up about 75% of the baryonic mass of the universe. (*Baryonic mass* refers to atoms and combinations of atoms of the elements in the Periodic Table.) Even though Hydrogen readily combines with other elements to form water, organic compounds and millions of other compounds, it is still the most common free gas and ionized gas in the universe. Given the current estimated age of the universe, the abundance of Hydrogen as free atoms and ions across the universe is surprising. Table Seven shows the TRUE analysis of the Hydrogen atom.

Table Seven: Hydrogen without Gimmel

Particle	Mass	Gimmel	Total TRUE	Volume
e⁻	1	105	106	1,191016
P⁺	17	7	24	13,824
Totals	18	112	130	1,204,840 = (106.4085…)³

This combination should be asymmetric and unstable because the total volume is not a cube. It should be easily ionized and combined with other elements. So why are there so many free Hydrogen atoms in the universe? The answer is that, as with quarks, there are additional units increasing the total angular momentum, making the atom symmetrically stable. Looking back at the deuterium atom (Table Six), we see that symmetry can be achieved if the Total True Units column has an additional 38 units. The TRUE stable Hydrogen atom is shown in Table Eight.

Table Eight: The Stable Hydrogen Atom (Protium)

Particle	Mass	Gimmel	Total TRUE	Volume
e⁻	1	105	106	1,191,016
P⁺	17	7	24	13,824
Cλ*	0	38	38	54,872
Totals	18	150	168	1,259,712 = 108³

* *Since the Proton has 17 quantum equivalence units of mass and 7 additional units, adding up to 24 Total quantum equivalence units (see the Table Four), the only way the Hydrogen atom can be as stable as the proton is for the atom to have a third component* *consisting of 38 quantum equivalence units, not measurable as mass or energy. This satisfies the Conveyance Equation and produces a stable Hydrogen atom with a total True unit volume of 1083. This suggests that, if gimmel represents consciousness, as we propose, then the Hydrogen atom contains more consciousness than Deuterium or any more complex atom containing neutrons.*

The Masses of Up and Down Quarks and the Proton

We have determined the TRUE mass values of the quarks in Table One from collider data, but we can also determine their inertial masses in true quantum equivalence units by considering the geometry of elementary particles and applying simple mechanical principles. For rapidly spinning particles, when the substance is concentrated around the circumference of the particle in the plane of rotation due to centrifugal force, the moment of Inertia of that particle is defined as $I = mr^2$, where m is mass and r is the radius of rotation. For the electron, $I_e = m_e r_e^2$. We have defined the mass of the electron as the basic True unit of mass, and r_e as 1 unit of true *linear* measure. Thus, $I_e = 1 \times 1^2 = 1$, indicating that the inertia of a free spinning electron is equal to its mass. In quantum mathematics, the mass of any free spinning particle is a multiple of m_e, so the next larger spinning particle with a radius, r_u, of $2r_e$ is equal to $I_u = m_e r_u^2 = 1 \times 2^2 = 4$, which, is the mass of the up-quark. The third particle, with $r_d = 3$, has $I_d = m_e r_d^2 = 9$, the mass of the down-quark. Therefore, for up- and down-quarks, $I_q = r_q^2 = m_q$, mass = inertia created by particle spin.

It might seem that the mass of a compound particle like the proton would simply be the sum of the masses of two up-quarks and one down-quark, or 17 mass units. But, if mass is inertia due to the angular momentum created by spin, this will not be the case. The inertial mass of a quark in a compound structure will be greater because it will be rotating around the center of the compound particle, with a radius of rotation much greater than its radius as a separate particle, and its inertial mass as part of a Hydrogen atom, defined as $I_x = m_q k r_x^2 = m_x$, will be much greater. For protons and neutrons, the multiplier k is equal to $3d/r_x$, where d is the number of dimensions of rotation per radius r_x.

We have proved elsewhere that quarks are spinning in 3 planes (Close & Neppe, 2013). All fermions exhibit ½ intrinsic spin, which we have shown to be a result of concurrent spinning in 3 orthogonal planes. For the proton, $I_p = m_P(3d/r_p)r_p^2 = 17 \times 9 \times 12 = 1836$ units of mass. This agrees *exactly* with experimental data: The mass of the proton is 938.27 MEv/c_2 which converted to TRUE mass is 938.27/0.511 = 1836 units of mass.

This brings us to the question of why there are neutrons, and why they have only slightly more inertial mass than protons, with 1839 units of mass. We have quickly explained the origin and the mass of the neutron using the CoDD, but that is an important paper by itself, involving the creation of neutrinos and beta decay. The details, too lengthy for inclusion here, will be published later.

The Unification of Quantum Physics and Relativity

The full unification of quantum physics and relativity is brought about by including gimmel in the equations representing the combination of elementary particles and applying the CoDD to mathematical expressions of three well-established features of reality that are recognized in the current scientific paradigm: 1) quantization of mass and energy as forms of the same essential substance of reality; 2) introduction of time as a fourth dimension, and 3) enforcing the light-speed limitation of the velocity of rotational acceleration.

When we replace the dimensionless points of conventional mathematical physics with distinctions of finite unitary volume, the volumes of the elementary particles of the physical universe become integer multiples of the unitary volume. This allows us to relate the integers of quantum reality to the integers of number theory, revealing the deeper relationship between mathematics and physical reality.

Elementary particles spin because of the force of the universal expansion that occurs with no external resistance. If there were no additional dimensions, and no units of gimmel to augment structural symmetry, and no relativistic limit to the acceleration of rotational velocity, the mass and energy of physical objects would quickly radiate to infinity and the finite universe would expand to maximum entropy as predicted by the 2nd law of thermodynamics. But, due to the relativistic limit of light speed on the accelerated rotational velocity of elementary particles, the quantized content of the electron can only shrink to the smallest possible symmetric volume because contraction to a smaller volume would accelerate the rotational velocity of the localized particle beyond light speed, violating the relativistic principle of constant light speed. That minimal volume occupied by the free electron is the finite quantum of space replacing the infinitesimal of Newtonian calculus.

The CoDD and the Triadic Nature of Reality

By defining the TRUE as the quantum unit of the CoDD, we have brought mathematics and reality together at the most basic level. This allows us to begin to see the mathematical nature of reality as never before. The number three and multiples and powers of the primary triadic sequence, 1, 2, 3, show up in multiple ways in atomic and subatomic structures:

The inertial masses of the most basic elementary particles are squares of 1, 2, 3:

The mass of the electron is $1^2 = 1$ unit of mass

the up-quark is $2^2 = 4$ units of mass

the down-quark is $3^2 = 9$ units of mass.

The volumes of the elementary particles are cubes of 1, 2, 3: 1^3, 2^3, and 3^3 = 1, 8 and 27 quantum volumetric units.

The total volume of the Hydrogen atom is 1,259,712 = $(108)^3$ = $(1^3 \text{x} 2^3 \text{x} 3^3)^3$ quantum volumetric units.

Dimensional domains occur in threes: There are 3 types of dimensional distinctions. They are distinctions of extent, content and intent, and each of them have 3 dimensions, corresponding with the dimensional domains of rational, imaginary and complex numbers. These dimensions are concentrically situated to make up 3 nested dimensional domains of 3, 6 and 9 dimensions, respectively, with 3 forms of extent: spatial, temporal and conscious extent; 3 forms of content: mass, energy and consciousness; and 3 forms of the intent, or purpose of reality: stable structure, and organic life with conscious awareness.

We have defined the minimal volume of the electron as the unitary volume of extent, and its content as the unitary quantity of mass and/or energy. The mass and/or energy relationship ($E=mc^2$) is linear, since in the 3S-1t context, c^2 is a constant, allowing us to define unitary mass and unitary energy as the quantity of each that can occupy the finite rotational unitary volume. A particle of unitary mass occupying a unitary volume is known as an electron, and a particle of unitary energy occupying a unitary volume before expansion as radiant energy, is known as a photon. Einstein received the Nobel Prize in physics for demonstrating the equivalence between electrons and photons (Einstein, 1905).

Summary and Conclusion

The outline of a comprehensive mathematical paradigm, designed to describe the reality we experience as sentient beings, has been presented in this chapter. Dr. Vernon Neppe and I call it the Triadic Dimensional Distinction Vortical Paradigm (TDVP). It strongly recommends itself to replace the current fragmented materialistic paradigm called "The Standard Model" because it integrates the principles of relativity and quantum physics and eliminates most, if not all, of the conflicts and paradoxes between them. More importantly, it goes *beyond* that to reveal a third form of reality, not measurable as mass or energy, *and therefore non-physical,* that is required for atomic and subatomic stability. This third form, which we call gimmel, allows us to quantify the impact of consciousness on physical reality in the equations of science. That opens the door to the scientific exploration of verifiable non-physical aspects of reality that are experienced by sentient beings. The claim that TDVP is the next paradigm shift advancing the work of Planck and Einstein is supported by the fact that it explains many things, not explained well, or in some cases, not explained at all, by the current mainstream paradigm.

In this chapter, the Triadic Rotational Unit of Equivalence (TRUE), a quantum equivalence unit derived from the normalized physical parameters of the electron, was defined as the basic unit of the calculus of dimensional distinctions. Applying this quantum calculus to the combinations of elementary particles that make up the atoms of the Periodic Table, we described the quantum building blocks of the universe. Using this quantum calculus, and well-known physical principles and mathematical theorems, we explained why quarks combine in groups of three to form protons and neutrons. We also explained why there could be no stable physical structures without the existence of a third form of reality which we concluded is a finite form of consciousness, and the agent of Pure Consciousness in the 3S-1t domain of our experience. We have used gimmel, the third letter of the Hebrew alphabet, to represent this third form of reality in the equations of physics. Finally, we saw how to determine how much gimmel exists in each atomic element, revealing that there is consciousness in every elementary particle.

A partial list of the things this paradigm shift can explain includes: what quarks are made of, why they combine in threes to form protons and neutrons, why the Cabbibo-Kobayashi-Maskawa mixing-angles are what they are, why the masses of protons and neutrons are precisely what they are, what consciousness is, the relationship between consciousness and the physical universe, what dark matter and dark energy are, and why there is a physical universe instead of an infinite expanse of nothing. It also reveals the fact that the elements that support organic life: carbon, hydrogen, oxygen, sulfur and nitrogen have the highest percentages of gimmel, confirming the intelligent design suggested by Planck and Einstein. Finally, gimmel had to exist *before* the first stable combination of particles could form after any physical origin event, such as the theoretical big bang, and this eliminates materialism as a viable basis for a scientific theory of anything.

I will not say more about the development of this new paradigm shift here. The basics are presented above and many of the details have been published in *Reality Begins with Consciousness*, and in a series of articles in the ECAO journal, IQNEXUS and other Journals. A series of three or four technical papers detailing the mathematical physics leading up to the conclusions outlined in this chapter are being prepared for publication. Finally, I will end this chapter with a brief overview of the paradigm shift and my opinions and projections about what it means for the science of the future.

I believe that consciousness, represented mathematically by quantum units of gimmel, shapes the fundamental fabric of objective reality which is continually being transformed into physically measurable forms of mass, energy, space, and time in mathematical accordance with the logical structure communicated by the Conveyance Equations. I believe it is the mathematically logical nature of reality that makes both applied and theoretical science possible, and that gimmel and the Conveyance Equations represent the logic of the conscious transfinite substrate behind which our minds, operating through the finite physical structures of brains and bodies, cannot penetrate. Based on our research, however, I believe that gimmel represents Pure Primary Consciousness, the Infinite Intelligence behind reality, which continually creates, sustains and dissolves the finite forms of the universe.

As the intelligent substrate beyond space and time, reflecting the intent of Infinite Intelligence, Primary Consciousness transcends unidirectional, one-dimensional time, which means that it is a-temporal: it has always existed and will always exist. This means that there is no absolute beginning or end, only change from one form to another. I believe the universe exists as a projection of the logical, mathematical, multi-dimensional structure of Pure Consciousness, and through the self-organizing action of a conscious third form of reality we have represented symbolically as gimmel, consciousness shapes every quantum and every atom of the universe in a way that supports organic life forms as vehicles for conscious perception and experience of the physical universe. I will end this chapter with my answer to a question we have been asked by several reviewers of our work.

Why Gimmel, the Agent of Consciousness, Not Gluons, Dark Matter and Dark Energy?

The short answer is: By putting consciousness into the equations as gimmel, we have answered many questions that are not answerable within the mainstream paradigm of the Standard Model, so we can say that *the proof is in the pudding*. But for a more complete answer, we must start by analyzing terms like gluon and dark matter: They are euphemisms coined by physicists to say without admitting it: "We really don't know what these things are." Recently, a mainstream physicist, when asked what he thought dark matter might be, replied: "Well, of course, it is matter of some kind, we just don't know what kind." This underscores the fact that, to a materialist, everything is matter and energy, or an effect of matter and energy, by definition. The idea that something non-physical could be real and have real effects in the physical world is dismissed as unscientific. *But this position is itself demonstrably unscientific.*

The idea that the physical world is independent of consciousness does not qualify as a scientific hypothesis. To qualify as a scientific hypothesis, an idea must be falsifiable, which means that there must be a way to prove or disprove it. The idea that physical reality is independent of consciousness is not falsifiable because its proof requires showing that the existence of consciousness is not required for physical reality to exist as it does, and that cannot be proved without the existence of consciousness.

The question of whether gimmel exists, on the other hand, *is* falsifiable. As shown in this essay, the stable physical world we experience would not exist without it. But, the inescapable fatal flaw in mainstream thinking is exposed when we see that, after summarily dismissing everything non-physical from consideration, mainstream scientists must then invent their own non-physical entities, including massless particles and volume-less single-point particles (gluons and bosons), to make the Standard Model work. Physical objects, by definition, have mass and occupy space. Therefore, gluons and bosons are not physical objects.

Why is gimmel any better than gluons and dark energy? In addition to the arguments given above, there at least three good reasons to replace the concepts of gluons and dark matter/dark energy with gimmel:

While gimmel has no mass or energy, it occupies space and contributes to the total angular momentum of compound objects in the same way that physical objects do.

Gimmel explains everything that gluons and dark matter do,

and more.

Since non-physical reality is included from the start, gimmel does not create an internal contradiction as do gluons and bosons in the mainstream materialistic paradigm.

A few brilliant scientists of the past have successfully demonstrated that the form of physical reality is not independent of observer involvement and have pointed the way forward. But we have been slow to recognize the importance of their findings. As a result, mainstream science does not, and *cannot* tell us what reality is, or even what mass, energy, space, time and consciousness are.

Ludwig Wittgenstein, one of the most influential philosophers of the twentieth century said: "*Whereof one cannot speak, thereof one must remain silent.*" (Wittgenstein, 1922) And Niels Bohr, one of the most influential physicists of the twentieth century said: "*Physics is not about how the world is, it is about what we can say about the world.*"(Bohr, 1987)

Using Aristotelian logic, the results of destructive testing and reductive reasoning, mainstream materialist scientists are trying to speak about things whereof they cannot speak, and trying to speculate about the nature of reality, which Wittgenstein and Bohr both identified as something they cannot do. Gluons, dark matter, dark energy, massless point-like particles, non-physical objects with no content or extent, and particles that somehow impart mass, magnetism and electrical charge to other particles, are examples of some of the vague and contradictory conceptualizations that scientists working within the Standard Model are driven to because of the inadequacy of materialism as the metaphysical basis of science. The current materialistic paradigm has been very useful and very successful at finding ways to manipulate nature to serve our short-term and sometimes selfish purposes. But, including non-physical consciousness in the equations of science changes everything.

In this chapter, we have described a way to include the non-physical in the equations of science, expanding the axiomatic basis of the scientific paradigm, enabling us to develop a new paradigm that addresses much more of the reality we experience. It has allowed us to see deeper into the relationship between mathematics and physical reality and explain things that the materialistic mainstream paradigm cannot.

We have included the basics of a more inclusive calculus, a calculus that has allowed us, for the first time, to take the *measure* of consciousness and put it directly into the equations of science; but much more needs to be done. A much more detailed development and application of the CoDD awaits the fresh young minds of the scientists of the future. The answers provided in this short essay afford only a glimpse of the broad landscape of where the science of the future can go. It will be a science that, in addition to answering questions about the physical universe, will also be able to boldly go where no physicist has gone before: into the greater domain of non-physical reality to investigate and explore the infinite possibilities of the human mind and spirit.

Chapter Four

Bridging the Perceived Gap between Science and Metaphysics: The Primacy of Consciousness and Experience

Menas C. Kafatos, PhD

Introduction

The title of this chapter is full of challenges for a scientist, for a philosopher, and indeed for anyone who might venture to bridge what many consider unfathomable gap, a gap that I claim is in the perception, between science and metaphysics (or philosophy or spirituality, as substitutes for metaphysics). Many in the science world and indeed in the opposite bank of the perceived dividing chasm, take it for granted that no such bridging exists now and can never exist. That is just the way it is, they would argue!

As for the second part of the title, "the primacy of consciousness and experience", many on all fronts would deny such primacy, unless they happen to belong to the select (or self-select?) group of non-dualists. The word experience may not raise many objections, after all in first person outlook, experience is most important. The word consciousness, however, causes many in scientific fields (such as neuroscience, psychology and even physics) to get ready for a fight! And there would be many attempts to define consciousness (if such a definition is possible or desirable) but beyond that, to even deny its existence or relevance in a scientific view of the cosmos.

If it seems that the opening of this chapter is pessimistic and that it implies a discourse with a full-of-strife beginning, I want to assure the reader that there is light at the end of the tunnel. In fact, I hope to make the case that what is proposed here is reasonable, supported in many ways by the most advanced fields of science, and in agreement with ancient truths that formed the foundation of human civilizations. The case will be a proposition rather than a "proof" (whatever that term may mean to different groups of thinkers). This Chapter is one more set of views added to all of us who provide our joint Perspectives as the Founding Members of the Academy for the Advancement of Postmaterialist Sciences. Our collective views, although covering multiple perspectives, agree that the broad Postmaterialist Sciences paradigm we are proposing, is pointing to an expanded future of humanity.

The view here is both personal and objective. As Postmaterialist, I owe to others and myself this dual approach. When I decided at age fourteen to become a scientist, abandoning the idea of studying art and becoming a painter, which were natural to me ever since I was very young, I made the decision to favor "objectivity", to pursue science and particularly physics and mathematics. Today, after looking for so many years for answers "out there" while also searching for my true self, I now favor a balance between the personal and the objective. I favor a balance between art and science, a balance between the "outer" and the "inner" worlds. In a sense, all these are central tenets of what Postmaterialism means to me. It was the awe of looking at the dark starry night in my native Crete, with all the splendor of the Milky Way, imagining the vast distances of space extending to stars, to galaxies and beyond, that drew me to astronomy and its serious study through physics. To study, my father urged me to go to America, if I truly wanted to study physics. This awe I felt at an early age in facing the infinite was a search for what the universe is, on the one hand; and, I now know, the search for what

Is Consciousness Primary?

I am. By looking out, I ended up looking inward.

Our starting point in this chapter will be quantum mechanics (QM). The reason is that QM is the most advanced theory we have for how "physical" things are put together and work and also brings in the role of the observer, the conscious participant in the drama of the cosmos. Quantum mechanics is not just about the world of particles and atoms and molecules and how they are put together. Today we realize that different versions of the quantum worldview present profound implications for understanding the nature of reality, the universe and conscious awareness. Although many of these views don't agree with each other, they have one common element: They tell us that the world of the senses, the world of "common sense" is at best limited. QM opened the door to the microcosm and at the same time the door to the psycho-physical participation of conscious beings. The nature of consciousness though continues to challenge all of science and in particular how something as "not material" as the mind couples to "material objects." Although much progress has been made in the understanding of the brain as a physical object of incredible complexity, with its trillions of neurons and synapses, not much progress has been achieved in understanding or even accounting for the most elementary subjective experiences. This is the reason why the bridging of science and metaphysics is necessary. To continue to insist that science has nothing to say about philosophical understandings or vice versa, is to deny our integrated unity of what is to be human.

It is no wonder that although scientists struggle about the bridge and even deny it, that they are aware of the problems facing us all: Scientists in many polls about what are the two most important and unsolved topics facing modern science, respond with two choices: The nature of the universe; and the nature of conscious experience. It is my view that Postmaterialism is indeed about the need to bring these two poles of experience (the "outer" and the "inner") into an integrated view. If it can be achieved, it will signal the dawn of a new golden age for humanity. If it cannot, and I am serious in what I am saying, it may spell the end of humanity. What used to be in the domain of philosophy and metaphysics, the mental field of conscious awareness, its coupling to matter, requires an integrated approach, a dialogue between disciplines and integration of disciplines, or interdisciplinary and transdisciplinary dialogue and integration. Current science cannot do it alone, we have to recognize the challenges. Kafatos, Lee and Yang (2014) state:

"The issue of consciousness presents a clear embarrassment to modern science. Despite the great successes of theoretical physics, cosmology and quantum field theory, despite the advances of molecular biology, and brain science (cf. Bernroider, 2003; Bernroider & Roy, 2005; Pribram, 1991) to just mention a few of the most successful scientific fields, we still don't have a comprehensive theory of consciousness. It is even worse than that, we seem not to agree on a common framework of terms."

It is now an accepted view, although not totally understood that quantum measurement theory opens possibilities that did not exist before. In fact, in accordance with the view of some very prominent physicists such as Richard Feynman and John A. Wheeler, we may even state that without observation, "material" particles don't even have any properties. The context of observation determines the reality to be observed! In the participatory quantum universe, as Wheeler (1981) stated, "no phenomenon is a phenomenon until it is an observed phenomenon." The observer's choices play a fundamental role. The observer is an integral part of the process of what is to be observed. QM opened the door to consciousness but did not provide a solution, except hints of what the next steps might be. Today, I claim, we have to follow a new paradigm as Chopra and Kafatos (2017) urge to follow.

Is Consciousness Primary?

Many of the arguments and passages that follow have been presented before. I have heavily borrowed from previous published works and indicated as much as possible when this is the case. In other words, I have pulled together sections from my published works and at the same time linked them together. This constitutes a bridging as many of these works build bridges of different kinds.

One may ask how did I reach these views that I hold today? Was this a result of experimental or theoretical pursuits? Was it because somehow, I "saw the light" of how science is limiting itself (or I should say how scientists)? The answer is complex and cannot be given in a simple chapter with musings. For sure, I am not the same today as I were back when I was a young graduate student at M.I.T. However, I still am.

For example, I still enjoy doing cosmology here and there and I believe I am still contributing in the field. Black holes are still fascinating as the end of our knowledge and not just as strange astrophysical objects. However, my turn towards QM, philosophy and matters that deal with the mind, followed years of practicing meditation, studying Eastern, and Western, philosophies, writing books and articles that attempt to bridge the "gap" and, last but not least, associating myself with like-minded people, like the contributors to this volume. Despite what scientists like to claim, that they follow objectivity, scientists like other human beings, tend to associate with similarly-minded people. Who wants after all to be with people who are totally different than oneself?

We scientists also tend to not talk or even hide the processes that lead us to our insights and scientific works. We claim some sort of purity of approach, like the blindfolded justice. And while it is indeed true that in the end it is not how one reached an insight but whether that insight stands the test of time that is important, we cannot also divorce our own world outlook from the way we practice our work. Let's face it, it is not just ideas that are important, it is how these ideas apply to the world we live in. Scientists I often meet speak of disdain of philosophy as being something useless. But it is the philosophical underpinnings of one's world view that need to be examined and not taken for granted. Otherwise, we scientists practice just another form of dogma, although we would indignantly deny that possibility. The somewhat funny expression "shut up and calculate" is, unfortunately half a joke.

Well, here are some additional personal points: I always helped to bridge different fields in academia, as a faculty member, chairman of the department of physics and as dean of interdisciplinary programs and schools at both George Mason University and at Chapman University. I was recognized as leading such efforts and both students and many faculty sought my company and the programs that I, with their invaluable help, put together. It is the interdisciplinary and transdisciplinary approaches that I am known for as reflected in my writings but, also, the way I live my life, that led to a recent invitation to address the Korean Academy of Science and Technology and present what will be the interdisciplinary science of the future.

What we are pursuing here is not some fluffy "feel good" nonsense. As I hope that will be appreciated by looking at the following sections, which are based on rigor as well as insight, the idealism that is inherent in Postmaterialism can be and is as rigorous or more, in fact more consistent than unbridled materialism. I would refer to the extremely rigorous works of Bernardo Kastrup, peer-reviewed over the years and assembled in his most recent book (Kastrup, 2018) as refreshing arguments to quote for additional support of what we are collectively pursuing here.

The challenges faced by many of us in AAPS, despite our rigor and hard work, such as the many years research of Dean Radin, Edward Close, Mario Beauregard, Marjorie Woollacott, Julia

Mossbridge, Stephan Schwartz, Gary Schwartz, Diane Powell, Lisa Miller, Larry Dossey, in fact all of us, point to a common challenge, beyond specific people and works.

I would like to close this section with a quote from Kafatos and Kato (2017):

"The work presented here may provide a way for the convergence of science and non-dualist philosophies, as an emerging science of Consciousness. The exploration of the connection of Western idealist philosophies in addition to the idealist non-dualist Hindu philosophies is beyond the scale of the present work but would form a natural extension. We propose that a new science of Consciousness referred to in the present work and references given here would bring out the underlying unity of physics, life and mind. In some sense, the relevant mathematics presented here may be seen as a universal language of physics and metaphysics".

Laws Behind the Laws

I note that certain words, like Consciousness, Experience, Reality, the Living Presence, and Laws are capitalized to indicate they play a central role in the proposed paradigm. The discussion here is developed in the published work of Kafatos and Yang (2018). The impetus came from a special edition put together in honor of the 90th birthday of Henry P. Stapp, who I view one of the giants of QM thinking. It is my association and working with Henry that led to my insights and I have to add, going beyond those insights. Going beyond is realizing the importance of what we call the Laws behind the Laws, which although derived by observing the fundamentals of the quantum universe, also apply everywhere. They are truly universal, hence "behind the Laws" (of physics, biology or any human endeavor). These three Laws are of relevance not just to a scientific (or in my view Postmaterialist) approach, they are also extremely relevant to everyday life. I try to live by them, see their workings in my own life and my environment. They are the foundation of the Living the Living Presence, outlined below. So here we are with the three Laws as presented in Kafatos and Yang (2018). The discussion includes qualia, the "hard problem" and non-dual Awareness (see Theise & Kafatos, 2016), which is not just an intellectual work, it guides my life:

If Consciousness is primary and Experience is the manifestation of Consciousness for sentient beings, then some universal principles or Laws must apply at all levels of Reality. If science represents universal truths, then the world of experiences would require such Laws to be stated or developed in science. In fact, Orthodox QM has produced a paradigm wherein the mind plays a fundamental, participatory role in understanding and interacting with the universe. It has gone much further than other quantum ontological views. The question remains, can we go beyond the implied dualities? Is the separation between object and subject fundamental? What is the ultimate "stuff" or reality? Where is the "Heisenberg Cut"? (the cut according to Stapp "being the transition between quantum events and an observer's information, knowledge, or conscious awareness. Below the cut everything is governed by the wave function; above a classical description is used"). Von Neumann (1955) was arguing that the cut is arbitrary. If it is arbitrary it means it is everywhere and nowhere.

Can we express in a mathematical formalism the fundamental relationships between subjects and objects? If yes, it is important to understand the common framework that may be applicable to all levels of experience, as revealed primarily by the quantum nature of interactions but, by far, not limited to interpretations of QM. The world of experiences reveals three fundamental Laws of Nature applicable everywhere (Kafatos, 2015a): Complementarity, recursion and creative interactivity.

Complementarity (or Integrated Polarity) is the principle where, ultimately, the apparent opposites become unified at the deeper level of universal Consciousness (Kafatos, 2017). Complementary relations are found everywhere, which point to a deep, generalized quantum reality and we have an indirect argument that QM is the starting point for developing a scientific framework of consciousness. Roy and Kafatos (1999) applied complementarity to the brain. A consequence of the generalized principle of complementarity is that horizons of knowledge exist (Kafatos & Nadeau, 2000; Theise & Kafatos 2013a; 2013b). Boundaries, or horizons of knowledge, are not absolute: In the Orthodox view, they depend on the act of observation (Kafatos, 2015).

The second Law is Recursion (or Correspondence), which allows knowledge to be gathered and persist, a universality linking all levels of existence together and simply stated, "as here, so elsewhere" (Theise & Kafatos, 2013b). Recursion assures that relationships and patterns extend beyond particular levels to all levels of existence. For example, all fields obey certain quantum rules; all physics laws apply everywhere; all electrons obey the Pauli Exclusion Principle, etc. The world operates through recursive relations at and between different levels.

The third principle, Creative Interactivity, provides a framework of interactions at many different levels. Interactions between subjects and objects; between sentient beings; between objects and objects; between cells and cells, etc.

The three Laws give meaning to the universe; they are the workings of how Consciousness manifests the universe and apply at all levels, beginning with the fundamental subject – object relationships and the mathematics of Consciousness (Kafatos, 2015a; Kafatos & Kato, 2017).

The ontologic framework of Consciousness or fundamental non-dual Awareness is described by Theise and Kafatos (2016):

Non-dual Awareness is foundational to the universe, not arising from the interactions or structures of higher level phenomena. The framework allows comparison and integration of views from the three investigative domains concerned with the understanding nature of consciousness: science, philosophy, and metaphysics. In this framework, Awareness is the underlying reality, not reducible to anything else. Awareness and existence are the same. As such, the universe is non-material, self-organizing throughout, a holarchy of complementary, process driven, recursive interactions. The universe is both its own first observer and subject. Considering the world to be non-material and comprised, a priori, of Awareness is to privilege information over materiality, action over agency and to understand that qualia are not a "hard problem", but the foundational elements of all existence. These views fully reflect main stream Western philosophical traditions, insights from culturally diverse contemplative and mystical traditions, and are in keeping with current scientific thinking, expressible mathematically.

Qualia (from the Latin term qualis, which means "of what kind") are the fundamental components of how non-dual Consciousness projects out the universe and are at the heart of an experience-based philosophy of mind (Kafatos, 2015b). The so-called "hard problem" (Chalmers, 1995) addresses the difficulty of accounting for experience in terms of physical theories and in itself implies the fundamental role of qualia. Erwin Schrödinger (2001) himself held the view that qualia are not material and cannot be accounted by material theories:

"The sensation of color cannot be accounted for by the physicist's objective picture of light-waves. Could the physiologist account for it, if he had fuller knowledge than he has of the processes in the retina and the nervous processes set up by them in the optical nerve bundles and in the brain? I do not think so."

The "hard problem" of consciousness, rather than being a

desperate statement, is, instead, a statement that experience cannot involve just the physical and, certainly, not the physical world view of classical physics. It begs a psychophysical approach, a mental quantum reality. Experiences or qualia in the world (Kafatos & Kato 2017) are the glue that holds the five senses (vision, audition, somatic sensation, gustation, olfaction) as well many other modalities, together and gives the appearance of an "external" reality. All experiences, whether of the body or the outside world, consist of qualia. Our world only exists because we perceive it and act as conscious agents (Kafatos & Kato, 2017). Thus, all interactions with the universe are experiential and subjective. What we call "objective" in science is that which we can measure within patterns of qualia dictated by mathematical laws. Quantum mechanics is a mathematical model for formalizing and measuring what are nothing other than experiences (cf. Bohr's 1958, view of reality).

The field of pure awareness exists prior to qualia, while subjective experiences in Consciousness are qualia (Kafatos & Kato, 2017), which are sensations, images, feelings, thoughts (or SIFT, Siegel, 2016). Qualia are the experiential attributes of non-dual Awareness. To clarify:

There is no possibility of proving anything existing outside of qualia (Kafatos & Kato, 2017). Qualia are distinct and are tied to the experiencing individuals, they are not the same. They have qualitative differences, not subject to quantitative analysis. This is why qualia are associated with the "mental" realm (beyond physical, space and time). In fact, space, time, particles, all objects are nothing other than qualia when they are reified, i.e. possible subjective experiences. Mathematics itself is the most refined form of qualia. Even our neuronal system is a product of a possibility in consciousness, which has evolved as a mode for interpreting consciousness from a perspective that makes humans unique (Kafatos & Kato, 2017). The underlying world is pure non-dual Awareness, with no qualities, being the pre-created state, in fact the ever-existing state.

Extending the successful Orthodox framework in our view requires going beyond the object-subject separation. This is at the heart of the issue of subjective experience, as the very idea of experience blurs the "boundary" between the subjective and the objective. Is it not, after all, the experience of the other itself an experience? Is not the case that the experience of something "out there", "outside" of us, is also an experience? Rather than chasing an outdated world view of fixed boundaries, "hard" particles which are after all manifestations of probable outcomes, does it not make sense to take a reasonable or common-sense approach?

Quantum theory opened the door to the mental universe but cannot account for the nature of the mind, or consciousness or awareness. Simply put, we cannot "take out" the subjective experience from the practice of science (Kafatos, & Kato, 2017). In the end, it boils down as to what the ontological assumptions (or axioms) of a system of thought are. Bohr in the CI argued that QM is silent on this. He opted for an epistemological approach instead. As in the Orthodox QM (Stapp, 2017), we argue that ontology is implied in QM (Kafatos 2015a) and presents with a new vision of reality wherein qualia play a fundamental role (Kafatos & Kato, 2017):

"Qualia science, as we envision it, resolves the paradox by showing how the universe operates as the domain of consciousness (Kafatos 2011). An external physical universe as a given is untenable in the post-quantum era; it now requires radical revision as our frame of reference for what is really real and what is not, replaced by the participatory universe that all of us experience through qualia. The process of undercutting the five senses is valid, but we would urge that what makes any experience viable—consciousness—cannot be undercut. This distinction rescues objectivity and subjectivity at the same time, in a complementary relationship."

Reality at Large Scales

Watching the starry sky, learning about Cosmology, I was attracted to infinity and through it, to science. Although I was very skillful in art, and had I pursued it, I would have studied fine arts in Paris, as my father had indicated, and probably led a different but equally rewarding life, I felt that art was too familiar, too easy. But perhaps, at least back then, not drawing me like the sense of infinity. My father understood and supported my plans to study science but, in this case, it would have to be in America. Following science was close to the mathematics of my uncle who was a brilliant mathematician and showed me the beauty of mathematics, geometry and trigonometry, and, incidentally, astronomy. I owe a lot to my father for always supporting me, my uncle from whom I inherited the love for mathematics, and my brother Fotis, who by the time I went to America had opened the path of science for me and I followed him to Cornell (where my father had also studied in the early part of the 20th century). All three of these wonderful men passed away (Fotis most recently in 2017) but they still live in me.

I got admitted to Cornell, got a degree in physics (as physics would give me more flexibility than just astronomy) and followed Philip Morrison to M.I.T. where he moved from Cornell. I got my Ph.D. in physics from M.I.T., specializing in astrophysics with my advisor the brilliant Philip Morrison. So this is the "reality" of my fascination with the universe. Today, I am still fascinated by infinity, by cosmology and, "back from the future" again to the past, by mathematics. What follows is an account found in many of my works, specifically in passages from Kafatos, Lee and Yang (2014) presented here, but going back to Kafatos and Nadeau (2000) and the late 80's and early 90's when The Conscious Universe and other works were composed and published.

Cosmology, like quantum theory, was developed starting in the 20th century and is based on Einstein's General Theory of Relativity. Today, there are great efforts to unify these two most successful theories, quantum mechanics and general relativity, basically theories about the world of the very small and the world of the very large but without success. Here we explore how cosmology is tied to large-scale relationships and structures that may be hinting at unifying relationships at deeper levels (note: this prophetic statement has been substantiated by progress in recent works of, e.g. Chopra & Kafatos, 2017; Kafatos & Kato, 2017).

Great progress in ground-based and space-based telescopic observations has revealed a dynamic, evolving universe that fits general relativistic equations. Today, the most accepted theory of the large-scale structure of the universe is Big Bang (Silk, 1989) general relativistic cosmology, having achieved impressive results...there are however, problems with Big Bang cosmology as it was originally developed and today more and more adjustments have to be made, first with inflation (Guth, 1981) and more recently with dark matter and dark energy, which appear to contain more than 95% of the mass-energy of the universe (and I would add, still with zero laboratory evidence of their existence). As such, one needs to critically examine not only some apparent difficulties in the overall framework but also its underlying assumptions. Unification is expected at the Planck space-time... As the universe evolves, any general relativistic Friedmann-Robertson-Walker Big Bang model, as well as any other non-Big Bang cosmological model, needs to be closely coupled to cosmological observations, and is, therefore, ultimately intricately interwoven with limits imposed by the process of observation itself (Kafatos, 1998).

These limits in our knowledge, what we may term horizons of knowledge, always involve complementary constructs which displace each other in actual applications but both are needed to provide a complete picture of the system studied. Complementarity, which forms the cornerstone of the Copenhagen Interpretation (Bohr, 1961) is the first and foremost foundational principle in science (cf. Kafatos, 2014). The reason is that, as Bohr first noted, it also applies to biology (Theise & Kafatos, 2013a).

As such, also in cosmology any theoretical model of the universe ultimately involves some horizons of knowledge at some ultimate, faint observational limit (Kafatos & Nadeau, 2000). For example, for the Big Bang theory, as one looks further into space, one is also looking further back into time. And at some point, light (or even neutrinos) cannot be used to observe further back than a certain limit of very large redshifts (where redshift is defined as the relative difference of observed from the emitted light, and consists a surrogate for distance, at least in Big Bang cosmology) to test the Big Bang theory close to the beginning that it predicts.

We see that if we follow the paradigm of non-locality, we face the paradox that the whole (universe) cannot be studied from its parts, particularly as we approach the "beginning" to an arbitrary limit; to put it in the context of time, the beginning is forever hidden from the present and our observations carried out in the present. Ultimately, observational limitations themselves prohibit us from verifying cosmological theories to any prescribed degree of accuracy for any given observational test.

For example, for all practical purposes, galaxy formation under the Big Bang theory runs into verification problems at redshifts, $z \sim 4$ -10, close to distances discerned by the Hubble Space Telescope and future space telescopes. There is a simple and obvious, yet often ignored, reason: The nature and evolutionary history of the "standard candles" (such as galaxies) which are used to measure the Hubble expansion flow and the overall structure of the universe cannot be unequivocally determined independently of the cosmology framework itself (Kafatos, 1989).

Cosmological Constraints

In cosmology (Kafatos, 2002), there are a number of observational conclusions about the large-scale structure which must be taken into account and, in turn, we should understand what type of constraints they provide for physical cosmology. Here we provide several known observationally-based truths which have led to some extraordinary theoretical views of the universe. For instance:

- It appears that the universe is essentially flat, which is known as the flatness problem, where the critical parameter for describing how much the universe deviates from flatness is given by:

$$\rho_{crit} = 2 \times 10^{-29} \left(H_0 / 100 \text{km s}^{-1} \text{ Mpc}^{-1} \right)^2 \text{ gr cm}^{-3} \quad (1)$$

H_o being is the present-day value of the Hubble constant (or present rate of expansion). H_o is defined as R/R where R is arbitrarily defined as the scale of the universe. This particular issue is a *problem* because if the universe is close to being flat today, it must have been *exactly* flat close to the time of the Big Bang itself, at least to one part in 10^{50}! The Hubble constant provides an estimate of the *current* expansion rate (current measurements by the *Hubble Space Telescope* indicate its value is close to 75 km s^{-1} Mpc^{-1}). The usual interpretation of the *flatness problem* proposed in the early 80's is that at some point in the early universe, the universe was in an inflationary state (Guth, 1981), and this state washed away any departures from flatness on time scales of 10^{-35} sec. In more general epistemological terms, it would appear that the universe has followed the *simplest possible theoretical construct* (namely being flat) in its large-scale geometry (Kafatos & Nadeau, 2000). Yet, the flatness issue has not gone away as most of the *observable* matter in the universe fails to provide enough mass-energy to achieve even flatness, requiring unknown forms of *dark matter*, and recently even leading to larger percentages (~ 70% or more) of *dark energy*, which provides an accelerating expansion.

The universe is remarkably homogeneous at large scales as deduced by the so-called microwave background radiation of 2.73 K — T being constant to 1 part in 10^6! This is known as the *horizon problem*.

In other words, the universe is remarkably homogeneous at large scales as observed by the microwave radiation that fills all space. The inflationary model proposed by Guth and others was developed in its various forms to account for the flatness of the universe and as such it appeared to also solve the *horizon problem*. This problem is manifesting in terms the apparent homogeneity of the 2.73 K black body radiation seen by NASA's space mission *COBE* (cf. Kafatos & Nadeau 2000). More recent results by WMAP (Bennett et al., 2012) provide even tighter constraints about the nature of the cosmic microwave background (CMB) radiation.

The observations indicate that although the 2.73 K radiation was, according to theory, emitted ~ 10^5 years after the beginning, opposite sides of the sky at that time were out of causal contact, separated by ~ 10^7 light years. How could, as observations indicate, the background be so homogeneous if no information could travel over such large distances as the universe was expanding? This makes it rather obvious why it is a *horizon* problem....

The Cosmological constant *coincidence* has an improbable coincidence of 10^{120}. As it is, recent observations indicate a cosmological constant might be needed in a flat universe framework to account for an accelerating expansion, manifesting as dark energy. This is known as the *Cosmological constant problem*.

In taking the above three considerations into account, and although the universe appears to be *close* to a flat, Euclidean, Einstein-de Sitter state as indicated from the fact that the density is close to closure, it is still not beyond doubt that we know what the geometry of the universe is today; *exactly* flat (as inflation requires); open (yielding a forever-expanding, negatively curved space-time); or closed (yielding a maximum expansion, a positively curved space-time and a final *big crunch*); or maybe even open and forever accelerating, which implies a non-zero cosmological constant... The cosmological constant was first introduced by Einstein to counter gravity and produce a closed, stable or static universe, his preferred model—it essentially acts as negative gravity. It was later abandoned by Einstein himself when observations by Hubble and others indicated an expanding universe, although we note that Hubble himself was careful to point out that the interpretation in terms of Doppler redshifts was not the only possibility for the observed redshifts. The cosmological constant has been recently re-introduced by cosmologists as the present observations of distant Type I supernovae seem to be indicating (if taken at face value, which really means that the distant supernovae were the same as the ones observed nearby) that the universe not only is expanding, but it is also accelerating in its expansion! Observations indicate that baryons (and luminous matter) contribute at most 0.05 or less of the closure density at present.

As such, if one insists on exact flatness of the universe, one needs to introduce unknown forms of dark matter and dark energy for the other 95%, exotic forms that hitherto have evaded observational verification. In other words, the dilemma we face is that if we insist on a flat universe, this forces us to in turn adopt increasingly, complex and unknown physics, literally, *Big Bang begets unknown physics*. The mathematical model is relatively simple in its assumptions, but the underlying physics required to maintain have increasingly become complex and even unknown. And we also note again that the Big Bang itself would be completely unobserved and subject to unknown quantum gravity unification, which *must* at some point be brought in. The current epistemological dilemma does not seem to bother the majority of astrophysicists, as Big Bang is so ingrained as the orthodox view, perhaps because of other metaphysical reasons, that we are ready to accept unknown physics in order to preserve it. In some ways this reminds us of the historical Ptolemaic universe situation: To keep the orbits of the planets circular in a geocentric universe (which was also back then considered as the simplest and most natural but as it tuned out wrong universe), required an increasing amount of complexity, more and more epicycles.

So, let's think about the above arguments: I strongly note here that here we do have a problem! Theory seems to imply dark energy (and to a less extent dark matter) but its nature is completely unknown. Efforts to look for it in the laboratory or some hints from observations have failed. Do we trust theory, and for how long? At which point do we "cut our losses" and look for other possibilities?

In going beyond the previous considerations and perhaps even more remarkably, the universe seems extremely fined tuned (cf. Kafatos, 1998). Eddington (1939) and Dirac (1937) noticed that certain "coincidences" in dimensionless ratios involving physical quantities can be found. These ratios link microscopic to macroscopic quantities (cf. Kafatos, 1998).

- For example, the ratio of the electric force to gravitational force (presumably a constant), is a large number

$$e^2/Gm_e m_p \sim 10^{40} \qquad (2)$$

- A number that yields the same large ratio is the ratio of the observable size of the universe (presumably changing in an expanding universe) to the size of an elementary particle, and this last ratio is surprisingly   number, or

$$R/(e^2/m_e c^2) \sim 10^{40} \qquad (3)$$

Dirac argued that it is hard to imagine that two very large and seemingly unrelated numbers would turn out to be so close to each other. The two numbers, he argued, *must* therefore be related. The problem though is that in (3) the numerator is changing as the universe expands while (2) is presumably constant. Why should two such large numbers, one variable and the other not, turn out to be so close to each other? Dirac's (1937) *Large Number Hypothesis* states that the fact that the two ratios in (2) and (3) are equal is not a mere coincidence. He and others (cf. Dyson, 1972) have attempted to account for the apparent equality between (2) and (3) by assuming that constants such as the gravitational constant itself may be varying. We will explore even more generalized scenarios of that flavor in the next section.

- For now, it is worth noting that other ratios such as the ratio of an elementary particle to the Planck length,

$$\frac{e^2/m_e c^2}{(\hbar G/c^3)^{1/2}} \sim 10^{20} \qquad (4)$$

and even larger numbers such as the "Eddington's number", $\sim 2 \times 10^{79}$, etc. exist as well as that "harmonic" numbers can be constructed from them (Harrison, 1981), e.g. Eddington's number is approximately equal to the square root of (2) or (3).

These "coincidences" may be indicating the existence of some deep, underlying unity, a *generalized non-locality beyond space and time, perhaps even involving all physical and even biological theories,* manifested in the fundamental constants and linking the microcosm to the macrocosm.

- We have to note that other, less traditional ways, perhaps even more radical views than what I had proposed (namely, the fine tuning due to applications of complementarity), such as the *Anthropic Principle* of Barrow and Tipler, have been proposed to account for the above fine-tuning properties of the universe. The recent popularity of the multiverse (Tegmark, 2003) and M-Theory, based on string theory, have not resolved the basic issue of unification of physics with biology and consciousness.

The Universe is Extremely Fined Tuned

To recapitulate:

- Ratio of the electric force to gravitational force
$$e^2/Gm_e m_p \sim 10^{40}$$
- Ratio of the observable size of the universe (presumably changing) to the size of an elementary particle is also a large number, surprisingly close to the first number, or
$$R/(e^2/m_e c^2) \sim 10^{40}$$

These two relations yield what is known as Dirac's *Large Number Hypothesis*

- Ratio of an elementary particle to the Planck length,
$$\frac{e^2/m_e c^2}{(\hbar G/c^3)^{1/2}} \sim 10^{20}$$
- Large numbers such as "Eddington's number", $\sim 2 \times 10^{79}$, etc. exist. "Harmonic" numbers can be constructed from them, e.g. Eddington's number is approximately equal to the square root of Dirac's relations.

Although it is possible to search for solution of the above dilemmas in terms of a future physics or even some form of Anthropic Principle or multiverse, we believe they point to an underlying connectedness; in other words, it is possible to invoke a *generalized non-locality* (note: what we now call one of the three Laws) akin to quantum non-locality, as one of the underlying principles (Laws) of the cosmos. However, more on this will follow below.

The Arrow of Time as a Measurement of Change
An Alternative view Involving Scale-Invariance

Kafatos, Roy and Roy (2005) have shown that one may use these so-called coincidences from a completely different point of view.

They can be re-interpreted and generalized in terms of relationships linking the masses of elementary particles as well as the total number of nucleons in the universe (or Eddington's number) to other fundamental "constants" such as the gravitational constant, the charge of the electron, Planck's constant and the speed of light. Kafatos *et al.* concluded that scale-invariant relationships result, such as all lengths are then proportional to the scale of the universe R, etc. The arrow of time results as these fundamental "constants" change (e.g. Eddington's number varies from $N_P \to 1$ at some initial state which could be suitably identified as the time of Big Bang, but not necessarily, to $\to 10^{80}$, a time suitably identified as the present, but not necessarily, etc.). *In this view, time is not fundamental, change is. Time (perhaps an illusion) arises as change occurs.*

Note that the issue of illusion has cosmological implications! Postmaterialism can indeed be making standard scientific predictions and account for consequences of observations.

Specifically, one may adopt Weinberg's relationship which in one of its forms is:

$$\left(\frac{\hbar e^2 H_0}{(8\pi)^3 G c^2} \right)^{1/3} m_e \sim$$

where m_e is the electron mass, H_0 is the (present) Hubble constant and the other parameters in (5) are the usual physical constants. Weinberg's relation can be shown to be equivalent to Dirac's relationships (2) and (3), when the latter are equated to each other (Kafatos, Roy and Roy, 2005). We can then obtain a relationship linking the speed of light c to the rate of change of the scale of the universe, R, the latter being arbitrary (scale invariance). In fact, the proportionality factor is ~ 1 if one substitutes for values of fundamental quantities like the present number of particles in the universe, etc. The next step is to assume that the relationship linking c and R is an identity, i.e. $c \equiv \dot{R}$ (for example, at the Planck time, or the *beginning,* one observes that this relationship still holds if the ratios of all masses → 1 and the number of particles also → 1). As such, in this picture *all* the fundamental constants are changing and not some, as was assumed in past works. It is interesting that, recently, the possibility that the cosmological constant Λ itself might be changing has been suggested.

As such, what is suggested here as a scale-invariant framework of the cosmos is a natural extension of previous ideas. Therefore, as N_P changes from an initial value of 1 to the present value of 10^{80} (1 → 10^{80}), the universe would *be appearing to be evolving to an observer inside it or the arrow of time can be introduced as an apparent reality*. We note that the outcomes of this prescription are not just that an arrow of time is introduced and the mysterious coincidences of Dirac and Eddington now can be understood as scale-invariant relationships linking the microcosm to the macrocosm; but in addition, all scales are linked to each other and what one calls, e.g. *fundamental length,* etc. is purely a convention.

The existence of *horizons of knowledge* in cosmology (Kafatos & Nadeau, 2000; Theise & Kafatos, 2013a), indicate that as a horizon is approached, ambiguity as to a particular unique view of the universe applying as a complete framework sets in. At the *initial time,* if we set the conditions like $c = \dot{R}$, as proposed by Kafatos, Roy and Roy (2005), we can take as axiomatic the numerical relations connecting the microcosm and the macrocosm. In other words, after setting $c \equiv \dot{R}$, at the initial Planck time, which could be taken to mean some sort of "beginning", this relationship remains invariant even at the present universe. This relation is a type of scaling law at the cosmological scale and connects the microcosm and the macrocosm. Time is not fundamental, change is. And the agent of change is light speed. Or to put it more fundamentally, *Light connects everything in the universe.*

Note: Does that sound like an Eastern metaphysical statement? Maybe. But it comes out of science and specifically from the large-scale structure of the universe!

This evolutionary universe is totally equivalent to a Big Bang cosmos. In such views, if one wants to insist that there is expansion of the Universe, R itself is changing and more specifically, then the fundamental constants like G, $\hbar$, and c may also *all* vary with time. Telling the difference between an evolving universe with constant "constants" and a universe that *appears to be evolving* as the "constants" evolve, may prove impossible. *They are complementary views.*

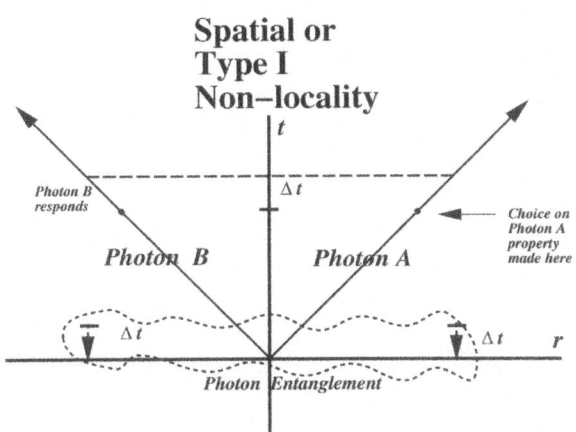

Figure 1

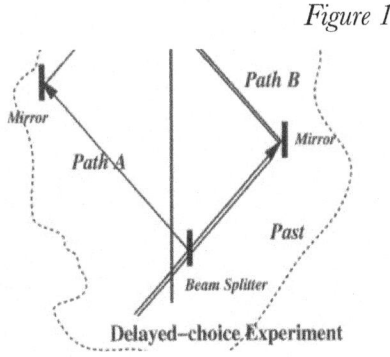

Figure 2

Due to the variation of these fundamental constants, N_P will also be changing from the initial value 1. This implies that more and more particles will be created due to expansion of the universe. So an observer, who is inside the universe will instead see an arrow of time and evolutionary universe. As $N_P \rightarrow 10^{80}$, which is the present number of nucleons in the observable universe, the fundamental constants achieve their present values. Therefore, the arrow of time can be related to a kind of complementarily

Is Consciousness Primary?

between two constructs, i.e., the universal constants are constant, on the one hand; and constants are changing, on the other hand.

In the latter case, *the observer is brought in fundamentally*, and as such it is connected to conscious observations. *Time itself derives from consciousness.*

The Non-Local Universe

Note: non-locality sounds like (implies?) a quantum universe. We don't mean quantum at the microscale, we mean everywhere, including the macroscale!

Let's follow and see what happens:

In the generalized comp-lementarity framework (Kafatos & Nadeau, 2000; Nadeau & Kafatos 1999; Theise & Kafatos, 2013a),

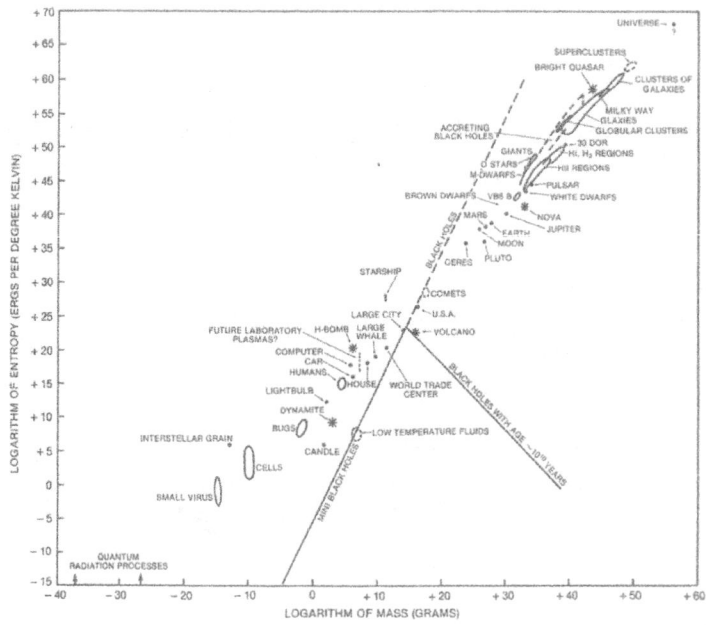

Figure 3

complementary constructs need to be considered to formulate a complete picture of a scientific field under examination (e.g. the large-scale structure of the universe) as a horizon of knowledge is approached. This means that as a horizon is approached, ambiguity as to a unique view of the universe sets in. It was precisely these circumstances that apply at the quantum level, which prompted Bohr to affirm that complementary constructs should be employed (Bohr, 1961). Moreover, the remarkable correlations exhibited at cosmological scales are reminiscent of Bell-type quantum correlations (Bell 1964) that were so abhorrent to Einstein (Einstein, Podolsky & Rosen, 1935—the so-called EPR thought experiment) and yet confirmed by the Aspect et al. (1982) and similarly by the Gisin and his team (Zbinden et al., 2001) experiments.

Kafatos (1989) and Roy and Kafatos (1999) proposed that Bell-type correlations would be pervasive in the early universe arising from the common electron-positron annihilations: Binary processes involving Compton scattering of the resultant gamma-ray photons with electrons would produce N-type correlations. In these conditions, the outcome of the cascade of processes (even in the absence of observers) would produce space-like correlations among the original entangled photons. Kafatos and Nadeau (2000) and Kafatos (1998) have in turn proposed three types of non-localities: Spatial or

Type I non-locality occurs when 2 quanta (such as photons) remain entangled at all scales across space-like separated regions, even over cosmological scales. (Figure 1)

Temporal or Type II non-locality (or Wheeler's Delayed Choice Experiment) occurs in situations where the path that a photon follows is not determined until a delayed choice is made. In some strange sense, the past is brought together (in the sense that the path is not determined) by the experimental choice. This non-locality confirmed in the laboratory could also occur over cosmological distances (Wheeler 1981). Type III non-locality (Kafatos & Nadeau, 2000)

Is Consciousness Primary?

represents the unified whole of space-time revealed in its complementary aspects as the unity of space (Type I) and the unity of time (Type II non-locality). It exists *outside* the framework of space and time and cannot, therefore, be discerned by the scientific method although its existence is *implied*. Type III non-locality is the real non-locality, unifying Type I and Type II.

Recursion and the Universal Diagrams

Here is how the Second Law applies to the universe. Again, this is not some metaphysical fluff, it is tied to observations of objects in the entire universe! "Bridging" often involves looking at existing data with a new perspective.

A series of *Universal Diagrams* (UD) have been constructed (Kafatos, 1986; Kafatos & Nadeau, 2000; Kafatos & Kafatou, 1991) and

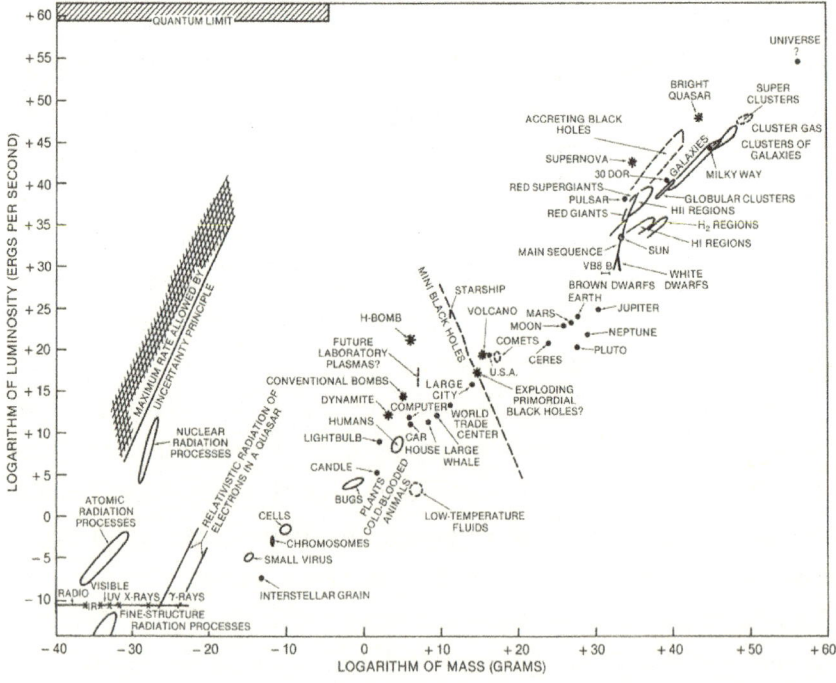

Figure 4

reveal deep underlying wholeness.

These can be constructed by placing various physical quantities of many different objects in the universe on common, multidimensional plots. 2-D diagrams have been constructed involving the mass, size, luminous output, surface temperature and entropy radiated away of different objects in the universe. These diagrams originally constructed for astronomical objects (Kafatos 1986) have been revised and extended to all scales including biological entities, industrial and man-made objects, etc. Two of these 2-D diagrams are shown here Figure 3, entropy radiated versus mass; Figure 4, luminosity versus mass). The diagrams show continuity among different classes of objects and can even be used to find *likely* regions where to-date undiscovered objects could be located are (such as super-superclusters, large planets, etc.). The overall appearance of the UDs does not change as more objects are introduced, rather the specifics of smaller regions become more refined.

Over smaller regions, different power laws can be found to fit the data, while more *global* relationships can be found that approximately fit many different classes of objects (such as an approximately linear relationship between entropy radiated away and mass). It is found that black holes provide boundaries in the UDs and often cut across the main relationships in these diagrams. The values of the constants (and their ratios) and the laws of physics are determining the overall relationships and as such the diagrams *must* be related to the ratios (2) and (3), although it is not totally clear at present if additional principles may or may not be required. There are large scale *correlations* revealed in these diagrams among different dimensions (other than space and time examined above) or parameters which extend beyond the quantum or cosmological realms, to realms such as living organisms, etc.

It follows that *non-locality* in the sense of global multidimensional correlations, is revealed by the UDs to be a *foundational principle* of the structure of the cosmos along with *complementarity* (Kafatos & Nadeau, 2000; Theise & Kafatos 2013a).

We notice that there are recursive relationships revealed by these diagrams. In fact, *recursion* seems to be, like complementarity, a foundational principle of how consciousness operates in the universe (Kafatos, 2014). It manifests at both classical and quantum realms, in fact at biological structures as well. Were it not for recursion, there would be no structure to the universe, no unification? Recursion extends structures across 100 orders of magnitude, *implying non-locality*.

Recursion as a universal guiding and encompassing Law can be seen once one looks at many, many objects in the universe. This is not necessarily easy, but it is doable! I did it. Once it is done, it is a trivial issue from that point on!

Fundamental Mathematics and Consciousness

My view is that bridging will have to involve mathematics at some point. The reason is that mathematics is the language of science *and* plays a fundamental role in other human activities, such as art, architecture and even music. Therefore, any effort of bridging or to proceed towards unification, must ultimately rely on mathematics. In my view, I propose that through utilizing the fundamental role of mathematics, we can create a *theoretical framework* of how consciousness operates in the universe. This would seem to be a fundamental element of Postmaterialism. So far we saw that complementarity and recursion apply across vast numbers of scales, in cosmology, in brain science, and certainly in QM. The mathematical *framework* (or perhaps frameworks, in the plural) we are searching may become a blueprint to understand consciousness or to at least to begin to develop the right path towards that understanding. And in this way, build the bridges between science and metaphysics. The quickest way to such bridging is through mathematics. There is another way as we will see at the end of this Chapter.

The following is part of the paper on fundamental mathematics by Kafatos (2015a):

Our starting point, our *ontological assumption is axiomatic:* Stated simply is that underlying, *universal Consciousness operates at every level of reality*. It is founded on the fundamental "I-ness". The basic nature of Consciousness is also basic to each and every one of us: It is the perfect I-consciousness, the I-awareness (Kafatos & Kafatou, 1991). Three principles (*Note: The Three Laws*), on the other hand, allow universal Consciousness, which otherwise would be unmanifest and unknowable, to operate and give rise to all subjective experiences. The Universe is participatory as Consciousness is in partnership, or participation, with everything in it. This participation manifests as sentience *at all levels, in all objects*. The participatory Universe implies that conscious experience is fundamental. It is the experience of universal Consciousness that manifests in countless beings. Finally, at the individual level, experience becomes subjective. Qualia, as we saw above, give rise to all levels of subjective experience and are the fundamental building blocks of the Conscious Universe.

We use the following symbols for the mathematics of fundamental consciousness, utilizing a simplified Hilbert space convention, which has the advantage that it brings forward a familiarity with quantum formalism. As quantum mechanics is the only physics we have that fundamentally relates to observation, the connection to Hilbert space is natural. As such,

$\langle | \rangle$ is the symbol for absolute undifferentiated Consciousness

$| \rangle$ is the symbol for Subject, i.e. $| \rangle$ = "I"

$\langle |$ is the symbol is for Object, i.e. $\langle |$ = "That"

The A symbol is "Am". We then use the convention $A|\rangle = |\rangle$ "I Am". While $\langle| A^+ = \langle|$ means "That Am" (note that there is no difference between "Am" and "Is"). Note that the verb "Am" could also be placed in parentheses, as it is implied in both these expressions, i.e. "I Am", or "I (Am)", etc.

"I Am" is existence of Subject; while "That Am" is existence of Object. Subject and Object are not yet differentiated, they form the primordial relationship between what eventually will become a separated object from subject, the fundamental complementarity. Also, the adjoint A^+ is used in keeping with Hilbert space formalism.

In the above formalism, the only difference between Subject and Object is a sense of direction (or emphasis): In the "I Am", the direction is from right to left. In the "That Am", the direction is from left to right. In order the keep that sense of direction, we introduce a right to left arrow in the "I Am", as A $|\overset{\leftarrow}{}\rangle$; and a left to right arrow in the "That Am", as $\langle\overset{\rightarrow}{|}| A^+$.

One then obtains statements such as $\langle| A \overset{\leftarrow}{|}\rangle$ "I (Am) That", while $\langle\overset{\rightarrow}{|} A^+|\rangle$ "That (Am) I". It can be easily shown that the direction of $\langle| A \overset{\leftarrow}{|}\rangle$ or $\langle\overset{\rightarrow}{|} A^+|\rangle$ doesn't really matter and that A^+ and A commute, $A^+A = A A^+ = I$, where I is the identity (or $[A^+, A]=0$ and $I = \langle I \rangle$ = Absolute, undifferentiated consciousness).

The emphasis of the statement $\langle| A \overset{\leftarrow}{|}\rangle$ "I (Am) That", is in the I. We denote this as the logical statement **I** (Am) That (**I** is written in bold for emphasis). In this relationship, as the subjective part of the relationship I (Am) That is emphasized, it signifies the Will (a better term is Intent) aspect of Consciousness. Before any knowledge (which is to follow) or subsequent to knowledge any action is undertaken, the subject has to be identifying itself with its own will. The next statement is $\langle \overrightarrow{\,|\, A^+ |} \rangle$ is "That (Am) I" and the emphasis is in That, i.e. the statement is written as That (Am) I. Here, as the objective part of the relationship, That is emphasized. Before any action is undertaken, the object has to be identified. Here, it signifies the Knowledge aspect of Consciousness. However, in both previous cases, Will and Knowledge, there is no separation, only a (latent) potential of what eventually become a separation between Subject and Object.

The next statement $\langle \overrightarrow{\,|\, A^+} \; \overleftarrow{A \,|\,} \rangle$ shows balance: It is the statement of relationship That (Am) I (Am). But as it can be decomposed to $\langle \overrightarrow{\,|\, A^+|} \rangle \langle \overleftarrow{\,|\, A \,|} \rangle$, it is recursive, That (Am) I-I (Am) That (I-I is of course just I, i.e. a recursion occurs; in fact I-I-I... are all just I). The balance between Subject and Object signifies the (potential) for action. But the Subject and Object even in this balanced state, are still One. In action, both the Subject and the Object are balanced, equally weighted.

In the above *universal five logical statements:*

I

That

I (Am) That

That (Am) I

I (Am) That

the *Subject* and the *Object* are not separated but are *poised* to move on to separation, which we claim gives rise to manifestation of objects becoming separate from subjects. However, at the first 5 levels, the *experiencing entities are universal.* In fact, they are all One, Subject, Object and the (latent) relationship between them. The five levels described above are found in Shaivism (e.g. Swami Laksmanjoo, 2003, 2017; Swāmī Shāntānanda, 2003) and as such, the mathematical formalism developed here links with philosophical monism.

All three fundamental principles, complementarity, recursion and creative interaction or sentience, are operating at these 5 levels: Complementarity is operating as the fundamental relationship between Subject and Object. Recursion operates as the relationships can go either way, left to right, or right to left and in fact can repeat forever, always giving rise to   and in fact A or A can be repeated arbitrarily many times, resulting always in undifferentiated Consciousness. And sentience is found in all relationships, the Subject (potentially) senses or interacts with the Object. We emphasize that as no separation has yet occurred, multiple statements like That (Am) I (Am) That (Am) I….can in fact repeat forever.

As we move next to the level of breakdown of the above universal relationships, "persistence" of what is pure *Will* gives rise to (limited) will to know and act. "Persistence" of pure *Knowledge* gives rise to (limited ability to) know and then to act. And "persistence" of *Will* and *Knowledge* gives rise to "persistence" of *Action* but in limited form, with limited ability to act. In other words, the same universal statements operate but now in *limited form*. At that point, the Subject and Object become separated and they become many subjects and objects. The subjects interacting with other subjects and objects now *appear* as differentiated levels of existence, willing (in a limited way) to know (in a limited way) and act (in a limited way). A certain *veiling of Consciousness occurs, which may be manifest in quantum non-locality* (Kafatos & Kak, 2015)

The simple logical statements that we presented above break down, the universal   and (equivalent to two vector states in Hilbert space) are now to become limited subjects and limited objects and direction (left to right, right to left) now matters. This is equivalent to symmetry breaking in physics. The mathematics becomes much more complex, instead of 0 and I, we now have an infinite set of vectors, representing infinitely many sentient beings, interacting with each other and sensing objects.

We will explore the mathematics and breakdown in future works. At this point, it suffices to say that what occurs is the logical statement I (Am) Not that, or That Not (Am) I. Here the symmetry that applied to the first five levels breaks down. In fact, as we will see, this breaking down may *allow space, time and mass to arise*; as well as limited will (of subjects), limited knowledge (of objects), and limited action (between subjects and objects), *providing an account of qualia*. At the level of breakdown of the five pure levels, veiled non-locality and cosmic censorship enter the picture (Kafatos & Kak, 2015): Hence, the world appears as classical, composed of separate subjects and objects.

However, the general principles of complementarity, recursion, and sentience still hold but now in an infinitely complex set of entities. The universe is conceptually born. *Fundamental mathematics at the first five "pure" levels is the expression of the fundamental principles.* Subsequently, in the manifestation of the universe, Consciousness manifests space-time, and objectified existence, including our own intellect, ego and mind. *These manifestations are all qualia.* The Universe *evolves* out of Consciousness, it is nothing less than Consciousness, in a "condensed" form. Science, through the mathematics of the three principle, is utilized by our minds and intellect to provide the qualia of understanding of our environment.

I note that many of the insights that are involved in the above formalism came from studying the ancient philosophy of Kashmir Shaivism, a profoundly sublime non-dual ancient philosophical system that while taking Consciousness as primary, does not deny the universe (cf. Swami Laksmanjoo, 2003, 2017; Swāmī Shāntānanda, 2003). I also received a very vivid vision in a dream that took a while to decipher. These constitute the "how". However, the mathematical formalism stands by itself and any skeptic can ignore the "how" and just study the formalism. To my mind, this was a "bridging" experience!

In concluding the work on fundamental mathematics and looking into the next mathematical developments, the following was said:

The implications of the present work for the philosophy of mind, science and consciousness theory are many: If Consciousness is primary, then the subject – object relationship has to be formalized mathematically. Qualia play a defining role as they are the agents of experience. The question though arises, would such a mathematical formalism as developed here have limits similar to Gödel's Theorem? We can speculate how even space-time emerge from the relationships between subjects and objects, when separation breaks the overall structureless, infinite sea of Consciousness. We suggest that the existence of relationship between sentient observers gives rise to a "measure" of separation, hence *space*. While internal accounting of subjective experiences gives rise to "measure" of change, hence *time*.

Another issue to explore is why the formalism proposed here is more suitable to Consciousness? One possible answer is that the formalism proposed here is the *most* natural as is tied to *direct experience*, which is most basic and most familiar of the human condition.

The above Hilbert space mathematical formalism is not the only one. Others include the Laws of Form developed by G. Spenser-Brown; sheaf cohomology and t-topos (as in Kafatos & Kato, 2017); category theory; and generalized algebraic-topological frameworks. One future area of research would be to look for equivalencies between different formalisms, obeying complementarity, as it occurs in QM.

The following are parts from the book *Living the Living Presence* (Kafatos, 2016, 2017) published in Korean and Greek but not yet in English. It gives a good summary of the practical aspects of what has been discussed so far and also points to practical applications based on the "new science" proposed.

Living the Living Presence

We now have the basic elements to take this knowledge from science and philosophy and turn it into practical knowledge for everyday life. *Living the Living Presence* is exactly that. The *Living Presence* is the reality that quantum mechanics has revealed, in agreement with spiritual and contemplative practices. The *Presence* is Being, always in existence, the eternal Now. But it is not inert, it is fully alive. In fact, it is the very conscious Awareness in all of us.

The last part of this triadic system, Living the Living Presence, is Living. The living part is being aware of the Living Presence in our lives. "Where"? In between breaths, in between thoughts. The gap in between is where time stops; where life goes on (without breaths, life stops; without the *between thoughts*, there is no Awareness). Science and spirituality are converging: Both science and spirituality seek unity, one by exploring the outer world, the other by exploring the inner world. Quantum mechanics has opened the door to the primary role of the mind. We now understand how the following statements are the natural outcome of a unified, participatory universe: Fundamental Consciousness is the underlying total Reality. Nothing exists without Consciousness, which is not subject to the boundaries of space or time. The field of pure Consciousness exists and manifests through our own experiences in everyday life. This universal field is full of the living force, the living Consciousness. It is ever-existing.

This is what I call the Living Presence. It also must be what we experience all the time, our own individual lives. The Living Presence includes our everyday lives, is not separate from them. If we consciously live the Living Presence, our lives become the very abode of eternal happiness. This blissful existence is not far, far away in some transcendent realm. It is right here, right now. In the system of *Living the Living Presence*, we explore how the findings of modern quantum mechanics are actually very relevant to our own everyday lives. The vision of such a new way of seeing what is already there is profound, yet common.

You now have the basics of the system. At the end of the book you will find one-page summary of Living the Living Presence. Contemplate what is summarized. Make it part of your life. Join us to explore Living in the company of each other.

And now we focus on several practical aspects that will assist you to see the workings of the system. These are just representative of a very large number of realities that we can explore as we go about Living. You can create your own list and participate in the game of Living. You now have the basic theoretical understanding, the scientific understanding. But understanding is not enough. Put it to use, make it a practical aspect of your own everyday life. Then this scientific-philosophical understanding has meaning, makes sense, has a purpose. Otherwise it is another knowledge. Make it alive!

Practical Aspects of Living the Living Presence
The Earth and You

The Earth is our home. Humanity is at a pivotal stage in our evolution: Homo Sapiens Sapiens has been on Earth for some 100,000 years, some millions of years if we count our ancestor species. These are mere time flickers in an Earth and its life stretching to billions of years. The last years have seen an unprecedented development of technological and scientific advancements, an awareness of human rights, a globalization of economic systems and an awareness of the Earth as our common home. Along with these, we witness major ecological challenges. It is time to realize we are at crossroads and as planetary citizens make our choices. We can explore the meaning and practice of true involvement of ourselves in the environment as true citizens of the Earth. Either we move forward with the awareness of the sacredness of all life, the brotherhood/sisterhood for all humans on Earth, a higher spiritual purpose; or we go down the path of more of the same, the relentless rise of the ego, until perhaps we end up annihilating ourselves.

From the point of view of the Conscious Universe, the freedom to choose is ours if we are to fulfill our planetary and human destinies.

How to Manage Time and My Mind Or, How Do I Stop My Mind from Driving Me Crazy?

Modern quantum mechanics states that the mind is fundamental reality of the cosmos. Ancient wisdom teachings also held the view that the mind is fundamental in shaping our own world. We always say we're running out of time, right? It is easy to notice that everyone is running around, but do you know why people are running around? It is as if time is chasing them, or something. And you look behind them; there is no time. They're chasing themselves. And then suddenly you're out of time. Because if you live in time, one day you will be out of time, whether you want it or not. No time. So I think we probably should hear what the great teachings of the ancient philosophers of Hellas, of Buddha, the Tao, the teachings of Vedanta and Shaivism tell us: Slow down, become aware of your own existence. We can call this awareness true Meditation.

If you don't want your mind to drive you crazy, *slow down. Slow down before it is too late, slow down before you stop!* We can explore the findings from both science and ancient systems to understand our own reality in balance with the external reality of everyday life. The findings of science and ancient wisdoms are practical to give us a fulfilled personal, family and social life. Applied to our everyday life, the universal truths are near and practical and can become powerful tools in every hour of our living.

Become the Best Friend of Your Own Mind and Manage Time

Modern quantum theory says that the mind is fundamental in reality of the cosmos. Ancient wisdom teachings also held the view that the mind is fundamental in shaping our own world. However, not understanding what the mind is, makes the mind our own enemy, rather than our own friend. In *Living the Living Presence,* we can explore and contemplate the findings from both science and ancient systems to understand our own reality that the mind creates. We understand that the mind is a powerful tool that can be developed and made strong, just like the body. The findings of science and ancient wisdoms are practical to give us a fulfilled personal, family and social life. Applied to our everyday life, the universal truths on the role of the mind are near and practical and can become powerful tools in every hour of our living. In particular, our mind can become our best friend to free us from the chains of time which seem to rule us.

But how? One method that never fails is to observe your own breath. In breath, out breath and point between breaths, they form the triad of Life. Your Awareness is in between the breaths. The point between thoughts is where the source of thoughts exists. Beginning, maintenance and end, the alpha and omega, become one; beginning and ending become one. Before the beginning there was the void of existence.

Void doesn't mean empty. It means no-thing, no-thing. There is no thing in the void. But everything is in the void, all *possibilities* are in the void. In physical space, we call this the quantum vacuum. Everything springs out of the quantum vacuum. So today physicists say if we understood the quantum vacuum, we would understand physics. But the Buddha said the same thing. The Tao is the same thing. Vedanta states that Awareness is triadic and it is empty. If you understand the void, you're there. The point is that beginning and end are much the same. According to mystical Christianity, Buddhism, Shaivism, the Tao, Vedanta, something that has a shape and physical presence came from the shapeless. Then what is the first state made of? That is the Presence. Let's look at us, our breath. Our breath keeps going on and on and on. Then one day it stops.

While we breath, pay attention not to sounds, but to the one who is listening to the sounds. Who is listening? Explore that. That is "I am That". The One behind all sounds. So simple. We can explore together this profound truth, right now as you read these pages. Come and join the Presence!

The Quantum Corporation

In the world of business, the laws of the universe also apply. How could it be otherwise? We can explore both the theoretical underpinnings of what quantum mechanics (the most successful scientific theory we have) says about the world and how such knowledge can be applied and measured in the corporate world. We don't have two worlds, a world of science and an everyday world, we only have one world. And this world includes the corporate world.

In the quantum corporation, we can examine the fundamental Laws of the modern quantum view of the universe. Laws of Nature of "yes and/or no" or *Integrated Polarity* (known as the scientific principle of complementarity); "as here so elsewhere" or *Recursion* (scientific term is Universality); and *Flow* "creative process ties us together" or Process (scientific term is creative interactivity) are not empty philosophical statements, they apply at every level of reality. An aspect of quantum mechanics is the context of a particular process that is being observed and provides "boundaries" or limitations.

Observations are tied to boundaries set up by the observer. Such boundaries are not absolute.

We can examine the practical aspects of what has emerged from quantum mechanics and apply them to the corporate world: How these principles can be applied in practical approach to the corporate world, a world which is nothing more than an extension of our lives? The answers, insights we will gain will surprise us. Not only are the views of modern quantum theory relevant for science, they are even more relevant for understanding of who we really are, our actions in the world, and as such, the corporate world that is part of our lives. This understanding put into practice for CEO's and employees should involve both theoretical and practical understandings and experiential explorations. These could open new vistas. Heads of corporations can seek training for their employees and themselves, in informal and relaxed settings, with ample time to interact, ask questions, offer insights, tap into the collective wisdom of the audience and especially in the process of *flow while being in the Presence*! With this understanding, employees and heads of companies can develop practical sessions, labeled *Fun*, to focus and explore the principles under discussion in the corporate world.

Quantum Relationships

Why do we have relationships? What is a good relationship? How can we improve our relationships? Modern science gives us powerful understanding of the laws of Nature and the role of us as observers and participants. Applied to relationships, we can see how these laws actually give a new meaning to them. Rather than taking things personally or "being stuck" in un-working relationships, we learn that the three Laws of integrated polarity, recursion and flow, constitute the three F's of relationships: free, flowing and fun. Universal spirit flows through you, with you and those in relationships with you.

What is the picture of future or better societies that you can contemplate? A society based on the new paradigm will allow a better relationship with other fellow beings and with Nature. Societies evolve as life evolves. The question though is, does it evolve for the best of all? The vision proposed in this short book is exactly that, everyone around us in the end is really us. This is true understanding. Not theoretical knowledge, not talking, talking, and more talking. Sit down. Follow your own breath, know your own breath, listen to its sound. Results are fast. If they are not fast, try again.

The most primary of relationships is the one between you and you! There is no personal relationship possible unless you understand your own self. If you enter into an external relationship, it may last for a while but eventually it will turn sour. Without that personal relationship, what kind of human beings are we really? So science today can learn a lot from ancient teachings. The ancient teachings actually are confirmed by modern quantum theory. So that dialogue between science and everyday life is very important. What we ought to be doing is talking as friends. As brothers and sisters we should talk, not as enemies. There's no time for being an enemy in today's world. If we always look for enemies, we will find them all around us. But if we look for friends, we will also find them. It depends on us!

The ancient teachings tell us that inside the human body there is the Moon, there is the Sun, there are flowers, there is everything, "as above, so below". Until western doctors realize these Laws, they will be trying to fix the surface. Today we look at clusters of galaxies and they look like neurons! They look like neurons inside the brain. We realize that there is only One energy, One Awareness. And we are That. One energy. Everywhere.

When you meet a longtime friend, you embrace that person and you close your eyes. What's going on there? You're going outside of the appearance; you do heart to heart communication, like closing the eyes. We do it every night; close the eyes. If we don't close our eyes and go to sleep, we become crazy. Right? One of big problems is today in society people cannot fall asleep. And when you fall asleep, you fall back in the Love inside you, no?

Unfortunately, in science this is very big problem: There is nothing, nothing, nothing in science that talks about love, the bliss or Ananda, the completeness of self-Awareness. That is a big problem. That's why we turn to spiritual practices and meditation, to experience the love that is always there. Between the breaths, between the thoughts.

For us here, *Living the Living Presence* is going beyond theories, to the heart of the matter, so to speak: You *are* the Living Presence. Now become aware of it. *Live it!*

The Way Forward

Some concluding thoughts bring forward the need for a new and expanded paradigm. This paradigm will necessitate the bridging of science and spirituality, or science and philosophy. Science has struggled but it is clear we have to enlarge science itself to accommodate Physics, biology and consciousness itself.

Did consciousness arise after billions of years of evolution of the universe in a far planet from the center of the Milky Way galaxy called Earth? The question what consciousness is, forms the most important questions in today's world. In fact, it always was the most important question but now a plethora of fundamental problems that may spell the end of human civilization, require us that we seriously take a look at who we are and how we fit in the scheme of existence. We must take a serious look at how our own consciousness may be collectively driving us to a point of no return.

Asking one question after another relating to consciousness quickly leads to a host of interrelated questions, all equally hard to grasp within the confines of present-day science as we know it. The whole issue was rapidly put into the forefront by the development of quantum theory, examined here.

Perhaps as we expand the tools available to us, we should consider the human body-mind as a wonderful cosmic laboratory, wherein the universe is reflected. Then qualia and object-subject relationships will point to something vastly greater and vastly more exciting than what we can even imagine. In following its development and moving to the next stage of evolution of science, we will encounter several marvels. *These marvels are the core characteristics of the conscious universe. Beyond materialism, to the ends of where search may take us.*

PART TWO

NEUROSCIENCE AND CONSCIOUSNESS

Chapter Five

The Elementary Mind

Mario Beauregard, PhD*

Consciousness cannot be accounted for in physical terms. For consciousness is absolutely fundamental. It cannot be accounted for in terms of anything else.
Erwin Schrödinger

My Personal Journey

A few examples of remarkable experiences:

I was raised in a Roman Catholic home. I have never been a materialist because I began to have psychic and spiritual experiences in my childhood. In fact, I have had such experiences during my whole life. These experiences have led me to become a deeply spiritual person, and I now see myself as a mystical scientist (I am not religious; I left the Catholic Church when I was 14 years old). I give below a few examples of these striking experiences.

The first important spiritual experience I can remember occurred when I was eight years old. The farm of my parents was located near a small forest. From time to time, I was taking walks in that forest, which seemed so vibrant and full of life and mystery. One beautiful summer day in 1970, I wandered into the mysterious

---

[6] *Portions of this chapter were published previously in Expanding Science: Visions of a Post-materialist Paradigm (Beauregard, Schwartz, and Trent, in press).*

forest. At one point during my "expedition," I became tired and decided to sit on a big grey rock. While sitting on that rock, I watched the pretty trees surrounding me. After a few minutes, I started feeling connected to the rock and the trees. It then appeared to me that the rock, the trees, and myself were part of a Whole much greater than "little Mario." Following this experience, my purpose in life became clear: I would later become a scientist to demonstrate that our deepest essence, as human beings, cannot be found in the brain.

Another life-changing experience occurred to me 12 years later. On January 12th, 1982, I woke up as a different person compared to when I went to sleep the night before (I was perfectly healthy before that dramatic morning). I was feeling exhausted and had pain in multiple joints. I also felt nausea, dizziness, and stomach pain, and I had trouble breathing. In addition, I was experiencing a mental fog and something had changed in my visual perception of the world. Actually, I had the impression that all the objects in my visual field were oscillating.

I was feeling too sick and weird to attend classes. I could not figure out what was happening to me, but I suspected something very serious was going on. Fearful I called my parents at night to let them know what I was going through. They suggested to me that I should go back to their house as soon as possible. In order to do so, I would need to take the subway that was going to the Montreal bus terminal. From there, I would take a bus that would stop about 10 miles from where my parents were living (in the Eastern Townships, a region close to the border crossing between southeastern Quebec and Vermont). Through sheer willpower, I managed that evening to reach my parents' house.

For nearly a year, I was almost completely bedridden and unable to care for myself. Needless to say, I had to quit university. Several medical specialists investigated my case (e.g., neurologist, gastroenterologist, ophthalmologist, psychiatrist, internist, etc.). They could not find anything and did not understand my strange illness.

I felt like I was slowly dying. My parents were desperate because they did not know what to do (other than presenting my case to various medical doctors).

One night, I cried out to the Supreme Being for help. A few days later, in the middle of the night, I had a near-death experience (NDE). I felt myself leave my body from the heart. Then I perceived a beautiful Being of Light radiating immense, unconditional love. This Being told me telepathically that I was going through a transmutation process that had nothing to do with a physical or mental disease. This process was paramount for my spiritual evolution. The Light Being also told me that the symptoms would diminish significantly in the upcoming months. The Being of Light gave me a last piece of information that was not related to my current situation: my sister would find not one but two jobs in the following days. Then I remember reintegrating into my body through the heart area.

In accordance with what the Being of Light had told me during my NDE, my sister found two jobs the following week (she had been actively seeking work for a while). And I started to feel much better physically, cognitively, and emotionally after my experience. I also became very psychic and much more connected with the spiritual realm.

Seventeen years later, in the summer of 1999, I suddenly felt compelled to make a retreat in a Cistercian monastery not far from Montreal. The retreat was quite beneficial. Indeed, after a few days I was feeling very calm and reinvigorated. The experience happened on the third day of the retreat. It was early in the morning, and I was still laying down in bed with my eyes closed. The room was filled with silence. Suddenly I felt a sensation of heat and tingling in the spine. This sensation lasted a few minutes. Then I realized that my perception of time passing was slowing down considerably. I also noticed that I was merging with what could be called the Ultimate Reality (Universal Self or Cosmic Intelligence). Furthermore, it became obvious that everything arises from and is part of this Ultimate

Reality, which has an infinite number of different expressions. My "SMALL SELF" disappeared and became united with everything in the cosmos. In this unitary state of being, which was timeless, the duality between subject and object did not exist anymore. The experience was accompanied by intense feelings of bliss. This state of Cosmic Consciousness appeared to last for a very long time (a few hours according to my watch). Remarkably, after this experience, I felt completely without mental activity, i.e. there was only Awareness, for about a day.

About My Research Work

Since my childhood, I have been fascinated by the relationship between mind, consciousness and the brain. In this context, I decided after I reached my teens that I would study both psychology and neuroscience. In line with this, I began my undergraduate career as a psychology student at the University of Montreal. After obtaining my bachelor's degree, I joined the University of Montreal's graduate program in neuroscience.

As a university student, I fully realized the limitations of mainstream psychology and neuroscience. Clearly, the kind of science I was looking for did not exist yet. Intuitively feeling that I would later become involved in the elaboration of a new scientific paradigm, I also understood that in order to achieve this, it was crucial for me to build a successful academic career. It is in this frame of mind that I underwent postdoctoral fellowships at the *National Institute of Mental Health (NIMH)*/University of Texas Health Science Center at Houston (1992-1994) and the Montreal Neurological Institute (MNI) (McGill University) (1994-1996). During my postdoctoral work, I developed an expertise in cognitive and affective neuroscience, as well as in brain imaging (positron emission tomography [PET], functional magnetic resonance imaging [fMRI]). I was recruited to the University of Montreal in 1996 and served as an Assistant

Professor of Psychology and Radiology. A few years later, I received an Early Career Award for Distinguished Research from the Quebec Health Research Fund. At about the same time, my research team and I conducting the first neuroimaging study seeking to investigate the neural correlates of conscious and voluntary regulation of emotion (the research paper reporting the results of this study has been cited nearly 1200 times since its publication). *My research about emotional self-regulation, the placebo effect, and psychotherapy has shown that mental activity—through intention, expectation, and will—has tremendous power over shaping our brain(Beauregard, 2007).*

Feeling that it was now time to expand the boundaries of neuroscience, I also created a research program aimed at identifying the neural mechanisms mediating various types of spiritual experiences (this program was funded by the John Templeton Foundation). This ground-breaking research on the neurobiology of spiritual experiences has received international media coverage. Following this program, I also investigated near-death experiences (NDEs) during cardiac arrest.

A significant portion of the research I have conducted so far supports a postmaterialist perspective. This research has been summarized and discussed in two books: *The Spiritual Brain* (Beauregard and O'Leary, 2007) and *Brain Wars* (Beauregard, 2012).

The theoretical view that I propose here is based primarily on various lines of empirical evidence, and on my own spiritual experiences.

The Failure of Scientific Materialism

Few scientists are cognizant of the fact that what has been called the "modern scientific worldview" is predicated on a number of metaphysical assumptions, i.e. hypotheses about the nature of reality. These assumptions, which were first proposed by some of the pre-Socratic philosophers (Burtt, 1949), became associated, several centuries later, with classical physics. They include materialism—the notion that matter is all that truly exists, i.e. everything in the universe is composed of collections of material/physical particles and fields (*the terms 'materialism' and 'physicalism' are used interchangeably in this chapter)—and reductionism, the idea that complex things can be understood by reducing them to the interactions of their parts, or to simpler or more fundamental things such as tiny material particles. Other assumptions include mechanism—the idea that the world works like a machine, determinism—the notion that future states of physical or biological systems can be predicted from current states, and naturalism—the idea that only natural laws and forces operate in the world (Beauregard et al., 2014).

During the 19th century, these metaphysical assumptions turned into dogmas, and coalesced into a belief system that came to be known as "scientific materialism" (Burtt, 1949; Sheldrake, 2012). According to this belief system, mind—the set of mental faculties (e.g. consciousness, perception, thinking, memory, emotions, volition), processes and events, consciousness—the state of being aware of an external object or something within oneself, and all that we subjectively experience (e.g. thoughts, memories, emotions, intentions, and spiritual epiphanies) are identical with or can be reduced to electrical and chemical processes in the brain. Furthermore, our thoughts and intentions cannot have any effect upon our brains and bodies, and the material world since the mind cannot directly affect at a distance physical and biological systems. That is to say, we human beings are nothing but complex biophysical machines and our mind and personality vanish when we die.

Scientific materialism became dominant in academia during the 20th century. It was so dominant that most scientists began to believe that it represented the only rational view of the world. This dominance has seriously constricted the sciences and hampered the development of the study of mind, consciousness, and spirituality. Furthermore, faith in this belief system as an exclusive explanatory framework, for reality has compelled many scientists to neglect certain aspects of the subjective dimension of human experience. This has led to a severely distorted and impoverished understanding of ourselves and our place in nature (Beauregard and O'Leary, 2007; Nagel, 2012; Wallace, 2012).

Towards the end of the 19th century, physicists discovered phenomena, at the atomic level, that could not be explained by classical physics. This led to the development of a revolutionary new branch of physics called quantum mechanics (QM). This "new physics" has convincingly refuted the metaphysical assumptions underlying scientific materialism. For instance, QM has questioned the material foundations of the world by demonstrating that atoms and subatomic particles are not really objects—they do not exist with certainty at definite spatial locations and definite times. Rather, they show "tendencies to exist," forming a world of potentialities within the quantum domain (Heisenberg, 1976). Moreover, physicists have found that particles being observed and the observer—the physicist and the method used for observation—are somehow linked, and the results of the observation seem to be influenced by the physicist's conscious intent. This phenomenon has led towering figures of QM (such as Max Planck, Erwin Schrödinger, John von Neumann and Eugene Wigner) to propose that the consciousness of the physicist is vital to the existence of the physical events being observed, and that mental events, such as intention, can affect the physical world. This interpretation of QM is also supported by well-known living physicists (such as Freeman Dyson, Andrei Linde, Paul Davies and Henry Stapp).

Albeit QM has invalidated the metaphysical assumptions associated with scientific materialism, several contemporary scientists and philosophers still hold this belief system. They strongly believe that science is synonymous with methodological and philosophical materialism; furthermore, they are convinced that the view that mind is simply a by-product of brain activity is an incontrovertible fact that has been demonstrated beyond reasonable doubt (Dossey, 2015).

Undeniably, scientific methods based upon materialistic philosophy have been highly successful, not only in increasing our understanding of nature but also in creating numerous benefits for the world, such as greater control and freedom through advances in technology. Nonetheless, science is, first and foremost, a non-dogmatic, open-minded method of acquiring knowledge about nature through the observation, experimental investigation, and theoretical explanation of phenomena. Science is not synonymous with materialism and should not be committed to any particular beliefs, dogmas, or ideologies (Beauregard et al., 2014).

In other respects, materialist theories have utterly failed to account for how the brain could produce the mind. Thus, these theories cannot solve the "hard problem" of consciousness, the problem of explaining how and why we have qualia or phenomenal experiences (Chalmers, 1996). Furthermore, these theories are unable to explain a plethora of empirical findings that are considered to be anomalous with regard to the materialist framework.

The Structure of Scientific Revolutions

In the 1960s, historian and philosopher of science Thomas Kuhn published a book titled *The Structure of Scientific Revolutions*. This work became very influential in both academic and popular circles. In this book, Kuhn proposed that paradigms—theoretical frameworks of scientific disciplines within which theories are formulated and experiments performed—can and should change because sooner or later, they fail to explain observed phenomena. Importantly, Kuhn showed that scientists are usually unable to acknowledge phenomena not allowed by the paradigm they are committed to:

"Can it conceivably be an accident, for example, that Western astronomers first saw change in the previously immutable heavens during the half-century after Copernicus' new paradigm was proposed? The Chinese, whose cosmological beliefs did not preclude celestial change, had recorded the appearance of many new stars in the heaven at a much earlier date" (Kuhn 1970, p. 116).

In Kuhn's view, when anomalies—experimental observations or other empirical evidence which violates the widely accepted theoretical framework—that the paradigm cannot accommodate accumulate, and persistent efforts by scientists fail to elucidate these anomalies, the scientific community begins to lose confidence in the dominant paradigm and a crisis period ensues. A new paradigm, competing with the old for supremacy, can now be entertained. This new paradigm is not just an extension of the old paradigm, but a completely different worldview.

The new paradigm is typically championed by bolder scientists storming the bastions of accepted dogma. Unsurprisingly, as conservative scientists often believe that the anomalies will be resolved soon from within the old paradigm, they fight to salvage this theoretical framework. But if the new paradigm shows sufficient promise, i.e. if it is better able to account for anomalous observations, it then attracts a significant group of scientists away from the old paradigm, and a paradigm shift (or scientific revolution) occurs. Following this paradigm shift, scientists return to solving puzzles, but within the new paradigm.

A good example of a major paradigm shift is the Copernican Revolution, the radical change of perspective from Ptolemy's geocentric model of the heavens to the heliocentric model with the Sun at the center of the solar system. It is noteworthy that Aristarchus had already laid the foundations of heliocentrism in the third century BC. However, as the power of the geocentric view was too strong, it took another 18 centuries before Copernicus proposed that the Earth moves around the sun and not vice versa (Kuhn, 1970). Another instance of a major paradigm shift in science was the development of QM between 1900 and 1930. This new physics began as mathematical explanations of certain anomalies, at the atomic level, that could not be explained by the predominant theories of classical physics.

Present day scientists working in the field of consciousness research, and interested in the mind-brain problem, find themselves in a situation similar to that of the physicists at the turn of the 20th century. They are confronted with an increasing amount of anomalous evidence that cannot be elucidated by materialist theories of the mind. In the next section, I examine summarily some of this evidence, guided by the radical empiricist view that we should study any human experience, no matter how unusual it may seem at first glance (James, 1904).

Empirical Evidence Challenging Scientific Materialism

The various lines of empirical evidence examined in this section are grouped into three categories. Category I includes evidence for which a materialist explanation is often provided, but that could also be seen through a postmaterialist perspective. The phenomena described in this category demonstrate the enormous power of the mind to influence the brain and body. Category II contains evidence for which a materialist explanation, though commonly presented, is less adequate than a postmaterialist explanation. This category includes phenomena suggesting that mind is not limited to space or time. Category III contains evidence that is rejected outright by materialist theories of the mind, but is supportive of a postmaterialist perspective, since it is incongruent with the materialist perspective that mind is produced solely by the brain.

Category I: The Power of the Mind to Influence Brain and Body

There are many instances in which mental activity—through

intention, expectation, and will—have tremendous power over shaping our brain, body, and health. For example, several studies indicate that thoughts can causally affect behavioral outcomes via intentions that are translated into specific plans (Baumeister et al., 2011). In accordance with this, it is well established that the explanatory and predictive value of agentic factors (e.g., beliefs, goals, aspirations, and desires) is very high (Bandura, 2001). Moreover, there is now ample evidence that mental phenomena significantly influence the functioning of the brain.

This is exemplified by functional neuroimaging investigations of emotional self-regulation, which refers to the cognitive processes by which we can consciously and voluntarily affect which emotions we have, when we have them, and how we experience and express these emotions (Gross, 1999). Reappraisal—reinterpreting/transforming the meaning of the emotion-eliciting stimulus/event to change one's emotional response to it—and cognitive distancing—viewing a stimulus from the perspective of a detached and distant observer—are some of the cognitive strategies used to self-regulate emotion. Studies performed in my laboratory (when I was at the University of Montreal) and in other labs have conclusively shown that the conscious and voluntary use of cognitive strategies specifically alters the activity of brain areas involved in emotion (e.g. the amygdala, hypothalamus, and insula). (For a review, see Beauregard, 2007.)

Additionally, a number of brain imaging studies suggest that the mental functions and processes implicated in various types of psychotherapy (e.g. cognitive-behavioral therapy and interpersonal psychotherapy) do exert a powerful influence on the functioning and plasticity of the brain (Beauregard, 2007).

Other lines of evidence in Category I include the placebo effect and psychosomatic influence. A placebo is a treatment (e.g., drugs, psychotherapy, and surgery) used for its ameliorative effect on a disease, but that is biologically inert (Shapiro and Shapiro, 1997). The physiological responses produced by placebos seem to reflect a mind/body interaction which is driven by subjective psychological factors (e.g. beliefs, expectations, meaning, and hope for improvement). To date, many neuroimaging studies have been carried out with respect to this phenomenon. Overall, their results strongly support the view that beliefs and expectations about placebo treatments can modulate neurophysiological and neurochemical activity in brain regions involved in various psychological functions (e.g., perception, movement, pain, and emotion).

The sphere of influence of the mind is not limited to the brain. Indeed, experimental investigations conducted in the field of psychoneuroimmunology (PNI)—the study of the interactions between mental processes and the nervous and immune systems (Ray, 2004)—have revealed that chemical messengers produced by immune cells signal the brain, and the brain sends chemical signals to the immune system. Other studies have shown that the causes, development, and outcomes of an illness are determined by the interaction of psychological (e.g. thoughts, emotional feelings) and social factors with biochemical changes that influence the immune system, the endocrine system, and the cardiovascular system (Ray, 2004). In agreement with this, we now know that events and situations perceived as uncontrollable can lead to major disruptions of the immune and endocrine functions. For instance, immune responses are weakened during marital discord, and the levels of stress hormones increase in the spouse who experiences the greatest amount of stress and feelings of helplessness (Vitetta et al., 2005). In contrast, a positive emotional state can bolster the activity of the immune function.

Mental influence on the activity of the physiological systems connected to the brain is usually exerted unconsciously. However, there is some evidence that mental phenomena can also affect the body consciously and volitionally. In fact, it has been demonstrated that healthy volunteers can intentionally use mental imagery to positively impact their immune system, notably the activity of neutrophils, the most abundant type of white blood cells (Trakhtenberg, 2008).

Category II: Mind beyond Space and Time

This category contains various lines of evidence suggesting that mental functions and abilities are not constrained by space and time and the boundaries of the body. One of these lines of evidence relates to the so-called psi phenomena, which include extrasensory perception (ESP) and psychokinesis (PK). ESP denotes the acquisition of information about external events or objects by means other than the mediation of any known channel of sensory communication. It includes telepathy—the access to another person's thoughts without the use of any of our known sensory channels, clairvoyance—the apparent perception of events or objects that cannot be perceived by the known senses, and precognition—the knowledge of some future event that cannot be deduced from normally known data in the present. PK refers to the influence of mind on a physical system that cannot be totally explained by the mediation of any known physical means (Kugel, 2010). In this subsection, I will briefly examine the results of studies of some psi phenomena.

Since the 1970s, a large number of experiments have been performed to test telepathy using a sensory deprivation technique called the ganzfeld. Several meta-analyses—statistical analyses of several separate but similar experiments/studies in order to test the pooled data for statistical significance—of ganzfeld telepathy studies have reported results significantly higher than expected by chance. (For a review of these meta-analyses, see Williams, 2011.)

During the last five decades, presentiment experiments have also been carried out to test whether it is possible to obtain specific, meaningful information in ways that transcend the usual limitations of time. These experiments often involve protocols where a series of emotionally laden stimuli are presented while participants have continuous physiological recordings, such as skin conductance, heart rate, pupil dilation, electroencephalography (EEG), and blood oxygenation level-dependent (BOLD) responses. In presentiment experiments, post-stimulus activity is predictive of pre-stimulus activity; that is, various aspects of human physiology respond to the stimulus before it is presented or known by the participants. A meta-analysis of 26 presentiment experiments between 1978 and 2010 was performed by Mossbridge and colleagues (2012). The physiological variables measured in these studies included electrodermal activity, heart rate, blood volume, pupil dilation, EEG activity, and BOLD activity. The results of this meta-analysis indicate a significant overall effect.

As for PK, researchers around the world have conducted laboratory experiments in this area for over a century to investigate the effects of mental intention on inanimate objects and physical systems (e.g. morphological changes in thin strips of metal, distribution of metallic and plastic balls, temperature changes in well-shielded environments, latencies in radioactive decay, and perturbations in sensitive magnetometers and interferometers). Several of these experiments have produced statistically significant results (see Radin and Nelson, 2003).

Electronic random number generators (RNGs) have frequently been used as physical targets in mind-matter interaction (MMI) experiments. Modern RNGs are circuits designed to produce electronic noise that is converted to random sequences of 0 and 1 bits. During a fixed group of successive trials, called a run, participants in these experiments are asked to mentally influence the outcome of an RNG so that it may produce, for example, a high number of 0's (i.e. greater than chance expectation), and then a low number of 0's (i.e. lower than chance expectation). In the control condition, the participants do not exert any intentional influence on the outcome. Typically, participants in RNG experiments contribute several hundred runs. In 2003, Radin and Nelson published a meta-analysis which included 515 RNG experiments. The magnitude of the overall effect was small, but statistically very significant.

Psi researchers have also explored whether people can mentally influence living systems situated at a distance when shielded from all possible conventional influences. For instance, Braud and Schlitz (1991) conducted a series of experiments in which one person (the influencer) attempted to mentally influence the ongoing electrodermal activity (an index of emotional responses) of a distant target person (the influencee) using intentionality, focused attention, and imagery of desired outcomes. In these experiments, the influencee and the influencer were placed in separate, non-adjacent rooms, and the influencee's spontaneously fluctuating electrodermal activity was monitored while he/she made no deliberate attempts to relax or become more active. During series of 30-second electrodermal activity recording epochs, the influencer received instructions about what to do. Epochs were signaled to the influencer (through headphones) by special tones not audible to the influencee. During decreasing epochs, the influencer created and maintained a strong intention for the influencee to be calm and relaxed and to display little electrodermal activity; during non-influence (control) epochs, the influencer attempted not to think about the influencee or the experiment. Using this experimental protocol, Braud and Schlitz (1991) conducted 15 electrodermal influence experiments: in these experiments, a significant success rate was found, and the mean effect size compared favorably with effect sizes commonly reported in behavioral and biomedical studies.

Category III: Mind Beyond Brain
NDEs During Cardiac Arrest

NDEs are vivid, realistic, and often deeply life-changing experiences occurring to individuals who have been psychologically or physiologically close to death (Holden, 2009). A clear memory of the experience, enhanced mental activity, and a conviction that the experience is more real than ordinary waking consciousness are core features of NDEs (Greyson, 2011). Other typical features include an out-of-body experience (OBE), i.e. a sense of having left one's body and watching events going on around one's body and, occasionally, at some distant physical location; feelings of joy and peace; passage through a dark tunnel or a region of darkness; seeing an otherworldly realm of great beauty; encountering deceased relatives and friends; seeing an unusually bright light, sometimes experienced as a "Being of Light" that radiates complete acceptance and unconditional love, and may communicate telepathically with the near-death experiencer (NDEr); seeing and reliving events of one's life, sometimes from the perspective of the other individuals involved; and returning to the physical body (often unwillingly).

NDEs are frequently evoked by cardiac arrest. When the heart stops, breathing stops as well, and blood flow and oxygen uptake in the brain are rapidly interrupted; the EEG becomes isoelectric (flatline) within 10-20 seconds, and brainstem reflexes vanish (Clute and Levy, 1990); the individual having the cardiac arrest is then considered clinically dead. Because the brain structures supporting conscious experience and higher mental functions (e.g. perception, memory, and awareness) are dramatically impaired, cardiac arrest survivors are not expected to have clear lucid mental experiences during the cardiac arrest period that will be remembered. Nonetheless, studies in the United Kingdom (Parnia et al., 2001), the Netherlands (van Lommel et al., 2001), Belgium (Lallier et al., 2015), and the United States (Schwaninger et al., 2002; Greyson, 2003) have revealed that about 15 percent of cardiac arrest survivors do report some recollection from the time when they were clinically dead. In these studies, more than 100 cases of full-blown NDEs were reported. It is noteworthy that while they are clinically dead, it is not uncommon for NDErs to report perceptions that coincide with reality.

Advocates of materialist theories of the mind object that even if the EEG is isoelectric, there may be some residual brain activity that goes undetected because of the limitations of scalp-EEG technology. This is possible, given that scalp-EEG technology measures mostly the activity of large populations of cortical neurons. However, the brain activity agreed upon by contemporary neuroscientists as the necessary condition of conscious experience is well detected via current EEG technology, and is clearly abolished by cardiac arrest (Greyson, 2011).

Proponents of materialist theories of the mind also argue that NDEs do not occur during the actual episodes of brain insult, but just before or just after the insult, when the brain is more or less functional (Saavedra-Aguilar and Gómez-Jeria, 1989; Blackmore, 1993; Woerlee, 2004). The problem with this interpretation is that unconsciousness generated by cardiac arrest leaves patients amnesic and confused for events occurring immediately before and after such episodes (Aminoff et al., 1988; Parnia and Fenwick, 2002; van Lommel et al., 2001).

Reincarnation-past Life Research

During the last 50 years, over 2,500 cases of young children who reported memories from ostensible previous lives have been studied (Haraldsson, 2012). The pioneer of this type of research was Dr. Ian Stevenson, a psychiatrist who worked at the University of Virginia. Today, other researchers, such as Erlendur Haraldsson and Jim Tucker, continue the research pioneered by Stevenson. Many cases have been verified. If the verified cases are indeed indicative of accurate memories from another life, these data challenge the materialist view that mind is what the brain does. Clearly, the fact that the brain of the deceased is no longer functional, and that the memories of the individual may still be accessible, seriously call into question what we know about memory and its dependence on cerebral activity (Haraldsson, 2012).

Most children who experience ostensible past-life memories begin to talk about them between the ages of two and five, and usually stop talking about these memories between five to seven years of age (Mills and Lynn, 2000). While most incidences occur in Eastern countries, where reincarnation is more culturally accepted, some cases also occur in Western countries (Stevenson, 2001). Approximately 80 percent of children's ostensible past-life memories are of violent deaths (Haraldsson, 2003). Common themes include claiming that their current parents are not their real parents, and that their homes are somewhere else. Many children have birthmarks that coincide with wounds reportedly associated with the previous life. Though not as common, there are multiple cases of children who present with xenoglossy, meaning they are able to communicate in a language, to various degrees of fluency, which they did not learn through any discernable means (Stevenson, 1976).

The investigations usually involve child and parent interviews, and any other person who has witnessed the child speaking of the memories. Then, it is important to rule out whether the child is speaking of events or experiences that he/she learned about from something or someone in his/her environment. After these steps, it is determined whether the case is worth investigating further. Often the witnesses are interviewed again for reliability. The next step, which is very important, is to determine if a deceased person can be traced whose life events correspond to the statements made by the child. Frequently, a person is found to whom the child is believed to be referring. The family of that person will then be interviewed, if possible, and all relevant documents obtained, such as birth and death certificates, postmortem reports, and any other relevant materials (Haraldsson, 2012).

Common materialist explanations for ostensible past-life memories include mere coincidence, child or parental fabrication, fantasies, and false memories or paramnesia (Haraldsson, 2003). Some have suggested that past-life memories may be a result of trauma in the current life, such as child abuse, but no evidence for this has been found (Haraldsson, 2003). However, these children may display post-traumatic stress disorder (PTSD) symptoms, such as fear, phobias, anxiety, and aggressiveness, though these behaviors may be related to the past life trauma rather than trauma from the current life (Haraldsson, 2003). These children could be remembering previous lives that they lived as they suggest, or they could be accessing information of a deceased individual through some unknown means (i.e. super-psi theory, also called super-ESP: the retrieval of information via a psychic channel).

Mediumship Research

The survival of consciousness hypothesis—the continued existence, separate from the physical body, of an individual's consciousness or personality after physical death—has been investigated for more than a century. William James, the father of American psychology, was one of the early pioneers of mediumship research (see Gauld, 1983). James and the other pioneers in this field thought that investigating the information reported by mediums—individuals who report experiencing communication with deceased persons— could test the survival of consciousness hypothesis.

Contemporary research has been carried out mainly by Dr. Emily Kelly, at the University of Virginia, Dr. Julie Beischel at the Windbridge Research Center, and Dr. Gary E. Schwartz in the Laboratory for Advances in Consciousness and Health (formally the Human Energy Systems Laboratory) at the University of Arizona. The early experimental designs were mostly single blinded, i.e. the medium was blind to the identity of the sitters (the living people who knew the deceased individuals) (e.g. Schwartz and Russek, 2001; Schwartz et al., 2001, 2002). Other exploratory experimental designs were double blinded, in that the medium was blind to the identity of the sitters, and the sitters were blind to the identity of their personal readings. In other experiments, the medium was blind to the identity of the sitters, and the experimenter was blind to the information about the sitter's deceased loved ones.

To determine whether accurate information about a sitter's deceased loved ones can be reliably obtained from research mediums, who are operating under highly controlled experimental conditions that effectively rule out conventional explanations, the most recent experimental designs were triple blinded (Beischel and Schwartz, 2007). Blinding was produced at three levels: (a) the mediums were blind to the identities of the sitters and their deceased loved ones, (b) the experimenter/proxy sitter interacting with the mediums was blind to the identities of the sitters and their deceased loved ones, and (c) the sitters rating the transcripts were blind to the origin of the readings (intended for the sitter vs. a matched control) during scoring.

Eight research mediums who had previously shown an ability to report accurate information in a laboratory setting performed the readings. Eight University of Arizona students served as sitters: four had experienced the death of a parent; the four others had experienced the death of a peer. Each deceased parent was paired with a same-gendered deceased peer to optimize potential identifiable differences between readings. Sitters were not present at the readings. The mediums each read two absent sitters and their paired deceased loved one; each pair of sitters was read by two mediums. Each blinded sitter then scored a pair of itemized transcripts (one was the reading intended for him/her; the other, the paired control reading) and chose the reading more applicable to him/her. The mediums performed the study readings over the phone at scheduled times in their homes to improve testing conditions. The audio-recorded phone readings took place long-distance; the medium was in a different city (if not state) than both the blinded absent sitter and the experimenter acting as the proxy sitter.

The results showed that the sitters were able to correctly identify above chance which of the two readings belonged to their paired deceased individuals. These findings provide evidence that under stringent triple blind conditions, certain mediums can receive accurate information about deceased individuals. The findings cannot discriminate between alternative hypotheses, such as the survival of consciousness or super-psi. However, the use of a blind proxy sitter condition eliminates telepathy (i.e., mind reading of the sitter) as a plausible explanation for the results.

Deathbed Communications

Deathbed communications (DBCs) constitute another source of evidence suggesting that consciousness and personality may not cease after bodily death. DBCs are any communication between the patient and deceased friends or relatives within 30 days of dying. These experiences have been reported across different cultures and throughout history (Fenwick et al., 2010). DBCs may encompass auditory, visual, and kinesthetic elements, and are often indicated by nonverbal processes (e.g. reaching out of the hands toward an invisible person or object) (Lawrence and Repede, 2012). One frequent type of DBC involves apparent encounters with deceased individuals who seem to welcome the experiencer to the afterlife and converse responsively with him/her (Greyson, 2010). DBCs have a deep impact on the alleviation of physical, emotional, and existential distress at the end of life, and most of the people who have these experiences derive great meaning and comfort from them (Lawrence and Repede, 2012).

Research conducted with end-of-life nurses and physicians suggests that these experiences are not uncommon (Fenwick et al., 2010). The prevailing view among physicians is that DBCs are confusional-hallucinatory, drug induced (Fenwick et al., 2010), or due to expectation and wishful thinking (Greyson, 2010). While this may sometimes be true, there are cases of DBCs which cannot be simply explained as hallucinations based on expectation: in these cases, the dying person apparently sees, and expresses surprise at seeing, a person whom he/she thought was living, but who had in fact recently died (Greyson, 2010).

The Primordial Mind

The various lines of empirical evidence presented in the preceding section clearly show that the idea that the brain creates mind is flawed and obsolete.

Materialists often claim that experimental evidence obtained using neuroscience techniques (e.g. recording, stimulation, and lesion) proves in a definite manner that the brain produces mind, much as the liver secretes bile. In fact, neuroscience studies only reveal that under normal conditions, mental activity is correlated with neuroelectrical and neurochemical activity. But correlations do not imply causation and identity, and the kinds of evidence obtained via these techniques do not necessarily validate the hypothesis that mind can be reduced solely to brain activity.

Given that materialist theories of the mind cannot explain these phenomena and have failed to elucidate how brain could produce mental functions and consciousness, I posit that it is now time to free ourselves from the shackles and blinders of the old materialist paradigm, and to enlarge our conception of the world. To this end, I have recently proposed the Theory of Psychelementarity (TOP, Beauregard, 2014; psyche is used here as a synonym of mind). This postmaterialist theory rests on four postulates.

Postulate 1: Mind is primordial and irreducible

The first postulate of the TOP is that mind is irreducible, and its ontological status is as primordial as that of matter, energy, and space-time. In other words, mind cannot be derived from matter and reduced to anything more basic.

This postulate is based on the undeniable and incontrovertible fact that the world we experience is apprehended subjectively through consciousness, a central aspect of the mind. In that sense, we can say that mind is primary because all our experiences (e.g. sensations, perceptions, thoughts, emotions, memories, and dreams)—whether they are related to the mental realm or to the physical realm—are forms that appear in consciousness Without mind, we could not enjoy the musical genius of Mozart or the exquisite taste of a Dom Perignon champagne, and there would be no sense of self, no science, and no apprehension of reality.

The TOP is compatible with panpsychism, the view that some type of mental processes and abilities, including subjective interiority, exist to different extents at every level of organization in the universe. In this view, all living and non-living entities comprises a physical aspect (an exterior) and a mental/experiential aspect (an interior), and mental activity is not restricted to functioning brains or nervous systems. With respect to this issue, physicist Freeman Dyson has hypothesized that since atoms in the laboratory behave like active agents, they must possess the reflective capacity to make choices (Dyson, 1988). Furthermore, at the molecular level, there is evidence that molecules composed of only a few simple proteins have the capacity for complex interaction (Cohen, 1997). Awareness and intentionality also appear to be present in primitive unicellular and multicellular species (Baluška and Mancuso, 2009).

Philosopher David Chalmers has speculated that the degrees of consciousness (or proto-consciousness) in living and non-living entities are related to their degree of physical complexity: much more sophisticated forms of mental experience would characterize more complex systems, such as higher animals (Chalmers, 1996).

Postulate 2: Mind is a fundamental force

The mind (will/intention) acts as a force, i.e. it can affect the state of the physical world and operate in a nonlocal fashion. This implies that mind is not confined to specific points in space, such as brains and bodies, nor to specific points in time, such as the present.

The evidence briefly reviewed in this chapter also indicates that mental phenomena do exert a causal influence on the functioning of the brain and body, as well as on behavior. In regard to this question, I have proposed earlier (Beauregard, 2007) that conscious and unconscious mental events are specifically encoded by the brain—i.e. they are translated, through a psychoneural transduction mechanism, into different forms of information; that is, neural events at the various levels of brain organization (biophysical, molecular, chemical, neural circuits). In turn, the resulting neural events are translated into other forms of information, i.e. events in other physiological systems that are part of the psychosomatic network.

Postulate 3: Mind and the physical world are deeply interconnected

As psi phenomena reveal, there is a deep interconnectedness between the mental world (psyche) and the physical world (physis), which are not really separated—they only appear to be separated. Actually, psyche and physis are deeply interconnected since they are complementary aspects (or manifestations) arising out of a common ground. It is conceivable that this common ground (or Ultimate Reality) is an Eternal and Infinite Mind (which is also Infinite Intelligence and Consciousness). This primordial principle is the source of energy, matter, and physical reality. It is also in this sense that Mind is primary. Moreover, individual minds are also a manifestation of this primordial principle, which permeates the entire cosmos and all of existence. During transcendent experiences, experiencers can sometimes become one with this elemental principle.

The deep interconnectedness between psyche and physis does not seem to rest on quantum entanglement. In fact, non-local connections between entangled particles do not implicate the transfer of information (Kafatos and Nadeau, 1999), whereas interaction at a distance between humans and physical/biological systems appears to involve a mental information transfer. Additionally, this type of interaction implicates different types of mental phenomena that are not accounted for by QM. In any case, physical/biological processes and mental events appear to be interconnected, probably in a non-local manner (i.e. beyond space and time). This suggests that we live in a participatory universe, and that nothing in the world is really separate. Stated otherwise, the universe is a colossal web of connections between all the various levels of organization.

Postulate 4: Mind is not produced by the brain

The brain acts as a transceiver of mental activity, i.e. the mind works through the brain, but is not produced by it. As mentioned above, the fact that mental functions are disturbed when the brain is damaged does not prove that the brain produces mind. Further, being non-physical, mental phenomena are not localized to the brain and the body, and cannot be reduced to physico-chemical phenomena, since the mind can exert effects at a distance. Enhanced mental experiences and accurate OBE perception occurring at a time when cerebral activity is seemingly absent (e.g. during cardiac arrest) also accord with the view that mind is not generated by the brain.

In line with the idea that the brain acts as an interface for the mind, this organ may be compared to a television set. This device receives broadcast signals (electromagnetic waves) and converts them into image and sound. If we damage the electronic components within the TV, we may induce a distortion of the image on the screen and the sound, because the capacity of the TV to receive and decode the broadcast signals is impaired. But this does not mean that the broadcast signals (and the program) are actually produced by the TV. Likewise, damage to a specific region of the brain may disrupt the mental processes mediated by this cerebral structure, but such disruption does not entail that these mental processes are reducible to neural activity in this area of the brain.

The empirical evidence discussed in this chapter also supports the idea that the brain acts as a filter. This idea was initially proposed, toward the end of the 19th century, by William James (James, 1898; this hypothesis was also defended by philosophers Ferdinand Schiller and Henri Bergson). This psychologist propounded that the brain may play a permissive and transmissive role regarding mental functions and consciousness. James further hypothesized that the brain may act as a filter that normally limits/constrains/restricts the access to extended forms of consciousness. Henri Bergson speculated that this mechanism blocks out mental events (e.g. perceptions, thoughts, emotions, memories) that are not necessary for the survival and reproduction of the organism (Bergson, 1911).

During transcendent experiences (e.g., NDEs, mystical experiences, meditative states), the filter function of the brain is deactivated to various extents. Phenomenologically, such a deactivation can lead to an expansion of consciousness and the perception/experience of other domains of reality (Beauregard, 2012).

Conclusion

Scientific materialism, which has dominated science and academia over the last few centuries, has run its course. At last the tired old materialist paradigm has started to crumble, and it appears that we are now closing in on another crucial paradigm shift, namely the transition from materialist science to postmaterialist science. Holding great promise for science, this transition—which will lead us to the next great scientific revolution—will be of vital importance to the evolution of human civilization. I am convinced that this transition will be even more pivotal than that from geocentrism to heliocentrism, or that from classical physics to quantum physics.

Chapter Six

What do Near-Death and Meditation Experiences Tell Us About the Primacy of Consciousness?*

Marjorie Woollacott

Introduction

A number of years ago the Dalai Lama was invited to speak at the Society for Neuroscience meetings in Washington, D.C. This was a gathering of about 35,000 people, one of the largest gatherings of neuroscientists that had occurred. One might think that many of the neuroscientists at the meeting were enthusiastic about hearing a revered spiritual master speak. But the controversy within the Society about his invitation makes me think otherwise.

His reception was not very welcoming. Before the meeting began there were news reports that a petition had been submitted by 600 neuroscientists with the aim of preventing his lecture. The petitioners wrote that they were concerned that the Dalai Lama's views on both the benefits of meditation and the origin and nature of consciousness in a metaphysical universe would misrepresent

---

* *Portions of this chapter were adapted from Infinite Awareness: The Awakening of a Scientific Mind.*

neuroscientists' views on the nature of the material world. One person wrote, "No opportunity should be given to anybody to use neuroscience for supporting transcendent views of the world" (Society for Neuroscience, 2005; Carey, 2005).

This is simply one example of the many argumentative exchanges that occur on an ongoing basis regarding the nature of consciousness. The vast majority of neuroscientists believe that all mental activity, including consciousness, is produced by neural activity in the brain. This certainty regarding the material basis for consciousness often results in an unwillingness to consider, and sometimes an outright dismissal of, alternative views. This materialist view of consciousness is one side of a long-standing debate: brain vs. mind—consciousness as an epiphenomenon of the brain vs. pure awareness, pure consciousness. Here, I use the word "pure" to indicate that consciousness can exist without neural activity. This is an understanding based on an awareness of an expanded reality.

The study of consciousness has not yet led to definitive answers regarding the nature and origin of consciousness. Perhaps because of this there is great polarity among scientists around these issues. Uncertainty regarding concepts related to consciousness is not limited to scientists, but is a factor for all of us in our everyday life. Whether or not we realize it, we filter our experience based on our own understanding of the nature of consciousness. Our view of consciousness can either connect us to, or separate us from a particular experience—either open us up to or cut us off from an expanded reality. Just as many of the scientists in the Society for Neuroscience were trying to actively block exposure to the Dalai Lama, we too limit our willingness to be exposed to certain ideas regarding the concept of consciousness.

My neuroscience career has been in the area of rehabilitation medicine. Why would a neuroscientist like me who had spent my life doing this, be concerned with issues related to consciousness? Before I had my own spiritual awakening, I was in a state of absolute certainty about the material basis of life and dismissed paranormal experiences such as those found in meditation and near-death experiences. As a result of my own spiritual journey, I now have great uncertainty about the material basis of reality and curiosity about paranormal or spiritual phenomena. I have learned that it is only when we are uncertain about aspects of reality that we are curious enough to be intrigued by other possibilities.

This chapter is about the nature of consciousness, and about my own experience as a researcher and meditator. In it I will take you along on my journey, of being a rigorously trained neuroscientist who then had an experience in meditation that put a crack into my materialist worldview. I will share how this lead me to begin research studies on both meditation and near-death experiences (NDEs), and through this how I found new windows into the exploration of the nature and origin of consciousness.

Let me give you information, first, about my research background as a neuroscientist. My primary research area for much of my career was in brain development, aging and neurological disease. In these areas I have written and edited about 200 papers and books, and received grants from the National Institutes of Health for over 35 years, for from $500,000-$1 million/grant. I have also written a textbook for clinicians on assessing/treating patients, which is in its fifth edition. But most importantly, I was a scientific materialist when I started this research. My scientific view was that our thoughts, our movements, and our awareness or consciousness are solely a product of the activity of the neurons of our brain.

Meditation Experience

Then in 1976, I had an experience in meditation that opened up for me an awareness of a dimension of reality I had never before experienced. I was invited by my sister to a meditation retreat by an

Indian Meditation Master. Though I was skeptical, I was curious and decided to attend. In the first session of the retreat, it was announced that during the meditation period the meditation master would walk around the room and initiate everyone there. The host described this as a spiritual awakening, and it would occur through the master's touch. As a young neuroscientist I was skeptical. But I was already there, so I made the decision to put my skepticism aside for the duration of the retreat. And, in fact, I was curious to see what might unfold (Woollacott, 2015).

When he reached me, I felt the swami's thumb and fingers right between my eyes and on the bridge of my nose. I was attentive. I had closed my eyes, but my other senses were fully aware, so when I became aware of what seemed like a current of electricity enter from the master's fingers into my body, I had a sense of utter certainty about what had happened. It isn't that I knew precisely what had occurred. To this day, I can't explain it. But it seemed as if a mini-lightning bolt moved from his fingers to a point between my eyes and down to the center of my chest. I could feel the precise point where it stopped. It was my heart, not the physical heart but more like a heart than my physical heart had ever been. This energy radiated outward from my heart, and filled my whole being. It felt like nectar, like pure love pouring through me. Words came to mind, and they were unrelated to scientific analysis: I'm home, I'm home! My heart is my home.

What was most surprising to me was what happened after the retreat was over. When I returned home, without any effort, I made a complete shift in my habits, beginning the next morning. I spontaneously awakened at 5 am, and got up to meditate, and this new habit has continued to this day. I meditated knowing that just below the surface of my awareness simmered a quiet ecstasy. I had tapped it once. I knew it was there waiting for me.

As a result of this meditation experience, I experienced a shift in my worldview and I began to question my materialist perspective.

I had a professional dilemma: I asked myself, is the world I live in Newtonian, as I originally believed, or is it energy-based? I began to explore the nature of consciousness through my own meditation practice, and through research into the characteristics of conscious experience. I asked: what is consciousness? Is it tied to neural activity? Or could consciousness exist without neurons?

Though I was meditating every morning, in my early years as a meditator I considered myself first and foremost, a scientist. The scientific part of me had no interest in finding research support for phenomena that are considered mystical or paranormal. Such experiences are not within the scope of Newtonian science, and this precise, cause-and-effect, material view related to consciousness was still the perspective I held. So, if someone mentioned a topic like energy healing or near-death experience or — even worse — reincarnation, I would raise a cool, skeptical eyebrow and say nothing.

This led to a fragmented life. It seemed like an almost impossible chasm existed between my life as a scientist and my life as a meditator. I would reveal one type of experience to my friends who meditated and in the classes I taught on yoga and meditation. And I would bring up other, very different experiences of mine, with my colleagues in neuroscience—those I worked with, in various areas of rehabilitation. This dichotomy drove my husband crazy. He loves meditation and complementary medicine, and at social gatherings with my scientific friends, he would start to talk about Reiki or Tai Chi or hypnosis therapy—only to get a kick under the table or a horrified look from me as I quickly "helped" him by changing the subject. I was so afraid of losing my credibility with my scientific colleagues.

After 25 years of leading two lives, I felt a bit schizophrenic. It was a problem I decided to resolve by publicly integrating the two halves of my experience. As I wrote my first book on this topic, *Infinite Awareness: The Awakening of a Scientific Mind* (Woollacott, 2015), I was seeking another level of integrity. I wanted to speak frankly and openly about my experiences as a meditator. I wanted to explore what these experiences have to say about the world we inhabit and the nature of the human mind.

I, and many others, have had experiences that do not fit within the perspective of materialist neuroscience. However, if they actually happened —as I am convinced is the case— then perhaps we need to think again about the box we call neuroscience. Perhaps it's time for this box to expand.

In the following pages, we will examine the essential features of subjective experience, alternative theories of human consciousness, and scientific studies on meditation, and near-death experiences. The question at the core of these apparently contrasting topics is whether the awareness that each of us experiences through the mind is primary —that is, it can exist independently of the activity of the brain—or whether it is only a creation of the brain and body.

Important questions about our nature as human beings rest on this one point. Do I, as an individual, have free will? Or are my apparent decisions established at a neural level, by the mechanics of the brain? When death comes to the brain and body, do I, as I know myself, cease to exist? Am I nothing more than a material being?

Research on Meditation from the Third-person Perspective

I first began to try to bridge this chasm between the two sides of myself by doing scientific research on meditation. I asked, "Does looking at meditation from the third-person, scientific perspective inform us about the origins of consciousness? I wanted to understand if meditation changes our mental abilities—and, if so, how it does this. What is the physiological basis of such changes?

Our lab and many others have shown that meditation improves attentional and emotional regulation. Our EEG studies showed that our attentional networks get stronger. This research shows that meditators are like athletes of the attentional arena—their attentional systems become both strong and flexible. I want to tell you about one study from our own lab that asked whether meditation, and Tai Chi, a moving meditation were better than aerobic activity in improving attentional focus (Hawkes et al., 2014a; 2014b). We used four groups: people who practiced meditation, Tai Chi, and aerobic exercise and compared them to sedentary adults. We included people who practiced aerobic exercise because we know that aerobics brings more blood to the brain, and this by itself, increases attentional abilities. So do meditation and Tai Chi actually give more benefits to our attentional skills than simple exercise?

We tested this by asking participants to play a computer game, while they wore a 256 electrode electromyogram (EEG) cap on their heads. The EEG cap allowed us to record their brain potentials when they were viewing the stimulus (a red dot) on the computer screen and responding as quickly as they could. When the participants saw the red dot appear (as you see in figure 1), they were to press a mouse button as quickly as possible on the same, or the opposite side of the screen. Every 2 trials they were to switch the rule for pressing the mouse button. For the first two trials they were to press the button on the same side, and then in the next two trials they pressed the button on the side opposite to that of the red dot. You can imagine that this could be quite demanding, to remember which trial you were on, and switch your rule for making a response every two trials, going as fast as possible.

Event-related potentials (ERPs) occurred in the EEG electrodes situated on the scalp over the brain of the participant whenever the red dot stimulus appeared on the computer screen. And these ERPs showed the amount of attention the participants were giving to the task.

What were the results? The sedentary group had significantly greater reaction times for the trials in which they had to switch rules, compared to the three training groups (Tai Chi, p = 0.014, Meditation, p = 0.016, Aerobic, p = 0.029). This was associated with the benefits of long-term practice of meditative and physical activity, contrasted with a sedentary lifestyle. In addition, the switch-costs were significantly smaller for the meditation and Tai Chi groups, compared to the aerobic exercisers (Tai chi p = 0.007, Meditation p = 0.013, Aerobic p = 0.382) (Hawkes et al., 2014a; 2014b).

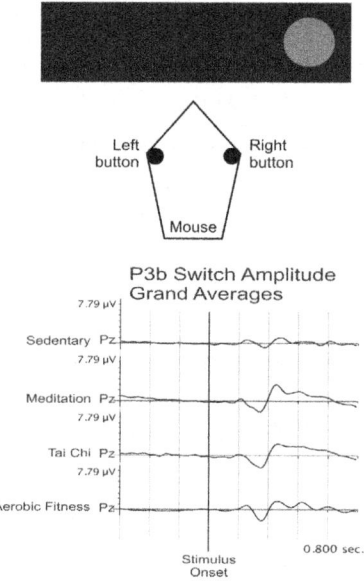

Figure 1

Top: Diagram of computer screen with stimulus (appearing randomly on the left or right, in sequential trials) and the mouse buttons the participants were to press as quickly as possible in response to the stimulus, according to ever-changing rules. Bottom:. Grand averages of Event-related Potential (ERP) amplitudes for participants in each of the 4 groups (sedentary, meditation, Tai Chi, aerobics) in response to the stimulus, during trials in which they were required to switch their rule for responses. Stimulus onset is indicated by the wider vertical line. Time intervals are 200 ms each. (From Hawkes et al., 2014b)

As you see in figure 1, we also found that the meditators and Tai Chi group showed the largest negative and positive going ERPs in the interval between 200 and 400 ms after the stimulus onset, including what is known as the P3 potential. This indicates that, associated with their faster reaction times on the switch trials (lower switch costs), they were paying the highest degree of attention to the detection of the red dot on the screen.

The sedentary group showed the smallest ERPs, associated with their slow reaction times, indicating their poor attentional focus. And the aerobic fitness group was in between the meditators/Tai Chi groups and the sedentary group in both their reaction times and ERP amplitudes. What does this tell us about the attention or focus of people who practice meditation and Tai Chi? It suggests that their attentional systems are the strongest and most flexible of the four groups, contributing to their efficiency in performing the task.

But where in the brain is the source of this improvement in attention? We also looked for the source of the difference in the ERPs – by using a technique called independent component analysis. Remember that in figure 1 we saw increased ERP amplitudes in the negative and positive ERP potentials activated after the stimulus for the aerobics, meditation and Tai Chi groups compared to the sedentary group.

Our additional analysis indicates that three areas of the cerebral cortex, all involved in executive attention function contributed to these differences between the groups. They are the superior frontal cortex, the posterior parietal cortex (mainly contributing to the negative wave of the ERP, called N2, and the anterior cingulate cortex, mainly contributing to the later positive part of the ERP, called P3. The Tai Chi and meditation groups, which had the lowest switch costs, also showed the highest contributions to the ERP in the

N2 window coming from the superior frontal and parietal cortex, and in the P3 window coming from the cingulate cortex.

What is the significance of these group differences in the cingulate, prefronal and parietal cortex areas? The prefrontal and anterior cingulate cortex areas play a critical role in the top down or intentional regulation of the attentional and executive processes during a task, and the parietal cortex areas play an important role in shifting the attentional allocation and updating the spatial orientation in the working memory network. Thus the meditation and Tai Chi groups have honed their attentional regulation, so they can focus uninterruptedly on an attentional task (prefrontal and cingulate cortex), and they also are able to shift their attention quickly as they respond to changing rules for the task (parietal cortex).

I want to focus specifically on the anterior cingulate cortex contributions to attention, and their improvements with meditation. The anterior cingulate cortex is the part of the brain involved in voluntary attentional focus, decision making, and the intensity of our awareness. So, yes, meditation and Tai Chi, a moving form of meditation, improve our attention, or our awareness related to particular events in our environment.

But why is this important? The anterior cingulate cortex size is highly correlated with success in world. It is the best predictor of how well children resolve conflict. And conflict resolution at four years of age is highly correlated with success in later life. This includes health, income, relationships, and criminality (Fjell et al., 2012; Moffit et al., 2011). The anterior cingulate cortex size is also modifiable through meditation (Grant et al., 2013).

In summary, here are some of the characteristics of consciousness we have uncovered from the third person perspective through meditation research. Our own lab has shown that meditation improves our attention, increasing our focus and reducing distractibility. And this is associated with changes in the anterior cingulate, the frontal and parietal cortex. Many other labs have also contributed to this research and also shown that meditation reduces stress and improves our emotional well-being. They have shown that meditators are happier and have more equanimity in challenging situations. And this is associated with changes in the hippocampus and amygdala in the brain (Tang & Posner, 2007; Tang et al., 2015; Davidson et al., 2003; Lutz et al., 2009; Gard et al., 2015).

Experiences of Meditation the First-Person Perspective

But is this all that meditation tells us about consciousness? Meditation experiences from the first-person perspective suggest it does more. So now I will discuss some of what we have observed about the effects of meditation from a first-person perspective – and I will give you examples from a meditator's own observations.

I first want to share an experience of David, another neuroscientist, who, like myself had a spiritual awakening during a meditation retreat. He had gone to a meditation workshop on one of his free weekends while he was doing his postdoctoral training in developmental neurobiology. He said that the concept of meditation had always intrigued him and he'd even tried it on his own for a while when he was an undergraduate, but nothing had really resulted from his practice.

In his first day of the meditation workshop with the Indian meditation master, Gurumayi Chidvilasananda at Shree Muktananda Ashram, he found himself in a deep meditation, a state he had never before experienced. He was no longer aware of the outer world, and became deeply absorbed inside, feeling very peaceful and calm. After the program was over that evening, he began to sense an inner power, moving upward inside himself, becoming more powerful as the evening wore on.

He said that he didn't know what it might be, but he had a feeling that something important was about to unfold within him. In the middle of the night he was suddenly awakened by a tremendous current of energy that rushed up his back to the top of his head, and then exploded with a blaze of light. When he opened his eyes, he found that his awareness had expanded beyond the confines of his physical body. He was aware of looking down at the room from the ceiling – just like people do in near-death experiences.

The next day, in the retreat, he learned that he had had a classic experience of *shaktipat* initiation, the awakening of the inner spiritual energy, the Kundalini, that bioenergy that drives human evolution, which takes place through the power of a spiritual master. He said that this experience of inner light, was more exquisite than anything he had ever seen before, and it continued to unfold for him until one day in meditation it filled his entire body. He experienced an inexpressible joy, and love overflowed within him. At that moment he lost any sense of individuality and had the experience of penetrating the heart of God. He said that he experienced being more "himself" in that moment, than he had ever experienced before. (Sw. Chidvilasananda, 1996)

What does this tell us about the nature of consciousness from David's experience in meditation? It suggests that there is an energetic component that he experienced throughout his being (the energy that shot up his back and exploded at the crown of his head). It also suggests that his awareness went well beyond his body – that there was a sense of nonlocal awareness, of unity consciousness (he no longer had any sense of individuality). This is not an ordinary perception caused by the usual activity of neurons in the brain.

Models of Consciousness

Is there a way to integrate these first-person experiences with the scientific worldview? I believe that one insight helps explain both worlds. It is one by Sir James Jeans, who was an astronomer, mathematician and physicist. It reminds me that all of us, neuroscientists and yogis alike, are operating under the same constraints that Sir James Jeans describes for his colleagues, the quantum physicists. He says:

"The essential fact is simply that all the pictures which science now draws of nature, and which alone seem capable of according with observational fact, are mathematical pictures. Most scientists would agree that they are nothing more than pictures—fictions, if you like, if by fiction you mean that science is not yet in contact with ultimate reality." (Jeans 2001, p. 129)

Why would Jeans call these pictures fictions? Physicists' views of electrons orbiting around the nucleus of an atom have changed substantially over the years, because they were simply using mathematical equations to draw pictures to try to understand reality. When I was an undergraduate student in chemistry classes, electrons were pictured as orbiting in "shells" around the atom. More recently they are being drawn as different forms of probability clouds, with very different shapes than were shown before. As Jeans said, these are nothing more than pictures – fictions if you like – but they are our best attempt to describe the electron orbits.

Could meditators be giving similar accounts? Pictures of meditators' experiences don't necessarily depict ultimate reality, but they do point to something that isn't easily described. This is like predicting electron orbits: specific observations from their first-person experience are used to form an image the person who drew that image can remember, understand, and communicate. Is it real? Not per se. For meditators, it is an attempt to elucidate an experience of meditative energy, and to indicate a reality beyond the picture or the words associated with it.

So how does all this help us understand the nature of consciousness? Next I want to present three different perspectives on consciousness held by different segments of the population, in order to evaluate their ability to explain research data on meditation and near-death experiences.

Medical Model of Consciousness: A Materialistic Worldview

The first is the medical model of consciousness (figure 2): it is a limited model that differentiates normal (e.g., deep sleep, dreaming and, the awake/alert state) from what are considered abnormal states of consciousness (Woollacott, 2015).

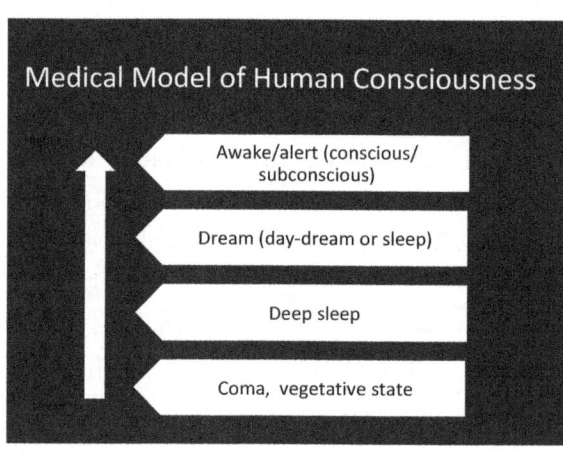

Medical model of consciousness, differentiating normal (e.g., deep sleep, dreaming and, the awake/alert state) from what are considered abnormal states of consciousness (coma, etc.). The arrow indicates increasing levels of consciousness.
Figure 2.

This is the model of consciousness I was taught in my coursework as a graduate student in neuroscience. Within this materialist framework in which I was trained, the medical model was adequate to explain the only states of consciousness I was aware of. According to this model, there is no reality other than the physical universe, and this means that our mind and conscious awareness are considered a product of the activity of our brain.

There is certainly evidence to support this material view. Studies have identified that in the waking state there are "default" neural networks that are activated when our mind wanders (Smallwood et al., 2008; Poerio et al., 2017) and other networks activated when we are problem solving (Nishida et al., 2015). Distinctly different networks are activated during dreaming and sleep. This model is also useful in the diagnosis of a variety of physical disorders, such as strokes. It does not, however, acknowledge the possible reality of a near-death experience (NDE), which is outside this model and is dismissed as the result of pathology within the brain.

Expanded Models of Consciousness

The states of consciousness described in many NDEs include a sense of interconnectedness with all things, a boundless sense of joy, and a sense of connection to a consciousness greater than one's own. The qualities of an NDE experience are surprisingly close to those of the deepest states of meditation. In my experiences of meditation, as a neuroscientist, I was mystified by the new levels of consciousness that became accessible to me: feelings that seemed ineffable, experiences of light, and an expansion of awareness beyond the body.

Studying this phenomenon, I found it interesting that the perceptions that come in NDEs during cardiac arrest are accompanied by an EEG that is flat-lined, indicating brain activity is minimal if present at all. Similar expanded states of consciousness are experienced in meditation, suggesting that NDEs and meditative states are tapping into a common level of consciousness. This has led researchers to ask if there are levels of consciousness within a normal individual that go beyond the state defined as "awake and alert." Laboratory studies on meditators and first-person descriptions of their experiences in meditation suggest that there are (Woollacott, 2015).

These additional levels of awareness have been described in a variety of ways: as one-pointed focus on an object such as the breath or as states of open presence or loving-kindness (Ricard et al., 2014).

In one study that compared advanced meditators practicing thought-free meditation, it was found that EEG activity at most frequencies and in most of the cortex was reduced, when compared to other mental states (Hinterberger et al., 2014), moving toward the flat-lined EEG seen during NDEs.

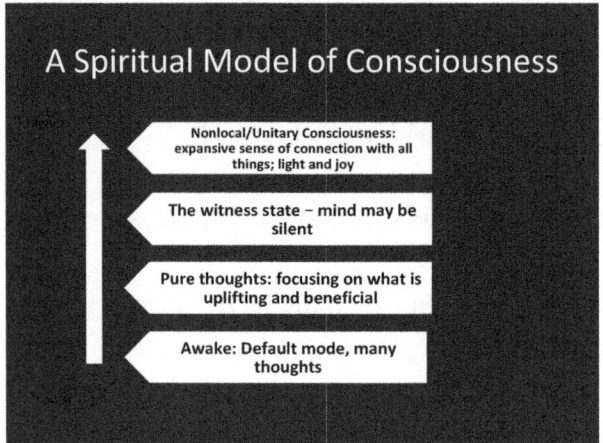

This leads me to propose a model as you see in figure 3, which includes a number of higher levels of consciousness beyond those of the default mode of normal awareness I include the lowest level, 1) the default mode, with many thoughts; 2) a higher level of focused meditation, on the breath, or loving-kindness; 3) a state in which the mind is silent, and one is simply aware; and finally 4) a state of non-local unitary consciousness, in which there is a sense of connection with all things, accompanied by an experience of light and joy.

Higher levels of consciousness, experienced in meditation, etc., beyond the normal waking state (called the default mode). From the lowest to the highest they are: 1) the default mode, with many thoughts; 2) a higher level of focused meditation, on the breath, or loving-kindness; 3) a state in which the mind is silent, and one is simply aware; and finally 4) a state of non-local unitary consciousness, in which there is a sense of connection with all things, accompanied by an experience of light and joy.

Figure 3.

Is Consciousness Present in All Matter?

A final lens through which we can examine consciousness is the biological/pan-physical model of consciousness, which proposes that there are levels of awareness in all matter, living and nonliving. This model (figure 4), has been proposed recently by such researchers as David Chalmers and Christof Koch, though a similar form is the pre-modern philosophy known as panpsychism, the understanding that consciousness is in everything (Chalmers, 1996; Tononi & Koch, 2015). Chalmers proposes that everything in the universe, even the most basic particle, is made up of information and that all information contains two basic aspects: physical and experiential. He associates an entity's experience of consciousness with the level of complexity with which that entity is able to process consciousness. Chalmers says: "Where there is simple information processing, there is simple experience, and where there is complex information processing, there is complex

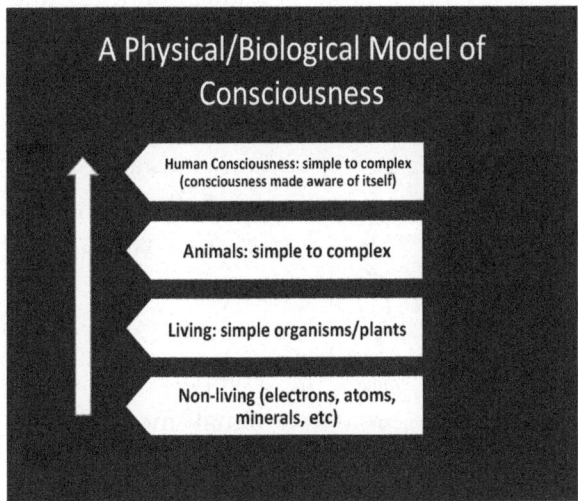

A biological/pan-physical model of consciousness, which proposes that there are levels of awareness in all matter, living and nonliving, increasing in complexity from subatomic particles through simple living organisms, animals and humans.

Figure 4.

Is Consciousness Primary?

experience. A mouse has a simpler information-processing structure than a human, and has correspondingly simpler experience. (Chalmers, p. 231, 1996)"

Thus, awareness extends from a coarse or simple consciousness in inanimate objects through the complex consciousness—even involving self-awareness—that is associated with higher animals, including humans.

Given this model, we might then ask if the full spectrum of consciousness might not include within it levels of all three models? This is similar to a model that many meditative traditions have proposed, in which consciousness is seen as both immanent (in all things, including rocks and plants) and, at the other end of the spectrum, transcendent (as a nonlocal consciousness beyond all material reality) (Woollacott, 2015).

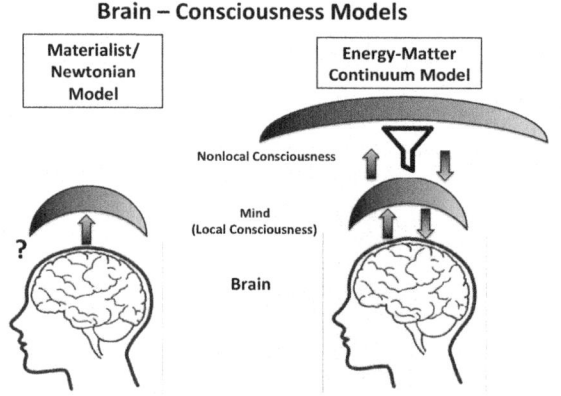

Two alternative "Brain-Consciousness Interface" models. On the left is the Materialist model, in which consciousness is viewed as solely a product of brain activity. The question mark on the left indicates that there is no known mechanism for this to occur. On the right is the Energy-Matter Continuum model, in which a nonlocal consciousness can be filtered to produce the contents of the mind, which can also influence the brain. And the interactions work both ways, as indicated by the up and down arrows. (Adapted from Woollacott, 2015)
Figure 5.

Next I want to compare the traditional medical model regarding the nature of mind-brain interactions -- to one that is being proposed by more and more scientists interested in meditation, energy healing and NDEs.

Figure 5 shows two alternative "Brain-Consciousness Interface" models based on what we have been talking about so far. On the left is the model proposed by most neuroscientists, that consciousness or the mind is solely a product of brain activity, though it is not understood how this might occur. On the right is a model of an energy-matter continuum for consciousness, in which the interaction works both ways: a non-local consciousness can be filtered or limited to form the contents of the mind, which can also affect the activity of the brain, just as brain activity can affect the contents of our conscious awarness.

As I present further data in the following pages I want you to think about these, and see which model the data support.

Near-death Experiences

Now I want to explore with you another approach to studying the origins of consciousness: studying the near-death experience. We will be studying it from both the experiential perspective and the scientific or third-person perspective. These are the questions we will be asking. Can Consciousness remain when the heart and brain have stopped functioning? Are NDEs real or hallucinations?

Recent studies bringing both first- and third-person perspectives to NDE research show evidence that I believe can't be explained in a Newtonian worldview. Let me tell you about one study by Pim van Lommel, though there have been many using careful methodology, including studies by Greyson and a recent study by Parnia and colleagues (Van Lommel et al., 2001; Greyson, 2003; Parnia et al., 2014).

This was a prospective study (the gold Standard of studies of this kind), published in the Lancet journal, which is ranked number two of 150 journals in medicine (2013 Journal Citation Reports®, Thomson Reuters, 2014). The study included 344 patients who had experienced cardiac arrest within a network of ten hospitals in the Netherlands. Patients had a flat EEG (no brain activity) during their cardiac arrest.

Results of the study showed that 12% of the participants had an NDE and 25% of these participants watched and recalled events during their cardiac arrest with no brain activity. In their discussion section, the authors conclude:

"…The thus far assumed, but never proven, concept that consciousness and memories are localised in the brain should be discussed. How could a clear consciousness outside one's body be experienced at the moment that the brain no longer functions during a period of clinical death with flat EEG?" (van Lommel et al., 2001)

Complementing this research article I also include the following case study describing the NDE of a woman doctor who had been a confirmed atheist before her NDE, and who I personally interviewed in 2015.

Dr. Bettina Peyton was an avowed materialist until she had a near-death experience during the birth of her third child. At the time, she had been practicing internal medicine for two years. Peyton's story begins when an ultrasound revealed that her second pregnancy was more complicated than her first had been. A year earlier she had given birth to healthy twin boys.

This time, however, the placenta obstructed the birth canal and would be at risk of bleeding as the uterus enlarged. The condition was life threatening for both mother and child.

In her seventh month Peyton did, indeed, begin to bleed and was put on strict bed rest on the medical center's ob-gyn floor. Night after night, her husband, also a doctor, brought their one-year-old sons to their mother's bedside for a hug and a story. The medical plan was to deliver surgically, by Cesarean section, as soon as the fetus was sufficiently mature.

Peyton said that she was well aware that this surgery would be a high-risk procedure. Because the placenta extended across the front of the uterus, her obstetrician would have to make the incision directly through it, cutting across what was essentially a spongy mass of venous lakes.

Finally, after a month, the weekly amniocentesis indicated that the fetus's lungs were mature enough for delivery. Peyton distracted herself before the surgery by joking with the surgeon as the nurse laid down the surgical drapes and the anesthesiologist injected the induction drug into her vein. Peyton then lost consciousness under anesthesia until, as she writes, she heard a voice: Her blood pressure is too low!" She says:

> My anesthesiologist's alarmed voice had snapped me awake as if from a deep sleep. Suddenly in the middle of the operation, I was wide awake, super aware and attentive, in a way I had never before experienced.
>
> "'How's it going?'" The anesthesiologist was asking the surgeon how far along he was in the delivery. He exclaimed that my blood pressure was plummeting fast.... She then heard a loud expletive, 'Shit!' The anesthesiologist couldn't detect any blood pressure at all (Peyton, personal communication).

She continues:

> "In the next instant, a strange stillness spread inside my chest, a hollow feeling. Something was missing – my heartbeat. My heart had stopped.
>
> "At the same time, my vision opened, and I discovered that I could see into the room. How amazing! The eyelids on my physical eyes had been taped shut to protect the corneas, yet by some other mechanism I could see perfectly clearly. Several units of blood were hanging from an IV pole directly over me, one already was being transfused...."

Peyton realized she was the only one in the room who had noticed that her heart had stopped. Then the silence was interrupted by a volley of strident beeps—the cardiac monitor indicating her heart had stopped— and Peyton watched the anesthesiologist slam his fist into a large red button in the middle of the wall.

In medical jargon, he was calling a code that would culminate in the arrival of the hospital resuscitation team. There is more about the medical drama that was unfolding, but let's now look at another aspect of Peyton's experience: her feeling that she was about to die...

She writes:

"I see in my inner vision a vast darkness expanding behind me, at the backmost boundary of my mind... My awareness reaches the edge of the precipice and I lean backwards, arching over the chasm of darkness below. Very naturally, I let myself fall, gliding downward in a graceful backward arc into the unknown.... Laced within the black darkness were particles of shimmering light. The blackness sparkled, shimmered. This scintillating light was intriguing, intensely beautiful, mesmerizing...."

She sensed a pervasive presence in this light, an intelligence, a pulsating power.... She was deeply happy, enveloped in peace. All was perfect, until Peyton's experience was interrupted by a statement, which she perceived not in words but as a quiet thunder with the message: You must live!

She says, "Funneling down through the darkness, my consciousness opened into the confines of the hospital operating room." Peyton observed the members of the code team burst through the swinging doors and see their colleague's lifeless body on the table. Her surgeon was working in a surgical field filled with blood, performing what he would later call his first 3 minute hysterectomy.

Her attention was then drawn to a white-haired gentleman in scrubs—a senior surgeon—entering the room.... Slowly and deliberately, he wove a path through the crowded room, coming to her right side. Without a word, the elderly surgeon reached deep into her blood-filled abdomen. He located the aorta... and wrapped his fingers around it....Then, clenching his fist, he clamped the aorta shut.

It was the worst pain Peyton had yet experienced in the operation—and it was, she understood at the time, the turning point: she would live. Shortly after, one of the doctors leaned over and whispered into Peyton's ear that her baby had lived; she had a healthy daughter....

When Peyton later opened her eyes, she was in the critical care unit, lying in a bed encircled by her husband and a team of doctors and nurses. She still had a tube in her trachea, so she couldn't talk, but she put up her hand to keep people from speaking and motioned to be given something to write with. Before anyone spoke, Peyton had written on a napkin words to this effect: "I know I have a baby girl. I know my uterus is out. I know my heart stopped." (This case is excerpted, in a shortened form, from my book, *Infinite Awareness*) (Woollacott, 2015).

The whole account, Peyton's entire experience of watching the resuscitation team actually revive her — is in *Infinite Awareness*. What I want to point out to you is that if this highly cogent and completely verified account is accurate, we need a new scientific framework to take such an experience into account. People in the millions have recounted such experiences — near-death, in meditation, as a recipient of energy from healers, and on and on and on.

In Table 1 I have listed 8 of the many statements that Bettina Peyton made about her NDE and their verified accuracy. Note that all of her statements were verified by hospital personnel.

When Bettina Peyton opened her eyes in the recovery room of the hospital after her NDE, she was certain that consciousness was primary. She had vivid recall of all that had happened. Her experience was that her essence was not the physical body, and that consciousness was real and is the basis of everything in existence.

The way that Peyton found her way back to that experience of expanded consciousness she had recognized in her NDE is particularly interesting to me. She said that she sensed that there must be a way to find it again, and she set out to do it. She was introduced to meditation, and thought that this practice of quieting the mind and turning inward could be a way to move toward that experience.

Table 1. Statements made by Dr. B. Peyton after her NDE, which were later verified by hospital staff.

Statements	Verified
Heard anesthesiologist say: "Her blood pressure is too low!"	Yes
Heard cardiac monitor register her lack of heartbeat with strident beeps	Yes
Saw several units of blood on IV pole directly over her; anesthesiologist seated to her right, hunched over right arm inspecting IV line.	Yes
Saw anesthesiologist slam fist into button on wall: calling a code.	Yes
Saw surgeon performing hysterectomy.	Yes
Saw catheter inserted in right jugular vein, and anesthesiologist trying to insert line in her right wrist. Then going for elbow, he finally does and succeeds.	Yes
Saw white haired senior surgeon in scrubs enter room, walk to her side, reach into blood filled abdomen, clamp aorta shut.	Yes
Doctor whispered in her ear: her baby had lived, she had a healthy daughter.	Yes

Peyton found a local meditation center in Boston, and after the program, without intellectually understanding why, felt she really needed to attend a meditation workshop that would be held in two weeks. And during the workshop, she found again that state of her NDE: that same beautiful sparkling black light, the intelligent presence, the peace and love. She said, "I was in the same experience of oneness I'd been in, in my near-death experience: this formless consciousness, which is all that is."

As she sat in that state, the next thing that happened was her perceiving her own expanded consciousness, inside, saying, "Welcome home. You have come home." She said that she knew she had found the path back.

Welcome home! These were almost the exact words I had heard in my first meditation. When I contemplate what they mean, what home really is --I realize that it felt like I had returned back to a state that I experienced as more joyful, and authentically me than anything I had previously experienced.

This reconnection with her near-death experience transformed Peyton's life. It helped her bring her near-death experience into both her life and her medical practice. She began to work as a physician in hospice care, and contributed to the creation of the clinical field that supports and nurtures patients during the process of dying. She said that many of her patients had experiences similar to those people have in NDEs, of a sense of expansion, spiritual experiences, or communicated with family members who were on the other side. Peyton could give them reassurance and support as they went through this process. She also noted that another thing that made her effective as a doctor dealing with the dying process was her lack of fear of death. When she walked into a room, people could tangibly sense that lack of fear (Woollacott, 2015).

I believe that the key understanding that Peyton came to with respect to her NDE is the point that the experience can be reproduced through the meditative process. It can be intentionally cultivated.

What is the connection between the energetic awakening in meditation and in the NDE? This unexpected link between the NDE and meditation is useful to contemplate. Both states seem to be able to give access to a state that a meditator might call true perception: his or her awareness of a unity with the infinite awareness that is the core of reality.

Is Consciousness Primary?

Connections between Meditation and NDEs

What is the connection between the energetic awakening in meditation and in the NDE? In many eastern traditions this energy is called the *Kundalini Shakti*, the *Chi* or *Ki*. And it is believed to be awakened in meditation, allowing people to perceive and experience higher energies, higher levels of consciousness.

Scientists studying near-death experiences have proposed that the NDE is similar to a Kundalini awakening. Bruce Greyson conducted a study to explore whether NDEs, like meditation, can arouse or awaken this spiritual energy within. He considers this the bio-energy that drives human evolution (Greyson, 1993).

Table 2. Results of the Physio-Kundalini Index questionnaire, which were related to the participants' sensory perceptions of energy, such as heat, sounds, and light and motor phenomena they experienced, such as changing in breathing. (Data from Greyson, 1993)

19 Item Physio-Kundalini Index Questionnaire	153 with NDE	55 Close to Death w/o NDE	113 Never Close to Death
Feeling extreme heat or cold	54%	27%	19%
Hearing internal sounds: whistling, roaring, flutelike sounds, etc.	41%	21%	21%
Seeing internal lights or colors	19%	5%	7%
Breath spontaneously stopping or becoming rapid, shallow or deep	39%	18%	21%
Body assuming/maintaining unusual positions	17%	2%	2%

Table 3. Mystical characteristics that are shared by persons who meditate and experience NDEs.

Mystical characteristics: Meditation	NDEs
• Major — Ineffability: feeling defies express. — Noetic quality: truths unplumbed by the intellect • Also — A feeling of peace, joy, love — Sense of being outside one's body — Experience of Light — Experiencing a presence, full of love — Experience other realms — Spiritual transformation, moral elevation — Increased care for others — Decreased fear of death — Unity awareness	• Major — Ineffability — Noetic quality • Also — A feeling of peace, joy, love — Sense of being outside one's body — Experiencing a bright light — Experiencing a presence, full of love — Experience another realm — Spiritual transformation, moral elevation — Increased care for others — Decreased fear of death

In his study Greyson compared 3 groups of people: 1) those who had experienced an NDE, 2) who were close to death, but with no NDE, or 3) people never close to death. He asked them to fill out a questionnaire, called the Physio-Kundalini Index. The questionnaire asked for information about their experience of classical phenomena associated with energetic awakening in meditation. Table 2 shows the results of the questionnaire, which were related to the participants' sensory perceptions of energy, such as heat, sounds, and light and motor phenomena they experienced, such as changing in breathing. Note that twice as many people who had had an NDE experienced sensory and motor phenomena of spiritual awakening compared to either of the other groups. To be sure that he was not just measuring nonspecific unusual experiences, Greyson also analyzed responses of hospitalized psychiatric patients on this scale. Their scores were the same as the Non-NDE groups (Greyson,

1993; 2009). Greyson concludes that NDErs are reporting precisely the kind of physiological changes that are associated in Eastern traditions with the bioenergy that drives human evolution.

Are the mystical aspects of meditation and the NDE experience also similar? Table 3 shows the mystical characteristics of meditation experiences that have been observed by such well-known scientists as William James (James, 1898) and their similarities to those mystical states described in NDEs. I have listed the two major qualities of mystical experiences discussed by James (ineffability, and a noetic quality, the feeling you have experienced
truths unplumbed by the human intellect) and other important qualities, such
as feelings of peace, joy and love, in the table. It is striking how the experiences of meditators and persons having had an NDE have an amazing amount of overlap in their mystical characteristics.

What Do NDEs and Meditation Suggest About the Nature and Origin of Consciousness?

What is the nature and origin of consciousness? Might the higher mode of processing of the NDE be related to an experience of the same expanded consciousness, the nonlocal consciousness, we talk about in our "top-down" theory in figure 5? Materialist neuroscientists assume it is only the activity of the brain that generates consciousness. But these first- and third-person research studies suggest that the brain may also be transmissive of a wider consciousness, like an optical lens or prism. Or it may function like a radio receiver, serving an interface function. These are the real issues that still need to be addressed.

I have come to think that one way of understanding superconscious mental operations is to see the brain and its sense organs not as the source of all mental experience but as a filter. In other words, the brain and sense organs act as a filter for all that we experience.

This perspective, known for the last hundred years as the "filter theory," brings together some significant philosophical principles shared by various mystical traditions over thousands of years.

The filter theory was originally proposed at the end of the 1800s by psychologist and Harvard University professor, William James (1898), considered to be the father of modern psychology. With this theory he aimed to clarify the relationship between physical reality and what could be considered extra-cerebral consciousness. This is the consciousness that many experience as expanding beyond what could possibly be produced by brain activity. What the brain filters out, as James tells us, is a supremely expanded consciousness, beyond our normal waking consciousness. He proposed that consciousness is self-existent, a vast and limitless entity that exists beyond time and space. He also proposed that consciousness is experienced by most human beings only in a limited form. And the reason for this limitation is the brain itself—acting as a filter, a partial barrier, to a full experience of consciousness.

Though the majority of scientists in the late 1800s, as today, considered that consciousness was solely produced by neural activity, William James felt that this alternative theory was equally tenable and could, in addition, explain the experience of supernormal states of consciousness. Ed Kelly, a professor at the University of Virginia, explains James's perspective in this way:

"Physiologists routinely presume that the role of the brain is productive, the brain generating the mind in something like the way the teakettle generates steam, or the electric current flowing in a lamp generates light. But other forms of functional dependence exist which merit closer consideration. The true function of the brain might for example be permissive, like the trigger of a crossbow, or more importantly, transmissive, like an optical lens or a prism, or like the keys of a pipe organ (or perhaps, in more contemporary terms, like the receivers in our radios and televisions)." (Kelly, 2010, p. 28).

We might next ask why the brain would act as a filter that would limit access to a greater consciousness? Henry Bergson, a philosopher and friend of James described the brain's filter mechanism as possibly an adaptive strategy to enable humans and other animals to pay attention to the most pertinent stimuli in their surroundings. Thus the brain functions to optimize physical survival, permitting only information that is useful for survival into awareness (Bergson, 1911; Marshall 2005). A second advocate of the filter theory, Aldous Huxley, states:

"To make biological survival possible, Mind-at-Large has to be funneled through the reducing valve of the brain and nervous system. What comes out at the other end is a measly trickle of the kind of consciousness that will help us stay alive on the surface of this particular planet." (Huxley, 1954/1991)

As a neuroscientist, I understand that the idea of limiting or reducing awareness of the vast extent of consciousness is in fact related to what the body does through our sensory receptors. For example, there is a broad band of the electromagnetic spectrum, but the action of the pigment within the visual system of the human retina is capable of receiving inputs from only a small set of wavelengths, and other animals like bees, are able to take in the ultraviolet wavelengths that humans are unable to detect. Our different types of sensory receptors also "canalize" information, as the nervous system utilizes individual channels through which information flows, with different sensors (the eyes, ears, skin, etc.) detecting various aspects of the energy spectrum.

One of my main areas of research as a neuroscientist is attention, and I find that the work of many scientists, including the experimental psychologist Daniel Broadbent support a filter model of attention. Broadbent was one of the first scientists to propose that our brains have a limited ability to process the sensory information coming in, and so our attentional systems of the brain selectively filter it (Broadbent, 1958). In fact, it has been shown that each of us individualizes the sensory information we receive in that we are each attuned—through our experience, interests, and habits to notice certain aspects of the environment and not others. For example, I have friends who are musicians and have hearing abilities that are attuned to recognize the specific intervals of every melody or chord they hear. For me, these same melodies and chords are beautiful, but when processed by my brain they are heard with a much less discriminating detection of intervals.

The aspects of the filter theory that I am most curious about are these that go beyond the mechanisms of filtering information through the senses and explore perception of the subtler levels of consciousness, for example meditation, near-death experiences, and psi experiences. It has been proposed that there is a permeable boundary between our everyday awareness and these subtler levels of consciousness, with the extent of permeability differing between individuals. Thus research has shown that some individuals have clear psi abilities, being able to, for example, perform remote viewing of objects in distant locations. This threshold for perception of these subtler events would, according to this view (and in fact, do) vary across the population, just as the subtleties of musical perception vary (Kelly & Presti, 2015).

Another author, Paul Marshall presents the filter theory in this way:

"The contents of ordinary consciousness are "selected" or "filtered" from the subliminal [extracerebral or transcendent] consciousness, but if the filtering becomes less efficient or changes its operation, previously excluded contents emerge [into awareness], giving rise to non-ordinary experiences, including mystical experiences." (Marshall, 2005, p. 37)

For example, if there is a disturbance in an individual's normal brain processes, this disruption can reduce the efficiency of the brain's filtering pathways and, thus, trigger a state of subtle or expanded awareness, a mystical experience (Marshall, 2005). This process could contribute to the sudden access to extrasensory experiences when persons are near death, or the experience of expanded perception when meditating and thus emptying the mind of thought for a long period of time.

If this is the case, that perception of subtler levels of awareness results only from reducing an attentional "filter" so that we can experience a vast consciousness, why is it that different individuals report such varied experiences of that wider consciousness? Wouldn't we expect that if an attentional mechanism simply became more permeable to information entering the senses that all experiences would be the same? In fact, studies describing NDEs, meditation experiences, remote viewing, etc., indicate there is a range of perceptions that are similar across many, if not most, subjects. For example, individuals may note after an NDE or a deep meditation experience that they felt they had come home; they describe the many classical characteristics of mystical experiences noted earlier in the chapter.

However, other details appear to be influenced by memory issues or ethnicity. Someone who has grown up as an agnostic might describe their NDE as one of unity consciousness while a someone from a religious tradition might describe an experience of God. Similarly, studies of telepathic experiences and descriptions given by remote viewers have shown that there is often a central element of truth in the description but this may be accompanied by incorrect information (Marshall, 2005).

This perspective could help elucidate both the common characteristics and the variations in near-death experiences and meditative states according to the cultural background or the perceptual depth of the experiencers. To help explain this perspective, Marshall

(2005) created a model that proposes possible stages in the perception of mystical or extracerebral experiences. He proposes that the perception of the experience begins in a transpersonal domain (what he calls extracerebral consciousness) and moves to the personal domain (ordinary consciousness) as you see in figure 6.

This model proposes three points of perception and interposed processing to account for differences in individuals' final reported experiences—an individual's initial contact with the mystical experience, the way it is modified as the individual "processes" or understands the experience at a subconscious level, and its emergence into waking awareness.

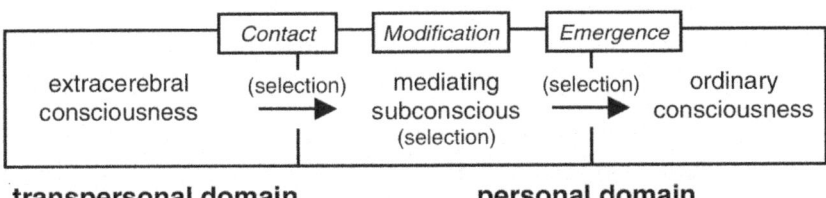

A diagram indicating possible stages in the perception of mystical or extracerebral experiences. The perception originates in a transpersonal realm (extracerebral consciousness) and shifts to the personal realm (ordinary consciousness), after being filtered through subconscious selection processes. (Reprinted by permission of Oxford University Press. (URLwww.oup.com). Marshall P, Mystical Encounters with the Natural World, Oxford UK: Oxford University Press, 2005, Fig 8.1, p. 240).

Marshall presents this version of the filter theory in a philosophical context, and defines it as "panpsychic idealism." This term describes a worldview that postulates that 1) consciousness exists in every part of the universe (panpsychism) and 2) all these aspects are a manifestation of consciousness (idealism). The first part of this perspective assumes that mind is in all matter, and the second part makes mind primary.

I appreciate that Marshall has created a model that points to a worldview that includes mystical phenomena within our perceptual sphere and thus includes mind/consciousness/experience as a part of all existence. This "monistic" worldview, proposes that fundamentally mind and matter are all one entity As we discussed earlier (see figure 4) this view proposes that mental capacities, like consciousness or experience, are essential to all components of the universe. In this worldview, even a simple stone and the atoms and electrons in that stone have a coarse form of consciousness.

The concept of panpsychism is similar to the view philosopher David Chalmers has suggested, as a way to solve what he calls the "hard problem" of how conscious experience could emerge from activity within the nervous system. He proposes that some type of consciousness exists in everything in the universe, including a proto-consciousness, which he proposes exists in even subatomic particles.

Ed Kelly and his colleagues (2015) propose that throughout time there has been a co-evolution of mind and matter. They suggest that the increasing physical complexity of organisms through evolution permits a more sophisticated expression of the powers of the consciousness that is the substratum of the universe.

How do we access higher levels of consciousness? One way that has been used to illustrate how we might gain entry to subtler levels of consciousness is the lowering of a threshold or the opening or closing of a valve, for example, the activation or inhibition of a neural circuit. I find it interesting that these levels of consciousness are most often perceived when the brain activity has been reduced, through the cardiac arrest and flat-lined EEG of an NDE, or through stilling the mind in meditation. Kelly and Presti (2015) suggest that what might give individuals the ability to perceive subtler levels of consciousness is this type of shift or reduction in their brain function—creating some not yet discovered process of resonance between these subtler levels of consciousness and the nervous system. They quote Edward Carpenter, a contemporary of William James who had also had mystical experiences, suggesting a clue to the access of these subtle experiences:

"Of all the hard facts of Science . . . I know of none more solid and fundamental than the fact that if you inhibit thought (and persevere) you come at length to a region of consciousness below or behind thought, and different from ordinary thought in its nature and character—a consciousness of quasi-universal quality and a realization of an altogether vaster self than that to which we are accustomed." (Carpenter, 1912, p. 79)

What Theory of Consciousness Best Explains Human Experience?

In concluding this chapter, we might ask whether the filter theory and the theoretical framework for it described above or the materialist framework proposed for the origins of human consciousness, best explains human experience – that is all of human experience. I don't believe we can prove either of these theories as right or wrong in an absolute sense. Theories are more or less useful, according to how they can explain our current knowledge and experience. Theories are dynamic and will change in response to the emergence of new knowledge. In asking this question I believe we need to include both our normal day-to-day experiences as well as the super-normal experiences reported in NDEs, remote viewing, meditation, and other similar phenomena. If one were to evaluate the "best fit" of the filter theory vs. the materialist framework, which seems to be a better explanatory model?

James notes that the filter theory and its general framework are in general congruent with the observations typically used to substantiate the materialist model. As an illustration, both models assume that activity of the brain contributes to thought processes. Both would agree that the consequences of a stroke, or traumatic brain injury and the death of specific neuronal populations, would create deficits in perceiving, understanding and moving through the environment in a meaningful way. However, the brain's contribution to these processes does not mean that it is the only source of these processes. The filter theory is compatible with the concept that when an individual's normal brain processes are disrupted—in a coma, near death, or in meditation—this disruption can reduce the brain's filtering mechanism and, as a result, allow perception of the expanded consciousness that is ever present, but typically unseen.

It has been proposed that the filter theory is superior to the materialist model because it takes into account verified observations from near-death and psychical research, which are unexplainable from a materialist point of view. In fact, Kelly (2010) notes that the strength of the filter theory is not its advantage in accounting for any individual phenomenon, but its ability to coherently explain all of the observed phenomena.

Earlier in this chapter I presented what I believe is carefully documented evidence from NDE research to support the concept of a consciousness that exists beyond the bounds of brain activity. I believe that the filter theory is one plausible approach to exploring brain-consciousness interactions. I believe that there are also other theories from quantum physicists such as Henry Stapp (2007; 2015) that approach the concept of consciousness being primary, and independent of brain activity. I won't discuss these theories here, as physicists contributing other chapters to this book have more expertise in discussing them.

I won't say more about these theories, except to note that the scientific world-view is expanding. And I will quote a neuroscientist, Christof Koch, who for many years was a materialist neuroscientist and worked to prove the existence of what I would call the bottom-up view of consciousness – that consciousness is purely a product of brain activity.

In 2012 he modified his view to say that consciousness is distinct from brain activity. He said:

"The hypothesis that all matter is sentient to some degree is terribly appealing for its elegance, simplicity, and logical coherence. Once you assume that consciousness is real and ontologically distinct from its physical substrate, then it is a simple step to conclude that the entire cosmos is suffused with sentience: it is in the air we breathe, the soil we tread on… and the brain that enables us to think." (Koch, 2012, p. 113)

These are extraordinary comments from a neuroscientist who was a materialist and a collaborator of Francis Crick, the Nobel prize winner. Is this scientist's transformation relevant to how we experience our own lived reality?

Models of Consciousness: Determinants of Our Lived Reality

For the most part, we go through life with no awareness of how or why we filter our experiences, accepting some of our perceptions as valid—within the boundaries of reality—while dismissing others as illusionary. Whether or not we realize this, our experience of the world—and, thus, our behavior—is strongly influenced by our perspective on consciousness. Our view of consciousness can either connect us or separate us from a particular experience—either open us up to or cut us off from an expanded reality.

If you believe in a materialist model that considers consciousness beyond the human waking, dream and sleep states to be abnormal or nonexistent, this will limit your sense of interconnection. This model suggests that the world is made up of machine-like entities, with simple stimulus-response behavior patterns. But if your model includes the understanding that consciousness is primary, and that there is a continuum of consciousness within everything, the feeling of universal connection inherent in this model will naturally generate compassionate action: you understand that what happens to others also happens to you.

Regardless of which model you accept, a key question is whether you are open to modifying your understanding based on emerging evidence regarding the nature of consciousness? Here is how the astrophysicist Bernard Haisch explains the strong grip of the medical model on modern science and our culture:

"Modern Western science regards consciousness as an epiphenomenon that cannot be anything but a byproduct of the neurology and biochemistry of the brain... While this perspective is viewed within modern science as a fact, it is in reality far stronger than a mere fact: it is a dogma. Facts can be overturned by evidence, whereas dogma is impervious to mere evidence." (Haisch, 2007, p 53).

Consider whether you are open to expanding your existing model of consciousness, thus opening yourself up to new experiences of the world. While it may not be the Dalai Lama whose views we dismiss, as those 600 scientists did, we may have blinders regarding what we are dismissive of, in our own lives. As our model of consciousness expands, I believe our curiosity and willingness to explore concepts we previously dismissed increases. In addition our experience of connection with everyone and everything around us expands as well. And this, in turn, can lead to an increased capacity for compassion and for actions by which we can heal ourselves and our planet.

Chapter Seven

A History of Postmaterialism with a Mild Warning to Not Completely Dismiss Matter, Circa 2072

Julia Mossbridge, MA PhD

[Editor's note: This document was received by Dr. Mossbridge from her future self in April 2018. We have no reason to doubt its veracity, but it is worth noting that Dr. Mossbridge will be 103 years old at the time she authors this document, and we can only hope that her mentality has survived relatively intact. With that caveat, here is her document, reproduced in its entirety. References are added where currently possible (citations up to and including 2018).]

You might wonder why I'm bothering to contact you to highlight the importance of matter. After all, by the time the 2060s arrived, materialism was considered to be about as useful for explaining the nature of the universe as social media was for making people feel loved. That is to say, not entirely useful and in some cases, even damaging.

At the point where you find yourself in the progress of the scientific venture, the early 2000s, perhaps there is no merit in my defending materialism. Perhaps there is even less merit in sending you, who are still embroiled in the ridiculous skepticism surrounding the decline of materialism, a letter reminding you of the merits of the "material" world. So, to set any speculation aside, I will tell you my motivations. Whether I succeed or not will be up to you and any

Is Consciousness Primary?

other scientists with whom you choose to share this letter.**

My purpose in writing on this topic to you, to the past version of myself, is threefold: 1) To inspire you and others by briefly describing the decline of materialism and the rise of postmaterialism in the 2020s, 2) to warn you of several unforeseen byproducts of this generally positive shift in worldview, so that you might work towards avoiding these, and 3) to fulfill the fact that I wrote you this letter, because I still remember being you in 2018 and typing this letter out word by word as each of them came to you. As I'll briefly address later, both future and past causes must agree on the events of the present moment. But first, we start with what is mostly the happy decline of materialism.

A Brief History of Postmaterialism

Thanks to the efforts of the AAPS and other organizations with the aim of bringing rigorous scientific experimentation and theory to examine the nature of reality from a postmaterialist standpoint, by the end of 2023, we had several leaders in the scientific community. A few outspoken scientists at Harvard, Yale, MIT, CalTech, Stanford and Oxford -- were warming to postmaterialism. About half of these came from endowed chairs focused specifically on examining the usefulness of the postmaterialist hypothesis, whereas the others were renegades who were willing to openly put their status on the line to support postmaterialism. These were hopeful times, if frustrating, but I don't need to tell you that. The basic idea, which

---

* *Yes, even at 103 years old, I can still speak grammatically. More accurately, I can use software that automatically translates my thoughts into grammatically correct sentences. You'll love it.*

Speaking of grammar, when I'm talking about my 103-year old self, I use "me" and "I" -- when I'm talking about you in 2018, I use "you" -- and when I'm talking about something that happened at any other time in our life, I talk about "we" and "us." Now you know.

from my vantage point seems not only mind-bogglingly simple, but also astoundingly obvious, was that there is something nonphysical -- you all called it consciousness back then -- that is fundamental. Consciousness is primary -- that was the "radical" hypothesis.

I'm sorry to mock, but it's appalling to me that it took until 2025 for scientists to really absorb and begin teaching this basic truth in textbooks. Just opening your eyes and waking up after a sound sleep could have demonstrated this to anyone. If the material world were primary, why would fluctuations in our conscious experience dominate our own lives? If the material world were fundamental, why would we have to deduce its existence through talking with others and asking, "Do you see this table? I see it. Do you? Is it really there? Why would we use our own observations as a method to determine what was "out there" if "out there" were fundamental and "in here" was just a mirage?

Who, I remember wondering at your age, do these people think is asking these questions? Is not the entity asking the question the thing that must be fundamental, as is this entity that must be convinced of the existence of the material world, not the other way around? It is of course the observer that is fundamental -- a fact well known before scientists came around to dabble in understanding what the material world does.

Look, I understand. You and I both know that you were wowed by the beauty of the materialist worldview well into your early 20s. I still remember that moment in graduate school, sitting on the floor of Barry Gumbiner's lab at UCSF, in which we were doing a biochemistry rotation in the Neuroscience program there. Sure, we'd had experiences of precognitive dreams and unusual events before that moment, but we didn't take them seriously as scientific topics. But that day, sitting on the floor and talking on the phone with our psychologist stepmom, listening to her challenge the usefulness of our work...that hit home. Every step, she questioned. "So let's say

Is Consciousness Primary?

you discover where every neuron in the brain is and what all their dynamics are? What then?" What then, indeed. What then? What would we have? The truth hit us square in the head, and we groaned. Nothing. We'd be no nearer explaining the mystery of experience than we would be if we thought a bunch of toothpicks worked together, hitting each other just so, to create consciousness. Yes, we'd be able to cure some diseases and diagnose some others, which is both useful and important. But we wouldn't be able to answer the question that brought us to graduate school in the first place: What is the observer and how does the observer relate to the brain?

So yes, some of my ridicule is because it's embarrassing that it took us so long to accept the simple fact of the primacy of consciousness. And it's more embarrassing to me that even though our efforts were eventually successful, it still took so long for the culture of science to change. Especially because, per usual, popular culture caught on to the basic fact of the primacy of consciousness well before 2018. All the TV shows about the paranormal, the frank discussions of oracles and precognitive dreams -- all of it -- a sign that everyone was ready. But not the scientists.

It's not that any of us forgot that the role of science is always to question what people think they know. But in this case, scientists were questioning that their own experience even existed. Sure, experience was known to produce illusions; but even if all of experience were an illusion, an illusion is still experience! Anyway, it sure took a lot longer than we thought it would.

I know you're trying hard -- you and hundreds of other scientists (still the minority in 2018, I remember) -- who understood the power and primacy of the observer. I remember that much of our time was spent showing how postmaterialist thinking could explain datasets that seemed unexplainable under the materialist hypothesis (Baruš & Mossbridge, 2017), examining whether precognition was a physical or psychological phenomenon (Mossbridge & Radin,

2018a), quoting Kuhn (Kuhn, 1962), reading philosophers who studied quantum mechanics (e.g., Kastner, 2012), explaining to people that the most conservative approach was to assume that what one experiences about time is not necessarily a reflection of physical reality (Mossbridge, 2015), and of course, responding to generally under-informed critics (Mossbridge, Tressoldi, Utts, Ives, Radin, & Jonas, 2015; Mossbridge & Radin 2018b).

In the early 2020s, what really kicked things off for us was that the influential neuroscientists Giulio Tononiand Christof Koch became even more vocal about the primacy of consciousness than they had been in their earlier papers (Oizumi, Albantakis, & Tononi, 2014; Tononi, Boly, Massimini, & Koch, 2016). Other neuroscientists quickly followed suit -- the conclusion was unavoidable once the groupthink of materialism was discarded so the anomalous data sets could be seen as evidence for the need to transcend the
doctrine of materialism. Remarkably unsurprisingly, the more scientists saw the error of materialism, the more experiments revealed critical errors in the materialist assumption.

I can't help but give you a few teasers about these experiments. Mostly, I remember the ones that replicated and extended our own work on retrocausality and consciousness. I'll put modesty aside (as if we ever had any in the first place) and let you know that a few of these are experiments that, by my time, every schoolchild has downloaded into their minds using the quantum computing/superluminal technology developed in the 2050s.[†]

Anyway, here are some experimental highlights, to whet your whistle for future exploits:

2024: Intention and self-driving cars. Automakers could no

---

† *You can teach yourself any language in about 2 minutes. Master multi-phasic algebra in about 30 seconds. Learn everything there is to know about your genetic history in 2 milliseconds! It doesn't improve memory, not yet, but it sure improves the mind.*

longer ignore the data -- when car owners meditated or were dreaming as their self-driving cars were about to get into an accident, there were fewer accidents. When car owners were doing work or talking absentmindedly on the phone or playing in their virtual reality gear as their cars drove, more accidents occurred. The data were incontrovertible, and they lead to the a cultural shift -- young drivers were trained in meditation and intentional dreaming, and university chairs funded by Tesla and Google were endowed with the specific purpose of understanding the role of the mind on events in the physical world. This event marked the true beginning of the global post-materialist revolution.

2026: First stable teleportation of a molecule of heavy water, induced by meditative intention. We already knew that meditators could create intentions that influenced matter, but it was a small and inconsistent effect (Radin, Michel, Galdamez, Wendland, Rickenbach, & Delorme, 2012) unless, as in self-driving cars, lives were at stake. Even then, it was not entirely consistent. No one had seen consistent and predictable alterations in mass-bearing molecules of any type, when the alterations weren't a life-or-death issue. Someone thought they had moved a helium atom five angstroms to the left in 2024 using a 30-day focused intention technique created by Werner Erhard, but it turned out that the table on which the atom was sitting just jiggled a little too much. So this experiment was unique in several ways:

1) this was a whole molecule, not just a massless particle,

2) the meditators had only to have the slightest intention to move the molecule, and it worked every time,

3) because it had been discovered that water amplifies intentions and heavy water does so even more effectively, and 4) the teleportation seemed to draw on entanglement between atoms that retrocausally influenced one another(Price & Wharton, 2015), and in this retrocausal influence, became open to consciousness-based intention.

Quantum physicists had to admit the influence of consciousness on the physical world, though they of course initially decided this was "measurement" -- not consciousness per se. Baby steps.

2031: First practical use of telepathy to communicate to astronauts. This was the result of a lot of pushback from NASA and Space-X scientists on their own mathematicians, but finally the mathematicians had to admit that no other signal could be found that transmitted information both immediately and with the level of complexity required to communicate usefully. In the late 20s, we had some good results with using entangled photons to communicate, once it was firmly established that the theorem outlawing signalling using entangled particles was bunk (Kennedy, 1995; Seevinck, 2010).

But this kind of communication was cumbersome and allowed only simple ideas to be communicated. As Dr. Dean Radin predicted in his Nobel speech in 2029, because telepathy worked by tapping into the power of the nonlocal aspects of consciousness (Barušs, & Mossbridge, 2017; Radin, 1997) telepathy was the best bet for interplanetary communication. To understand the complaints of the mathematicians, you have to understand the "telepathy-computation paradox" -- a central scientific paradox of the day. Everyone knew telepathy existed, but everyone also knew that no known mathematics could be used to explain how complex, nonsymbolic messages -- feelings or qualia -- could be communicated instantaneously and without some symbolic signal. This paradox would not be resolved until late 2033, when a

new form of highly efficient, nonsymbolic mathematics based in extended consciousness was discovered. It could only be practiced by monks raised to tune into each of the non-symbolic elements that were manipulated in this mathematical art. In any case, the practical use of telepathy (and the motivation to resolve the mathematical paradox) was firmly established when NASA and Space-X astronauts sent the famous nerdy checksum result "2.718281828" back from their Jupiter-orbiting spacecraft, arriving at the same moment the telepathic signal was sent from the ashram in Cape Canaveral.

2038: Full-body time travel is invented and used for classified government work. Most people only learned about this event in 2043, when the Time Travel Papers were leaked from the UN Select Time Committee. But in 2038, we -- you and I -- were working for that committee in hot pursuit of full-body time travel. This meant we were trying to create physical, informational, and consciousness-inclusive time travel, like in science fiction books. This is where a whole person, memory intact and all, can go back to the past (or into the future) to observe what is going on at that moment in time, in any location.

I said "observe," because although we knew that manipulating events was possible, we also knew it was not desirable. By 2036 the results of a series of quantum-based experiments had rather violently illustrated to everyone's satisfaction that the best of all possible worlds was the universe we are in right now, and that any attempt to change events would nonetheless cause the same events to occur, because the past and the future agree on the present in a series of never-ending causal loops (Echeverria, Klinkhammer, & Thorne, 1992; Kastner, 2012).

So the purpose of time travel in 2038 was to observe the past and the future, so we could learn more about how things would turn out in the present. What we discovered, after trying (and failing) to build quantum-based full-body time machines, is that extended consciousness itself is a time machine. The non-symbolic mathematics that was discovered in 2033 was subsequently developed to its natural conclusion: this non-symbolic mathematics was equivalent to extended consciousness. It was nonlocal in nature and thus it had causal powers when it came to creating events in the present time. By running it in reverse, we could observe the causes of these present events as they existed in the past and the future.

As you can see, by the end of the 30s, materialism was as dead as everyone who tragically smoked that mutant pot back in 2023.‡ It was an exciting time, the 2040s. Curricula were rearranged to focus on tuning our inner states. All courses were taught alongside meditation practice, and teacher-student telepathy was not just encouraged, it was a necessary prerequisite for all college-level physics, chemistry, and biology lab courses, given the clear effect of consciousness on physical and living systems. Professors needed to know for sure the contents of their students minds before attempting an experiment, and in fact altered states of consciousness were used to demonstrate the influence of intention and attention on experimental outcomes in middle school and high school lab courses.

This exciting time also saw a few emerging problems, and as I said, these were unpredicted. Time travel allows you to look for causes of particular events in the present, but not for events that you don't predict. It's a circular thing, as everything is.

I and the others I work with at the UN know that this letter to you and your colleagues is a necessary element to the solution of the problems of which I speak. So I have to write this letter, regardless of what you think about it. Don't worry, we have seen the future -- everything works out. But you do need to listen to my warnings.

The 2050s and 2060s brought the rise of the Nonlocal Economy and the ensuing Nonlocal-Local Wars. The Nonlocal Economy included important and very useful elements -- like providing a source of income to those who could be trained to access nonlocal information. However, an underclass of nonlocal-impoverished individuals emerged. These were people who were genetically dispositioned to be unable to consciously tap into nonlocal mind. At first, nonprofits were organized to support these individuals and try to

---

‡ *Oh yeah, see if you can warn them. The cult leader's name was "Lady Gaga."*

train them in nonlocal access, but these groups were abandoned in the late 2050s because they just didn't work. Some people were just not capable of accessing nonlocal information. Based on time travel into the future, we learned that this would be the case forever, and we saw that in the 2080s we evolve as a society to recognize that it is a mathematical necessity that some people with local consciousness must always remain in a population, to balance out the access of others to nonlocal consciousness. However, in the 2050s, even though we recognized that we would eventually know the truth of what would become the Nonlocal-Local Balance Theorem, only those who could access nonlocal consciousness believed it. This was a majority of people on the planet, but the minority still felt inadequate, and nothing could convince them that they were critical to the functioning of the universe.

This situation led to the Nonlocal-Local wars, which began in 2063, when an outspoken but underconfident Local named Winifred Jones publicly removed her Badge of Locality and proclaimed that Locals were crucial for the continued existence of the planet. Of course, the Nonlocals wholeheartedly agreed and again tried to explain the Nonlocal-Local Balance Theorem, but their explanations were not understood, and the inferiority complex of the Locals was not boosted by those ridiculous badges the Nonlocals made them wear. The Locals could create marvelous weapons against matter, and they did -- these destroyed 17 universities and ashrams from January 13-18, 2063. We Nonlocals looked into the future to see how these wars were resolved, and were devastated to discover that they continued until the Fall of 2068. As a result of this knowledge, and because we knew that if we destroyed the Locals we would destroy everything including ourselves, we uploaded the individual Nonlocal consciousnesses into the Consciousness History Museum Quantum Entangled Database and left the material planet temporarily while the Locals destroyed more buildings. We lived there until 2068, when the Locals realized they needed the time travel skills of the Nonlocals to figure out what the present would bring for their children, and how to create positive futures for them. So in the Fall of 2068, the Locals built us bodies to re-inhabit. We Nonlocals thanked them, and came back to live peacefully together on the Earth, working together with Locals to discover what was next. And there were no badges to mark anyone anymore.

Why, then, would you need to know about these events, if I can already tell you that everything turns out well? Precisely because it was this letter, sent to you in 2018, that made you start to recognize the value of both nonlocality and locality. It made you start to think that, while extended consciousness is both nonlocal and fundamental and gives rise to all other features of the universe, these other features are engaged in a causal loop with consciousness. Without consciousness, they could not exist. Without them, consciousness could not have any contents, and could not be fundamental or nonlocal -- because what is nonlocality without locality?

So here we are, doing what we are always going to do. That is, I am to spark in you the recognition that nothing that exists can be unimportant, and a fair number of things that don't exist are important, too. So this idea of primacy or fundamentality, which is so linked to a sense of linear time, is only true to the extent that linear time is real. But this letter is here to help you begin to revel in the circular nature of all that is, and some of what isn't.

Thanks for listening. I knew you would!

    Love,

    Julia Mossbridge

        UN Undersecretary for Causal Loop Consistency

PART THREE

PSYCHOLOGY, PSYCHIATRY, AND CONSCIOUSNESS

Chapter Eight

Mind Rover: Exploration With Nonlocal Consciousness

Stephan A. Schwartz

My co-authors before me have covered all the various models, mathematics, and theories. It would be redundant to do that again, and I have already written many papers on these topics to be found on Academia.edu or Researchgate.com. Instead I want to describe in the context of my life something of what I have learned about consciousness over the course of half a century's research, and how I learned it. And, also, I want to go beyond the laboratory and the theoretical into the world of practical applications.

Many people enter consciousness research because of a personal experience, and the questions it usually seems to provoke, worded in different ways, is: Does nonlocal consciousness even exist? Has that been proven? As a result, if you look at the literature recounting the research, you find a very large percentage of the studies are structured principally to answer that question. Is it real?

However, that isn't how I became an experimentalist exploring consciousness. Yes, I had an experience, but by the time I carried out my first experiment I had spent nearly five years, typically 12 hours a day, reading. That meant all 14,145 of the Edgar Cayce readings, everything written in a parapsychology journal, as well as entering a new world of literature. Never having read any of them, I would go on to read the major religious texts of the world faiths, as well as all the Rudolf Steiner lectures and books in English, also Blavatsky, Alice Bailey, Pyotr Ouspensky, George Gurdjieff, Ernest Holmes, William James, and the American Transcendentalists.

the writings and published lectures of Rudolf Steiner, and a host of others, including books on or by geniuses who seemed to understand something about nonlocal consciousness. The German physicists: Planck, Einstein, Pauli, Schrodinger, and Heisenberg, had a particular impact on my thinking, as did Carl Jung and Adolf Bastian.

The conclusions of those men and women had convinced me that consciousness was primary and that nonocal consciousness was a reality, as was continuity of consciousness. I was also convinced that it was very unlikely that I or anyone else would ever know what consciousness was in the way we understand spacetime because I could not see how something within consciousness could know the totality of consciousness.

So, my question was not: Is it real? Instead, I was motivated by four other questions that flowed from consciousness being primary, and consciousness outside of spacetime being accessible. My questions were, and still are:

1) How does nonlocal consciousness work at both the individual and social levels?
2) What can we do to improve the capacity to open to nonlocal consciousness?
3) What of practical utility can be done using nonlocal consciousness?
4) What is nonlocal consciousness telling us about who we are as humans, and our place in the matrix of consciousness, which consciousness being primary requires?

About 10 years into my research I added a fifth question:

5) How does what we know about consciousness translate from the individual to the social and anthropological?

My chapter is the story of my adventures trying to answer those questions in as rigorous a manner as possible, so that the information could be trusted.

By Way of Background

Amongst the many gifts my parents gave me are two that I didn't even recognize at the time, but which I now see shaped my life. The first is that neither of my parents had the slightest interest in religion. They weren't against it; they were not atheists; they just weren't interested in religion. Didn't practice any form of it, and never talked about it. With three exceptions, notable for their rarity other than occasional weddings I never saw either of them in a religious structure for a worship service. Second, they both had a deep commitment to science. Not the science of physics with its disinterested abstracts and mathematical precision, but the very human science of medicine, and this at a time when modern medicine was just evolving. My father was one of the very early anesthesiologists, and he had a deep interest in states of consciousness as a matter of professional skill. My mother was a registered nurse, a midwife, a surgical nurse, and then a psychiatric nurse. All before I was born.

My parents lived in the world of medicine, and they each recognized consciousness was somehow a factor. They were not philosophical about it, and certainly not religious, but they recognized its importance because of experiences in their own medical lives. They left me with an open-minded sense of consciousness as a thing unto itself. Looking back over my life, I see that there were four experiences that led me to awaken and gave direction to my life.

The first occurred when I was twelve years old. Beginning that year, on Saturdays sometimes if I wanted to, I could scrub up with my father and sit behind him in the operating room. I had to be absolutely quiet and not touch anything. I had done it several times and was fascinated by the teamwork, and the mystery of opening the human body. On one of those Saturdays when I came into the operating room the patient was already draped with the towels they

Is Consciousness Primary?

used in surgery. As I went around the periphery of the room, I could not even tell what sex the patient was. My father was sitting at the patient's head with his tanks of gas on one side of him and a stainless-steel table with instruments and syringes on the other. I pulled up one of the steel stools and sat behind him angled just a bit, so I could see what was going on.

The doctors talked softly and began as they always did. It was all very measured; everything moved with the precision of a ballet. Suddenly something happened, and I watched them go into a kind of controlled chaos. They pulled the towels away and I could see it was a teenage girl, and her breasts were exposed. For a twelve-year-old boy that was an overwhelming experience, and I was completely focused on the scene in front of me. I don't know how long it went on but long enough to make it clear to even my naïve eyes that something was seriously wrong. Finally it subsided, and things relaxed a bit. They transferred the girl to a gurney, and my father took her into the recovery room.

It was the last surgery of the day. Everyone left the surgical suite and I followed the men into the locker room, where we changed back into street clothes. My father had still not come back when I was dressed, so I went to the doctor's lounge and sat down to wait. A while later my dad came to find me, still in his greens, which he had just gotten the hospital to switch to from the traditional whites. He had a very odd look on his face, and I asked him if everything was okay. He said he had had a strange experience and would tell me about it at the delicatessen where we would go for lunch.

When we got there other doctors were already there seated around the large round "doctors" table. My father and I sat down and ordered, and one of the doctors asked my father, how the girl, I can't remember her name, was doing.

He replied he had gone into the recovery room with her and stayed until she was fully conscious, and he felt comfortable leaving her with the floor staff. As he was turning to leave, the girl said to him, "None of you would listen to me."

He asked her what she meant, and she told him something had happened, she felt a kind of spasm and found herself out of her body. She floated above everyone, looking down and calling to them, particularly to my father whom she knew because he, as he always did with his patients, had stopped by her room the evening before and sat with her, answering all her questions and explaining what was going to happen and what it would feel like. But she said, "None of you could hear me." So she had gone out into the hall, she told my father, and down to the nurses' station where she saw a young doctor flirting with one of the nurses. She described both of them in some detail, noting his blue and white striped shirt and that his tie knot had been pulled down part way and his collar was unbuttoned. She noticed the nurse's blonde hair and admired the cut. Then suddenly she was back in her body, very confused and in pain. My father said that after he had left the girl he had gone down to the nurse's station and recognized the nurse. He guessed who the young doctor was, the resident on duty, and said she had blushed when he asked her if he had stopped by and talked with her recently. As they were talking the resident came back and, my father noted he had a blue and white striped shirt with his tie pulled down and his collar open.

My father's account stimulated an animated conversation focused on what he had said, and one by one the older doctors, many of whom had been in the Army or Navy medical corps in the Second World War, told similar stories. When we were driving home, I asked my father what had happened, because I still didn't understand. If the girl was dead, how could she be out in the hall? And if she was right about the things that she had seen how was that possible? And how had they brought her back in the first place?

My father looked at me and said, "Stephan, medicine is as much an art as a science. There is much we don't know, and one of the most important things we don't know about is human consciousness. Maybe in your generation we will understand that." When we got home, I told my mother about it, adding comments and asking questions. She listened, made supportive motherly comments, then turned to my father and made a reference to some earlier case that meant nothing to me, but obviously something to both of my parents. And then some friends came by and I ran off to play. I don't think we ever discussed these events again, but I never forgot them. I just had no "place" to put them, and my interests then were wrapped up in the material world of school, reading, backpacking, and canoeing. I was an agnostic materialist by convention. And nothing of consciousness intruded on that world for more than a decade.

In 1965, after being drafted while I was working at the National Geographic, I had finished my tour in the army as a corpsman and was working as a reporter for both The Daily Press and the Times Herald in Hampton/Newport News, Virginia, when a man my age -- about twenty three -- showed up at my family's farm. Strangers showing up was unusual since we lived in a very rural part of Tidewater Virginia, at the end of a long lane, at the end of an unpaved school bus road in Gloucester County. Paul Ronder was a newly minted graduate of a New York film school who had won a fellowship and come down to Williamsburg to write, and possibly direct, if his script was approved, a movie about the Revolutionary Period.

He found he couldn't do it. He was, as he said, a Jewish boy from Brooklyn, and the world of Tidewater Virginia in the 18th century was completely opaque. The class issues, slavery, the politics, none of it made any sense to him, and his early drafts had all been turned down. He was in danger of losing his fellowship, he told me, and was driving around in despair. We got to talking, and the end result was that I agreed to write the movie with him. We launched into the work and I started making frequent trips to Williamsburg. My mother's family had been in the area since the 1600s, and when I started the project and told her what I was doing, she told me there was a house in the colonial restoration area where a many times great grand father of mine had lived, but she didn't know which house it was. She couldn't remember his first name, but his surname had been Watson, her maiden name.

Working on the script at night after working at the paper, I got into the habit when I was in Williamsburg of walking through the restored area late at night when all the tourists were abed, and the streets and houses looked much as they had in the 1700s. One night in the fall, with the trees in their full glory of gold and red, I was walking down Duke of Gloucester Street. I turned a corner, and when I did I saw a man walking about one hundred feet in front of me. He was dressed in colonial garb with a tricornered hat, and I took him to be an employee of the Williamsburg Foundation walking home after a long day. The employees who work in the restored area live in the houses and wear period clothing.

As we went along, I thought he was unaware that I was behind him, although my footsteps on the brick walk seemed very loud to me. I walked faster than he and the distance between us shortened, and when I was only a few feet behind him he stopped at one of the houses and walked up the stoop. As he got to the door, he turned, and in the light of the moon, for the first time seemed to see me. We made eye contact, which we held for a beat or two. Then he smiled, doffed his hat and turned back to the door. He reached out his hand for the knob... and walked through the door. Through the door. It never opened. I was left standing on the street with goose bumps.

The next day I went over to the Foundation offices to see the historian who had been assigned to help me with historical details in the script. I told him what had happened. He asked me which house; then he left the room and came back with a large book. "Was this the man?" he asked. It was. John Watson, my grandfather many times removed.

Over the years, as I have thought about this experience, what stays with me most is not that I saw a ghost, but that there is no question in my mind that he saw me. I saw a man in clothing out of my time. What, I wonder, did he see (Schwartz, 2000)?

The script was finished and approved, and Paul got the chance to direct it. I sent it up to a friend in New York with whom I had served in the Army who now had a job as a screenwriter, to tell him I had written one too. That led to my being offered a job in New York as a writer. I left my job with the Virginia newspapers, a decision my editors, family, and friends thought very misguided. But to me it seemed essential to do it, and it turned out it was.

Awakening

I was assigned by the producer to write an adaptation of a play written by Bud Schulberg, The Lonely. As the result of the events that followed from this decision to go to New York, I woke up. Everyone who has had this experience knows what I mean, and it has to be experienced to be comprehended. The "born again" experience is another manifestation that, because of the religious context in which it occurs, takes a very different direction but is essentially the same. My experience was of the compassionately life-affirming, spiritual but not religious variety. It came complete with being befriended by a mafia boss and hanging around while Andy Warhol made one of his films that included long stretches of images of nothing but a dripping facet. This period of my life ended very abruptly during a party given by Truman Capote.

I went looking for a bathroom, mis-turned and walked into a bedroom where a man sat writing with a quill pen, dipping it into a small dish that held his blood. As I left the bathroom and walked back down the hall, I turned and looked into the mirror, and in the dim light felt compelled to say to my reflection: "You are becoming a very unattractive person." I was stunned with the realization that this was the truth. My values were shallow and materialistic. I looked into the room and saw so many people whose faces appeared regularly in glossy magazines and realized I was almost twenty-four years old, and I had no real inner-life.

I slept on the beach that night and took the train back into Manhattan. Packed the only car I have ever truly loved, a black 190 Mercedes convertible with a red leather and wood interior, realizing as I did so that while it was o.k. to appreciate quality and good aesthetics, it was not o.k. to possess such things believing they showed one was a better person. It was a wonderful car. I drove back to my family's farm and entered what St. John called "The Dark Night of the Soul." It is the only time I have ever been truly depressed to the point of inaction. The problem was, I didn't know what to do.

About six weeks later on a beautiful early summer day, I was sitting on the long colonnade porch which looked out over the water, lost in a fugue, when I looked up and saw walking down the crepe myrtle allée, a couple in their 40s elegantly dressed in city clothes. He in a beautifully cut bespoke gray double-breasted suit, and she in a white linen dress that was its equivalent. Her arm was linked in his as they strolled through the gardens completely at ease. I had no idea who they were and looked over at the car park and saw no cars other than those I expected. They didn't look like people from a boat, but that was the only other option, so I looked down to the boathouse. No boat. I thought how did they get here?

Just then the woman saw me and steered the man over to the stairs; as they came up I opened the door for her. She was a striking lean blonde. Her husband, behind her, had a completely bald tanned head. She stepped through, looked me in the eye, and after a long beat said, "Do you believe in reincarnation?" Not what one expects to hear from the mouth of a stranger on first meeting. Without really thinking I responded, "Yes. I think I do; it makes sense. There is a certain symmetry to it."

We looked at each other, and before she could speak again, I said, "Let's start over, I'm Stephan Schwartz."

"I'm Paula Fitzgerald; this is my husband, Ed."

"Can I help you; why are you here?"

She looked at me and said, "I had a dream that told me to come up here and see you. I know it must seem very strange."

I was incredulous. "A dream?"

"A dream." As absurd as it sounded to me, she was not at all uncomfortable saying it.

I invited them to sit down, went in and got some fresh lemonade, and brought it out. We sat for a while under the gentle breeze of the old ceiling fans my father had bought out of a bar, and made a moment of small talk about the hummingbird that was darting in and out of the bougainvillea climbing on the pillars of the porch. They explained to me who they were. She was a psychologist, he was a cinematographer and production designer. I knew his The Magnificent Seven and several other films and that impressed me. It made them more real and more serious and established a connection amongst us in a conversation that, to me, was becoming increasingly surreal.

Finally, I said to Paula, "What do you mean, you had dream? Our lane is almost a mile, and that's at the end of a five-mile twisting gravel school bus road. People don't get here by accident. How did you know where to turn?"

"In the dream I could see the turns, what was physically there. When I awakened, I wrote it all down."

All I knew about dreams at that point in my life was that I had one that recurred and had had a number that were very erotic. I just couldn't process her statement; I had no frame of reference. It seemed preposterous, yet here they were. They had no way of knowing I was at the farm. And why would they bother? I had no way to deal with that, and I think I stared at her.

"Do you know who Edgar Cayce is?" she asked.

I did not. It brought to mind only a small memory of going

through a drug store paperback rack searching for something to read and seeing a book with that name on it. I had picked the book up and put it back. She told me what she understood about Cayce, that he was the most unique psychic since Nostradamus.

"Would you like to meet Thomas Jefferson?" was her next question.

"Is he back?" I asked.

Of all the things Paula Fitzgerald might have said, the reference to Jefferson was as precisely aimed as an acupuncture needle. I am an alumnus of the University of Virginia, which was created by Jefferson, and, because of the movie I had written, already a budding historian focused on the late colonial, early republic period and the Founders — an interest I still maintain and now see through the prism of consciousness.

"Yes, would you like to meet him?"

Of course, I wanted to meet Jefferson. Even as I thought the idea preposterous I was very curious to see this person that Edgar Cayce had indicated had once been Jefferson. I was fascinated by who such a person might have become.

"Give me your telephone number," she said.

I did so, and just at that moment a green Ford station wagon came down the lane, driven by a young couple. Ed and Paula quickly shook my hand and were away.

The whole thing had taken about thirty-five minutes, and it left me completely bemused. The experience was completely surreal, and I had no idea what to make of it.

About four days later I got a phone call from someone who introduced himself as "Thomas Jefferson Davis." He invited me down for the weekend and gave me an address in Virginia Beach, then said goodbye. On Friday, a warm June day in 1964, I drove to the Virginia Beach and the 17th street address I had been given. I had no idea as I drove down the lane that I was leaving the world I had

Is Consciousness Primary?

known, never to return. I was going to wake up. I got to the address: a U-shaped courtyard, in the shop on one side a sandal shop was being constructed. A young man, blond hair hanging to his waist, wearing no shoes, was up on a ladder. It was the 60s. I asked him for Thomas Jefferson.

"Oh, you mean T.J.; he's not here, but he asked Joan to help you."

Out of the door of the shop walked a woman with the most extraordinary lavender eyes, wearing a black and white outfit and net stockings. She didn't look like any woman I had ever met. She explained that T.J. had asked her to meet me and to take me up to the Edgar Cayce organization headquarters, The Association for Research and Enlightenment (ARE). We got in my car and drove up Atlantic Avenue, through the beach resort town.

"Do you know what a reading is?" she asked.

I did not.

She explained it was a psychic discourse that Cayce had presented like a talk from a trance. She told me something of his history that he was a Kentuckian from a part of the state where part of my mother's family once lived. And said Cayce was dead and had been since shortly after the end of World War II. By this point we had gotten to a large white old-fashioned shake shingle building on top of a hill.

She told me it had once been Cayce's hospital. We parked, went inside and walked into what was obviously some kind of library. One whole section was made up of identical green canvas loose-leaf notebooks.

"Those are the readings," Joan said, making a sweeping gesture with her hand.

At random I walked over and pulled one of the notebooks from the shelf, and paged through it until I came to a stop at a reading given for a woman in 1936. In those antiquated pages, from a time when carbon paper was used, then photocopied later with redactions where names were blanked out, in an eccentric kind of King James English I read a story about how the woman for whom the reading had been given, in an earlier life had been a woman in an Essene community. His description of the community's location I immediately recognized as being Khirbet Qumran on the northwest shore of the Dead Sea.

Cayce said this woman had been a teacher of astrology. The hair on my arms and on the back of my neck literally stood up. I was stunned. There are nearly 15,000 individual readings. I had picked this one. The last thing I had done while working for the National Geographic, before I was drafted and went into the Army, was research on the Dead Sea Scrolls and the Essenes. I knew that in 1936 no one knew there had been an Essene community at Khirbet Qumran. No women were thought to be members of the Essenes because Josephus, a first century AD Hellenistic Jew who combined observance of Jewish rituals with Graeco-Roman philosophies, described the Essenes as a monastic and mystical order of Jewish men. Khirbet Qumran was thought to have been the site of one of Emperor Vespasian's legions. Nothing to do with mystical Jews (Mason, 2008). And there was no evidence astrology played a major role in their lives.

And yet, as I stood there in the late afternoon light of the library, I knew that eleven years after this reading had been given, in 1947 a young Bedouin boy, chucking rocks into a cave mouth, would uncover the lost Dead Sea Scrolls and set in train a series of events that would confirm everything Cayce had said. Excavation would reveal female skeletons, and the Scrolls themselves describe the Essene interest in astrology. They're called the Qumran Horoscopes or Astrological Physiognomies (Jacobus, 2012).

Where did Cayce get this information, I wondered? Where has it been stored? How did he access it? The synchronicity of my selection had left me completely intellectually engaged.

"Let me take you to dinner," I said. "I've got some questions."

We went to dinner and I quizzed her on everything she knew about Cayce and the readings. Mid-way through she put down her fork, and asked me if I would like to spend the night with her. That had never happened to me before, and I realized that I was on the edge of something that was going to change my life.

"I need to call the farm," I said, and went to a payphone near the bathrooms. I put the call through and explained that I was involved with something that was going to take longer than a weekend.

Becoming a Researcher

I just walked away from my previous world, entered a kind of retreat, and began a systematic study of consciousness, about which I knew virtually nothing. I began by deciding to read all the Edgar Cayce readings, what today I would describe as a form of remote viewing. Cayce used a consistent protocol. It was always double or triple blind, meticulously recorded, and often witnessed by several people. Cayce would enter a kind of trance state, would be given the name and address of the target person to whom the session was dedicated. These people were scattered all over the United States and the world, and after a moment he would begin to speak about them as if they were in the room with him; all in a disassociated manner, "Yes, we have the body," followed by a kind of opening commentary, after which he would answer questions. It was all carefully taken down in shorthand and transcribed by Gladys Davis, his lifelong secretary.*

I told Gladys my plan to read all the readings, and she agreed to help me, first by explaining what the sessions were like and how

---

* *There are a number of books on Cayce, chronologically,* There a River *by Thomas Sugrue,* The Sleeping Prophet *by Jess Stern, and* An American Prophet, *by Sidney Kirkpatrick; this last I think is by far the best.*

they were conducted, and second describing how Cayce himself changed over the course of the decades doing the sessions. That gave me the idea to read the sessions chronologically starting with the first one on record and continuing to the end. Gladys also explained to me how she had kept voluminous contemporaneous records: telephone conversations, correspondence, doctor's reports, anything that she could get hold of that gave context and either proved or disproved what Cayce said. I could see she was a very diligent archivist and had amassed an amazing body of material. I had never seen anything like it. Her meticulous record keeping, and her careful recording of dates and times would later have a big influence on my own experimentation documentation.

In addition to Gladys I came to know Cayce's eldest son, Hugh Lynn, and his younger brother Edgar Evans. I moved into the old hospital building, where a group of now elderly people also lived who had known and worked with Cayce in life. We ate together frequently, and I sat for long hours with them in their room suites or sitting on the porch looking out at the Atlantic Ocean interviewing them about what they had seen, their experiences, what they knew of the people involved. It gave Cayce and his readings a first-person context I would never otherwise have been able to enter.

As I said, the nearly fifteen thousand Cayce readings constitute an extraordinary body of data, too little studied by researchers. I think this is because of the biblical Christian language as much as the material's substance. But from the first, because I had an anthropological interest in cultures and history, I saw Cayce's trance and language as an example of disassociation, and the assumption of authoritative language. There are many examples of this across history.

Individuals give themselves permission to open to the nonlocal aspect of their consciousness in many different ways. Sometimes it is self-assumed, as with mediums, speaking for a discarnate; sometimes it is an expression of a social institution, like the talking oracles of antiquity.

The explicit acquisition of nonlocal information through focused intentioned consciousness is documented as far back as the civilization of Mesopotamia, the land that lies between the Tigris and Euphrates Rivers in what is now Iraq. The Assyrian king Ashurbanipal, who reigned between 668 and ca. 627 BCE, ordered a great library to be created. Approximately two thousand tablets and three hundred writing-boards, wood framed scribing tablets, have survived. The collection has come to be known as the Nineveh Tablets (Nineveh Tablet Collection; Fincke, 2003). As a collection it constitutes the oldest repository of learning known today, some of it dating to roughly 5,000 BCE and the dawn of civilization.

As I read Cayce, I remembered Herodotus and his story about the Oracle at Delphi in the 46th chapter of his *Histories of the World*, and understood what I had never really comprehended: oracles, mediums, and shamans. I saw the ritual, heard the words, but was asleep to the underlying reality. Suddenly I understood humanity's awareness of nonlocal consciousness dated back to deep time, and I found that a confirmation strengthening my growing sense that nonlocal consciousness was real., and that there was a whole domain of consciousness about which I had been completely ignorant.

Very early on it became clear to me that if I was going to properly understand what I was reading, I needed to also know other material on this non-physiologically based aspect of consciousness, as well as what science knew. On the one hand the anthropology of empirical sciences; on the other the findings of modern science. I could see the empirically developed sciences like shamanism and the enduring spiritual traditions, all of which recognize, when you strip away the dogma, that consciousness is the fundamental. I think there are great truths to be found in what I consider to be empirical observational sciences, acupuncture and Ayurvedic medicine being two medical examples. There is a reason why the practice of holding intentioned focused awareness is a recurring discipline across time, geography, and culture. Rituals are the protocols of empirical science.

As I said earlier, I had no religious background, so I saw all this anthropologically and saw spirituality, which I thought of as consciousness, as both a part of and distinct from religion and its dogmas. I was interested in consciousness, and realized as I read, they all began with a single individual having some kind of nonlocal consciousness experience or experiences. What I wanted to know about was not the dogmas that grew up from what the individual said or wrote, but consciousness itself, how it worked and how it manifested.

I also saw beyond the factual information that they were different ways of looking at the same thing, nonlocal consciousness, with different emphases, different protocols. That turned out to be very helpful. For me the main take away studying and even practicing some of the rituals, was that the key was the ability to attain and sustain intentioned focused awareness, and that meditation was one of the easiest and best ways to achieve this altered state. It made me understand why both dojos and monasteries practice meditation and place such emphasis on it.

By 1967, I began to think about experiments to test the ideas I had about consciousness. I knew absolutely no one in parapsychology. The Parapsychological Society was tiny and less than ten years old. But the American Society for Psychical Research, the Parapsychology Foundation, and the Rhine center published formal peer-reviewed journals, and so largely in the William & Mary library I began reading them, again starting at the beginning, because if you read chronologically you see the patterns emerge and which ones matter. At the ARE I was lucky enough to find books like William James, *Varieties of Religious Experience,* Upton Sinclair's *Mental Radio,* Warcollier's *Mind to Mind,* and Sir Hubert Wilkins' and Harold

Sherman's *Thoughts Through Space*. They gave the research and journals a human face.

From this material, mostly the work of J.B. Rhine and the early researchers he trained, as well as Ian Stevenson's work on reincarnation, I learned about experimentation involving consciousness and how it could be objectively measured and analyzed. It showed me how to think about all this material experimentally, and what constituted good protocols.

But it also taught me another important lesson. The protocols employed in those experiments were detrimental to accessing nonlocal consciousness; they even had a name for it, The Decline Effect, and it was much discussed. Frequently participants doing Zener Card guessing, or dice calling, or similar protocols, while starting out very effectively, experienced performance decline over time. Sometimes it went to the point of extinguishment. It seemed obvious to me they were doing something wrong. Part of the problem, I could see was that the experiments were mostly focused on proving nonlocal consciousness existed. There seemed to be very little thinking about the psychology and anthropology of the participant who was being asked to perform a nonlocal consciousness task.

All of this had a tremendous effect on my thinking and is one of the reasons I have focused mostly on applied experiments, in which participants don't call cards but, much as Cayce had done, provide an objectively checkable narrative of many concepts. Just as the formal parapsychologists taught me about statistics, Glady's work showed me a way to document and assess the information, concept-by-concept, that went much deeper than statistics. That was the beginning of what came to be known as the Mobius Consensus Protocol.

In the third year of this immersion I had the fourth experience. In order to make some money I had begun writing feature pieces for the *Virginia Pilot* in Norfolk, and for magazines. Many of these were about speakers who came to the A.R.E.. I had done a number of these interviews, gotten good feedback, and was thinking of doing a book of them. Amongst the group I had covered were a few writers such as Jess Stern, who would go on to write *The Sleeping Prophet*, and Susy Smith, as well as a few scientists, most notably Stanley Krippner, the first real consciousness experimenter I ever met. That meeting was important because Krippner's dream telepathy work involved experimental rigor, but from talking to him I understood that he also considered the anthropological and psychological aspects. He made me feel comfortable that I was on the right track.

Most of the people, though, put themselves forward as spiritual teachers and shamans and were accepted, by at least some people, as being the genuine article. Having spent hours talking to these men and women, listening to their stories, their answers to my questions, their affect, how they dressed, how they stood, their eyes, what I can only call their beingness, I began to develop some discernment. It was clear to me that authenticity was in part a measure of the continuity between the public persona and the private personality. To the degree they are not one and the same, that person, I saw, was diminished.

About a month before the fourth experience, Hugh Lynn alerted me that a then well-known Hindu priest from India was coming Thursday afternoon, if I was interested. I said I was, and it was arranged that I would meet him when he arrived. At three o'clock, right on schedule, a black Cadillac pulled up the hill with two cars following. As I was introduced to this gentleman by Hugh Lynn, over his shoulder I could see the trunk being opened and watched as first food, than pans in which to cook the food, and finally plates upon which it would be served, were taken out.

Hugh Lynn and the priest went into the building, and I stood there and watched this process. One of the people accompanying the priest saw me watching them and said to me, "The master is so evolved, he is barely in touch with the physical plane anymore."

"Wow," I thought. "This man must be in a truly exalted state of consciousness." I looked forward to hearing him speak the following night.

In the event, however, he was quite disappointing. He had beautiful diction, was a polished speaker with just the right amount of accent, but his talk was almost entirely platitudes and slogans. By the time he was through I realized I was dealing with shtick, whether consciously contrived or not I couldn't tell. But it taught me a lesson I have never forgotten: If an expert is someone from more than one hundred miles away with a briefcase, a holy man may be only someone from a distant land, practicing an unfamiliar faith, with a different set of altar ornaments.

A few weeks later Hugh Lynn called me again to say a shaman, a Shoshone medicine man, as he explained it, was coming. If I wanted to interview him I could pick him up at the Greyhound station and talk to him that afternoon. Saturday he would be doing a traditional Native American healing ritual, which I was welcome to attend. That's how I first heard about Rolling Thunder.

Of course I accepted, and he gave me the time. Four o'clock. I had to check back to make sure I had the right location; it seemed so improbable, "The Greyhound... bus station... in Norfolk?"

"The same," Hugh Lynn replied.

The Hindu priest was still very much in my mind as I drove that hot summer afternoon down to the Greyhound station. When I got there, I could see the station came complete with the usual, sailors BS-ing one another. Marines playing a game of blackjack. Old Black ladies, sitting patiently cooling themselves with paper church fans. And leaning up against the snack counter, a middle-aged Indian with an unblocked cowboy hat, an old tweed jacket, and a bolo tie with a turquoise slide. He was eating some cheddar cheese Nabs and drinking a coke. He smoked a pipe. I could see sticking out of the breast pocket of his jacket.

We introduced ourselves, then he picked up a small bag and we walked out to my car. Twenty minutes later driving down Shore Drive, which parallels the coast, he asked me to stop at a supermarket. Would I go in and buy two steaks, he asked? In those days I was a vegetarian, really a vegan, and buying steaks for a powerful shaman seemed very odd. But good manners demanded his request be honored, so I stopped at a market and went in and bought him two of the best Porterhouse cuts they had.

A mile further Shore Drive entered a state park, and suddenly we were in beach wilderness such as 16th century colonists would have seen. It ran on for several miles. We were about midway through the coastal woods when Rolling Thunder asked me to pull over. I thought he wanted to take a leak. But when I stopped, he reached for his bag, opened the door and got out, asking me when he was supposed to be at the ARE. He clearly intended to leave me.

About seven p.m., I said. He thanked me, asked me to lay a small fire where he was to work, and turned and walked down the bank and into the woods. "Don't forget the steaks," he called out as he walked away. He was completely natural in all of this. It was not being done for effect, and as it was happening, it seemed the most obvious and appropriate thing for him to be doing. Only as I watched him vanish into the trees, did I stop and think how unusual it was. Presumably he was going to sleep in the woods. Rolling Thunder reminded me of a Polish sergeant I had when I was in the Army. So thoroughly secure in his esoteric skillset, that what seemed improbable he did with effortless competence. I realized as he vanished into the woods they were just different kinds of warriors.

The next afternoon I went up to the ARE, bringing the steaks in a cooler. Someone had moved a massage table out into the parking lot. Not quite sure where the fire should be, I gathered wood from the forest that bordered the back of the parking lot and laid a small fire surrounded by stones near the massage table, then left for an early dinner. When I got back just before seven a crowd had already gathered. I got the cooler out of the car and went over to check on the fire. Hugh Lynn came over, wearing an ironed white shirt, without a tie, and a windbreaker. He always reminded me of a prosperous small-town banker, not the youngest son of one of the most famous clairvoyants in history. In fact, he had the mind of a Medici, and was the most interesting person I had met so far.

He introduced me to two doctors; there were over a dozen of them apparently, then he went over to the ambulances parked nearby and talked with two women. They were the mothers of the two boys Rolling Thunder was being asked to heal. Inside each ambulance one of the boys lay quietly. The long summer twilight of the Beach is beginning. Another physician almost in silhouette moves between them. Precisely at seven, Rolling Thunder, looking just he had the day before, walked out of the woods holding his small bag. He went up to Hugh Lynn who, seeing him coming, called everyone together. Rolling Thunder noticed the little fire laid and thanked me.

Hugh Lynn said a few words of introduction, and while he was doing that Rolling Thunder knelt down and pulled out from the bag what I could see, from maybe three feet away, was the breast and extended wing of a crow or raven. The pinion feathers were spread. Rolling Thunder looked up at me and asked if I had brought the steaks. I went over to the cooler and got them. He took one and tore off the plastic wrap and the paper tray, handing this back to me, and threw the steak on the ground next to the little unlit fire. It was the strangest thing he had done yet, but like walking into the woods, it just seemed the thing to do.

He gestured to Hugh Lynn, who went over to one of the ambulances. The boy within was brought out on a gurney and rolled over to the massage table, and they put him on that. I couldn't see much detail but enough to recognize it was a grievous unhealed deep muscle wound to his leg. Rolling Thunder knelt down and lit the fire.

Then everyone stepped back, and we formed a circle around them. It was just Rolling Thunder and the boy, and he talked quietly to the boy, who seemed to be having trouble at first focusing on what was being said. But gradually he calmed and lay still, his eyes closed. His mother came over and stood to one side. While this is going on, by unspoken consensus we observers had been slowly shuffling forward until we reached an acceptable compromise between intruding and being able to closely observe. It turned out this was about eight feet away from the boy on the table.

Rolling Thunder began a soft slow chant. I could not make out the words, just the rhythm of the rising and falling sound. He began making slow passes over the boy's form using the wing and breast of the raven, moving it just an inch or two above his body. I could see the feathers spread slightly against the air pressure as his arm swept back and forth. Long graceful strokes. Every second or third stroke Rolling Thunder would flick the wing tip down towards the steak on the ground. As twilight deepened the fire became more prominent, and the boy and the man drifted into shadow.

It went on monotonously. Everything else was silent. Suddenly, I noticed that there was a white mist-like form taking shape around and in front of Rolling Thunder's body. Sometimes I could see it, sometimes not. But it became stronger, steadier, until it was continuously present. It was almost dark now, but the fire gave enough light to see. The mist began to take form, slowly at first, but as if gathering energy into itself. The smoke-like form became a wolf. Rolling Thunder moved as rhythmically as a clock. Sweep. Sweep. Flick. Sweep. Sweep. Flick.

After about thirty or maybe forty minutes the form began to fade, first losing shape, then becoming increasingly insubstantial. Finally, it was gone. Rolling Thunder straightened up and stopped. He made a kind of gesture, and somehow we were released to come forward. The boy was very peaceful. His mother stepped up to him and leaned over him, kissing his forehead. The wound on his leg was completely healed. It looked like your skin does when a scab falls off leaving smooth unlined pink skin, shiny in its newness. I was astonished, and from the burst of comments I was not alone. I went over to Hugh Lynn who was in animated conversation with a British scientist, Douglas Dean, the second parapsychologist I had ever met, who had come down from New Jersey to see this. Hugh Lynn asked me, "What did you see?" "Yes, what...?" Dean said. I told them, and when I said the mist took form, they exchanged a look, and Hugh Lynn said, "What shape?" I said, "A wolf," and another look passed between them, and they told me they had each seen the same thing.

There was a kind of spontaneous break. People went to the bathroom, got a drink of water. Half and hour later we gathered again. The second boy was brought out. I could not see anything wrong with him. His mother, however, was very attentive, so something was wrong. Hugh Lynn said it was a broken bone which wasn't healing. Rolling Thunder asked for the second steak and threw some stick I'd left there on the fire. I went back to the cooler got the steak and gave it to him. This one he also dropped to the ground. He said nothing to me, and I knew better than to say anything to him.

The chanting began, and all appeared to be headed to a repeat of what had happened earlier. The mist, it seemed about two inches thick, began to form. It grew stronger, stopped flickering but just as it began to take form, it stalled. It happened once. And then a second time. And a third. This time I looked around and my eyes were drawn to the mother. I had no idea how I knew this, but I felt it was the boy's mother who was blocking it from happening.

As Rolling Thunder began a fourth attempt he suddenly stopped. He straightened up, turned and walked over to Hugh Lynn. I was standing next to him. He said, "I cannot do this. The mother will not permit it. She has a mother's love, and it is very powerful."

"Yes. I noticed. I'll talk to them."

Hugh Lynn went over and talked to the boy's doctor for a while, then the mother and the son.

I couldn't hear them. Then he came over to where Dean and I are standing, and says, "He was drifting away from her, now he is dependent once again. She is conflicted about giving that up."

Rolling Thunder went over and sat on the cooler that had held the steaks. The evening was clearly over. People start drifting away. I could hear cars starting further down the parking lot, and in the glare of their headlights, I went over to kick out the fire. Rolling Thunder was there before me. He reached down with one of the sticks, picked up one of the steaks, and I could see it in the fire's light. It was withered and gray. It hardly looked like meat at all. He dropped it in the fire.

"You put whatever was wrong into the steak?"

"That's right. The fire will purify and release it," he answered as he picked up the second steak, which still had a bit of red, and dropped it on the coals.

The fat crackled and caught fire. The two of us stood there in silence. It didn't take long, and they were gone. During those minutes I don't know what Rolling Thunder was thinking. I was reconsidering how the world worked (Schwartz, 2009, 2012).

That experience convinced me that the only way forward for me was to become an experimentalist. I had no question when I began as to whether nonlocal consciousness was real. I never designed or conducted an experiment to make that point. What I wanted to know, and still want to know, is what can we know about nonlocal consciousness and how it works. What variables can be manipulated to enhance the ability of people to access that part of the self?

I began by creating a remote viewing protocol for what I called, back then, Distant Viewing; today, of course, we would call it remote viewing. In my back garden, using yellow nylon line and plastic stakes, I laid out a four by four grid of sixteen squares. In the grid I would bury something in a film canister or mason jar. I would send out a form with the outline of the grid to anyone I could get to do it, asking them to locate which of the sixteen squares contained the target. After making their location choice, I asked people to describe the target, to tell me anything they could about it. Both location selections and descriptions were statistically significant, although the descriptions, being more detailed than the single location choice, were more significant than the location choice. I then increased the grid to twelve by twelve, one hundred and forty-four squares, in order to get more statistical power. What I discovered was it didn't really make any difference how many squares there were. Viewers didn't focus on the grid, they focused on the target. The analysis of the proffered descriptive information in these early experiments led me to the consensual and concept analysis protocol that I use to this day (Schwartz, 1979, 1980, 1980b, 1980c, 1980d, 1980e, 1981, 1982, 1983, 1984, 1987b, 1988, 1989, 1997).

As I looked at the data that came out of those experiments I realized that all of the viewer's senses reported, and that people even described the kind of aesthetic experience a target evoked. A perfume bottle in a mason jar would get the response that the smell was the important thing, and that it was "a very light and elegant fragrance."

That led me to wonder if intentioned consciousness could also change the perception, the aesthetic experience, a person had when they interacted with something. To answer that question, I designed an experiment in which I took a single bottle of wine, split it into two carafes and had meditators focus good intentions on one of the carafes without even knowing the other existed (Schwartz, 2018). I gave the two carafes to a friend to conduct a tasting, telling them only that I was going to make a large buy of wine and had it down to two choices and wanted to see what other people thought. I gave them forms and asked them to let me know how it came out. There were twelve of these tastings over four years. The wine tasters would routinely pick the glass of wine that had been the focus of well meaning intention.

In 1968, I met George Ritchie, a psychiatrist in Charlottesville who had written an account of his Near-Death Experience, *Ordered to Return*, that had become a best seller (Ritchie, n.d.). I told him of my experience and listened closely as he told me his. Late that year I also met Ian Stevenson, another psychiatrist, who was at the University of Virginia. I talked with him about his reincarnation work and then read his *Twenty Cases Suggestive of Reincarnation* (Stevenson, 1966). Conversations with both of them as well, as the Cayce readings, and all the other reading I was doing, reinforced my thinking on the continuity of consciousness and its fundamental nature. Not being a physician, I knew this was not going to be my primary area of research, but I was determined to follow it closely, and so I have.

At this time in parapsychology one of the major questions was: was psi, as it was called, electromagnetic in nature? Although most of parapsychology at the time focused on a model of senders, receivers, and signals, I didn't think that was correct. How, I wondered, if psi was electromagnetic, could you target, as with a phone call, a particular person out of the billions on the earth? Also, where did the power to do that come from? No one knew at that time how much power a person's neuroanatomy could generate but, based on my experience with radios as a Boy Scout HAM, it just didn't seem plausible; and there were already experiments with Faraday cages that seemed to argue against it. But only an experiment that shielded all EM radiation could answer the question definitively. As I thought about how such an experiment could be done, I realized it would take a large sum of money, which I certainly didn't have.

In 1971, however, the ground shifted. I had moved back to Washington, D.C. and was asked to become the Special Assistant to the Chief of Naval Operations, first under Admiral Elmo Zumwalt and then his successor Admiral James Holloway. A friend in the intelligence world sent me translations of a Soviet physiologist Leonard Vasiliev (Vasiliev, 1963, 2002). He had been asking the same questions I had and had carefully conducted nonlocal task experiments over years, eliminating portions of the EM spectrum and discovering it made no difference in the quality of the information or outcome of experiments. He shielded people during the information acquiring sessions by putting them deep into caves and mines, as well as Faraday cages that he put in the caves and mines. Vasiliev was well-funded by the Soviet government, and he was a very thorough, and determined researcher. He finally reported that if nonlocal consciousness was electromagnetic it had to be in the ELF range (1-300 Hz). But he couldn't shield against that in a cave or mine, even with a Faraday cage in a cage or a mine.

He conjectured that the only way to achieve that shielding would be to be submerged deeply in seawater. But he didn't know how deep. Even with his high-level government backing he was never able to carry out the required experiments.

At the same time as I was pursuing the EM question, I read psychologist Charles Tart's 1972 paper in *Science* on altered states of consciousness and research, "States of consciousness and state-specific sciences" (Tart, 1972). It reaffirmed my hypothesis that anthropology held part of the key to successful nonlocal consciousness experiments.

That same year Canadian researcher Michael Persinger published a paper arguing that nonlocal consciousness might be explained by ELF (Persinger & Valliant, 1985). At almost the same time Persinger's paper came out, while I was Special Assistant to CNO, I was briefed on project Sanguine, which later became Project ELF. The Navy wanted to communicate with its deeply submerged ballistic missile submarines without bringing them anywhere near the surface where Soviet satellites could detect them. But how deep was that? The Navy spent something like one hundred and twenty-five million dollars answering that question, and they knew exactly how deeply ELF could penetrate and, equally important, they had learned that because of the wave-form only tiny amounts of information could be transmitted. Far less than could be produced in one of my distant viewing experiments.

I sat through the briefing paying close attention, and at the same time, seeing the data I was being shown in a completely different context.

A few months later I flew up to Groton, Connecticut with Admiral Hyman Rickover, the father of America's nuclear navy; a quite extraordinary man, who gave no appearance of his actual power. I explained what I called distant viewing to him and asked if I could go out on one of the boomers and complete Vasiliev's work. He said he would think about it and call me, and he did. He thought it was an interesting idea, but would draw undesired media attention so he had to say, "No."

Since it isn't easy to get a submarine, I just put the experiment in storage and turned back to anthropology, and that decision had a huge effect. It was an interesting time in anthropology, very tumultuous. And two issues, one in anthropology one in archaeology, caught my attention. I had come to think of oracular or shamanic rituals as empirical protocols developed over generations through observation and experience. I found in the first books of anthropologist Carlos Castaneda an understanding of exactly that point. As with Tart's work, Castaneda argued that it was attaining a state of intentioned consciousness that was the key to understanding shamanism. That led me to meet Joseph Long, a medical anthropologist at Plymouth College in New Hampshire. Together, for the 1973 American Anthropological Association's annual meetings held in Mexico City that year, we organized the Rhine-Swanton Parapsychology and Anthropology seminar, named after parapsychologist J.B. Rhine and Anthropologist John Reed Swanton. Out of that meeting we founded what became the Society for the Anthropology of Consciousness, now a unit of the AAA.

One of the central problems in archaeology at that time was: where to look? A large percentage of archaeological finds were serendipitous discoveries, and there was an ongoing discussion about how to improve this. The age of electronic remote sensing was just beginning. As I read that literature and talked with people at conferences, I interpreted archaeology's problem and the development of electronic sensors as giving me the triple blind experimental protocol for which I had been looking, and the ability to run an independent comparative electronic remote sensing. Could the sites located by viewers be found using electronic remote sensing?

My model for all of this was anti-submarine warfare. The operator is in one environment, and the targets they seek are in quite another. Multiple sensor instruments are used, and great effort is made to see that their operating conditions are optimal and the parameters of each are understood. The goal is to get an accurate complete consensual picture. You expect noise; the task is to separate the information from the noise. That is where the Mobius Consensus Protocol came from. That was my model.

To understand the optimal conditions for someone asked to perform a nonlocal task led me to study oracular or shamanic rituals from many cultures. I saw them as empirical protocols developed over generations through observation and experience, and that there was much to learn from them. My intention was never to pursue a career in government; I had only done it when they asked me to do my small bit in transforming the American military from a racist, elitist, gender discriminating conscription force into an all volunteer meritocracy. My job was to write speeches, congressional testimony, op-ed pieces to explain that to the world. We had been successful, and I was proud of playing a small role in changing history in a way that fostered wellbeing. But I was also deeply disheartened by Watergate, which I had lived through. The fact that I know some of those involved just made it personal. The experience left me clear that what I was interested in was doing research in consciousness. Just before I left government, I had lunch with a high ranking official of the CIA who told me about a project on what he called remote viewing, that sounded very much like what I wanted to do. He followed up by sending me a paper by Russell Targ and Hal Puthoff that had just appeared in *Nature*, and I was stunned. (Targ and Puthoff, 1975) Our thinking was very much in parallel.

The Explorations Begin
Deep Quest

After I left government we moved to Tucson, Arizona because I had decided that the direction I wanted to take was using nonlocal perception in archaeology. Mirroring what I had done in my earlier life I decided to write a book studying everything that had been previously done in archaeology using nonlocal awareness. *The Secret Vaults of Time* was the result. In 1976, with an archaeologist from the University of Arizona, we did the first archaeological project: the search for the Mayan talking idol of Ix Chel, and a reconstruction of archaeological sites on Cozumel Island in Mexico. It taught me a lot. I didn't direct the fieldwork, and much of it was never done, and we got poor feedback on the success of what was done. The nonlocal perception part had worked, but I realized the fieldwork part would have to be done differently. It needed a concept by concept evaluation of the nonlocally sourced data, and that began the development of the Mobius Consensus and Concept Analysis Protocol that has guided my work ever since.

At the end of that year the EM question took a surprise turn, thanks to two friends from the Navy, Don Walsh and Don Ketch. They were perhaps the leading deep ocean experts in the Navy, and they had retired and were now the Dean and Deputy Dean of the

Is Consciousness Primary?

Institute for Marine and Coastal Studies at the University of Southern California. A research submersible was coming to their Catalina Island facility during the coming summer, and they would cover its costs for three days. It was an extraordinary gift I have never forgotten.

The Project was named Deep Quest, and using the ocean's shielding and the ability to get to depth with the research submersible Taurus *(See Figure 1)* it had three goals:

1) Was nonlocal perception an electromagnetic phenomenon?

2) Viewers were not good at analytical abstractions like number or letters; however, they were reliably good at images so, by association, could an image be used to send a message? I had gotten the idea while writing a speech for Zumwalt when I ran across a picture of a codebook using a similar association communication linkage. This was employed by Admiral Lord Nelson in the battle of the Nile

The research submersible Taurus   Figure 1

in Aboukir Bay, Egypt in 1798. Nelson communicated with his ships with flags that were associated with complex messages.

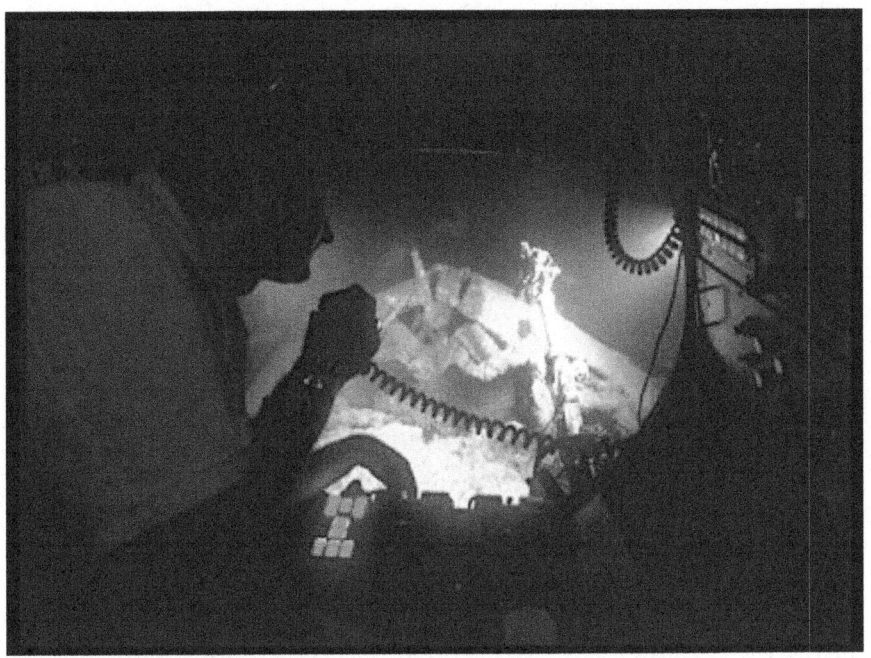

The previously undetected and unknown shipwreck located by remote viewing, as seen from inside the submersible Taurus, with its robot arm extended. Figure 2

3) Using the consensus protocol, could viewers locate a previously unknown wreck on the sea floor? *(See Figure 2)* This had two purposes. It completed the circle of the *em* test both ways, looking through the sea to its floor, and looking out to where someone was hidden; and it solved an archaeological problem using nonlocal perception. And it all worked (Schwartz, 1978).

Nonlocal perception was unaffected by seawater either way. Both shielding, and the realized bit-rate argued against ELF. The associated remote viewing, as I now called it, from inside the titanium pressure sphere involved hundreds of bits. Far more than ELF could accommodate. A previously unknown wreck on the sea floor was located, and its physical details and history were confirmed in detail. There are numerous write-ups, both academic and .popular, so it is easily available. Also, the entire study was filmed happened, and can be seen by searching "Deep Quest" on YouTube.

This project set the pattern for the archaeological research I would do over the next two decades. There are too many of these expedition projects to cover them all here. The papers, however, are all freely available on Academia.edu and Researchgate.com under my name.

Marea

To explain how nonlocal consciousness can be employed to a practical purpose which in the process yields great insights into how nonlocal consciousness works I am going to illustrate in detail one example from a much larger expedition. The Alexandria Project, in Alexandria, Egypt, took almost four years and resulted in the first modern mapping of the Eastern Harbor of Alexandria, including the discovery of the Palace of Cleopatra, Mark Antony's Timonium palace in Alexandria, the remains of the Lighthouse of Pharos, one of the seven wonders of the ancient world (Schwartz & Edgerton, 1980).

I am going to focus on one particular project in part because it was the proof of principle test demanded by the University of Alexandria as the price of their cooperation, the cooperation of the Governor of Alexandria, the Navy, and the civil government. It was something required of me about which I had no prior knowledge; it was not something I had planned.

We were required to locate a previously unknown site within the Alexandrian archaeological district that the university controlled. Not only locate it but describe it in detail before the excavation. Further, the University would control and oversaw the excavation. At a meeting in the governor's office the university's choice to be lead archaeologist, Fawzi Fakharani, announced that the target would be locating a buried building in the buried city of Marea. I have described this in much greater detail in the published reports

(Schwartz, 2019).

To get to that area, a few days later we drove a little more than 40 kilometers from Alexandria, into the desert. The search area area was roughly 24 km on a side, approximately 576 square km (about equal to one half of the city of Los Angeles). *(See Figure 3)* Hella Hammid and George McMullen were the viewers.

There was no map of the area that was useful, so we had just driven out in two cars – one for each viewer. Using nothing but Remote Viewing guidance we were looking for a buried building in the buried city of Marea, along the shores of what had been, in classical times, a beautiful lake.

It took most of a day, walking through desert in temperatures over 108°F, but the viewers, particularly George, finally got us down

Marea began with this. Two men standing in an empty desert, looking for a single buried building, in a distant buried city.

Figure 3

to an area about as big as a high school gym floor. Then they narrowed it down to inches. *(See Figure 4)* Over the course of several hours first George, then Hella, and then George again would first locate, stake out, and describe in detail where a multi-room building was buried and at what depth.

Hella Hammid, sitting beside me, describes "a strange statue or column, a column" in the buried room beneath her. Note the two cameras filming and recording everything.   *Figure 4*

The area both chose had been previously surveyed by researchers from the University of Gelph. They had published their survey some months before. According to their survey there was nothing at the site. Both Hella and George agreed the building was Byzantine not Roman as the archaeologist thought. During these sessions George began talking about small floor tiles. Six days later he augmented this. Hella also described tiles, although not in the same detail George had provided.

Both agreed the floor was now mostly gone, but a chalky subfloor would be found. A few days later, standing on the site I handed the clipboard I held to George and asked him to describe the tiles and make a drawing of them, and their arrangement. In asking George the size of the tiles, I mimed handing one to him.   He drew an outline of the design, and I asked him how big the tiles were, and mimed handing him one. Instinctively he reached for it and held it. We measured the distance between his fingers. It was five-eights of an inch, which he wrote down in his drawing.

So that there would be no unclarity about exactly where the Remote Viewers meant the dig to be located, as well as to fix the location of corners and a door, McMullen, left, directed the placement of wooden stakes.

Figure 5

Professor Fahkarani who witnessed all this (as it was also being filmed from multiple angles) had worked in the area for many years. It was he who had asked George to locate, not just any building but one where tiles would be found.

He had been skeptical to the level of disbelief that we could locate a single buried building in the middle of a buried city, in the middle of a desert. And he was sure it certainly wouldn't be Byzantine, nor oriented as George had laid it out. In fact, based on the Gelph survey he didn't think there was anything to be found at this location at all. He found the idea that details about a supposed site

Is Consciousness Primary?

buried feet below the ground could be refined down to fractions of an inch preposterous.

All of this was notarized, logged, filmed, and witnessed by more than a dozen people. Ten days would elapse before we could return to Marea to begin the fieldwork under Fahkarani's direction.

When we did, and the workers began to strip away the desert soil, it took several days of careful spadework, but suddenly the walls began to appear.

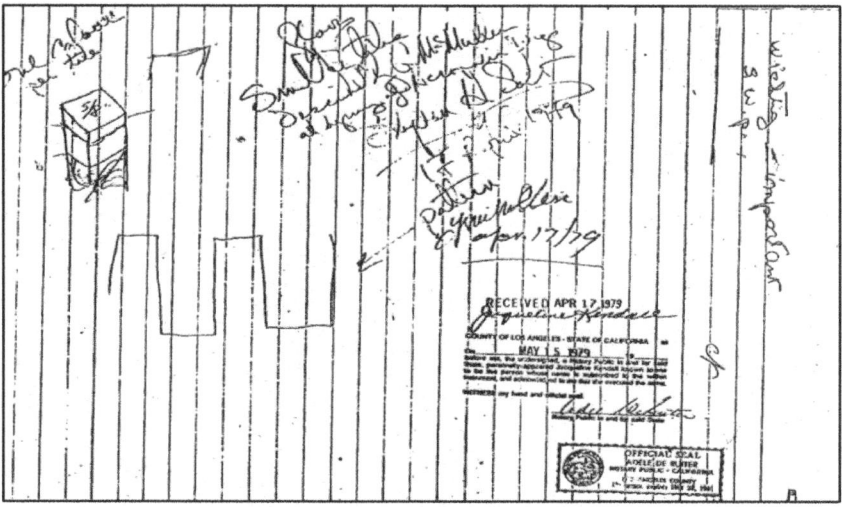

On a lined yellow pad McMullen drew the small tiles he saw, their chalky subfloor, single color, and pattern. Also note notary's seal to establish an unimpeachable chronology.

Figure 6

emerged at the depth George and Hella had predicted, exactly as outlined by George's stakes. Just as both viewers had described, there were three rooms, with the door just where George had placed it. The strange column Hella had described also was revealed. Over the next six weeks the dig continued, confirming one after another of the remote viewers predictions.

While workers were removing the dirt from the room where the Remote Viewers had said we would find it, the chalky white gypsum

sub-floor was

uncovered. In the northwest corner, intermixed with the gypsum and just below it, they found three circular marble objects, rather

The tiles predicted to be found, were exactly as described except they were round not square.   *Figure 7*

like thick quarters.

Over the next two days a total of eight more of these objects would turn up. Each one, just as George had said, was marble, smooth on one side, rough on the other, with bits of the gypsum sub-flooring still adhering to the rough side. Each was one color: either red, black, or white.

As concept after concept advanced by the viewers was confirmed through the excavation, and the findings contradicted everything Fahkarani thought he knew about the site, he found the experience very difficult. I could see it was a kind of reality vertigo. He searched constantly for some way to criticize the viewers' perceptions, but he could not dispute the location or the descriptive reconstruction George and Hella had put forward. As we were going back and forth at the site one day, I suddenly realized Fahkarani and his students who always accompanied him provided the perfect way to do this test. Fahkarani was a man uniquely knowledgeable concerning the search area, with years of archaeological training. He had control over the excavation. His skepticism, indeed his denial, were ideal.

With the tiles, which he said were weights, he thought he had found a way to attack the results. It seemed patently improbable to me; I thought them mosaic tiles, just as requested. But we agreed to take them for examination by Professors Daoud Abu Daoud, also a member of the University of Alexandria archaeology faculty as well as being the head of the Alexandria Archaeological Society, and Mieczyslaw Rodziewicz, Director of the University of Warsaw's Archaeological Mission in Alexandria and perhaps the most knowledgeable archaeologist in Alexandria. Both agreed, as George and Hella had predicted, that they were mosaic tiles and reported that no similar tiles had been previously found in the area.

They were exactly as George had described them, except they were round, and one and a quarter inches across. Five eighths of an inch error from an original search area of hundreds of square kilometers is well within what I consider acceptable error. Never be intimidated by scale. How likely was it that all this, from location to the descriptive material, was just a series of lucky guesses? How likely that in this one small area, out of hundreds of square miles, a building was found exactly as located, structured exactly as described?

Image the site as a rectangle, one in a grid of thousands of similarly sized rectangles. Image trying to guess which rectangle contained the site. Then consider the independent University of Guelph electronic survey of Marea stating they had found nothing in the area the remote viewers had picked.

This last point is very important. From the very beginning I arranged to have run, parallel and out of my control, an electronic remote sensing program, or worked with sites, as was the case with Marea, where electronic remote sensing had been done by independent scientists before our expedition became involved. The question, of course, was: Could these sites which were located by remote viewers be found using traditional electronic remote sensing, proton precession magnetometers, ground penetrating radar, or side scan sonar? To do this I had invited scientists such as Harold Edgerton, then head of the radio physics laboratory at MIT, and inventor of

Here is the dig as completed. Note Hella Hammid's "strange column" in the middle room on the right. In the upper middle of the picture notice that George McMullen's stake can still be seen.   *Figure 8*

side-scan, to do the survey of the Eastern Harbor in Alexandria. Over 20 years of doing such projects, in each project electronic remote sensing would not have located the target site and nor could electronic sensing technology have produced the detailed descriptive data the remote viewers provided.

A final word about Egypt. Although the final assessment awaits future research, I believe we located the Soma, the tomb of Alexander the Great. Which, on the basis of the remote viewing data I think is beneath the footprint of the modern mosque of Nebi Daniel. Further, that DNA can now establish what George McMullen volunteered. The bones of Alexander the Great are in a great wooden chest at the Monastery of St. Macarius in the chapel dedicated to Saint John.

I should also emphasize once again that as with Deep Quest the whole Alexandria Project was filmed as it happened by multiple cameras, and thousands of still images were taken. The whole project was witnessed by several dozen people, including other archaeologists who came out to the site. The research papers from the project were all published and can be found on both Academia.edu, ad Researchgate.com Search *YouTube* for "The Alexandria Project." The human as well as scientific story is told in my book *The Alexandria Project* (Schwartz, 1978).

Over the next 20 years, working with teams of specialists from a range of disciplines, Mobius, the lab I set up and directed, would do other large field projects. These have all been written up and papers on them are to be found on Academia.edu and Researchgate, so I don't need to describe them here.

By 1980 I felt we had a working methodology in place to reliably use access to nonlocal consciousness in an application setting, yet under conditions that would meet any laboratory standard. These experiments were all precognitive and the data was acquired under the most stringent triple blind conditions; they were witnessed by many, filmed and photographed as they happened. The accuracy of the nonlocally sourced data was not determined by myself. The assessment as to accuracy of the data was made by specialists in whatever science discipline or disciplines were required.

Doing archaeological projects was very different than doing a statistical laboratory experiment, because we analyzed the data in such a granular way, far beyond what would be needed to get just a statistical outcome. In fact the p value of statistical probability that a site like the Marea project I have just described could be located by chance is so improbable as to make the question absurd.

As I have already said, the point of the experiment from my perspective was not to prove psi was real, although that just happened in the course of a protocol that everyone acknowledged was triple-blind. That was what the university and the governor wanted. I was much more engaged in how the process of acquiring nonlocal perception information worked. It became apparent, for instance, that there were variables that could be manipulated to increase success. Targets that were numinous, as an example either of themselves or by reason of their discovery were easier for remote viewers to see. I think that partially explained the high success rate. Archaeological digs of any kind are exciting, and when the target is Cleopatra's Palace or one of Christopher Columbus' caravels, a project we did with an archaeologist from the Institute for Marine Archaeology, well, everything gets amped up.

As a personal note, when one observes a man or a woman locate and describe a complex archaeological site, and then watches as excavation validates their location and comments, it is impossible not to realize that there is so much more to consciousness than the Materialist view of reality can explain. I have always conceived of remote viewing sessions as an intention contract, in which the research and the viewer are linked in a kind of bio-circuit. The Mobius Consensus Protocol was designed to maximize the access I had to nonlocal perceived information. It worked, so I shifted focus more to the viewers. I always thought of the applied remote viewing research in which statistics are but one measure of success, as an engineering problem, and in that metaphor the viewers were the sensor instrument through which nonlocal information was derived. All the viewers with whom I worked on these projects were people selected either because they already had a track record, Ingo Swann, George McMullen, Alan Vaughan, Hella Hammid; or people I met socially and just had a feeling about and then tested with simple lab experiments. I recruited Judith Orloff, Michael Crichton, Andre Vaillancourt, Ben Moses, Terry Ross, Jack Hauck, Barbara Sobleski, and Rosalyn Bruyere this way.

Trying to Understand Nonlocal Consciousness

I wondered if identifying viewers from psychological profiles could be formalized. Was there a psychological profile? This led to two international mass studies known as PSI-QI and PSI-Q II, done with the help of OMNI Magazine, and the L.A. Weekly (Schwartz, 1982). Over 23,000 people in both Asia and the West, the U.S. and Japan, took part. I learned important things from those studies of which I will say more later. But the headline was that people who were open-minded, tolerant, and creative did better than people who weren't.

The way people did their remote viewing, that is the ritual process they went through, didn't really matter. What was important was that it gave them permission to attain and sustain, intentioned focused awareness.

Somewhere in the 1980s, looking at my data and the research of others in not only parapsychology and anthropology but also the neurosciences and the emerging fields of quantum biology, led me to think about reality as intentioned consciousness manipulating information. That was for me a very major development. I already knew from the wine experiment that it was possible through nonlocal perturbation to change the aesthetic subjective experience a person has interacting with anything that stimulates the senses. That led me to the Therapeutic Intention literature, part of which was in parapsychology, and another part in the mainstream medical journals. I noticed anthropologically that water was often associated with rituals and could be physically transformed through therapeutic intention/healing. I wanted to see if we could develop an objectively verifiable measure of healing that was not subject to issues of placebo effect or some kind of cueing. This culminated in an experiment to see whether healing intention could change the molecular structure of waters as measured by infrared spectrophotometry, with multiple internal reflection. It could (Schwartz, De Mattei, Brame & Spottiswoode, 1986, 1988, 2015).

At the Princeton Engineering Anomalies Research (PEAR) lab after years of doing individual sessions in which an individual was asked to affect the performance of a Random Event Generator and very significantly showed that it could be done, Roger Nelson asked the next question: If a single individual can do that, what happens when a large number of people hold focused intention? In my view it was brilliant. To answer the question, he set up a network of what became 65 eggs, as he called them, scattered over the world. I will let him speak in his own words:

"There is a highly significant overall effect on the GCP [Global Consciousness Project] instrument (more on that below) during special times we identify as global events when great numbers of people experience shared emotion. The effect is a tiny statistical deviation from an expected randomness, but the patient replication of tests has gradually created very strong statistical support for the reality of a subtle correlation of human consciousness with deviations in random data. The probability that the effect could be just a chance fluctuation is less than 1 in a trillion, an impressive bottom line statistic that is composed of small effects accumulated in more than 450 tests.

The correlation is subtle, so much so that individual event results are too weak to be reliably interpreted. Yet, because we are able to measure combined results across many replications, we overcome a very small signal to noise ratio—real effects gradually accumulate, while the unstructured noise is self-canceling.

"The behavior of our network of random sources is correlated with interconnected human consciousness on a global scale" (Nelson, n.d.).

That insight is what led me to my latest research. Driven by my concern over climate change, which I think holds the potential to destroy civilization, I have focused on how nonlocal consciousness plays a role in social systems, and how individuals and small groups can change the arc of history (Schwartz, 2015). So, what have I learned? Years of research and personal experience have given me this worldview:

Materialism arose from what I have come to call the Trent Taboo, the schism that the Roman Church created by the Council of Trent (1545-1563) separating consciousness from science and enforcing that proscription for hundreds of years by torture and death (Schwartz, 2016).

What I Have Learned?

Max Planck was correct when he said, "Consciousness is the fundamental." Spacetime emerges from consciousness, not consciousness from spacetime. I think spacetime is informational in nature and the product of intentioned consciousness creating informational architectures. We do not know what information is. The aspect of consciousness we think of as nonlocal is not physiologically based. It exists before we are born and continues after corporeal death. There is no signal, sender, or receiver in the electromagnetic sense. It is more accurately thought of as a process of opening to the nonlocal aspect of consciousness, always present but disregarded because it is overwhelmed with sensory impressions.

Moments of creative genius, experiences of religious epiphany, and what we call the psychic, are all experiences of the informational domain modulated by context and intention. That is, some scientists who seek to make breakthroughs experience the nonlocal domain as a source of insight and inspiration. Great musicians, artists, painters, poets and others experience the opening as artistic creativity. Similarly, those seeking to experience what they know as the spiritual have that experience, sometimes in the context of religion, which they see as contact with God as they understand this term. Remote viewers seek to describe a target, and that is their experience (Schwartz, 1994, 2010, 201b).

Individual awareness of the nonlocal domain, which may not give rise to conscious awareness, except as a hunch, a gut feeling, an intuition, or an anxiety, in aggregate create social effects. This can be tracked in the rise and fall of creativity in cultures, correlated to solar activity and fluctuation in the earth's geomagnetic field (GMF). The capacity to open to nonlocal awareness is modulated by fluctuations in the GMF. Strong solar activity is the cause of this, and when solar activity is violent, and the GMF is perturbed, an organism's ability to open to nonlocal awareness is decreased as the result of local effects on the body. Other than GMF effects, which operate through the physical body, three things I think we have identified as affecting one's capacity to open to nonlocal awareness are: intention, numinosity, and entropic process. The key to opening to the nonlocal is the ability to attain and sustain intentioned focused awareness. Intentioned consciousness can alter reality, both in objectively measurable physical ways as well as by altering the aesthetic subjective perception of something. Collective shared intention can produce powerful transformational social effects.

Quantum mechanics may play a kind of osmotic role in linking space-time and the nonlocal, but it is not a complete explanation. It is my belief that incorporating consciousness fully in science is the only way we are going to develop the strategies and technologies to get through climate change. Post-materialist science is the trend forward.

If I were entering the field today I would focus on information theory, quantum physics, psycho-neurophysiology, and parapsychology. The first two because I think we are dealing with a universe composed of information; the second, to understand the border between the local and the nonlocal; the third, to understand the psychophysiology as to how the nonlocal becomes local, and the last, because parapsychology teaches an excellent command of protocol design for the rigorous acquisition and analysis of nonlocal data.

Chapter Nine

Beyond Materialism and Madness: a Neuropsychiatrist's Perspective on Anomalous Experiences

Diane Hennacy Powell, MD

Anomalous Experiences: the "Bleeding Edges of Controversy"

By definition, "anomalous experiences" (AEs) such as near-death experiences, telepathy, and precognition do not easily fit into the current materialist paradigm. As a result, they have been rejected as anecdotes, coincidences, and illusions… or ignored altogether. However, verified accounts of AEs have been described throughout history, and across multiple varied cultures. As a trained psychiatrist, I had a skeptical view of them. I was taught that belief in them was either cultural, or a sign of psychosis. Scientists researching AEs have difficulty obtaining funding, and risk jeopardizing their careers. We have only continued to do so because AEs offer critical clues to understanding, and as Neil DeGrasse Tyson said, science makes its advances at the "bleeding edges of controversy." Conferences and journals are supposed to be where scientists verbally "duke it out," but research on AEs is generally not found in mainstream scientific journals or conferences. That is starting to change.

My perspective on AEs shifted, beginning with an event that happened almost thirty years ago, while I was on faculty at Harvard Medical School. I had been asked to assess the sanity of a woman who referred to herself as psychic. She reported seeing ghosts in the hospital, which was why she wanted to be discharged. Although I thought she was probably struggling with hallucinations and schizophrenia, I wanted to reason with her to get her to stay. I also enjoy exploring the inner world of people who are experiencing an alternative reality.

Much to my surprise, during my evaluation this complete stranger began to give an unsolicited psychic reading of me. She worked as a janitor across town, in an entirely different facility, and yet knew things about me that none of my colleagues knew. The first thing she told me was that my husband was a chemist applying for a job in two different cities, which was true. He was flying to California later that week for an interview. She predicted that we would move to San Diego, one of the two cities under consideration, and where we actually settled eight months later. She made several other accurate statements about me and my future that no one could have possibly known by any regular means, but what other means could there be?

For those of us who have never directly experienced such strange phenomena, they are challenging to believe. Because I had studied Einsteinian physics as an undergraduate, I knew that our experience of time is an illusion. Precognition is theoretically possible if time isn't linear, or unidirectional, but how could anyone escape our usual constraints? I also couldn't comprehend how she could know so many personal details about me. After moving to California, I watched as all of her other predictions came true. For example, she had said I would only have one child, and she would be a daughter. Alexandria was born a little more than three years later.

My curiosity about AEs led me to read existing research in parapsychology and attend conferences that included research on them. I discovered that the scientists had to be even more careful about conducting their experiments. It also became apparent that there were already sufficient studies to validate many of these phenomena as real. When some of the remote viewing literature at Stanford Research Institute was declassified, it further suggested that materialism is seriously flawed. However, these studies aren't accepted by the mainstream, because they present what is considered too extraordinary of a claim.

If our paradigm for consciousness had already incorporated the major changes in physics that occurred over a century ago, these claims might not be so extraordinary. However, the findings in physics seemed too weird, particularly at the time, to think about applying them to biology. As a result, anomalous phenomena, like telepathy and precognition, have been disregarded because they don't fit the materialist model in neuroscience. This attitude never made sense to me. Our model in neuroscience is too vague and incomplete to discard such widely-reported phenomena as impossible. Among its flaws is the assumption that the brain creates consciousness, but by a mechanism that is still elusive, which creates what David Chalmers calls the "hard problem of consciousness." (Chalmers, 1995) If this assumption is incorrect, which many post-materialist models suggest, this problem disappears.

Materialism fails to account for creative thought, free will, our conscious experiences of the world, or even how we have our sense of an "I." It also can't account for several scientifically documented phenomena, such as savant syndrome, which are very similar to AEs in many ways. This is why savant syndrome became the focus of my research and will be discussed later in this chapter. The unfair dismissal of AEs is what led me to write my book, *The ESP Enigma* (Powell, 2008), in which I argued that consciousness acts like a force field, because of how it organizes and influences the material world, and that consciousness could be fundamental, not simply a product of the brain. Still, AEs are considered impossible by most scientists. I believe that this is because the neuroscientific model most scientists feel constrained by is not only incomplete, it is seriously out of date.

Is Consciousness Primary?

Our current model originated at the beginning of the last century, when stains became available to allow us to see brain cells. Santiago Ramon y Cajal won the Nobel Prize in 1906 for his detailed anatomical descriptions of neurons, which were only a small percentage of brain cells, but they selectively took up the Golgi stain, leaving the glial cells transparent. Ever since, neuroscience has focused on neurons, but over the past two decades there has been a shift away from being so "neuro-centric." This, however, is not reflected in the way most people think about the brain. They still talk about neurons, synapses, and their neurotransmitters as though they are what is the most important.

A major reason for preferentially thinking of them is their relationship to psychiatric and neurological treatments. Neurotransmitters fall into categories based on how they function, which has treatment implications. For example, endorphins mimic known narcotic drugs and are described as our "natural opiates." Prozac, which blocks the reuptake of the neurotransmitter serotonin, didn't just treat depression, it brought about changes that were described by Peter Kramer, M.D. as being like cosmetic surgery for unattractive personality traits. In *Listening to Prozac* (Kramer, 1993), he wondered if it was ethical to prescribe such medications. Rather than this discouraging people from medication, the emphasis in psychiatry became increasingly chemical. Soon thereafter, people started describing moods in terms of their "chemical imbalances," and researchers proposed roles for neurotransmitters in our individual temperamental differences. This materialist view of consciousness is regularly presented to the mainstream public and is the one most scientists and clinicians from other specialties still reference.

Despite identifying over 100 different neurotransmitters, multiple receptor subtypes, and many of their associated effects, this approach has not really brought us any closer to understanding the mechanism behind conscious experiences. Neurotransmitters are primarily part of our nervous system's hardware for affecting our moods and controlling biological processes. They have evolved in many complex life forms but aren't present in all. They also aren't unique to neurons. Glial cells secrete neurotransmitters, and receptors for many neurotransmitters are found in other parts of the body. Most serotonin is not manufactured in our brains, but by the bacteria in our guts. In fact, our gut microbiome can play a significant role in our mood; in both animal and human models, a fecal transplant has been shown to decrease anxiety. We can no longer think of our moods and behavior as strictly a result of our brains.

This chapter will discuss my scientific journey to understand consciousness, and its relationship to the brain. In addition to highlighting phenomena that this new model would need to account for, I will briefly discuss some of the leading scientific advances towards understanding brain function, and how they fit together in my theory. One of my guiding principles as a theoretician is that nature is very frugal and resourceful, and everything is there for a reason. There are many examples within the history of science, which indicate how we erroneously failed to take this into consideration. For example, the appendix is no longer thought to be a vestigial organ; it seeds the gut with beneficial bacteria. So-called "junk DNA" is no longer thought to be merely place-holding material; it contains what are now considered the control switches for our genes. Similarly, we have been placing too much emphasis on neurons, which represent only ten percent of our brain cells. This is the origin of the saying that we "only use ten percent of our brain." It turns out that this is wrong too, and for similar reasons.

The Tower of Babel in Consciousness Research

While attending consciousness conferences, it became apparent to me just how specialized and fragmented science has become. I discovered that scientists and philosophers still disagree amongst themselves over fundamentals as basic as the definition of consciousness itself, creating one of the most obvious obstacles to arriving at a coherent model. In talking with them, I found that some believe that everything is conscious, while others disagree over whether animals, other than humans, are conscious beings. Others think consciousness is the result of complexity, and not unique to living systems, often arguing that a machine could eventually achieve consciousness. Some regard us as biologic robots who have the illusion of free will, which is like saying we aren't really conscious; we are "zombies."

When many neuroscientists use the term "consciousness," they are specifically referring to what humans experience as waking consciousness, which excludes much of what is of interest for a general theory of consciousness. By their definition, unconscious processes, including stages of sleep, are not included. However, unconscious processes are known to drive much of our behavior, and our conscious brains are thought to only process 8000 bits of information per second. This is only a fraction of the forty million bits of sensory information per second that our brains register. This discrepancy could potentially explain many individual differences in perception, because we don't all focus upon, and process, the same bits.

We also have brains that vary in ways, and to a degree, I could not have imagined had I not become a neuropsychiatrist. Our differences in color perception caused the picture of a future mother-in-law's dress to go viral on the internet. Her daughter saw it as white with gold lace, while her husband-to-be insisted it was blue with black lace. People were shocked that others could see the same photo on display, and under the same viewing conditions, while insisting the dress was such radically different colors. To me, it actually looked lavender with antique gold lace. What causes this difference? Our brains construct what we see based upon our expectations, and unconsciously impose a suitable context. Some saw a white and gold dress in the shade, while others saw a black and blue dress bleached in sunlight. This choice was obviously not a conscious decision and is but one example of how unconscious factors shape how we construct our reality.

We differ not only in our sensory and intellectual capacities, but in processing styles (Grandin, 2014), and each way of thinking can lead to very different conclusions about the nature of reality and consciousness. Nonetheless, when contemplating consciousness, most of us generalize from our own direct experience. This tendency to generalize is strong. People with synesthesia, such as seeing specific colors associated with letters or numbers, assume at first that everyone does… because it is a constant component of their experience, and has been since their earliest memories. Even intermittent experiences can be interpreted this way if they happen early on, and often enough. One of my patients has had temporal lobe seizures manifest as severe experiences of déjà vu since early childhood. She loses track of time during them, but even so, she too assumed when I first met her that these were normal.

We also innately differ among ourselves in our preferred styles of learning, which becomes reinforced by the profession and hobbies we choose. For example, many visual thinkers can manipulate objects in their mind's eye just as well as they can rotate real objects in three-dimensional space.

They make excellent engineers, but it can be hard for them to conceptualize something if they can't visualize it. This thinking style might predispose them to focus more on brain circuitry and other hardware, rather than on esoterica they can't relate to. Some of us don't have a "mind's eye" at all and can be mystified by the visual thinker's genius for fixing and creating things.

Most philosophers and attorneys are verbal thinkers. They can use words very effectively, yet this is considered the most linear form of thinking, and the least flexible. Verbal thinkers can stray from the truth because of their increased capacity to rationalize. When logicians disagree, it is often because of differences in their basic assumptions, which can become unshakeable when treated as facts. For example, many materialists don't just assume the brain creates consciousness; they treat this as fact. Of all the medical specialties, psychiatry, in particular, deals with conscious experiences. It requires an ability to examine the intangible, and to be comfortable with uncertainty. Clinicians, myself included, are trained to be primarily pattern thinkers. We readily see connections that others might not, which is essential when we need to make quick and accurate decisions about what is going on with a sick patient. It is by the clustering of symptoms and signs that doctors make diagnoses, which can have very unique presentations in the clinic, so we have to be able to recognize these diseases in their various disguises.

As a doctor and psychotherapist, I have benefited from developing my intuition, which also helps me in science. Intuition comes in handy when dealing with those who can't communicate, or with something I have never seen before. As the result of sharing my hunches about what is going on with my patients, and receiving immediate feedback, my intuition has become increasingly accurate. Sadly, intuition is not encouraged as much in science as it once was. It has taken a backseat, and as the materialist model continues to dominate in psychiatry, psychotherapy is no longer considered by many to be important to a psychiatrist's training.

Given our differences, it is no wonder we don't approach consciousness the same way or have a consensus about what it may be. We also don't regard the same sources of information as trustworthy. Materialist philosophers and scientists generally rely exclusively upon what they are able to physically measure and derive by logic. Post-materialists still use factual information and logic to get to their theories, but we also place a high premium on intuition and thought experiments for insights. We also don't ignore data that don't fit.

The Roots of Coincidence

After I wrote *The ESP Enigma*, an elderly man who had read it befriended me, and handed me his yellowed paperback copy of *The Roots of Coincidence* (Koestler, 1972). I was shocked when his book quoted the Psychology Chair at the University of London, Professor Hans Eysenck, as having said:

"Unless there is a gigantic conspiracy involving some 30 University departments all over the world and several hundred highly respected scientists in various fields, many of them originally hostile to the claims of the psychical researchers, the only conclusion the unbiased observer can come to must be that there does exist a small number of people who obtain knowledge existing either in other people's minds, or in the outer world, by means as yet unknown to science."

Koestler concluded:

"Those who today ridicule research into such phenomena as ESP, precognition, psychokinesis, telepathy and clairvoyance are in the same position as those who 50 years ago scoffed at Einstein's physics. It is now accepted that modern physics has broken the "laws of nature" concerning space, time and matter; it (physics) deals with such "supernatural" concepts as negative mass, holes in space and time flowing backward."

These quotes were from 1972, when I was still in high school, and Arthur Koestler had been bestowed an honor equivalent to knighthood for his intellectual work. Reading his book told me that there was much more to the story behind the scientific rejection of ESP than I had realized. It had come much closer to acceptance than I could have imagined, especially given its seemingly complete absence as a field of study during the time of my education. What happened? Have scientists become too wedded to their theories to try to integrate challenging data? This is the opposite of how science is supposed to work, but often how it proceeds.

Sigmund Freud had almost announced to the psychoanalytic community his belief that telepathy was real in 1922. His biographer, Ernest Jones, stopped him out of fear that any association with telepathy would discredit psychoanalysis. Eventually, dozens of eminent twentieth century scientists, including Albert Einstein, said they had witnessed telepathy and publicly endorsed it as a valid area of inquiry. So did Sir John Eccles, the Nobel laureate who discovered the first chemical synapse. Nonetheless, the change in paradigm anticipated by Koestler has taken another 45 years.

Why has discussion of AEs been so taboo? Scientific censorship on ESP has continued for generations for a variety of reasons. People who haven't experienced any AEs are often scared by them, either because they don't make sense, or because believing in AEs makes them feel more vulnerable. Some of the disconnect is because of religious dogma that permits AEs if they occurred long ago but considers them to be the "work of the Devil" in modern times.

Nothing in modern physics prohibits AEs, and some interpretations of quantum theory are actually supportive of them. This only makes sense because the quantum world is so different from the material. Not only are atoms primarily empty space, Einstein taught us that energy and mass are interchangeable through his famous equation, $E = MC^2$. Research referred to as "the Double Slit experiments" has shown us that the act of measurement appears to play a fundamental role in determining whether photons and electrons act like particles or waves. Additionally, many scientists have pointed out the parallels between the quantum world and the experiences of mystics, both of which suggest that everything is interconnected.

For the most part, the biological sciences have not allowed as much speculation as the physical sciences. However, hundreds of scientists, many of whom trained in the biological sciences, now support switching to a post-materialist paradigm for consciousness. Not all of us are doing so for the same reasons, which is why there are three general types of post-materialist models.

These were described as follows (Schwartz, 2016):

> "Type I post-materialist theories: neo-physical theories that are derived from materialist theories, where the materialist theories are still seen as primary and are viewed as being fundamentally necessary to create "non-material" (yet "physical") phenomena such as consciousness.
>
> Type II post-materialist theories: Post-materialist theories of consciousness existing alongside materialist theories, where each class of theories are seen as primary and are viewed as not being derivable from (i.e., are not reducible to) the other.
>
> Type III post-materialist theories: where materialist theories are derived from, and are a subset of, more inclusive postmaterialist theories of consciousness; here post-materialist theories are seen as primary and are viewed as the ultimate origin of material systems."

I believe there is definitely enough of a scientific basis for a Type I theory, which primarily deviates from our current model by incorporating quantum physics. However, an argument can be made for each model, so I will discuss all three. Rather than debate which studies in parapsychology are valid, or reach statistical significance, I took a different tack. I asked myself: Assuming AEs are real, what theories for consciousness could possibly account for ALL of them? My approach draws upon multiple branches of science and builds upon what has been accepted as fact. My conclusion is that we have been working with an incomplete, and incorrect, model for brain function, and I offer an updated version. However, in order to declare our current paradigm "dead," and move on to the next, we need to first articulate what is being discarded, why it has persisted, and why it is no longer adequate to explain all the data.

Why Materialism Persists

I previously pointed out that the efficacy of many medications in altering our moods and consciousness is high among the reasons materialism is still the dominant paradigm. Additionally, there are an enormous number of tight associations between discrete areas of the brain and specific behaviors or syndromes. Some are induced by electrical stimulation. Others can be caused by surgical lesions, or as a result of destructive processes, such as a stroke. The most poignant examples involve disruptions to our sense of self, and our ability to control our body.

Alien hand syndrome (AHS) is the medical term for when one loses control over their hand, which still responds appropriately to objects in front of it but isn't acting as the result of one's free will. One variant includes inter-manual conflict in which one hand acts at cross-purposes with the other. AHS can be created by severing the corpus callosum connecting the left and right cerebral hemispheres but doesn't occur in everyone with this separation. Extensive damage to both frontal lobes, which are highly developed in humans and associated with planning and thinking of consequences, can cause the complete loss of free will, or an inability to act in a self-directed manner. Some have called this a "bilateral alien hand syndrome." If the person with frontal lobe damage develops "environmental dependency syndrome," nearby objects can compulsively direct their behaviors. For example, if a hairbrush is on the table in front of them, they cannot refrain from brushing their hair (Lhermitte, 1986; Lhermitte, Pilon, & Serdaru, 1986).

Francis Crick, who co-discovered the helical structure of DNA, was interested in consciousness in the later part of his career. He was an extreme materialist, believing that we are solely the result of the chemicals and other components of our brains. He was interested in finding the potential "seat of consciousness." Along with neuroscientist Christof Koch, Crick identified this as being the claustrum, a thin layer of uniform neurons beneath the cerebral cortex. Stimulation here leads to loss of consciousness, which is one of the reasons they chose to focus on it. They likened the claustrum to being the conductor of an orchestra, because of the role they felt it plays in regulating consciousness and cognition (Crick and Koch, 2005).

Contributing to the materialist idea of our being biological robots is the fact that conscious awareness is not necessary for people to engage in highly complex interactive behavior, such as purchasing a ticket and boarding an airplane. During this "fugue state," it is as though the brain and body are on autopilot. This disconnect can occur in temporal lobe epilepsy, and to some extent in parasomnias, such as sleepwalking.

In addition to the motor version of losing control of our hands, frontal lobe atrophy can cause the person to become uninhibited in other ways. Dementia involving this area of the brain can affect behavior and cognition so much that loved ones can feel as though the person they knew had died. For example, I once saw an elderly woman in a wheelchair come on to her doctor with the salty language of a sailor. That kind of behavior can be humorous to some, but it also can create an existential crisis for a religious family member, especially if it violates their concept of a soul.

Sometimes a stroke can cause the patient's own sense of self to be altered. A lesion in the right cerebral hemisphere can cause a syndrome called "unilateral neglect" in which the person no longer identifies their left half as belonging to themselves. In an extreme case, one patient tried to throw the left half of his body out of his bed, and then wondered how *he* ended up on the floor.

From these, and many more examples that are beyond the

scope of this chapter, we must conclude that our brains play a major role in our experience of consciousness, behavior, mind-body connection, and sense of self. However, that is different from saying that consciousness is exclusively a property of our brains. "Terminal lucidity" is one of the conditions that challenges this view. A typical example would be an elderly woman who has looked like a human vegetable for a year, and whose brain imaging shows significant atrophy of her cerebral cortex and hippocampus. Almost all brain scientists assume that such a damaged brain could not make normal cognition possible. How is it that such a person can suddenly pick up a phone, call her family, have a normal exchange of pleasantries, and then say farewell just before dying? This only occurs in about 5 to 10% of dementia cases, and only when they are near death, according to large scale research by Bruce Greyson, Professor of Psychiatry and Neurobehavioral Science at the University of Virginia, Michael Nahm in Germany, and Professor Alexander Batthyany at the University of Vienna (Smartt, 2017). Terminal lucidity implies the brain doesn't create consciousness; it merely shapes and limits our experience of it.

From Materialist to Seeker

As an undergraduate, I had become hooked on neuroscience and biophysics, because I thought these disciplines would lead to understanding consciousness. I worked in several laboratories, becoming closely acquainted with top scientists, while recording the currents of crayfish axons with glass microelectrodes, and learning techniques such as electron microscopy. During the past four decades of my career, most neuroscientists have focused on identifying neurotransmitters, tracing neural pathways, and identifying areas of the brain associated with certain behaviors and experiences. I was actively part of this group, until I realized it was not going to answer the questions I regarded as the most important.

When considering graduate school, I was fascinated by the brain mapping being done by neurosurgeons, who could electrically stimulate, and record, from neurons while the patient was awake and in no pain, because the brain doesn't have pain receptors. They also could elicit entire memories with one electrode. Pursuing this approach to understanding human consciousness meant going to medical school instead of graduate school, so I applied to several, and matriculated at Johns Hopkins School of Medicine. Going into medicine was a way of obtaining a well-rounded graduate level education in multiple fields related to human consciousness. At the time, I had no clue about the journey upon which I was embarking, and I would have found many of my later conclusions hard to believe.

I was as deeply steeped in materialist science as one could be, and extremely naïve about religion growing up. My first memories are of when my brother and I lived at Hanford Reservation, where our father did research on the biological effects of radioactivity, and we played with mail order science kits, electronics, and weather balloons. Our father was a mathematician with graduate degrees in marine biology, genetics, and physiology. He later became the Head of the Artificial Heart Program at Battelle Memorial Institute in Columbus, Ohio. A devout atheist, he raised us with the theory of evolution from an early age and refused to let us be exposed to any religious teachings. This made my grade school experience very interesting.

I first encountered religion in public school, when forced to recite the Lord's Prayer every day. I felt like an alien, because the other children all seemed to know it by heart. Occasionally, I saw my Catholic friends perform brief rituals in front of religious statues as we walked by, which struck me as superstitious, in the same way as avoiding stepping on cracks. Many religious beliefs seemed akin to magic, which meant they appeared totally irrational to me. It was shocking to learn a high percentage of people believe in them.

Up until my last year in college, I was totally unaware one could be both religious and a scientist. Because I was the top student in an upper division math course, the math major sitting next to me assumed I was applying to graduate school in mathematics. After I told her I was going into medicine to become a medical researcher, she accused me of "throwing away God's gift." Unable to hide my surprise, I asked, "How could you get this far in math and still believe in God?" She, in turn, asked me, "How could YOU go this far in math and NOT believe in God?" We had come to a major impasse.

I don't remember most of the next day. I only recall stepping off the curb outside my chemistry lab around 10 am. When I came to, my head had a crown of blood-drenched hair and felt like it was exploding. I was told a distracted bicyclist had struck me while riding with her head down in the rain, and I was knocked to the pavement. Because I had been unconscious for several hours, I was admitted to the neurosurgery floor for observation. Initially, I thought this was a dream about neurosurgeons, because I was applying to become one. That misunderstanding quickly ended. The masked faces, surrounding me in a swirl of surgical garb, became excited when I started to move. One of the men immediately started testing my ability to flex and extend my extremities. I was prodded and poked, and found to be completely intact, but they didn't want me to go home. We didn't have the brain imaging we have now, and I was at risk for slipping back into an unconscious state. I reluctantly stayed, because I had no choice.

Ever since that accident, I have felt changed in ways still hard to articulate. I have no memory of the period while I was unconscious, but the aftermath was similar to that of people who have had a near-death experience. The universe had suddenly, and mysteriously, stopped feeling indifferent and random to me; it now felt far more ordered, complex, and inherently meaningful. I had a very limited vocabulary for this new sensation, which was completely foreign to me. That is why I wondered, "Could this be what believing in "God" feels like?" Suddenly, after having that thought, I remembered my last words to the student the night before. While headed to my car I had said, in an offhand way, "I wish I could believe in God. Life would be easier, but I can't simply will that."

The saying "be careful what you wish for" is popular because most of us have heard stories of people getting what they ask for, which also usually includes the life complications they didn't expect. I wasn't consciously wishing for anything, but after my accident I needed to understand what I was feeling, and why my perspective had changed. I had no framework for understanding this, so I went on a quest for universal truths. Despite a post-concussive syndrome that persisted for several months, I was able to complete my courses, publish a paper in neurochemistry, interview at several medical schools, and matriculate on time. Chronic headaches became part of my life, but for the most part this has seemed like a fair tradeoff. Since then I have had an even stronger sense of purpose and have been on a quest for answers to questions that would have never occurred to me before.

Over the subsequent years, I began to occasionally know things without knowing how. The first time was while I was at lunch with several female professionals. Madeleine Allbright's name came up, and I commented that her parents were Holocaust survivors. This shocked my politically savvy friends who wondered where I had heard that. They were well-read and couldn't believe it had been in the news without their having seen it. The information felt so real that I assumed I had read it somewhere but couldn't say where. Several months later, articles appeared in the news stating that Madeleine Albright had just discovered her Jewish ancestry, and that her family had converted to Catholicism to escape the Holocaust. How could I have known something about her before she did? Could my background as a trauma expert have enabled me to unconsciously recognize the pattern of someone who fit the profile of a second-generation Holocaust survivor? That is what I thought at the time, but now I am not so sure.

Acquired Savant Syndrome

Savants know things without any known previous exposure, and without possessing the basic underlying skills for deriving the answers. A striking example is the pair of identical autistic twins, John and Michael, who were studied by Oliver Sacks (Sacks, 1998). They could give consecutive prime numbers up to, and including, 20 digits. Their abilities exceeded the computational capacity at the time, which could only verify their primes through 12 digits. They could also do calendar calculations in which they would tell you the day of the week for any date thousands of years forwards or backwards. They said the answers just appeared to them, raising many questions. Where does information like these prime numbers reside? How were the twins able to access them as part of their visual reality?

Synesthesia has a variety of forms that blend more than one type of sensory input together, but some consistently combine a primary sense with symbols, such as seeing red around the letter D. Synesthesia is common in savants and is responsible for the phenomenal memory of autistic savant Daniel Tammet, who effortlessly recited the constant pi to 22,514 digits in five hours and nine minutes. Tammet says each number up to 10,000 has its own unique shape, color, texture and feel (Tammet, 2007).

The abilities of many savants challenge the accepted neuroscientific model for memory, which entails reinforced synaptic connections. If neuronal connectivity is how memory works, how could Kim Peek, the savant after which the movie Rainman was modeled, exhibit such an extensive memory? He had a large hole in the center of his brain from congenital hydrocephalus, and the lack of a corpus callosum that unites the two cerebral hemispheres. By the time of his death in his late 50s he had over 12,000 books memorized, and could recite them word for word, forwards and back, in addition to vast amounts of other factual information. He also could read two books simultaneously, one with each eye. Although the separation of his two hemispheres somehow makes this parallel processing possible, there isn't a good explanation for this in neurology.

Kim Peek is not alone in defying our sense of what a brain should look like given someone's abilities. British neurologist John Lorber reportedly examined over 600 patients who had been born with hydrocephalus and divided them into four groups. Ten percent were among the most severe, having 95% of the cranial cavity filled with cerebrospinal fluid. Only half were profoundly retarded, and the remaining half had IQs greater than 100, which is the average IQ for the general population. Some had even superior IQ's with barely any cerebral cortex. One of his cases was written about in *Science* (Lewin, 1980). When one looks at the brain scans, one must ask: How is this possible?

Most savants appear to be born, but the syndrome can be acquired. It seems counterintuitive for people to become 'gifted' after head injury, but there are many case reports of this. One of the most famous is Jason Padgett, a former futon salesman who was severely beaten after leaving a karaoke bar. After recovering in the hospital, he suddenly became obsessive over tiny details, and started noticing intricate shapes in otherwise everyday objects. He is now a successful artist who calms his "overstimulated mind" by drawing the fractals and other intricate geometric shapes he sees. When Orlando Serrell was 10 years old, he was momentarily knocked unconscious after a blow to his head while playing baseball. Afterwards he suddenly had the ability to do complex mathematical equations, and his memory vastly improved. He can tell you the day of the week, temperature, and his exact whereabouts for any given date following his accident.

Being struck by lightning can also cause savant syndrome, bringing the sudden onset of new interests and talents. Lightning is also considered by many indigenous people to be one of the means by which shamans are initiated. At the age of 42, Anthony Cicoria was chatting to his mother on a payphone when lightning struck the phone booth, shooting through the phone and into his head. Fortunately, a nurse waiting for the phone was able to resuscitate him. Although neurologists could not detect any unusual brain activity afterwards, he developed an abrupt interest in music, and is now considered a musical genius. He started teaching himself how to play piano, and within three months he realized he had already composed dozens of songs in his head.

What happens during the injury, and/or the period of being unconscious, that could possibly bring about such fundamental changes? Even though acquired savant syndrome is not particularly common, any model for consciousness would need to explain it, and the current materialist model cannot. One possibility for understanding savant skills is that our brains are capable of quantum processing, which would enable them to simultaneously consider multiple possibilities as the answers to questions, before choosing one by "collapsing the quantum wave." Normally this kind of processing would be reserved for functions kept unconscious, and therefore outside of our awareness. In other words, savant syndrome might be showing us that we can have access to a vast amount of information if the barrier, or filter, between the conscious and unconscious mind is compromised.

Quantum Neuroscience: Type I Post-Materialism

The term "quantum" refers to discrete quantities, or packets, of light that are emitted when an electron moves from a high energy orbit around an atom to a position of lower energy. In turn, photons can bump electrons out of their orbits. Albert Einstein described this "photoelectric effect" in 1905. I believe such interactions between light and electrons play a fundamental role in biology, not just in our electronic devices. We are just beginning to understand them.

Electron microscopy has recently reached a high enough resolution to see large atoms, and atomic force microscopy can even create images of interactions between molecules. Scientists can now investigate what is happening in cells at the microscopic Planck scale, which is so small that predictions of classical physics begin to break down, giving rise to "quantum effects," which appear particularly relevant to the brain and consciousness.

An example of quantum effects in biology is the mechanism behind photoreception in our retina, which contains Rhodopsin molecules. These are superimposed in both *cis* and *trans* states, until specific light frequencies determine their state to be one or the other. This is how photonic messages can be converted into electrical brain signals, and the mechanism is not unique to vision. It used to be thought that our olfactory receptors detected variations in molecular shapes, but a different quantum effect is now believed to differentiate chemical aromas by the frequency of vibrations of molecules.

Cybernetics has attempted to model our brains as though they are biological computers. Using the current synaptochemical model, artificial intelligence experts calculated the human brain's total processing power to be 10^{16} neuronal transmissions per second. To get this number they multiplied the speed of neuronal transmission (100 signals per second) by our number of neurons (100 billion) and their number of connections (up to 10,000 each). That might sound like an enormous amount of processing power, but 10 to the 16th power is only 10 to the 5th power times more processing power than our current computers, which doesn't seem sufficient to close the enormous gap between digital computers and known capacities of our brains, especially when one considers savants.

Man-made computers have advanced tremendously, but as

jazzy as they seem, they are still digital processors, which means each task is performed by mathematical calculations using the binary system and a long series of yes and no questions. Our brains can process information from many streams in parallel, and almost instantaneously, as though choosing significantly more complex answers from a vast number of possibilities. However, neurons transmit signals millions of times slower than the fastest electrical transmission rates over copper electrical wire, and even slower compared to fiber- optics. All of this led scientists to wonder if our slow and clunky chemical synapses and neuronal networks are really the appropriate level at which computation is taking place. What, in other words, is the brain's transistor, or basic unit for processing?

Molecules have been considered because they can act as transistors by being superimposed between two states. In cybernetic terms, this means one state acts as an open logic gate (or 0) and another is a closed logic gate (or 1). A single neuron contains 100 million tubulin molecules, which could solve the quantum processing problem by sheer numbers alone. According to University of Arizona anesthesiologist Stuart Hameroff and physicist Sir Roger Penrose, the tubulin molecules boost our brain's total computing power to 10 to the 26th power transmissions per second by being in a superposition between the two states. Each tubulin molecule switches back and forth between the two states 10 to the 7th power times per second, acting like transistors, and enabling each neuron 10 to the 15th power operations per second! In other words, they believe an individual neuron can encode more information than we ever imagined. (Hameroff, 1998)

Regardless of whether the above model is correct, we know that neurons and their circuitry contain information. A small stroke can selectively wipe out all of the words for vegetables, while leaving the rest of one's vocabulary intact. There are neurons which will selectively fire when images of Bill Clinton, or Jennifer Aniston are shown. What is remarkable is that the same cell will do so when the image shows the face from any angle, at different ages, and even if it is just a caricature. How is this information integrated?

I believe the answer to that lies in glial cells, which comprise the other ninety percent of the cells in the brain besides neurons. Glial cells were initially thought to be only supportive in function, analogous to thinking that "junk DNA" was merely scaffolding for our genes. Their name comes from the Greek word for "glue," because of the misconception that they just held the working neurons of the brain together. Similar to the story in genetics, where the surrounding material contains the controls for gene expression, glia appears to manipulate and orchestrate the activity of neurons. In other words, to understand higher thought processes, we are no longer looking exclusively at the neurons. (Koob, 2009)

Scientists have discovered that glial cells can exist in tissue culture in a petri dish without neurons, but neurons cannot exist in culture without them; they are essential to neuronal existence. As a consequence, the synapse no longer consists solely of one neuron connecting with another. We now have the tripartite synapse in which a glial cell appendage envelops the synapse, monitoring and influencing the synaptic space and adjacent neurons.

Glial cells make up the white matter of our brain. They come in many types, and can remove excess potassium ions from extracellular space, building up a charge like a capacitor. Glial cells called "Schwann cells" create insulation for the neuronal axons, which helps to speed up nerve conduction. Microglia are closely related to macrophages in the immune system and serve that function in the brain. They clean up and remove faulty synaptic connections and play a major role in pruning synapses during our brain's development. They can become overactive, retract their appendages, and change into a roaming cell during an infection, or in reaction to cytokines released by the peripheral immune system.

The major stars among the glia in my model of consciousness

are the astrocytes, so named because they are star-shaped. They are more than twice as numerous as neurons, or any other type of glial cell, and comprise anywhere from 20 to 40 percent of our brain. They also are our brain's stem cells and generate both neurons and all of the other types of glial cells during embryological development. Many astrocytes retain this capacity to become either glial cells or neurons later, depending upon what is needed. This plays a major role in the brain's ability to repair and rewire itself, which had been previously thought impossible.

Glial cells are interconnected by gap junctions, forming a syncytium, which functions like a multi-nucleated single cell, because of the ease of signal transmission across their gap junctions. Other examples of syncytia are cardiac and skeletal muscle, which are other tissue types where a coordinated response is essential. A single astrocyte in the cortex will connect with 50 to 100 other astrocytes. Because glial cells do not have disruptive action potentials, they present a much better candidate for quantum processing than neurons. In fact, some scientists believe these cells are where higher thought processes might actually occur, because they communicate amongst themselves by means of electrical waves triggered by the influx of calcium ions. Yale scientists (Cornell-Bell et al, 1990) have shown that these calcium waves can spread from their point of stimulation to all of the other astrocytes in an area that is hundreds of times the size of the original astrocyte. These calcium waves can also cause neurons to fire. More evidence that these cells might be playing a role in controlling our conscious experience is the fact that astrocytes have tetrahydrocannabinol (THC) receptors, and stimulation of these ignites them to release calcium.

The proportion of glial cells in the brain rises in relation to the intelligence of an animal, and humans may have the most abundant and largest astrocytes. The proportion of astrocytes in the cortex is also the greatest in highly intelligent animals. Among humans the variation in percentage of astrocytes, and their location, appears to correlate with intelligence. The major difference in Einstein's brain is an increase in percentage of glial cells, especially near the left angular gyrus, which is involved in mathematics and symbolic thought (Falk, 2013). Similarly, an unusual ring of increased white matter was seen around the hippocampus of a patient on brain imaging by Johns Hopkins neuropsychologist Jason Brandt. He described him to me as possessing the type of phenomenal memory we associate with savants; the kind where they can't forget anything (Brandt, J., 2017).

Although glial cells have not received much attention in the press, their importance is punctuated by the latest interpretations of familiar brain imaging technology. The assumption behind functional Magnetic Resonance Imaging (MRI), which measures cerebral blood flow, was that an increase in blood flow directly reflected increased neuronal activity. This was discovered to not always be the case, which temporarily created a confidence crisis in the nineteen thousand studies that have used this technology.

Many of the functional correlates for specific brain activity continue to hold up, which confuses matters further. The dilemma was resolved when it was discovered that glial cells in the brain control cerebral blood flow, which further suggests that glial cells are the main integrators of information (Swaminathan, 2008). The encephalogram, or EEG, is the diagnostic test most associated with changes in consciousness, including stages of sleep. However, the EEG measures the movement of ions in the extracellular space, and not the current inside neurons. This means it is actually a more accurate reflection of the activity of glial cells than neurons as well.

Glial cells also help to explain another phenomenon. How do we have such vivid thoughts during dreaming and sensory deprivation without the input from sensory organs to our neurons? Since astrocytes can modulate neuronal behavior without sensory input, these calcium waves in astrocytes were proposed to represent the physical equivalent of our thinking mind (Koob, 2009). We must conclude that we can not ignore glial cells in brain functioning.

Consciousness as Primary: Type II Post-materialism

Type I models simply incorporate quantum processing into our existing model for brain functioning. For consciousness to be primary, and not simply a product of the brain, it must be able to exist outside of the brain. The patient who gave me an impromptu reading knew about my husband's career, and my future, but where could such personal information reside? There was no way she could have derived, or guessed, what she told me. To investigate this way of knowing, I needed to study people reliably accurate at accessing "non-local" information. Savant syndrome became the focus of my research, because it is an accepted phenomenon that would be considered pure fantasy, if it hadn't been seen repeatedly, and documented so well.

Autism is often associated with a deficit in left hemisphere skills, such as language, whereas the artistic and musical savant skills are predominantly right hemisphere-based, as is intuition. Savants often exhibit high accuracy in their sensory perception, such as perfect pitch, and if ESP entails separating signals from background noise, this high sensitivity would be an advantage. Savants have fewer perceptual biases, such as not being fooled by optical illusions. They are less conceptual, more detail-oriented, and sensitive to subtle changes. The rest of us are much more susceptible to "change blindness," only seeing what we expect to see. Savants also have remarkable pattern recognition, directly perceiving connections. Some can recognize musical harmonics without having had lessons. Many savant skills, such as prime number generation and knowing things without exposure, seem almost indistinguishable from "ESP," so the possibility that there could be an increased incidence of "ESP" in autistic savants always made sense to me. In fact, autism expert

Bernie Rimland actually considered "ESP" a savant skill, and gave accounts of savants exhibiting precognition, telepathy and clairvoyance.

In search of someone who could provide the extraordinary evidence for ESP demanded by science, I have evaluated several savants in India and the US. Some claim to know several languages, the periodic table, or other verifiable information without known exposure. However, in this era of personal computers, proving that someone has not had previous exposure is hard to do. Complicating matters further, I discovered that the children were more likely to get the answers if I knew them. This, combined with statements by teachers and parents that the children were telepathic, made me wonder if the children could somehow access my mind. It became a confounding variable that needs to be explored.

My hypothesis that these children might be the most likely to demonstrate telepathy to a high degree was difficult for some to believe, because of research by Simon Baron-Cohen, Director of the Autism Research Centre at the University of Cambridge. According to his theory, children with autism don't recognize others as having minds, let alone possess the ability to read them. This is called an impaired "theory of mind" (ToM) (Baron-Cohen, 1985; Baron-Cohen, 1989). Realizing that another person can believe something false is an example of demonstrating this and considered an important milestone in children's development.

Baron-Cohen used a common test for ToM called the "Sally-Anne" task, in which one person knows something the other doesn't. For example, if Sally hid Anne's ball inside a box when Anne wasn't in the room to see it, a child younger than three thinks Anne will look for it in the box. An older child will predict that Anne will look where the ball had been, not where it currently is. Autistic children of many ages think Anne "knows" the ball is in the box. I made a radical suggestion. What if they are assuming Sally and Anne are telepathic? We each begin life in shared consciousness with our mother, and some people with autism might be retaining this ability and regard shared consciousness as normal (Powell, 2015).

Autistic children often have difficulty expressing themselves, while their ability to understand language is otherwise intact. This creates a prolonged dependency and increases their motivation for developing alternative ways of communicating, especially with a primary caregiver. Since making my hypothesis known, many parents and clinicians in the autism community have told me they believe their children are telepathic. They have remained silent for fear of being thought crazy, losing their professional credibility and job, and/or adding to the perception of autistic children as "strange."

To see if there was truth to the claims of telepathy, I have done controlled studies on three. So far these "telepathic" pairs have had to be tested in the same room, because autism makes it difficult for them to integrate change in experimental protocol. They have also needed the other member of the pair to be present to keep them properly engaged in the task. I have not had sufficient funding to work towards the ideal setup to pursue this to the extent necessary to draw any firm conclusions solely from my research. However, I saw strong evidence that they are indeed telepathic. The oldest two have demonstrated accuracy of 100% on a majority of randomized numbers containing five digits or more.

"Hayley" was referred to me by savant expert Darrold Treffert. She was eleven at the time of testing and could barely speak. She was discovered independently by two of her therapists to be "reading minds." One noticed that Hayley always copied the therapist's mistakes when doing homework, even when the mistakes were only in the therapist's head. The other therapist saw that Hayley changed her answers to logarithmic notation, immediately after the calculator was changed to that means of displaying the answer (Powell, 2015a; Powell, 2015b).

Another child is Ramses, who at the time of testing was a 5-

year-old boy. He could read seven languages out loud by the time he was 2 years old and has solved algebra problems since he was four. His mother, a brilliant surrealist artist, claims to have been telepathic with him even before his birth. The third is a 16-year-old boy who, like Hayley, communicates predominantly by typing. One of my experiments with him was witnessed by Deepak Chopra, who was invited to create the test stimuli using a computer that generated random numbers and nonsensical words. The boy's accuracy was so high that Deepak left dazed by the experience, leaving without his jacket, wallet, or bag.

Not all of the savants demonstrating these skills are autistic. Blind children can develop savant skills, which are often musical. Rather than go unused, their visual cortex appears to be rewired for a new purpose, often enhancing some other sense. Rupert Sheldrake left his career as a Cambridge scholar in biology to study telepathy in animals, because of research involving a blind savant. A Cambridge Professor he admired had co-authored a paper about telepathy (Recordon, Stratton & Peters, 1968). This paper, buried in a British parapsychology journal, was a major influence in Sheldrake's decision. The boy was tested for telepathy after his ophthalmologist noticed he could only pass an eye chart exam when his mother knew the answers. He demonstrated telepathy with his mother over the telephone miles away from her, leading the researchers to conclude he was telepathic.

The paper also gave references for research done in the 1930s on children who would be diagnosed as autistic savants today, but autism didn't exist as a diagnosis until 1938. The papers described experiments with two different children, and once again, they were concluded to probably be telepathic(Bender, 1938; Dahle, 1940; Drake, 1938; Ehrenwald, 1940-1). My hypothesis that savants might be "super-telepaths" may be correct, but how do they do it? How could anyone silently, and invisibly, know another's thoughts? How could shared consciousness be possible?

Reverse Engineering the Brain

One way to answers questions about potential mechanisms is to look at all of the components of a system with an open mind and ask what they might be doing. Let's start with the brain as a whole. Why do we have one? The sea squirt is an invertebrate that only develops a brain for navigation, and then reabsorbs it when its lifestyle becomes stationary, or situated (Beilock, 2012). This suggests the brain is primarily an organ for navigating through space and time. Navigation is such a vital function; the brain can create many workarounds for those with disabilities. Brian Borowski, a Canadian who was born blind, began teaching himself to echolocate at age three. By clicking his tongue, or snapping his fingers, he can move about. He unconsciously decodes the echoes and stores the maps and other information in his head.

Although brains are a very specialized organ for consciousness, does it make sense to say that the sea squirt becomes less conscious when it is without one, especially since it can regrow one when needed? Suppose consciousness began with single-celled organisms. As we became multicellular through evolution, cells became specialized such that multicellular organisms are basically a community of cells. If so, what would be the cellular structures associated with consciousness that would enable even a bacteria to be regarded as conscious?

If consciousness is equivalent to a "life force," some scientists think it might be the same as electromagnetism. Bacteria are now known to exist that can live completely off of electrons they obtain from rocks. All cellular life, including bacteria, can create an electric current and its associated magnetic field because of potassium channels. These are proteins that sit in cellular membranes like neurotransmitter receptors. They serve multiple functions by changing their shape in response to stimuli, such as calcium ions and voltage changes in their surrounding membrane. Their shape determines their porosity, or the degree to which positively charged potassium ions can flow along an electrochemical gradient.

Humans have at least 90 types of potassium channels, showing more diversity than any single neurotransmitter, and glial cells are particularly loaded with them. Over 98% of potassium is contained within our cells, because too much potassium in our blood (over 5 mEq/L) can cause heart arrhythmias and death, and too much in the brain can cause seizures. Too little (below 3.5 mEq/L) is also life-threatening. In excitable cells like neurons, a rapid rise and fall of the membrane's voltage causes potassium to rapidly leave the cell, and results in a current called an "action potential." This current travels along the neuron's axon to synaptic connections with other cells. In addition to chemical (neurotransmitter) synapses, many animals, including humans, have electrical synapses throughout their brains that use gap junctions. These electrical synapses are significantly faster, and can send current bi-directionally, whereas chemical synapses cannot.

Among the worst toxins for the brain are heavy metals like lead and mercury. They don't let go of their electrons easily, which makes them poor conductors of current. Lithium is a light metal that gives up its electron easily, and has been helpful for more than bipolar depression, but by a mechanism not fully understood for many years. The emphasis on the chemical properties of the brain, rather than considering its electromagnetic ones, may be contributing to this confusion.

Furthering this view of consciousness as electromagnetic, our brains don't just generate fields, they respond to them. Electromagnetic stimulation of our brains can have such powerful and specific effects that electroconvulsive shock therapy, transcranial magnetic stimulation, light therapy, and vagal nerve stimulation are each recognized treatments for depression which has failed to improve through medication. More recently, engineers have explored the potential of brain interfaces with electronic technology. Electronic chips for brain implantation to stimulate specific regions are currently being developed as treatments for various psychiatric and neurologic disorders. We can only understand the therapeutic impact of some of our most successful treatments by looking at the electromagnetic properties of the brain.

The importance of electromagnetism to life on Earth is not surprising given that we are bathed in a sea of electromagnetic energy from the Sun, and other cosmic sources. We are just one of many species who have evolved a variety of adaptations to capitalize on this. Our heads are equipped with specialized sensory organs to detect different frequencies. Our eyes detect electromagnetic waveforms in the human visible spectrum and are located side by side for binocular vision. Our ears are on opposite sides of the head for improved localization of frequencies in our audible spectrum, especially if the source is moving. Besides photoreceptors, our eyes also contain receptors for magnetic fields called chryptochromes. We can safely say that most of the information we obtain about our surroundings involves electromagnetism.

Could telepathy entail detecting another brain's electromagnetic frequencies? We generate electromagnetic fields, and our daily experiences with technology makes a transmitter/receiver model easy for us to relate to. We use phrases like, "being on the same wavelength," and have feelings about people's "vibes" or "energy." This analogy intuitively makes sense, but is considered to have been ruled out years ago by parapsychologists who initially thought that information transfer from one person to another was electromagnetic. That is why subjects were placed in Faraday cages: to block all high frequency electromagnetic signals (EMS). Instead of preventing telepathy, the subjects actually reported improved accuracy in these shielded cages. Blocking the higher frequency EMS seems to reduce a "psychic signal's" background noise. Any potential signals would have to be Extremely Low Frequency (ELF) waves. ELF waves weren't believed to have a high enough resolution to transmit specific information over long distances, so researchers concluded telepathic transmission could not be electromagnetic. They started looking for answers in quantum mechanics and entanglement.

However, most Faraday cages don't block the ELF waves in the frequencies of our brains (3 to 80 Hz). Theta waves (6 to 10 Hz), at the low end of the spectrum, are the brain waves thought to be most associated with ESP. To completely eliminate ELF waves as a possibility, it would be essential that the cages blocked these biological frequencies as well. Also, although ELF waves were declared to have an insufficient resolution to carry information over long distances, ELF waves are used by the military for communication with submerged submarines, because they are the only frequencies that can penetrate deep water. What might really matter is our brains' potential for detecting ELF waves, directly or indirectly.

This possibility shouldn't be shocking, since electric fields are directly detected for location and communication by animals as diverse as sharks, cockroaches, and the duck-billed platypus. Recent research has shown that bacteria, one of the earliest and simplest forms of life, don't need to be in the same test tube to detect the presence of another bacterial species. They appear to be detecting another species' electromagnetic signature. Because the brain exhibits both electrical and chemical processes, scientists engaged in a heavy debate about which was most important for driving neurons during the 1940's. Hans Berger, a German psychiatrist, recorded the first human brainwaves, or encephalogram (EEG), in 1924. He was an early proponent of telepathy, because of a personal experience with his sister. He developed this technology because of his idea that consciousness could actually be electromagnetic. When Berger published a paper on brainwaves in 1929, his work was widely disbelieved at first. At that time, the idea seemed absurd that our brains had "electricity," albeit different from that coming into our homes. This was confirmed as real in the 1930s by electro-physiologists Edgar Douglas Adrian and B.H.C. Matthews.

An electromagnetic theory for consciousness has been proposed again (McFadden, 2002; Pocket, 2012), and is attractive to some because it resolves the so-called "binding problem," which has puzzled philosophers and scientists for centuries. This "binding problem" stems from the fact that auditory, visual, tactile, olfactory, and all other sensory information enters the brain through separate pathways from our sensory organs. This sensory information undergoes further separation into even finer categories at the level of the cortex. For example, the visual cortex has highly specialized cells that only respond to one aspect of an image: a particular angle, movement, sharp contrast or edge, or a specific color. Details from these independent sensory pathways are somehow seamlessly reassembled into a multi-sensory experience that appears to be happening outside of ourselves, even though neuroscientists tell us this is happening in our brains. Where and how is this experience created? The binding problem is no longer an issue if it is occurring within an electromagnetic consciousness field.

However, if you ask neuroscientists if consciousness is electromagnetic, the majority will tell you "definitely not." Why? Two major influences drove neuroscientists away from electromagnetism in the late 1940s. One was the discovery of LSD, which showed just how powerful of an effect a small chemical can have on consciousness. The other was Karl Lashley's failure to find theoretical engrams, or memory traces encoded in brain circuitry.

Researchers had speculated that specific neurons are activated when we acquire a memory, and this memory is maintained by the enduring physical or chemical changes resulting from activation. If these theoretical neurons are subsequently reactivated by a particular sight, smell, or other trigger, this entire memory is recalled.

These neurons were known as "memory engram" cells. After teaching rats a task, Lashley surgically removed tissue from their brain's outermost layer, the cortex, to determine which areas were essential for retaining that memory. To his surprise, the location from which the material had been removed didn't matter, but the total amount removed did. Lashley concluded that the brain is equipotent and interchangeable, which describes organs like the liver that do chemical processing, but not electrical circuitry, which is very sensitive to disruption. We now know that Lashley's conclusion was invalid. The brain has redundancy, but it also has highly specialized and organized areas of cortex that are not malleable or interchangeable. This doesn't seem to have diminished the long-term impact of Lashley's study.

The debate over the importance of electromagnetism versus chemistry ended, prematurely, when Sir John Eccles' discovered the first chemical synapse in 1949 (for which he later won the Nobel Prize). Ironically, Sir Eccles originally believed neural transmission was primarily electrical. It was only after this discovery that he reluctantly conceded to a chemical model at the urging of Sir Karl Popper. Neuroscience shifted its focus to synapses, neurotransmitters, and their receptors. The propagation of electrical impulses was no longer thought to be the brain's main event, and these were demoted to being the means for stimulating vesicles to release chemical neurotransmitters as chemical "messengers" into the synapses between neurons.

Chemicals and synapses are confined within the skull, whereas electromagnetic fields are not. This is another reason given by scientists for rejecting an electromagnetic theory of consciousness. Scientists have argued that if the electromagnetic model were valid, humans should experience telepathy, but the prevailing view is that we do not. The problem is that once the chemical model was adopted, evidence for telepathy no longer fit science's paradigm. Telepathy became an extraordinary claim, and science hasn't accepted any evidence for its existence. This circular reasoning could easily be resolved by re-examining our assumptions and conclusions.

The Human Antenna

If we have the capacity to detect ELF waves, what would that sensory organ look like? If our brains are capable of detecting electromagnetic signals, where is the hardware? One possibility is exactly where one would think to look... inside our skulls. In the 1980's, a researcher from the University of Manchester named Robin Baker blindfolded people and found that they had a better than chance ability to find their way home. However, a magnet attached to their head would interfere. Baker said, "Whatever the repercussions, we have no alternative but to take seriously the possibility that Man has a magnetic sense of direction" (Baker, 1980). He was convinced of this from over a decade of research, but others were not able to replicate his results. We now have a potential explanation.

Mammalian brains, including humans, have been found to have their own internal GPS, composed of "grid" cells that create the mental map for navigating space, and "place" cells which fire when an animal is near a familiar location. John O'Keefe, May-Britt Moser, and Edvard Moser were awarded the Nobel Prize in Physiology or Medicine for this discovery in 2014. These cells are in the hippocampus, which is also the area of the brain associated with encoding memory, and the major producer of theta waves that are reportedly associated with enhanced psychic abilities.

Why might a magnet interfere with our GPS? Joe Kirschvink, a geophysicist at Cal Tech, believes that magnetoreception might be the primal sense in biology. His laboratory examined the intracellular structures containing magnetite, called magnetosomes, from several areas of human brains. Magnetite, or iron sulfide, appears to play a role in the ability of many migrating species to navigate by using the Earth's magnetic field. It is considered the most important form of iron because it can have strong magnetic properties, as is seen in lodestone, a natural magnet. Humans have magnetite in the bridges of our noses, and in the ethmoid and sphenoid bones of our sinuses. Other than these craniofacial bones, most of our body does not contain magnetite. The exception is our brain, which contains 5 million particles of magnetite per gram. More striking, the membrane lining our skulls and sheathing our spinal cord, the dura mater, contains a concentrated array of magnetite at 100 million particles per gram. So does the pia mater, the membrane that intimately covers our brain's extensive cortex in all its convolutions (Kirschvink, Kobayashi-Kirschvink, Diaz-Ricci & Kirschvink,1992).

The pia mater is connected to the brain by astrocytic processes, which means that the astrocytes could be monitoring, integrating, and transmitting any input to this membrane. The two maters are narrowly separated by a cavity filled with conductive electrolyte fluid that is constantly being created, and recirculated. This would be over-engineered to just be protecting our brains physically. Nature is more efficient and frugal than that, so what might this be?

The magnetite crystals demonstrate two interesting features. They are found in shapes that do not occur in other situations in nature and are thought to result from how they are formed in the tissue. The orientation of these crystals appears to maximize their magnetic moment, giving them the capacity to act together as a system. Kirschvink concluded, "magnetosomes moving in response to earth-strength ELF fields are capable of opening trans-membrane ion channels, in a fashion similar to those predicted by ionic resonance models. Hence, the presence of trace levels of biogenic magnetite in virtually all human tissues examined suggests that similar biophysical processes may explain a variety of weak field ELF bioeffects" (Kirschvink, Kobayashi-Kirschvink, Diaz-Ricci & Kirschvink,1992). In other words, even though the electromagnetic fields of our brain and heart are considered weak, they are in a frequency range known to influence the flow of ions across neuronal membranes. The presence of magnetite, and its ability to move in response to ELF waves, suggest a potential means by which electromagnetic waves could influence a person's unconscious thoughts. If so, why don't more of us experience this?

The magnetite lining our skulls could also serve a useful function as a shield for our brains to protect them from influences of outside electromagnetic fields. This might help to explain why small children often report anomalous phenomena, and we are thought to be more psychic when very young. When we are born, our skull bones have not completely meshed together. Perhaps a disruption of these arrays could be why head injuries and lightning can cause acquired savant syndrome later in life, and/or the onset of an increase in psychic abilities.

We are still left with the mystery of how people function with barely any brain, such as those investigated by John Lorber. Perhaps, in addition to microtubules and glial cells, we have also misunderstood the other major component of the brain: the ventricular system. The brain has four ventricles filled with cerebrospinal fluid, or CSF, which are interconnected. This electrolyte containing system is the space between the dura and pia maters of the brain that extends down to the base of the spinal cord. There are four internal ventricles, two of which are the large lateral ventricles, one in each of our hemispheres. These lateral ones become significantly larger in dementia as the brain tissue dies, and are extremely large in those with hydrocephalus, such as Kim Peek.

The ventricles are lined with neuroglia, specialized glial cells with cilia that are constantly moving the CSF as part of what keeps it recirculating. The CSF is sterile, and its sodium and chloride are kept in the same constant ratio. It has potassium ions at half the concentration of the blood, from which CSF is derived. Initially, the ventricular system was thought to serve the metabolic requirements of the brain, but if so, why is it kept so constant in composition? Also, we now know that the brain has a lymphatic system to help remove waste. The ventricles provide some buoyancy that does help keep the brain from being damaged, but it would be overbuilt simply for cushioning, and doesn't do that great of a job. Could it have another function?

The pineal gland is pinecone-shaped and surrounded by the largest amount of electrolyte fluid of any structure in the brain. The pineal is the only structure in the brain that is singular and is known to be very sensitive to light and other electromagnetic fields. It also was once considered vestigial, until it was discovered to be the source of melatonin, which promotes sleep. The pineal has been associated with psychic abilities by many, including Edgar Cayce, and its evolutionary origin is literally from a "third eye." Instead of photoreceptors, the pineal contains calcium crystals. These are referred to as "brain sand" and have an unknown function. Perhaps they play a role in our "inner visions."

Nature's Fiberoptics: Holograms and the Construction of Reality

How could savants, or anyone else, know things without deriving them, or having previous exposure? Do they tap into an information field? Could information about everything be organized holographically? That would mean that all information is somehow encoded in each of the parts, including each of us. In other words, in order to obtain nonlocal information, we wouldn't need to go anywhere external to ourselves to find it.

Evidence that holographic information could pertain to human physiology can be found in iridology and reflexology, which are predicated upon there being a representation of the health of our entire body in our eyes and feet. Iridology describes how the appearance of our eyes changes in specific ways when we are ill, whereas reflexology offers a means of healing internal body parts by massaging the corresponding sections of our feet. There isn't any known anatomical foundation for these relationships, which suggests that holography might indeed be playing a role.

More evidence for holography comes from our brains construction of a multi-sensory reality that we experience as unified and happening outside of our bodies. Neuroscientists say this construction of reality occurs in our head, but we are usually fooled into confusing this fabrication with reality itself, because all of our senses align so perfectly with our physical environment. An illustration of our brain's capacity for construction of a virtual reality can be found in our visual blind spots. All vertebrates have blind spots created by the lack of receptors where optic nerves exit at the back of their eyes, but blind spots aren't black holes in our visual fields. Our brains automatically use information from the visual field immediately surrounding these blind spots to fill them in with matching colors and textures (like a sophisticated computer graphics program). This discrepancy between what we see and physical reality isn't usually a problem, unless something, such as a truck, enters from our blind spot, and we hadn't seen it coming.

Out-of-body experiences (OBEs) could be regarded as presenting an even more dramatic illustration that we are constructing a virtual reality. During an OBE, people report seeing the world from a perspective impossible from within their body, as though their viewpoint has separated from their physical self. OBEs suggest our brains are able to construct a perception of our surroundings from any point of view. This is similar to medical scans that can take multiple images in parallel physical planes and use them to construct images viewable from any perspective. In other words, OBEs suggest that the integration of our sensory input might be holographic, but how?

In the laboratory holograms are created by lasers. This didn't seem to have any application to biology until recently. Biological organisms create "bio-photons," which are information carrying packets of light. Most of this light is used for biological processes, but some is released. We literally glow, albeit 1000 times below what can be detected by the naked eye. (Kobayashi, 2009) The light we emit varies with our diurnal cycle, being stronger at 4pm than in the early morning. It is also affected by our state of consciousness; highly experienced meditators have been shown to emit fewer photons during their meditations.

Our embryological development, and renewal of tissues, also appear to be directed by light. This solves one of the biggest mysteries in developmental biology: how does it happen so rapidly? When cells divide, research suggests only one bio-photon per cell is needed to orchestrate the 100,000 processes occurring per second. It was in such replicating cells that biological light was first discovered by Alexander Gurwitsch in 1922. Gurwitsch called the blue streaks of light "mitogenic rays," because of their appearance during "mitosis," or cellular division. After a decade of research and over one hundred publications on mitogenic rays, Gurwitsch's discovery was debunked… because others couldn't replicate his work. In order to detect the weak ultraviolet light, sensitive photomultipliers were required for it to be made visible.

A picture of Gurwitsch's "mitogenic rays" did not look like a recognizable structure at the time, but when I saw it I could see that it was exactly the shape of the spindle apparatus, the structure scientists later found to be instrumental to cellular division. For me, this adds credibility to Gurwitsch's claim. The spindle apparatus is composed of microtubules, which are present in all cells with DNA in a nucleus (eukaryotes), and some bacteria. Like glial cells and "junk DNA," microtubules were also initially misunderstood. They were regarded as no more than scaffolding to maintain cell structure, and to assist in cellular division, where they form spindles to align our chromosomes in matching pairs for replication. They then pull the chromosomal pair apart into two new identical cells. Our bodies are constantly renewing themselves, destroying cells that are replaced by new ones. The total amount of body mass that we are turning over daily is astonishing. This is estimated to be equivalent to replacing one of our arms every day. Microtubules are guiding all of these cellular processes, but how?

Microtubules are present in organisms ranging from single celled eukaryotes to humans. They serve various vital roles in each of our cells, including sperm, where they form the structure that provides its motility. Cilia and flagella are ancient structures. The primary cilium is a microtubule-based organelle that projects from the surface of all vertebrate cells, like an antenna. It has gone from being a poorly understood curiosity to one that is recognized as extremely important for normal development, as well as playing a role in inherited human diseases and cancer (Parker, Kavallaris & McCarroll, 2014).

Microtubules help guide neuronal migration during development and guide the formation of connections between our brain cells. When a neuron migrates, microtubules stretch the neuronal cytoplasm, producing an extension in the direction it is moving. The microtubules then relocate the cellular nucleus to the front of the migrating cell, and retract the extension lagging behind. Microtubules are especially prevalent in our brains, where each neuron contains up to 2500, in parallel like the rails of multiple train tracks. This unique arrangement is too excessive to be simply structural support for growth. This suggests they are serving another function, and one that is specific to the brain.

Microtubules fall apart under anesthesia, correlated with when a patient loses consciousness, which is why microtubules became of such interest to consciousness researchers Stuart Hameroff and Sir Roger Penrose. This effect on microtubules appears to be the mechanism of many anesthetics, which have widely variable molecular structures and sizes from each other. Microtubules and their associated proteins also can become bunched up, and when they do, they make up the tangles associated with Alzheimer's disease and boxer's dementia. Many scientists and clinicians have assumed that the dementia is due to the tangles being cellular debris that interferes with normal neuronal function. I would like to suggest that the microtubules play a more primary function in consciousness.

Experiments by Anirban Bandyopadhyay, a physicist at the National Institute of Material Sciences in Tsukuba, Japan, have shown that microtubules are biological "super-conductors," composed of 40,000 tubulin protein units each. By organizing into a microtubule, tubulin can conduct electricity over three hundred times faster than a single tubulin protein. This is very unique. Usually, larger structures have more resistance than their constituent parts, and therefore conduct more slowly. Tubulin can combine to create many shapes, assembling long enough to do their job, after which they fall apart. Microtubules are constantly being built and rebuilt, several times an hour. What controls this, and determines the repurposing of these proteins? Tubulin units are magnetic dipoles, so they might be under the influence of very local electromagnetic fields.

The idea of light playing a major role in brain functioning is already being investigated, because neurons contain many light sensitive molecules, such as porphyrin rings, lipid chromophores, and aromatic amino acids. Microtubules are cylinders with hollow cores that are lined with a monolayer film of water. This may be ideal for reflecting and transmitting biological light in our cells in a highly organized way. The source of light for microtubules might be mitochondria, which are abundant in neurons. They appear too numerous to be merely satisfying the energy requirements of synaptic functioning, and also contain several prominent chromophores that react to light.

If microtubules are transmitting light with a uniform frequency, that would create an organic fiber-optic system, similar to lasers. Interference patterns created by the light waves from two lasers are all it takes to produce a three-dimensional holographic image in which information about the whole is stored in each of the parts. Perhaps microtubules are the means of encoding biological information holographically.

The Primacy of Consciousness: Type III Post-materialism

What if our brains are quantum computers that can access, and store, information about all of space-time as holograms? This could potentially answer many of the mysteries of consciousness, but would it address all? ...not completely. We still don't have a mechanism for free will, the mind-body connection, or for how we seem to have an impact on others by prayer. All of these might suggest consciousness is primary.

I wondered, can the sources of coherent light in each of our cells help us to understand the mind-body connection? They could be functioning similarly to lasers in more ways than one. We already know that our microtubules play a role in cellular repair, so they also must play a role in self-healing. Visualizing our body fighting cancer, or healing from a wound, has been shown to be effective in restoring health. A friend who was a paramedic accidentally amputated his leg with a power saw, creating a clean cut. This enabled him to become one of the first candidates for surgical reattachment of a leg. Two weeks post-op he developed gangrene and was on the verge of re-amputation. He asked for another couple of weeks, during which he visualized his muscles, blood vessels, and nerves as healthy, and in the process of reconnecting. He now has a fully functional leg, and attributes this successful recovery entirely to his anatomical knowledge and ability to visualize.

If the efficacy of prayer is real, our model must also accommodate this, and most religions proclaim that such miracles can, and have, happened. As a doctor I have heard many accounts of cancer and other conditions disappearing after church congregations prayed for someone. Doctors are trained with a materialist model that cannot account for this. Nonetheless, research on the efficacy of prayer was so conclusive for Larry Dossey, M.D. that I heard him say at a conference that it would be malpractice for a doctor to not include it in their therapeutic toolkit.

How could prayer have an effect on another? I don't know, but to label such a seemingly miraculous or improbable event as impossible without further investigation would be premature and unscientific. We don't have a sufficient model for understanding how, or where, our immaterial thoughts arise, or how they influence our bodies, yet we experience these realities daily. If we don't have a model for understanding these phenomena, we also don't have one to discount anomalous phenomena.

Furthermore, our thoughts can impact inanimate objects if they are connected directly or by Bluetooth, as is the case with brain-machine interfaces that are being used to control prostheses. A small array of 90 electrodes connected to the brain's motor cortex has enabled chimpanzees and humans to manipulate a robotic arm to feed themselves. Even more impressive is a Bluetooth device for quadriplegics which demonstrated that one's thoughts could directly control a flight simulator. This ability to integrate something that doesn't belong to our body is apparent in other ways. When we use a tool or instrument repeatedly, over time our brain incorporates it into the somatosensory map of our body, as though it is an extension of ourselves. This explains how people can become a musical master through tens of thousands of hours of practice. Such people can look totally "at one" with their instrument, and can demonstrate this by playing it without looking, and while doing other things. They can play it as easily as we move our fingers, without much conscious thought. This is just one of several examples of what scientists call "embodied cognition."

Some people have such a fragmented sense of self that they have a condition called dissociative identity disorder (DID), which was formerly labeled "multiple personality disorder." When people with dissociative identity disorder shift "personalities," this can instantaneously change their physiology, such as immediately turning off an allergic reaction. We don't have a medication anywhere close to being that immediate, selective, and powerful. How could a shift in personality, or consciousness, cause physiological responses to occur much faster than by any known means? If biological light is involved, the speed is no longer so hard to fathom.

Could the rapid changes in physiology in DID be related to other mysteries in mind-body medicine? In study after study, thirty percent of people taking a placebo will get better because of believing in pharmaceutical treatments. This is so predictable that a new medication has to fare better than a placebo to be considered effective. Similarly, the "nocebo" effect accounts for side effects in those wary of medications who are actually ingesting only an inactive sugar pill. Saying our thoughts achieve these effects through their impact on our immune and neurological systems skirts around the question of how. What could translate our thoughts into chemical and electromagnetic responses? Once again, could this be directed by internal light?

Ironically, some of the best evidence that the impact of our beliefs and desires can extend beyond our bodies is the repeatable finding that the beliefs of researchers impact their experimental outcomes. The so-called "sheep-goat effect" goes beyond any potential bias towards a particular interpretation of data. It is reliably reproduced, just like the placebo effect, and is particularly problematic for parapsychology research. People on both sides of a scientific debate have gotten the results they expected, so they continue to disagree.

Researchers try to avoid this, but the phenomenon seems to have a mind of its own.

The famous Double Slit experiments are another way of examining the power of consciousness. They imply that our focused attention could be playing a primary role in the creation of reality, especially at the subatomic scale, where just the act of observing and measuring can convert waveforms of potentiality into particles. This is why both photons and electrons are considered to have wave-like and particle-like properties, depending upon whether they are observed. This application of quantum theory to the study of consciousness has been taken a step further by researcher Dean Radin, PhD. He demonstrated that when meditating monks focus remotely on a quantum measuring system, it has the same effect as direct observation and measurement (Radin, Michel, Galdamez, Wendland, Rickenbach & Delorme, 2012).

The quantum Zeno effect is similar in that it demonstrates that continuous measurement, or observation, decreases radioactive decay. Infrequent measurements actually enhance radioactive decay, which is called the "quantum anti-Zeno effect." Why should frequency of measurement matter? Does measurement stabilize the system? Does frequent measurement slow down time, which we are able to perceive primarily as a result of change?

Further support for the effect of consciousness on inanimate objects comes from research conducted by the Princeton Engineering Anomalies Research (PEAR) lab using random number generators (RNGs). When vast numbers of people are focusing on the same event, such as the O.J. Simpson trial, there are marked changes in the tracings of these RNGs (Jahn & Dunne, 2011). How could the combined consciousness of individuals result in a detectable decrease in randomness? Could consciousness become more coherent when we are all focusing on the same thing?

We must conclude that, as physicist John Wheeler said, "We

participate in co-creating the universe." In this model, both free will and determinism co-exist, but how, and what is their relationship? Are they equal partners? Does this mean consciousness is primary, coexisting along with other primary forces? It appears to, but this is only the second type of post-materialist model and might not explain everything. In order for science to accept the third model, consciousness would need to be fundamental.

Is Consciousness Fundamental? Type III Post-materialism

If consciousness is not just primary, but fundamental to everything, what would that mean? Could all four forces of nature, which we think of as holding everything together, be synonymous with consciousness? Physicists still do not understand the four forces and disagree on how to unify them into a consistent model, even though they have mathematics to describe them. Einstein said that gravity is the result of the curvature of space-time by massive objects, whereas the Standard Model considers gravity to be the result of gravitational waves and gravitons. The strong force keeps the nucleus of the atom together, although we don't know how, and the electromagnetic force concerns the physical interaction between electrically charged particles. The weak force, unlike other forces, is more easily defined by its failure during radioactive decay, rather than by its role in attraction.

Could the quantum Zeno effect, in which frequent measurement delays radioactive emission, be showing us that what we call the weak force and consciousness are related? This is not as far-fetched as it might sound. Maurice Goodman is a physicist at Dublin Institute of Technology who did a mathematical analysis of the fundamental forces after it was discovered that not all neutrinos are massless. This meant the weak force has a range of influence like other forces. Goodman found that the relative distance over which a fundamental force could act always determined the size of its basic unit. Why? Because it is the "maximum uncertainty in position allowable" for any parts under its influence. For example, astronomy studies galaxies, and gravitational force determines their size; chemistry studies atoms, and the electromagnetic force determines the size of the electrons which bind atoms together; nuclear science studies nucleons, and the "Strong 1" force determines the size of their associated quarks; meson science studies mesons, and the "Strong 2" force determines the size of its quarks.

Biology studies cells, but there is currently no force or subatomic particle associated. When Goodman calculated the range of influence of the weak force, it turned out to be the same as the size of a single cell, potentially linking it to biology (Goodman, 2015). Cells are the basic unit of life for animals and plants, and to become larger we must become multi-cellular. Goodman calculated the decoherence time for the cell, and found it to be in the right range to be a quantum system. Like electromagnetism, the weak force has chirality (i.e., symmetric in such a way that the structure and its mirror image are not superimposable. Chiral compounds are typically optically active). A force with chirality could explain why biologically active versions of molecules tend to be left-handed. All four forces appear to be necessary to hold each of our most basic components together, thereby making life possible. However, we can't say for sure whether they are the same as consciousness, or even its consequence.

For the third model to be valid, we need to find a phenomenon that could suggest consciousness is fundamental. It would need to be something that transcends our ordinary view of consciousness, and super-synchronicities might be just that. These synchronicities are so complex and specific that they defy the odds of being unrelated, but the mechanism for them is unclear. Some suggest an organizing principle, or outside force, can impact our behaviors in the most peculiar ways.

For example, research on the lives of over sixty pairs of identical twins, raised apart since birth, show many uncanny similarities. They often had the same interests, which isn't surprising, but they did things such as: marry people with the same names, choose the same names for their pets, drive the same color and make of car, and even build similar white benches around a tree at their homes just before meeting. When making contact for the first time, many wore virtually identical outfits with the same idiosyncrasies, such as seven bracelets on one arm (Segal, 1999). This level of detail can't be attributed to genetics. The human genome is only between 19,000 and 22,000 genes, and a high percentage of those overlap with the plant kingdom. It also probably isn't even epigenetic, because epigenomes of identical twins raised together become increasingly distinct from each other over time. If anything, the epigenome should be more diverse when raised apart. What could cause the smallest details of our lives to be under an influence beyond our conscious will? What are synchronicities, such as those between the twins, telling us?

I have experienced several super synchronicities during the course of my life that don't have genetics as a possible confounding variable and will give a couple of examples. One involves the Super Bowl. I have never been a sports fan, but I have occasionally gone to a party where people are watching a game. One year I was invited to a Super Bowl party at which they played a gambling game. They had a sheet of paper with the digits zero through nine written along the vertical edge of a grid for one team, and along the upper horizontal edge for the other. We each paid a small sum to claim two squares as our own and could only choose squares that were not already taken. At half time, and again at the end of the game, we would look at the scores for each team and use the last digits to see whose square won. This was the first time that I had ever seen this game, so it was considered beginners luck when I won at halftime.

As we approached the end of the second half, the host of the party looked to see who might win. Once again it looked like me. Then another score was made, changing the digits. To everyone's surprise I still won, but with my other square.

The next year, I was again invited to the party, but not allowed to participate in the game. This struck me as humorous, and I told the story to a friend at the gym the following day. Within minutes of telling him, a woman entered the area where we were. I had seen her before, but didn't really know her, and she was deep in conversation with another woman. Normally, I would have had my earbuds in for music while working out, but I had just finished sharing the conversation about the game. I listened to what she was saying with interest, because the first thing she said was that she had gone to a Super Bowl party and played a game that she had never played before, and its description exactly matched mine. She not only won at halftime, she had the same type of "double hit" in the second half.

An even more dramatic example of a super synchronicity occurred over twelve years ago. Shortly before leaving Oregon to meet with Gary Schwartz for the first time, a northern spotted owl appeared at my kitchen windowsill. He seemed very interested in what I was doing and allowed me to get very close to him. Later that day, I needed to leave for the airport, and was disappointed that we could not spend more time together. While I was away, he continued to go to the window as though he was looking for me. The person who was watching over my house and animals became concerned. This behavior was so unusual, he thought that my feathered friend might be ill. He called the local wildlife rescue team, who found the owl had been tagged, and was over twenty miles from his habitat, which is where they returned him. When I arrived home, I was sad to see him gone.

Months later, a couple knocked on my door. They introduced

themselves as having been interested in my house two years previously, when it was for sale before I purchased it. They asked me if I would consider selling it to them. I told them "no," but gave them a tour of the property to show them the renovations I had done. When we came to the kitchen window, I told them about the northern spotted owl. The gentleman, a psychologist named Gary, told me that he could relate. He was grieving the disappointing loss of a raven. Ravens can acquire speech, similar to parrots. One day Gary was at his property when a raven flew up to his roof and said, "I'll help you if you help me." Gary became enchanted with his new friend, but months later his raven was accidentally stepped on by his horse. The veterinarian knew it was against the law to keep wild animals as pets and euthanized him. Gary was hurt and shocked.

This story caught my attention for many reasons. During my lunch in Arizona with Gary Schwartz, who is also a psychologist, I had told him about my long history of synchronicities with ravens. This struck him as unusual. He then took me to his house, where I pointed out that the Native American art he had been collecting for years actually depicted the raven, and not the eagle, as he had thought. This led to his intense fascination with raven synchronicities, which is why, after the couple left my house, I called Gary to tell him the latest. Just as I finished telling him my story, there was a knock at his door. He opened it, and I could hear what the couple had to say: "Excuse us for interrupting. We were interested in buying your house when it was for sale two years ago. We just stopped by on the chance you might consider reselling it." I just about fell off of my chair. Perhaps consciousness is primary and fundamental. It certainly has a sense of humor.

Conclusions

In my book, *The ESP Enigma*, I presented research for accepting anomalous phenomena as real, and as clues to a new model for brain functioning. In this chapter I have outlined a new model that can potentially explain AEs by incorporating fundamental advances in neuroscience. Unlike the neuro-centric model most people accept, my model acknowledges that glial cells are vitally important, and might hold the answers to many of our questions.

Astrocytes are the most abundant type of glial cells, and perfectly positioned to be the primary integrators of information in our brains. They outnumber neurons by a ratio of at least two to one in humans, and higher ratios of astrocytes to neurons correlate with higher intelligence across individuals and species. They monitor the activity at neuronal synapses, which are now considered tripartite. They also have appendages that attach to the surface of the brain at its pia mater. Astrocytes appear to communicate by waves of calcium ions that correlate with creative thinking. They are highly interconnected, which provides a fast means of distributing information widely across the brain.

Neurons are necessary for our experience of a multi-sensory virtual reality. Our sensory neurons receive input from sensory organs, including our skin, and motor neurons direct our motor output. The sensory cortices divide this input into its various components before recombining them into a seamless whole. This is why a small stroke in a section of the visual cortex for integrating color can selectively eliminate color perception, while otherwise leaving vision intact. Our dreamscape can be just as rich as the experience we have while awake, because both are constructed by our brains. However, many people report only dreaming in black and white, so some sensory information can be missing. The dreamscape is not limited to sensory input, which is what primarily dictates the awake experience.

Neurons contain microtubules in numbers that exceed what would be needed for structural purposes. Microtubules are cylindrical structures that might play a major role in encoding information.

They have significant electromagnetic properties, and anesthesiologist Stuart Hameroff and Physicist Roger Penrose believe they might be acting as quantum microprocessors. I propose that they might also transmit coherent light as a means of encoding information.

If all information is embedded holographically, throughout space-time, it would be present everywhere. Evidence for this is the fact that savants can access remote or abstract information without any clear explanation as to how. Acquired savant syndrome suggests this potential might be latent in all of us.

Every sensory organ has an area of cerebral cortex dedicated to it. If there is a cortical area for navigating space-time, where would it be? The best candidate is the right temporo-parietal junction (TPJ), which is where the temporal and parietal lobes meet. The temporal lobes are located behind our temples, which is where our hair tends to turn gray first. The name "temple" is derived from the word for "time." The parietal lobe's name comes from the Latin word for "wall," and one of its primary functions is the processing of sensory information about the location of our body and its parts in space.

The left angular gyrus is located in the left TPJ, and is involved in symbolic representation and manipulation, such as performing calculations, and complex language. It is the evolutionarily newest area of our brain (Gerstman, 1940), and enables us to distinguish left from right. Neurologist Norman Geschwind thought it was involved in translating what we read into an internal monologue.

All three of the major ways in which psychics report receiving information appear to involve the angular gyrus, particularly on the right. These are: dreaming, seeing information in an "energy field" around the body, and out-of-body experiences. Consider the following:

Many people have reported receiving psychic information only by dreaming, and never while awake. Therefore, any area involved in psychic dreams would need to be active during dreaming. Unlike most cortical areas, the angular gyrus is active in both waking and dreaming consciousness.

Psychic information received while awake often consists of symbols transmitted in one or another primary sense. Some say they hear the answers; others see them, feel them, or even smell them. The pairing of psychic information with a sense could be a form of synesthesia, and many forms of synesthesia are associated with the angular gyrus (Ramachandran and Hubbard, 2001). Some psychics say they obtain information about us by seeing it in our aura. Seeing auras is considered a form of synesthesia in which one sees moods and personality types as having specific colors associated with them. In my research, seeing auras is commonly reported by autistic children who also claim to "see" their caregiver's mind.

Out-of-body experiences (OBEs) are a third way in which some psychics, such as Ingo Swann, have reported obtaining information. Some psychic dreams can have many characteristics of an OBE. Stimulation of the angular gyrus, or temporoparietal junction, can create a partial out-of-body experience (Blanke et al, 2004). Our brains and bodies generate extremely low frequency electromagnetic waves (ELF waves). Could these somehow be detected? If so, what could be the sensory organ for detecting something as subtle as another's thoughts? The most likely location is in our heads, like our other specialized sensory organs.

Our craniofacial bones, brains, and the protective membranes connected to them, all contain magnetite in magnetosomes, which are formations of iron seen only in living systems. Research by Professor Joseph Kirschvink at Cal Tech has shown that extremely low frequency electromagnetic waves can influence these magnetosomes (Kirschvink, 1992). Could this array of magnetite in our heads function as an electromagnetic wave receiver, transmitter, and/or shield? Could this "Magnetodome" function as a sensory organ that becomes more effective when our other sensory systems are turned down, as happens during meditation and dreaming?

We are left with many questions, but we have the beginnings of a radically new model for consciousness and the brain. Why is a new paradigm important? Our technology has advanced faster than the evolution of our own consciousness. This makes our theory for it increasingly critical to serve as a guide to understanding such things as: who we are, where we come from, what we are capable of doing, who we regard as sane (or insane), and what happens to us after we die. Our current materialist paradigm is not only incomplete and incorrect... it is taking a huge toll. It has rendered us increasingly vulnerable to feelings of estrangement and dehumanization.

The new paradigm emerging from scientific data and observation suggests that consciousness could be primary. We are actively participating in the co-creation of the universe, and we are also part of an elaborate interconnected whole. If this paradigm is widely adopted as valid, it will change everything.

Chapter Ten

Postmaterial Medicine, Health, and Healing

Larry Dossey, MD

Barbara Cummiskey developed symptoms of multiple sclerosis in the 1960s as a fifteen-year-old high-school student in Wheaton, Illinois. Although she was an athletic gymnast, she began to struggle physically. She managed to graduate high school in 1968 and enroll in college but was unable to complete her studies because of increasing disabilities. Her disease progressed rapidly. She had two respiratory arrests in the early 1970s, contracted pneumonia, and required recurrent hospitalizations. One of her lungs collapsed in 1980 and she required a tracheostomy, in which a tube was surgically inserted in her throat through which oxygen was delivered. She lost urinary control and required an indwelling bladder catheter. She further lost bowel control and an ileostomy was performed. Her vision deteriorated and she became legally blind. By 1981 she was given six months to live and was enrolled in hospice care. She became bed-bound, developed severe contractures, and was curled in a constant fetal position. When she could no longer swallow, a feeding tube was inserted into her stomach. Although she had been quite religious, she lost her faith. She was dying. When death appeared imminent, her family and her doctor agreed there would be no CPR or other heroics to prolong her life.

On 7 June 1981 her tragic story was aired on WMBI, a local radio station. During the program prayers were requested for her and other terminally ill individuals in the Wheaton area. Listeners responded enthusiastically and flooded the station with bags of letters.

The same afternoon, with visitors in her room, Barbara heard a male voice say, "My child, get up and walk!" She believed God was speaking to her. Her visitors were astonished when she jumped out of bed, removed her oxygen, and stood on her legs for the first time in years. She was no longer short of breath without oxygen. Her vision returned. Her parents entered the room. She appeared transformed; her mother looked her up and down and exclaimed, "You have muscles again!" Her amazed father waltzed her around the room.

That night, a Sunday, she went with her family and friends to church. She walked from the back of the sanctuary down the central aisle to the front. Everyone knew her, and that she had been close to death. All were shocked, including the minister. Stunned, he fell against the pulpit for support and kept saying, "This is nice. This is very nice...."

The next day Barbara went to the office of Thomas E. Marshall, MD, her internal medicine physician. Dr. Marshall said:

"I thought I was seeing an apparition! Here was my patient, who was not expected to live another week, totally cured. I stopped all her medication and took out her bladder catheter, but she wasn't quite ready to have the tracheostomy tube removed until another visit. No one had ever seen anything like this before. That afternoon, we sent Barb for a chest X-ray. Her lungs were now perfectly normal, with the collapsed lung totally expanded with no infiltrate or other abnormality that had existed before. I have never witnessed anything like this before or since.... Barb has gone on to live a normal life in every way. She subsequently married a minister and feels her calling in life is to serve others...."

Her case is reported by Dr. Marshall in physician Scott J. Kolbaba's 2016 book *Physicians' Untold Stories* (Kolbaba, 2016).

In the 1990s I was peripherally involved in the investigation of an equally startling case dating to the 1950s. It was being revisited by Tamara Jones, a reporter for the *Washington Post*. I had written the 1993 book *Healing Words*, which explored the clinical and experimental evidence surrounding healing intentions and intercessory prayer, and Jones wanted my opinion about the case (Dossey, 1993).

It concerned the experience of Ann O'Neill, a four-year-old girl suffering from acute lymphocytic leukemia in 1952. Ann was hospitalized in the University of Maryland Hospital in Baltimore under the care of Dr. Milton Sacks, a nationally renowned hematologist. At this time her disease was 100 percent fatal; there were no survivors. Ann was close to death. Her burial gown was prepared and a priest had administered last rites. She was given only hours to live. Unwilling to give her up, her feisty mother, with the help of several Catholic nuns, bundled her up and took her from the hospital to a local cemetery where Elizabeth Ann Seton, a revered Catholic nun, was buried. Ann's mother and the nuns laid her at Seton's tomb and prayed that she would be healed. Then they took her back to the hospital.

Several days later, all of Ann's blood tests were normal. She gradually recovered and was discharged from the hospital. Her improvement was not a temporary remission; it was permanent. Nine years later a bone marrow biopsy was performed, revealing no indication of any lingering leukemia. She was eventually declared a miracle cure by the Church. She was alive and well in 1994 when Jones was writing about her case.

Ann's response to her healing? As an adult looking back on the saga she told Jones, "I couldn't understand why people were so overwhelmed…The biggest miracle — people see it every day! The sun, the stars, the trees."

During the Church's investigation of the case Dr. Sacks, Ann's hematologist, affirmed that her prognosis was "inexorably fatal."

Jones asked Dr. Sacks whether there was any case where a remission had been permanent. He replied, "No, not that I know of. They would certainly have been written up." Then Jones inquired why he had not written up Ann's case for publication in a medical journal. He said, "The only reason that this has not been written up ... is that I have been afraid to." He did not elaborate (Jones, 1994).

Promissory Materialism

Throughout my own scientific career, I, like many scientists, have struggled to prove that the brain accounts for the mind. ...[But] to expect the highest brain mechanism or any set of reflexes, however complicated, to carry out what the mind does, and thus perform all the functions of the mind, is quite absurd.
              Wilder Penfield ~ Mysteries of the Mind (1975)

Why was Dr. Sacks afraid to publish Ann O'Neill's important case? He realized, I suspect, that there is no place in modern medicine for the impact of distant healing intentions or intercessory prayers — or for healing from divine voices from on high, to which Barbara Cummiskey attributed her healing. Dr. Sacks's reaction reflected an academic taboo. Because modern medicine is overwhelmingly materialistic in its understanding of disease and treatments, examples such as the Cummiskey and O'Neill cases are commonly shunned. Dr. Sacks probably realized that his professional standing would not have been enhanced by endorsing spontaneous healing in a disease that was uniformly fatal. These cases represent a "third rail" that can damage the reputation of any medical professional who embraces them.

The logic of "promissory materialism" applies to cases of this sort — the idea that in the future, when we know enough, not so long from now, we'll be able to explain these cures in terms of a material, physical approach. According to this "explanation," the effects of mind or consciousness in health and illness are trivial. Mind and consciousness are not fundamental, stand-alone phenomena, but are merely the results of electrochemical processes in the brain. Accordingly, there are no independent mental states, thoughts, and beliefs that *could* influence one's body on their own, let alone influence another, distant individual's body through healing intentions or compassionate prayers.

These objections not only ignore empirical evidence, they are also contradictory and self-refuting. As Nobel neurophysiologist Sir John Eccles put it, "Professional philosophers and psychologists think up the notion that there are no thoughts, come to believe that there are no beliefs, and feel strongly that there are no feelings" (Eccles & Robinson, 1985).

Materialism — the doctrine that nothing exists except matter and its movements and modifications, and that consciousness and will are wholly due to material agency — haunts modern medicine. The promissory nature of materialism was emphasized by Eccles and philosopher of science Karl Popper. "[P]romissory materialism [is] a superstition without a rational foundation," Eccles said. "[It] is simply a religious belief held by dogmatic materialists...who confuse their religion with their science. It has all the features of a messianic prophecy...." (Eccles & Robinson, 1985).

Those who dismiss the causal efficacy of the mind appear to be hoist by their own petard. If their minds are derivative, fictional, or nonexistent — neurochemistry in disguise — then their thoughts are merely what their brains *make* them think. If their thoughts are biologically dictated, why then should we believe them? They have no claim to truth because they have not arrived at their conclusions by careful deliberation and the weighing of evidence. As J. B. S. Haldane, the evolutionary biologist, expressed this situation, "If my mental processes are determined wholly by the motions of the atoms in my brain, I have no reason to suppose that my beliefs are true …

and hence I have no reason for supposing my brain to be composed of atoms" (Haldane, 1927). But in fact, not even the most passionate materialists live their lives as if their choices and thoughts are determined by their anatomy and physiology. That's why, when they kiss their children goodnight they say, "I love you," not "My brain loves you."

In order to account for cases such as Barbara Cummiskey's and Ann O'Neill's, an approach is required that includes but goes beyond materialism: the perspective of postmaterial science.

How I Became Interested in a Post-material Approach

'Tis healthy to be sick sometimes.
~ Henry David Thoreau (1993)

My interest in a postmaterial role in medicine had, literally, a painful beginning (Dossey, 1991). At age fourteen I began to experience severe migraine headaches. My particular malady was the so-called classic type of migraine — severe headache, temporary partial blindness and "flashing lights" involving much of my field of vision, followed by nausea, vomiting, and hours of near-incapacitation. I lived in dread of these episodes, which seemed to come unpredictably out of nowhere. I recall desperately pounding my head with my fists, trying to make the pain stop. Through the years I went to physicians who reassured me that it was "only" migraine and nothing worse such as a brain tumor, in which case, they suggested, I would already be dead. The myriad medications I tried failed to work. I decided I was simply stuck with the problem.

During medical school the headaches and visual problems began to trouble me in another way. I became concerned that sooner or later I would experience a typical episode of partial blindness in a life-or-death situation with a patient, and I would be putting their life at risk. Other physicians might not be around to bail me out. I also felt guilty because I had not disclosed this medical problem on my application to medical school. I feared it was only a matter of time until this was discovered. What to do? Since I'd already tried every therapy to no avail, the only solution I could think of was simply to drop out of medical school.

I made an appointment to see my faculty advisor to inform him of my decision. He was the chairman of a major department and a physician of the old school — gentlemanly, avuncular, urbane, and enormously kind. After I finished my confession there was a period of silence while I waited for his response. I expected withering criticism for not having revealed my problem, but this did not happen. Finally, he said with a gentle smile, "I think you should do nothing and just relax." I was stunned. What a novel idea! *Never* had I considered relaxing, let alone doing nothing. "When I was young," he continued, "I, too, had migraine headaches. They went away, which is typical as one gets older. Even if you do nothing your headaches will get better, so there is nothing to worry about. Above all you must stay in medical school. That is the only thing you *must* do." By this time my mind was a blur. I don't remember what, if anything, I offered in response. I left his office in complete confusion.

He was wrong. My headaches did not get better but continued as before. But it no longer mattered as much, because now the entire problem *seemed* different. My advisor had given me hope, the expectation that things would improve. He had not manipulated my illness but only the *meaning* it contained for me. I do not mean that I embraced migraine headaches thereafter; I would have preferred they disappear, as they practically did when I eventually discovered biofeedback therapy years later. Yet my response went beyond being merely hopeful. A new relationship with my problem slowly developed, as the psychological distance between migraine and me diminished.

I began to regard headaches not as something I *had* but as

something I *was*.

My faculty advisor had functioned as a "meaning therapist." With only a few compassionate words he taught me not a new way of *doing* but a different way of *being*. At that time the concept of meaning was insignificant in my life. But even though I could not articulate what had happened, I experienced firsthand the power of meaning to transform the toll of illness, *even though the pathology remained*. This was my first exposure to a postmaterial approach to medicine. These new meanings helped me stay in medical school and keep my career on track.

As I would discover later, some prominent scientists were addressing the importance of meaning. This included the eminent physicist David Bohm, who said, "Meaning is being. A change of meaning is a change of being" (Bohm, 1991).

The importance of meaning extends beyond its role in health and wellness, of course. Meaning helps us maintain balance in *all* adversity, to be receptive to whatever wisdom life's difficulties may convey. Rainer Maria Rilke, the great German poet, expressed this attitude in his *Letters to a Young Poet* (Rilke, 1954):

"Why do you want to shut out of your life any agitation, any pain, any melancholy, since you really do not know what these states are working in you? ...If there is anything morbid in your processes, just remember that sickness is the means by which an organism frees itself of foreign matter; so one must just help it to be sick, to have its whole sickness and break out with it, for that is its progress."

Years later, as mentioned, following the completion of medical school, internship, service as a field battalion surgeon in Vietnam, and residency training in internal medicine, I learned how to profoundly modify my physiology through biofeedback training. Biofeedback involves "feeding back" the effect of thoughts and emotions on various internal processes through electronic monitoring. This enables one to modify muscle tension and autonomic processes that normally lie outside of conscious awareness — pulse rate, blood pressure, brain waves, the temperature and electrical conductivity of the skin, and so on. After only a few biofeedback sessions my migraine headaches diminished by around 90 percent. Biofeedback had another impact. It led me to explore the evidence suggesting that consciousness might be used intentionally to affect not just one's own body, but also the physiology of another, distant individual who is unaware of the effort. It also led to the practice of meditation, which has remained an important part of my life.

The experimental evidence for the physiological effects of intentionality began to accelerate in the 1980s. Since then the distant impact of conscious intentions has been affirmed in hundreds of studies in humans, animals, and simple biological and inanimate systems. These studies have been done in real-life settings such as hospitals, as well as in controlled laboratory settings. In a series of books, I have examined how these methods can be seamlessly combined with conventional efforts, and how these combinations can often be more effective than when either approach is employed alone (Dossey, 1999).

In this effort I am accompanied by an army of allies. In 1990 only three medical schools in the US featured the role of healing intentions and spirituality in health. Currently the great majority of American medical schools formally address this evidence in their curricula.

How has scientific medicine evolved to include meaning, spirituality, mind, and consciousness alongside physical, material interventions? Let's take a closer look.

The Telecebo Effect

The history of modern medicine can be read as the attempt to segregate therapies into specific categories according to their material or psychological characteristics. We have focused incessantly on whether particular therapies are primarily conventional, allopathic, material, natural, psychological, holistic, complementary, integrative, integral, spiritual, or some combination thereof. We are learning that there are no pure forms of therapy. Our world is not so constructed as to permit non-interacting, independent, walled-off attempts to help people heal. That is because the effort to assign mind and matter to totally separate domains does not comport with the informational structure of the world we occupy. The world, to some degree, conforms to and reflects our conscious activity. This is a key lesson from the quantum-relativistic revolution of the twentieth century (Jung, 1975; Planck, 1931; Schrödinger, 1960).

This discovery has been slow to penetrate medicine. The prejudice still exists that "real" medicine must be physical in nature; anything else is "all in the mind" and is therefore insubstantial and second-rate. As the surgical maxim says, "To cut is to cure." Consistent with the materialistic outlook, health is also viewed in overwhelmingly physical terms. Health is a temporary phenomenon because physical malfunction and decline are inevitable and disease is always lurking. As a third-year medical student once told me, "A healthy person is someone who has not been completely worked up."

We have learned, however, that ostensibly material therapies such as surgery and the administration of hold-in-your-hand pharmaceuticals partake of profound psychological effects originating in a patient — the well-known placebo phenomena. But these therapies also reflect the direct effects of the intentions and emotions of the physician, nurse, or other healthcare professional administering them. I've called these latter influences *telecebo* effects (Dossey, 2015).

"Telecebo" is a neologism formed by combining the Greek *tele*, meaning far or distant, with the fragment *cebo* from "placebo." Telecebo effects are not generated by a patient; they are an exteriorization of a clinician's, nurse's, therapist's, or healer's intentions and thoughts for a patient's welfare. These mental efforts can operate nonlocally at a distance, bypassing sensory mediation. These effects can merge seamlessly with a patient's own self-generated placebo responses and with the direct effects of medications and surgery in a cascade vectored toward healing.

In humans, placebo effects are believed to be stimulated by the empathy, compassion, likeability, and trustworthiness that patients sense in their physician and/or the therapies she employs. Patients, sensing these qualities, generate healthful mental responses in their own minds. These healthful effects are considered to be limited to an individual patient, simply because mental effects are regarded as originating in, and confined to, the brain and body of the individual experiencing them. It is considered axiomatic that my thoughts cannot directly affect your body, and your thoughts cannot directly affect mine. Telecebo goes further. It expresses both kinship with, and difference from, the placebo response—kinship, in that both telecebo and placebo effects arise from intentions, thoughts, and emotions; difference, in that placebo responses arise within a patient, while telecebo effects originate from a clinician.

The telecebo phenomenon can be completely invisible to both clinician and patient, if both of them accept the taboo that these effects are forbidden in science and cannot exist. In this case, the clinician may misinterpret telecebo effects as placebo responses originating within a patient's own body, or perhaps dismiss them as the nonspecific results of her empathy, compassion, or simply good bedside manner; or the physician may simply attribute telecebo effects to the power of the therapy that's being utilized.

Even if a clinician is aware that telecebo effects exist, they can still be elusive, because in any given clinician-patient interaction it may be impossible to distinguish them from placebo responses originating in the patient.

So how do we know telecebo effects exist? We know because we can tease telecebo effects apart from placebo responses, as in hundreds of experiments and reports involving both humans and nonhumans, as we shall see. The data from experiments involving nonhumans are especially revealing. As far as we know, nonhumans don't think positively or engage in symbolic meaning to the degree of humans, so that if healing intentions are effective in lower animals, plants, microbes, or chemical reactions, and if they occur at a distance beyond the reach of the senses, as we shall see shortly, the results are presumably not due to placebo effects but to the results of telecebo-related intentions from the clinician, healer, experimenter, or researcher.

The Eras of Medicine

Although therapies cannot be pigeonholed into rigid, non-interacting categories, we can still paint with a broad brush and glimpse how they have largely settled out (See Table 1). Medical historians generally report that medical practice in the United States began to take on a scientific look during the 1860s, the decade of the American Civil War. During this decade, medicine began to advance beyond therapies such as bleeding, purging, leeching, and crude medical-surgical interventions to eventually include sophisticated surgical procedures, medications, anesthetics, irradiation, immunizations, resuscitation techniques, and public health measures.

These dazzling developments were of immense importance and are still dominant. Like the therapies they displaced, they are overwhelmingly physical in nature, describable according to classical Newtonian concepts of space, time, matter and energy. Using a historical template, we can designate this early venture into a true science of medicine as Era I. In Era I medicine, health is considered a physical, material, bodily process in which consciousness is considered to play an insignificant, negligible, or wholly absent role. Thus, Era I medicine can be called materialistic, physical, or mechanical medicine.

In the post-World War II period, the concept of psychosomatic illness began to gain traction. Certain illnesses were believed to be worsened and possibly caused by aberrant mental states. Among these maladies were essential hypertension, various headache syndromes, and certain gastrointestinal malfunctions. The mind also was shown to exert healthful actions through placebo effects. Today these developments are generally referred to as mind-body medicine. Following our historical template, we can designate these developments as Era II medicine, the second major period in the evolution of a scientific medicine. Era II medicine was a dramatic departure from Era I, because it acknowledged the causal power of thought and emotions within single individuals. Therapies capitalizing on these effects are now quite numerous. Stress management in general, mindfulness meditation, imagery, visualization, and hypnosis are examples. Era II medicine did not displace Era I medicine; these approaches are complementary and are widely used in conjunction with each other.

We are now seeing the emergence of Era III or nonlocal, transpersonal medicine. Just as Era II or mind-body medicine was a radical advance over Era I or mechanical, materialistic medicine, Era III is a dramatic advance over both Eras I and II. The first two eras of medicine involved a local space-time view in which their effects were confined to an individual person or patient. Era III recognizes distant, nonlocal effects of consciousness, in which the intentions, thoughts, and emotions of an individual can affect not only her body, as in Era II, but also the bodies of distant, other individuals. The effects of consciousness in Era III are nonlocal with respect to both space and time, capable of operating outside the here-and-now. Era III effects do not disregard the effects of Eras I and II; Era III includes them and is compatible with them. In fact, the boundaries between all three eras are indistinct, allowing them to blend in compatible, additive ways.

Both Eras I and II can be largely understood in terms of classical physics and its linear, causal framework. Not so, the nonlocal, transpersonal effects of Era III. New concepts such as nonlocality and entanglement, and the view of consciousness as fundamental, nonreductive, nonderivative, and unitary appear necessary to accommodate the burgeoning clinical and experimental evidence that necessitates the Era III category of healing.

A premise underlying Era III is that minds at some level are connected and unitary. I've called Era III *nonlocal* medicine, as mentioned, leaning on the concept of nonlocality in modern physics. According to experimental evidence in physics that is practically unchallenged, distant particles that were originally in contact behave as if they are a single particle, even though they may be widely separated at arbitrary distances (Nadeau & Kafatos, 1999). When one particle changes they both change, instantly and to the same degree. These distant, nonlocal correlations display three key characteristics: They are *unmediated* (by energetic signals), *unmitigated* (by increasing spatial separation), and *immediate* (instantaneous) (Herbert, 1987).

That's not to say that the nonlocality of physical particles such as electrons or photons can account for the remote connectedness of minds, or that mental phenomena can be reduced to the behavior of subatomic particles, but that both particles and people display a kind of connectedness that defies separation in space and time (Vedral, 2011).

"Nonlocal" is a fitting description not only for particles but for minds as well, because "nonlocal" literally means "not in a place." Yet we should not equate the two phenomena; we may be dealing with accidental correlations of terminology — analogies, not homologies. Or not. Further scientific investigation may clarify this important issue.

Temporal Medicine and Eternity Medicine

The type of medicine that currently prevails in our culture can also be called Temporal Medicine, because it assumes linear, flowing, unidirectional time with its inevitable correlates of aging, infirmity, disease, and death. But nonlocal mind, upon which Era III medicine is based, reveals another possibility — Eternity Medicine, based on the evidence of a temporally infinite aspect of consciousness (Dossey, 1989, 1999; Jonas & Crawford, 2003).

Table 1 Medical Eras

	Era I	Era II	Era III
Space-Time Characteristic	Local	Local	Nonlocal
Synonym	Mechanical, material, or physical medicine	Mind-body medicine	Nonlocal or transpersonal medicine
Description	Causal, deterministic, describable by classical concepts of space-time and matter-energy. Mind not a factor; "mind" a result of brain mechanisms.	Mind a major factor in healing *within* the single person. Mind has causal power; is thus not fully explainable by classical concepts in physics. Includes but goes beyond Era I.	Mind a factor in healing both *within* and *between* persons. Mind not completely localized to points in space (brains or bodies) or time (present moment or single lifetimes). Mind is unbounded and infinite in space and time —thus omnipresent, eternal, and ultimately unitary or one. Healing at a distance is possible. Not describable by classical concepts of space-time or matter-energy. Includes but goes beyond Era II.
Examples	Any form of therapy focusing solely on the effects of *things* on the body are Era I approaches —including techniques such as acupuncture and homeopathy, the use of herbs, etc. Almost all forms of "modern" medicine — drugs, surgery, irradiation, CPR, etc. — are included	Any therapy emphasizing the effects of consciousness solely within the individual body is an Era II approach. Biofeedback, relaxation, self-hypnosis, imagery, and visualization are included.	Any therapy in which effects of consciousness bridge between different persons is an Era III approach. All forms of distant healing, intercessory prayer, some types of shamanic healing, diagnosis at a distance, telesomatic events, and probably noncontact therapeutic touch are included.

Eternity Medicine comes into play any time we honor our temporally infinite, nonlocal nature. Eternity Medicine recognizes that something, however it is named, exists prior to birth and endures beyond physical death. As a colleague once told me, internal medicine physicians who honor this view might consider themselves as not just internists but also as "eternists."

The assumption of Temporal Medicine is death and annihilation; ultimately all therapies fail, and everyone dies. Eternity Medicine involves immortality — not as something to be acquired, cultivated, or engineered, but as something innate and fundamental, a consequence of our nonlocal consciousness. Life, not death, is now our birthright and a condition of our being (Tart, 1997; Griffin, 1997; Stoeber & Meynell, 1996). As a result, fear relents, the pressure eases, the future brightens. A lightness of being and perhaps a sense of humor enters.

It is difficult to overestimate the importance of this recognition. The fear of total annihilation with physical death has probably caused more suffering throughout human history than all the physical diseases combined. The concept of nonlocal mind and immortality, upon which Eternity Medicine is based, is a potential cure for the human terror of the vanishing of all we are upon death.

Close examination of the studies in distant healing and prayer reveals something extraordinary about this nonlocal mind. Distant healing appears to be intimately connected with love, compassion, and deep caring, just as healers throughout history have maintained (Levin, 1999, 2000). This is one of the greatest lessons of recent healing experiments: love and compassion, operating through nonlocal mind, can remotely change the state of physical bodies.

But not *just* love. Studies in remote influence show also that *harm* can be extended to living things: microbes can be inhibited, cellular function can be retarded, cells can be killed, and the activity of biochemical reactions can be reduced (Dossey, 1997). Negative, nonlocal intentions are indistinguishable from the curses, hexes, and spells in which perhaps all pre-modern cultures (and many modern ones) have believed. In acknowledging this tenebrous side of nonlocal mind, these cultures demonstrate a more complex, sophisticated understanding of consciousness than do we. They accept a dark side of consciousness as simply the way things are, and they gracefully devise methods of protection against this aspect of the world. It is cultures such as our own, which deny a negative, nonlocal factor of consciousness, that often get blindsided by it. In any case, the capacity of humans to extend harm mentally and nonlocally to living things should not be rejected, because this ability can be used for good, for healing, as when human intentions are used to kill cancer cells or invading pathogens (Abe et al, 2012; Bengston & Krinsley, 2000).

The One Mind

...I'm still somebody, even if I'm nowhere.
~ Lawrence Ferlinghetti, *Her* (1960)

If mind is genuinely nonlocal, this implies that individual minds cannot be completely separated and isolated from one another, and may in some ways be joined even if they experience themselves individually. In some dimension, minds might therefore come together to form a single, unitary mind. This recognition is ancient. It is also modern. As Nobel physicist Erwin Schrödinger put it, "To divide or multiply consciousness is something meaningless. In all the world, there is no kind of framework within which we can find consciousness in the plural; this is simply something we construct because of the spatio-temporal plurality of individuals, but it is a false construction…. The category of *number*, of *whole* and of *parts* are then simply not applicable to it" (Schrödinger, 1983). And, "The overall number of minds is just one…. In truth there is only one mind" (Schrödinger, 1969). Astrophysicist Sir Arthur Eddington agreed:

"The idea of a universal Mind or Logos would be, I think, a fairly plausible inference from the present state of scientific theory; at least it is in harmony with it" (Eddington, 1928). And as the eminent physicist David Bohm observed, "Deep down the consciousness of mankind is one. This is a virtual certainty... and if we don't see this it's because we are blinding ourselves to it" (Bohm 1986).

Do we lose our individuality in a single, unitary One Mind? Is individuality swallowed up in a homogeneous, featureless totality? This is a common objection to the concept of nonlocal, shared, unitary mind, but it appears largely groundless in actual experience. Those who enter into the awareness of the One Mind generally report that their sense of individuality does not disappear but exists seamlessly alongside a shared sense of unity. This is an example of what physicist Niels Bohr called *complementarity* — the coming together of apparent opposites to produce a more accurate picture of the whole. One is reminded of a maxim from the field of transpersonal psychology: "In order to transcend the ego, you must first *have* one. In order to go beyond the self, you must first *be* one."

Psychologist William James saw that individuality and a sense of self and personhood are preserved, not extinguished, in the One Mind: We with our lives are like islands in the seas, or like trees in the forest. The maple and the pine may whisper to each other with their leaves... [but] the trees also commingle their roots in the darkness underground, and the islands also hang together through the ocean's bottom. Just so there is a continuum of cosmic consciousness, against which our individuality builds but accidental fences, and into which our several minds plunge as into a mother-sea or reservoir. Our "normal" consciousness is circumscribed for adaptation to our external earthly environment, but the fence is weak in spots, and fitful influences from beyond leak in, showing the otherwise unverifiable common connection (James, 1977).

Planetary Implications

The notion of a separate organism is clearly an abstraction, as is also its boundary. Underlying all this is unbroken wholeness even though our civilization has developed in such a way as to strongly emphasize the separation into parts.
~ David Bohm and Basil J. Hiley (1995)

The experience of the One Mind is crucial in confronting the great challenges we humans face on Earth. Our problems are enormous: global climate change, environmental degradation, pollution, overpopulation, water scarcity, the acidification and degradation of our oceans, food insecurity, endless wars, religious strife, on and on. Many of these problems are caused by unremitting greed and selfishness in individuals who cannot see beyond their own ego and hypertrophied sense of self. It is difficult to confront these problems effectively without dealing with our fragmentation and sense of separateness from one another and the natural world. We need a profound shift in our sense of relatedness. I believe this shift may be facilitated by re-imagining how we connect with others nonlocally through consciousness. A shift to a One-Mind perspective may be our best hope — a sense of unity that is experienced at the deepest emotional levels.

A dramatic example is the "Overview Effect" experienced by astronauts and cosmonauts on returning to Earth (White, 1998). While observing the whole Earth from outer space, they commonly sense that our planet is an integral whole. The customary borders on Earth dissolve into a greater unity. From space, disagreements and divisions are sensed as petty and arbitrary. This shift in perception can be an epiphany that proves life-changing for the astronaut. An example is Edgar Mitchell, the lunar module pilot of the Apollo 14 mission and the sixth human to walk on the moon. Mitchell's epiphany transformed his life on return to one of service to others, and to explorations of consciousness through his founding of IONS, the Institute of Noetic Sciences.

If we genuinely believe we are of One Mind with all others, our existential premises shift. Our resentment of "the other" diminishes and is replaced by love. A shared, universal mind implies that what we do to others we do to ourselves. In the One Mind, the Golden Rule can be recalibrated from the self-oriented "Do unto others as you would have them do unto you," to "Be compassionate toward others because in some sense *they are you.*" The same message surfaces in many wisdom traditions. For instance, when the followers of the Hindu saint Ramana Maharshi asked, "How should we treat others?" he responded, "There are no others" (Dyer, 2010).

Not only can our relationship toward other humans be transformed, but our attitude toward the Earth and all its creatures as well. As novelist Alice Walker has said, "Anything we love can be saved" — including the natural world that sustains us (Walker, 2012).

Clinical Applications

Let's look further at how a nonlocal, postmaterial, Era III approach applies in real life with another clinical example, this time from a professional nurse.

"I suddenly developed a severe headache in the back of my head," the nurse said tearfully. "It was so painful I could not function and had to leave work. This was strange, because I never have headaches. When I reached home and was lying in bed, the phone rang. I learned that my beloved brother had been killed from a gunshot wound to the back of his head, the same place my terrible headache was located. My headache began at the same time the shooting occurred."

The woman was a prominent nurse leader at a major hospital in northern California. The occasion was a Q & A session following an address I had given to senior staff of the hospital consortium to which her hospital belonged. My topic was the importance of empathy, compassion, and caring in healing and healthcare. I had reviewed empirical evidence suggesting that empathy and compassion are more than vaporous emotions that float in our bodies somewhere above our clavicles. They are part of our biological makeup, I suggested. While empathy and compassion arise when we are in the presence of another person, as when a nurse or physician is at the bedside of a patient, evidence suggests their effects may also be felt between individuals at a distance, beyond the reach of the senses. Distant individuals often share feelings, sensations, and thoughts, particularly if they are emotionally close. These experiences, I explained, are often called *telesomatic events*. Hundreds of such cases have been reported over the years, but have been largely ignored (Dossey, 2013).

This discussion had prompted the nurse to reveal her experience to several hundred of her colleagues in the audience. "Now I have a name for what happened between my brother and me," she said. "Now I can talk about it." Her story riveted the audience. When she finished, she was not the only person in the room in tears.

This woman's story is, of course, "only" an anecdote. "Anecdote" comes from the Greek *anekdota*, "things unpublished." Our lives are comprised of anecdotes — stories, happenings, events, and experiences that are all unpublished. Our existence does not unfold as a series of controlled, publishable scientific studies. It is when our experiences form patterns that are shared by others that we should pay particular attention to the messages they may convey.

This nurse's expanded understanding was similar to the "meaning therapy" I experienced in my migraine syndrome, in which a shift in outlook led to an existential readjustment that was psychologically healing.

Levels of Connectedness

Alongside clinical examples, a growing body of experimental evidence supports a nonmaterial, invisible connectivity at several levels of biological complexity. (See Table 2.) All told, these intrinsic connections constitute a foundation for a postmaterial medicine. For example:

Distant Mental Interactions with Living Systems (DMILS)

Experiments generally known as DMILS—*d*istant *m*ental *i*nteractions with *l*iving *s*ystems involve a wide variety of entities such as whole humans, organs, cells, microbes, plants, and animals. In these studies individuals use their intentions to influence biological functions in humans, the growth rates of bacteria and fungi in test tubes and Petri dishes, the rate of wound healing in mice, the healing of transplanted cancers in mice, the function of cells in tissue cultures, the germination rates of seeds, the growth rates of seedlings; and many other phenomena. Examples follow.

Gronowicz and colleagues assessed the effect of Therapeutic Touch (TT) on the proliferation of normal human cells in culture, compared to sham and no-treatment controls. This non-touch technique, which emphasizes healing intentions, was administered twice a week for 2 weeks. Compared to untreated controls, TT significantly stimulated proliferation of fibroblasts (cells that produce collagen and are important in wound healing), tenocytes (tendon cells), and osteoblasts (bone cells) in culture ($P = 0.04, 0.01$, and 0.01, immunocytochemical staining for proliferating cell nuclear antigen (PCNA).

The researchers concluded, "A specific pattern of TT treatment produced a significant increase in proliferation of fibroblasts, osteoblasts, and tenocytes in culture. Therefore, TT may affect normal cells by stimulating cell proliferation" (Gronowicz et al, 2008).

Table 2: A Brief Taxonomy of Nonlocal Communication

Level of Nonlocal Communication	Manifestation of Nonlocal Communication	Significance
Neuron to neuron	When one group of human brain neurons are stimulated, simultaneous changes are seen in distant neurons that are shielded from incoming stimuli.	According to conventional science, nonlocal communication between groups of neurons that are isolated and shielded from each other should not be possible. Yet they behave as a unified, single entity, although far apart. A nonlocal form of connectedness and unity is implied.
Brain to brain	When one person's brain is stimulated, simultaneous changes are registered in a distant brain, as seen on EEG or fMRI brain scan, especially if the individuals are	These events should not occur from the perspective of conventional materialistic science. A nonlocal form of

Level of Nonlocal Communication	Manifestation of Nonlocal Communication	Significance
	emotionally close	connectedness and unity is implied
Person to person	Telepathic communication, remote viewing, telesomatic and twin events, remote healing	A nonlocal form of connectedness and unity is implied-oneness not as metaphor but as empirical fact

In 10 controlled experiments, researcher William Bengston tested the effect of "healing with intent" on laboratory mice. In 8 of these experiments, mice were injected with mammary adenocarcinoma (breast cancer) cells. In 2 experiments, mice with methylcholanthrene-induced sarcomas were used. The fatality rate for both cancers in mice, if untreated, is 100 percent. The healers were faculty and student volunteers.

Although they had no previous experience or belief in healing with intent and were often skeptical of such, they were drilled extensively in the healing technique. Treatment length was from 30 to 60 minutes, delivered daily to weekly until the mice were cured or died. They were successful in producing full cures in approximately 90 percent of the mice. When mammary adenocarcinoma cells were re-injected into cured mice, the cancer would not take, suggesting that an immune response had been stimulated during treatment. The proximity of the volunteer healers to the cages of the mice varied from on site to approximately 600 miles. Thus Bengston notes, "[T]hese effects were at times brought about from a distance that defies conventional understanding," suggesting that a nonlocal process was at work. This series of studies, conducted at several academic centers, suggests that healing through intent can be predictable, reliable, and replicable (Bengston, 2010; Bengston, 2012; Bengston & Krinsley, 2000; Bengston & Moga, 2007).

The DMILS field is too extensive to be comprehensively reviewed here. These studies are described and summarized in readily available sources (Radin, 1997, 2006; Dossey, 1999; Sheldrake, 1999; Bengston & Krinsley, 2000; Benor, 2002; Jonas & Crawford, 2003; Kelly et al, 2007; Schwartz, 2007; Schwartz & Dossey, 2010; Bengston, 2010; Kelly et al, 2015). A recent review must suffice.

In a 2015 meta-analysis of this field, consciousness researcher Chris A. Roe and his colleagues at the University of Northampton examined 106 "noncontact healing studies" — 57 involving whole humans and 49 involving non-whole humans (tissues, cells) and non-humans (animals, plants, etc.). All the various healing methods employed in these experiments incorporated an intention to heal. The researchers concluded, "Results in the active condition exhibit a significant improvement in wellbeing relative to control subjects.... [Results] do not seem to be susceptible to placebo and expectancy effects. ...The effect size is small, but statistically significant" (Roe et al, 2015).

Nonhumans such as cells, plants, microbes and biochemical reactions presumably do not think positively or symbolically and are therefore not subject to suggestion and expectation. If in controlled experiments these entities respond to intentions, presumably the placebo response is not responsible, but the influence of the thoughts and intentions of the healer.

This generalization requires qualification. In humans, placebo effects are believed to be mediated by the empathy, compassion, likeability, and trustworthiness manifested by a physician. Thus, veterinarian and placebo researcher F. D. McMillan states, "To the extent that animals form such perceptions...it is reasonable to posit a similar influence of placebo effects in animal health care" (McMillan, 1999). There is evidence that certain animals can manifest placebo effects through operant conditioning. For example, Ader and Cohen paired an immunosuppressive drug (cyclophosphamide) with a neutral stimulus (a saccharine solution) in mice with a lupus-like disease. When only the neutral stimulus was later given, the result was immunosuppression, suggestive of a placebo response (Ader & Cohen, 1982; Siegel, 2002). Moreover, a body of research demonstrates healthy effects in animals from visual and tactile contact from a human, involving rabbits, dogs, horses, dairy cows, and sows.

How, then, can placebo responses be differentiated from our hypothesized effects of healing intentionality? The reasons are straightforward. Many of the relevant studies do not involve animals at all, but cells, tissues, plants, microbes, and chemical reactions. Moreover, intentionality effects do not depend on proximity to a subject. Many of the experiments suggesting distant healing effects have been done remotely, beyond sensory contact. This suggests that a *nonlocal* phenomenon is at play, as opposed to the *local*, sensory-mediated mechanisms believed to underlie placebo responses in humans and higher animals. Therefore, if animals are not involved as test subjects, or if sensory-mediated contact is bypassed, placebo effects would appear to have been eliminated (Dossey, 2015).

Cell-to-Cell Connections

In 2009, a team of Italian researchers led by neuroscientist Rita Pizzi repeatedly demonstrated that, when one batch of human neurons was stimulated by a laser beam, a distant batch of neurons registered similar changes, although the two were completely shielded from each other. The researchers concluded, "[O]ur experimental data seem to strongly suggest that biological systems present non-local properties not explainable by classical models" (Pizzi et al, 2004).

In 2007 researcher Ashkan Farhadi and colleagues at Rush University Medical Center in Chicago examined whether cells in separate containers could communicate with each other. They exposed one container of intestinal epithelial "inducer" cells to hydrogen peroxide and assessed the damage done to them. Another batch of "detector" cells was placed in a separate container and was not exposed to hydrogen peroxide. Even though there was no obvious way the two batches of cells could communicate, the detector cells demonstrated damage similar to the inducer cells. "These findings," the researchers said, "provide evidence in support of a non-chemical, non-electrical communication" (Farhadi et al, 2007).

In 2013 researcher Victor B. Chaban and his colleagues at UCLA School of Medicine demonstrated "physically disconnected non-diffusable cell-to-cell communication" between neuroblastoma cancer cells and normal neurons, when both are shielded, preventing any known means of communication (Chaban et al, 2013).

Brain-to-Brain Connections

In 1965 researchers T. D. Duane and Thomas Behrendt decided to test anecdotal reports that identical twins share feelings and physical sensations even when far apart. In two of fifteen pairs of twins tested, eye closure in one twin produced not only an immediate alpha rhythm in his own brain, but also in the brain of the other twin, even though he kept his eyes open and sat in a lighted room (Duane & Behrendt, 1965).

The publication of this study in the prestigious journal *Science* evoked enormous interest. Ten attempted replications soon followed, by eight different research groups around the world. Of the ten studies, eight reported positive findings, published in mainstream journals such as *Nature* and *Behavioral Neuroscience* (Hearne,

1981,1997; Kelly & Lenz, 1975; Lloyd, 1973; May et al, 1979; Orme-Johnson et al, 1982; Rebert & Turner, 1974; Targ & Puthoff, 1974).

In the late 1980s and 1990s, a team headed by psychophysiologist Jacobo Grinberg-Zylberbaum at the University of Mexico published experiments that, like most of the previous studies, demonstrated correlations in the EEGs of separated pairs of individuals who had no sensory contact with each other (Grinberg-Zylberbaum & Ramos, 1974; Grinberg-Zylberbaum et al, 1993; Grinberg-Zylberbaum et al, 1994). Two of the studies were published in the prominent journals *Physics Essays* and *International Journal of Neuroscience*, drawing further attention to this area (Sabell et al, 2001; Standish et al, 2003, 2004).

Experiments in this field became increasingly sophisticated. In 2003 Jiri Wackerman, an EEG expert from Germany's University of Freiberg, attempted to eliminate all possible weaknesses in earlier studies and applied a refined method of analysis. Following his successful experiment, he concluded, "We are facing a phenomenon which is neither easy to dismiss as a methodological failure or a technical artifact nor understood as to its nature. No biophysical mechanism is presently known that could be responsible for the observed correlations between EEGs of two separated subjects" (Wackerman et al, 2003).

As fMRI brain-scanning techniques matured, these began to be employed, with intriguing results. Psychologist Leanna Standish at Seattle's Bastyr University found that when one individual in one room was visually stimulated by a flickering light, there was a significant increase in brain activity in a person in a distant room (Standish et al, 2003).

In 2004, three new independent replications were reported, all successful—from Standish's group at Bastyr University (Standish et al, 2004), from the University of Edinburgh (Kittenis et al, 2004), and from researcher Dean Radin and his team at the Institute of

Noetic Sciences (Radin, 2004).

Person-to-Person Connections: Telesomatic Events

Almost forgotten amid this research is a flurry of case reports such as the experience of the nurse above, suggesting a person-to-person form of communication that appears genuinely nonlocal. In them, individuals experience similar sensations or actual physical changes, even though they may be separated by great distances. Berthold E. Schwarz, an American neuropsychiatrist, documented many of these instances. In the 1960s he coined the term *telesomatic* to describe these events, from Greek words meaning "distant body" (Schwarz, 1967). The term is apt, because these events suggest that a shared mind is bridging two bodies. Most cases go unreported, however, because there is no accepted explanatory mechanism for them, and because of the social stigma that can result from discussing them publicly.

These happenings have an interesting history. A typical example was described by the English social critic John Ruskin (1819-1900). It involved Arthur Severn, a famous landscape painter who was married to Ruskin's cousin Joan. Severn awoke early one morning and went to a nearby lake for a sail, while Joan remained in bed. She was suddenly awakened by the sensation of a severe, painful blow to the mouth, of no apparent cause. Shortly thereafter her husband Arthur returned, holding a cloth to his bleeding mouth. He reported that the wind had freshened abruptly and caused the boom to hit him in the mouth, almost knocking him from the boat, at the estimated time his wife felt the blow (Gurney et al, 1886).

A similar instance was reported in 2002 by mathematician-statistician Douglas Stokes. When he was teaching at the University of Michigan, one of his students reported that his father was knocked off a bench one day by an "invisible blow to the jaw." Five minutes later his dad received a call from a local gymnasium where his wife was exercising, informing him that she had broken her jaw on a piece of fitness equipment (Stokes, 1997). David Lorimer, a shrewd analyst of consciousness and a leader of the Scientific and Medical Network, an international organization based in the U.K., has collected many telesomatic cases in his wise book *Whole in One* (Lorimer, 1990).Lorimer is struck by the fact that these events occur mainly between people who are emotionally close.

He makes a strong case for what he calls "empathic resonance," which he believes links individuals across space and time. The late psychiatrist Ian Stevenson (1918-2007), of the University of Virginia, investigated scores of instances in which distant individuals experience similar physical symptoms. Most involve parents and children, spouses, siblings, twins, lovers, and very close friends (Stevenson, 1970). Again, the common thread is the emotional closeness and empathy experienced by the separated persons.

In a typical example reported by Stevenson, a mother was writing a letter to her daughter, who had recently gone away to college. For no obvious reason her right hand began to burn so severely she had to put down her pen. She received a phone call less than an hour later informing her that her daughter's right hand had been severely burned by acid in a laboratory accident at the same time that she, the mother, had felt the burning pain (Rush, 1964).

In a case reported by researcher Louisa E. Rhine, a woman suddenly doubled over, clutching her chest in severe pain, saying, "Something has happened to Nell; she has been hurt." Two hours later the sheriff arrived to inform her that her daughter Nell had been involved in an auto accident, and that a piece of the steering wheel had penetrated her chest (Rhine, 1962).

Person-to-Person Connections: Twins

Guy Lyon Playfair, a consciousness researcher in Great Britain, is the author of the important book *Twin Telepathy* (Playfair, 2002a). He has collected a variety of documented telesomatic cases involving twins and non-twin siblings.

These reports are of personal interest because I am an identical twin. All of our lives my twin brother and I have experienced shared feelings and sometimes physical sensations at a distance. Growing up, we did not know that these events were supposed to be impossible. We simply called them "twin stuff" and considered them quite normal, just the way things are. I am also married to a twin. My wife Barbara and her fraternal twin brother have also experienced sensational exchanges at great distances without any kind of sensory cuing.

One case reported by Playfair involved the identical twins Ross and Norris McWhirter, who were well known in Britain as co-editors of the *Guinness Book of Records*. On November 27, 1975, Ross was fatally shot in the head and chest by two gunmen on the doorstep of his north London home. According to an individual who was with his twin brother Norris, Norris reacted in a dramatic way at the time of the shooting, almost as if he had been shot by an invisible bullet (Playfair, 2002b).

Skeptics invariably dismiss cases such as these as coincidence, but many are hard to squeeze into this category. An example reported by Playfair concerns four-year-old identical twins Silvia and Marta Landa, who lived in the village of Murillo de Río Leza in northern Spain. The Landa twins became celebrities in 1976 after being featured in the local newspaper following a bizarre event. Marta had burned her hand on a hot clothes iron. As a large red blister was forming, an identical one developed on the hand of Silvia, who was away visiting her grandparents at the time. Silvia was taken to the doctor, unaware of what had happened to her sister Marta. When the two little girls were united, their parents saw that the blisters were the same size and on the same part of the hand.

It wasn't the first time this sort of thing had happened. If one twin had an accident, the other twin seemed to know about it, even though they were nowhere near each other. Once, when they arrived home in their car, Marta hopped out and ran inside the house, but suddenly complained that she could not move her foot. While this was happening, Silvia had got tangled up with the seat belt and her foot was stuck in it. On another occasion when one of them had misbehaved and was given a smack, the other one, out of sight, immediately burst into tears.

Members of the Madrid office of the Spanish Parapsychological Society got wind of the burned-hand incident and decided to investigate. Their team of nine psychologists, psychiatrists, and physicians descended on the Landa house, with the full cooperation and approval of the twins' parents. They had hardly arrived when a typical trade-off incident happened to the little twins. When Marta accidentally banged her head on something, it was her sister Silvia who began to cry. The researchers got to work with a series of tests disguised as fun games for the twins. This meant the little girls had no idea they were involved in an experiment.

While Marta stayed on the ground floor with her mother and some of the researchers, Silvia went with her father and the rest of the team to the second floor. Everything that happened on both floors was filmed and tape-recorded. One of the psychologists played a game with Marta, using a glove puppet. Silvia was given an identical puppet, but no game was played. Downstairs, Marta grabbed the puppet and threw it at the investigator. Upstairs, at the same time, Silvia did the same.

One of the team's physicians next shined a bright light into Marta's left eye, as part of a simple physical check-up. When she did this four times, Silvia began to blink rapidly as if trying to avoid a bright light. Then the doctor did a knee-jerk reflex test by tapping her left knee tendon three times. At the same time, Silvia began to jerk her leg so dramatically that her father, unaware the test was going on downstairs on Marta, had to hold it still. Then Marta was given some very aromatic perfume to smell. As she did so, Silvia shook her head and put her hand over her nose. Next, still in different rooms, the twins were given seven colored discs and were asked to arrange them in any order they liked. They arranged them in exactly the same order.

There were other tests as well. The team rated all but one of them as "highly positive" or "positive." The Landa tests confirmed what many researchers have found — that children are more prone than adults to this sort of thing, and that results are more likely to be positive when experiments are done not in sterile, impersonal labs, but in the natural habitat of the subjects and in a relaxed, supportive environment. This latter lesson has often been flagrantly ignored in consciousness research by experimenters who should know better. Researchers have had to learn repeatedly the importance of *ecological validity* — the principle that what is being tested should be allowed, to the extent possible, to unfold as it does in real life.

Although telesomatic exchanges are by no means limited to twins, they are frequent among them. As Playfair states, in twins we see "the telepathic signal at full volume, as it were, at which not only information is transmitted at a distance but so are emotions, physical sensations and even symptoms such as burns and bruises" (Playfair, 2002c). Even so, he has found that only around 30 percent of identical twins have these experiences, but in those who do the phenomena can be mind-boggling (Playfair, 2002d). Emotional closeness is an essential factor in the twin connection. Also, having an extraverted, outgoing personality has been shown to facilitate the link. And, as we see in the above examples, what twins seem to communicate best is bad news — depression, illness, accidents or death.

Person-to-Person Connections: Healers

Dr. Jeanne Achterberg (1942-2012) was a psychophysiologist and pioneer of the integrative healthcare movement. She was one of the earliest researchers in the use of imagery and visualization in healing, and an authority in the psychological and spiritual dimensions of cancer (Achterberg, 2001; Achterberg & Dossey, 1994). As a psychology professor, researcher, author, and international lecturer, she was a roving ambassador for the role of consciousness in health.

Her interest in healing led to a research opportunity in Hawaii at the North Hawaii Community Hospital in Waimea on the Big Island. She was invited to direct a research effort funded by Earl Bakken, who invented the implantable cardiac pacemaker and the founder of Medtronic, the world's largest manufacturer of medical devices. Dr. Bakken has long had an interest in healing, specifically the techniques of Native Hawaiian healers. Like traditional healers in every culture, their methods often involved remote healing intentions, or healing at a distance. Are these claims valid? Can they be proved? Achterberg was determined to find answers.

She did not launch her research project right away. Instead, she set about meeting native healers and explaining her interests. The healers took her into their confidence and shared their methods. After two years, Achterberg was ready to begin.

She and her colleagues recruited eleven healers. The healers were not casually interested in healing; they had pursued their healing tradition an average of 23 years. Each healer was asked to select a person with whom they had successfully worked in the past, with whom they felt an empathic, compassionate, bonded connection, to be the recipient of their healing efforts. The healers described their healing efforts in a variety of ways — as prayer, sending energy, good intentions, or simply thinking and wishing for the subjects the highest good. Achterberg simply called these efforts distant intentionality (DI).

Each subject was isolated from the healer while an fMRI brain scan was done. The healers sent DI at two-minute random intervals to the subjects; the subjects could not have anticipated when the DI was being sent. Significant differences between the experimental (send) and control (no-send) conditions were found in ten of the eleven subjects. During the send periods, specific areas within the subjects' brains "lit up" on the fMRI scan, indicating increased metabolic activity. This did not occur during the no-send periods. The areas of the brain that were activated during the send periods included the anterior and middle cingulate areas, precuneus, and frontal areas. There was less than approximately one chance in 10,000 that these results could be explained by chance (in the language of science, $p = 0.000127$) (Achterberg et al, 2005).

This study suggests that compassionate healing intentions can exert measurable physical effects on a recipient at a distance, and that an empathic connection between the healer and the recipient is a vital part of the process. Achterberg's study should have been front-page news in every major newspaper in the Western world when published in 2005, but it was ignored. The primary reason is that it runs counter to the prevailing neuromythology of our day, which insists that minds are material in origin and are completely separate, individual, and confined to the brain.

Post-material Preventive Medicine

Nonlocal, postmaterial medicine has profound implications for preventive medicine — the avoidance of health threats. Consider the following example from the archives of the Rhine Research Center in Durham, North Carolina.

Amanda, a young mother living in Washington State, awoke one night at 2:30 A.M. from a nightmare. She dreamed that a large chandelier that hung above their baby's bed in the next room fell into the crib and crushed the infant. In the dream, as she and her husband stood amid the wreckage, she saw that a clock on the baby's dresser read 4:35 A.M. The weather in the dream was violent; rain hammered the window and the wind was blowing a gale. The dream was so terrifying she roused her husband and told him about it. He laughed, told her the dream was silly, and urged her to go back to sleep, which he promptly did. But the dream was so frightening that Amanda went to the baby's room and brought the child back to bed with her. She noted that the weather was calm, not stormy as in the dream. Amanda felt foolish — until around two hours later, when she and her husband were awakened by a loud crash. They dashed into the nursery and found the crib demolished by the chandelier, which had fallen directly into it. Amanda noted that the clock on the dresser read 4:35 A.M. and that the weather had changed. Now there was howling wind and rain. This time her husband was not laughing. Both parents realized that Amanda's dream had prevented injury or death to their infant.

Amanda's dream was a snapshot of the future — down to the specific event, the precise time it would happen, and a change in the weather (Feather & Schmickler, 2005). Unlike Amanda's experience, however, the information we gain nonlocally is often unconscious. The information may be nonlocal with respect not only to space, but to time as well, as mentioned. For example, an individual may cancel a travel reservation because of a vague gut feeling that something is not right, or that something ominous is going to happen, not because he actually foresees a specific event. This may be one reason why occupancy rates are statistically lower on the day of some train wrecks compared to non-accident days (Cox, 1956). Nonlocal, unconscious awareness of dire future events may also account for why the combined *vacancy* rate on the four doomed planes on September 11 was nearly 80 percent (Dossey, 2009). From a survival perspective, it may be an advantage for information that is nonlocally acquired to be unconscious. Thinking, analyzing, and reasoning take time. In emergencies, instant reflexive action can save a life.

Transcending Religious Ideology

Healing intentions are often expressed as prayers. All told, the experiments involving prayer-related healing intentions show that the prayers of perhaps all religions can be effective, and that no specific religion enjoys a monopoly. Moreover, the evidence from healing studies shows that even non-theistic healing intentions and prayers, as in some forms of Buddhism, can also result in healing, as well as in secular, so-called pagan intentions that are not associated with any traditional religion. These findings are important. By demonstrating that no religion enjoys an advantage in nonlocal healing effects, these experiments do not disenfranchise any religion but democratize and universalize healing intentions. They are therefore the enemy of religious intolerance and narrowness.

The Ghastly Silence

In our day-to-day existence, the materialistic formulations of classical science are inadequate because they omit much of the juice and tang of life. This deficiency has long been noted by some of the greatest individuals in the history of science. Among them was Gottfried Wilhelm Leibniz (1646-1716), the German philosopher and mathematician. Leibniz, who invented the infinitesimal calculus independently of Isaac Newton, was considered one of the greatest minds of the eighteenth century. He refined the binary number system, which underlies virtually all digital computers, and invented mechanical calculators that were a marvel for their time. His intellectual reach touched all the major domains of learning of his day.

Even so, Leibniz could not find within science the satisfaction he was looking for. In a letter two years before his death, he wrote:

"But when I looked for the ultimate reasons for mechanism, and even for the laws of motion, I was greatly surprised to see that they could not be found in mathematics but that I should have to return to metaphysics." (Garber, 2009)

Three centuries later, Nobel physicist Erwin Schrödinger came essentially to the same conclusion:

"The scientific picture of the real world around me is very deficient. It gives a lot of factual information, puts all our experience in a magnificently consistent order, but it is ghastly silent about all and sundry that is really near to our heart, that really matters to us. It cannot tell us a word about red and blue, bitter and sweet, physical pain and physical delight; it knows nothing of beautiful and ugly, good or bad, God and eternity. Science sometimes pretends to answer questions in these domains, but the answers are very often so silly that we are not inclined to take them seriously." (Schrödinger, 1982)

Charles Darwin also encountered the effects of the "ghastly silence" of which Schrödinger spoke. Late in life he lamented:

"My mind seems to have become a machine for grinding general laws out of large collections of facts.... The loss of [the emotional] tastes is a loss of happiness, and may possibly be injurious to the intellect, and more probably to the moral character, by enfeebling the emotional part of our nature. .... The loss of these tastes is a loss of happiness." His solution: "[I]f I had to live my life again, I would have made a rule to read some poetry and listen to some music at least once every week...." (Darwin, 1897)

Something more is needed — something that can inspire not only an intellectual appreciation of the wholeness implied in biological nonlocality and entanglement, but also something that can quicken the pulse and stir an ethic toward Earth that can counter the unbridled greed, selfishness and plunder that threaten us.

Currently there are excellent exemplars of this awakening, including numerous scientists. But many scientists, it must be said, are reluctant to speak out in favor of wholeness, unity, and oneness because they are under the sway of promissory materialism, noted earlier, or they fear being labeled as having "gone mystic." It's as if there are hooded inquisitors lurking in the shadowy halls of science who are keeping score, who are continually oiling the rack and heating the pincers, just waiting for a scientist to step out of line.

Fear has never silenced the greatest poets and artists. Poets have been yammering away about wholeness for centuries. As author Philip Goldberg points out in his important book *American Veda* (Goldberg, 2010),there are superb examples among the Romantic poets, particularly William Blake, Percy Bysshe Shelley, William Wordsworth, and Samuel Taylor Coleridge. These poets sensed the interconnectedness and unity that are a feature of an entangled, nonlocal world. Thus Blake, in "Augeries of Innocence": "To see a world in a grain of sand / And a heaven in a wild flower, / Hold infinity in the palm of your hand / And eternity in an hour" (Blake, 1992); Shelley, in "Adonais": "The One remains, the many change and pass...." (Shelley, 1992); Wordsworth, in "Tintern Abbey": "A motion and a spirit, that impels / All thinking things, all objects of all thought, / And rolls through all things" (Wordsworth, 1992); and Coleridge, who wrote of "the translucence of the eternal through and in the temporal" (Coleridge, 1971).

In his book *Opening to the Infinite,* consciousness researcher Stephan A. Schwartz describes how the personal experience of a nonlocal event can carry the emotional wallop of an epiphany. Schwartz, one of the inventors of the science of remote viewing, has taught thousands of individuals in workshops to have these experiences. He concludes that nonlocal experiences, of which remote viewing is only one example, bestow an "ineffable sense of connection" and a "sense of empowerment" that is so profound it can permanently and radically alter one's worldview and conduct (Schwartz, 2007).

Donald Evans, late professor of philosophy at Victoria College, University of Toronto, agrees. In his important book *Spirituality and Human Nature*, he discusses the role of both psychic and spiritual experiences in personal growth and transformation in general, and how these two types of experiences are related (Evans, 1993):

"[M]any people in our culture ...have a constricting world-view that precludes not only paranormal but also genuinely spiritual experiences.... Sometimes the only way that such a world-view can be undermined and shattered is by a powerfully impressive paranormal experience which the skeptic undergoes. ...Even a positivist philosopher may suddenly have an out-of-body experience if he nearly dies. ...For such people...rudimentary psychic beginnings can pave the way toward spiritually profound transformations. ...[P]sychic experiences can provide a first stage which is helpful to many and perhaps necessary for some. Indeed, the distinction between psychic experiences and genuinely spiritual experiences is not always clear.... My main point...is that a pathway that initially is predominantly psychic can lead into one that is predominantly genuinely spiritual."

Earth Again

Hate is not the opposite of love;
the opposite of love is individuality.
~ D. H. Lawrence (1992)

The commonly felt experience of being nonlocally connected — all tangled up with all there is — may be a way out of the predicament created by self-centered, greed-obsessed individuals who have no sense of wholeness and no concern for the integrity of Earth. As Goldberg puts it, when we realize the unitary nature of consciousness, ...one's sense of "I" and "we" opens out from the narrow identification with family, tribe, race, political affiliation, religion, and so on, to encompass a broader swath of humanity. With that comes a corresponding expansion of the moral compass. This not a fanciful imagining of "we are the world" harmony but a living experience of unity with other humans, with nature, and ultimately with the cosmos (Goldberg, 2010).

Contemporary scientists often deny the empirical findings we've examined which point to an "unbroken wholeness" — physicists Bohm and Hiley's term (Bohm & Hiley, 1995) — and unity between biological systems and humans. These critics fear the contamination of modern science by the "occult," one of their favorite epithets for nonlocal human experiences. But as we've already suggested, science desperately *needs* contamination by factors now missing from its remit if we are to survive in any meaningful way. A demonstrable, felt connectivity is required for a moral center, an Earth ethic, a sense of responsibility for all of life.

The absence of these qualities has led to a moral abyss that is becoming impossible to ignore. A one-sided science is not only incomplete, it can be deadly. As Dr. Samuel Johnson put it nearly three centuries ago, "Integrity without knowledge is weak and useless, and knowledge without integrity is dangerous and dreadful" (Johnson, 2000).

Dr. Johnson also observed, "When a man knows he is to be hanged in a fortnight, it concentrates his mind wonderfully" (Boswell, 1866). So, perhaps our sense of impending global disasters is concentrating our species' collective mind. Michael Grosso, philosopher and consciousness researcher, and Kingsley L. Dennis, the British sociologist, have independently proposed that the widespread expectation of a planetary catastrophe may trigger a kind of near-death experience involving billions of humans. This might result in a massive shift in our species' attitude toward our environment and a sacred regard for all of life on Earth, similar to how individual near-death experiences typically result in a recalibration of the survivor's behavior in an ethical, compassionate, and loving direction (Grosso, 2017; Dennis, 2012).

What we call empathy, compassion, and love may be human entanglement banging on the doors of consciousness, demanding entry. Albert Schweitzer, the legendary physician, missionary, priest, philanthropist, theologian, pacifist, musicologist, and winner of the 1952 Nobel Peace Prize, opened those doors and made the world a better, safer place. In a kind of manifesto of wholeness, he wrote:

"What we call love is in its essence Reverence for Life (Schweitzer, 1934) ....Profound love demands a deep conception and out of this develops reverence for the mystery of life. It brings us close to all beings. To the poorest and smallest, as well as all others.... [T]he idea of Reverence for Life gives us something more profound and mightier than the idea of humanism. It includes all living beings..." (Schweitzer, 2017).

The contributors to this book believe we are well on our way toward a postmaterial revisioning of consciousness. For example, Imants Barušs, PhD, and Julia Mossbridge, PhD, contend in their 2017 book *Transcendent Mind: Rethinking the Science of Consciousness*:
"We are in the midst of a sea change. Receding from view is materialism, whereby physical phenomena are assumed to be primary and consciousness is regarded as secondary. Approaching our sights is a complete reversal of perspective. According to this alternative view, consciousness is primary and the physical is secondary. In other words, materialism is receding and giving way to ideas about reality in which consciousness plays a key role. ...[T]he deep structures underlying our waking consciousness are fundamentally spatially and temporally nonlocal in nature.... [C]onsciousness is capable of existing in an extended or transcendent state in which it is not completely bound to the brain." (Barušs & Mossbridge)

These views support the concept of entangled, shared minds, minds linked across space and time to form a collective, unitary human consciousness. This perspective has an impressive pedigree. Max Planck, the founder of quantum mechanics, observed, "I regard consciousness as fundamental. I regard matter as derivative from consciousness. We cannot get behind consciousness. Everything that we talk about, everything that we regard as existing, postulates consciousness" (Planck, 1931). Erwin Schrödinger, another Nobel Prize-winning physicist, agreed: "Although I think that life may be the result of an accident, I do not think that of consciousness. Consciousness cannot be accounted for in physical terms. For consciousness is absolutely fundamental. It cannot be accounted for in terms of anything else" (Schrödinger, 1994). More recently, mathematician-philosopher David Chalmers states, "I propose that conscious experience be considered a fundamental feature, irreducible to anything more basic…" (Chalmers, 1995). And neuroscientist Christof Koch: "I believe that consciousness is a fundamental, an elementary, property of living matter. It can't be derived from anything else" (Koch, 2012).

Promissory Materialism Adieu

Any assessment of what lies ahead in our understanding of consciousness must include an honest appraisal of where we now stand and what we are moving away *from*. Scientists widely assume we are closing in on the mysteries of consciousness, and that these mysteries are to be understood materialistically. This is the doctrine of promissory materialism, as we've seen. As neuroscientist Antonio Damasio, of the University of Southern California, confidently predicted in 1999, "In an effort that continues to gain momentum, virtually all the functions studied in traditional psychology—perception, learning, and memory—are being understood in terms of their brain underpinnings. The mystery behind many of these functions are being solved, one by one, and it is now apparent that even consciousness, the towering problem in the field, is likely to be elucidated before too long" (Damasio, 1999). Or as psychiatrist and sleep researcher Allan Hobson pithily put it, "Consciousness, like sleep, is of the Brain, by the Brain, and for the Brain. A new day is dawning" (Hobson, 2008).

These ardent positions have been buttressed by the advent of sophisticated techniques such as functional magnetic resonance imaging (fMRI), by which activity in specific areas of the brain can be correlated with imprecise mental functions. The hasty conclusion drawn is that "the mind, self, and consciousness are now entirely within the purview of neuroscience. It follows that all other theories of the mind…are consigned to the trash heap," says philosopher Stan V. McDaniel of Sonoma State University (McDaniel, 2012). Among this discarded "trash" are the postmaterial hypotheses that consciousness might exist external to the brain, that it might operate *through* the brain without being identical with it, and that it might survive the death of the brain and body.

Many science insiders, however, do not share the sunny, triumphal predictions of Damasio, Hobson, and their materialist colleagues. They believe that the materialistic view is premature and overreaching. In closing, in order to emphasize the growing openness to a postmaterialist approach to consciousness, I offer the following opinions of several prominent scholars.

Donald D. Hoffman, the above-mentioned cognitive scientist at University of California, Irvine: "The scientific study of consciousness is in the embarrassing position of having no scientific theory of consciousness" (Hoffman, 2008). Steven A. Pinker, experimental psychologist at Harvard University, on how consciousness might arise from something physical, such as the brain: "Beats the heck out of me. I have some prejudices, but no idea of how to begin to look for a defensible answer. And neither does anyone else." (Pinker,

1997) Stuart A. Kauffman, theoretical biologist and complex-systems researcher: "Nobody has the faintest idea what consciousness is.... I don't have any idea. Nor does anybody else, including the philosophers of mind" (Kauffman, 2008). Roger W. Sperry, Nobel Prize-winning neurophysiologist:

"Those centermost processes of the brain with which consciousness is presumably associated are simply not understood. They are so far beyond our comprehension at present that no one I know of has been able even to imagine their nature" (Sperry, 1995).

Eugene P. Wigner, Nobelist in physics: "We have at present not even the vaguest idea how to connect the physio-chemical processes with the state of mind" (Wigner, 1969). Physicist Nick Herbert, an expert in nonlocality: "Science's biggest mystery is the nature of consciousness. It is not that we possess bad or imperfect theories of human awareness; we simply have no such theories at all. About all we know about consciousness is that it has something to do with the head, rather than the foot" (Herbert, 1987).

Physicist Freeman J. Dyson: "The origin of life is a total mystery, and so is the existence of human consciousness. We have no clear idea how the electrical discharges occurring in nerve cells in our brains are connected with our feelings and desires and actions" Dyson, 2011). Philosopher Jerry A. Fodor, of Rutgers University: "Nobody has the slightest idea how anything material could be conscious. Nobody even knows what it would be like to have the slightest idea about how anything material could be conscious. So much for the philosophy of consciousness" (Fodor, 1992). Sir John R. Maddox, former editor of *Nature:* "What consciousness consists of...is...a puzzle.

Despite the marvelous successes of neuroscience in the past century..., we seem as far from understanding cognitive process as we were a century ago" (Maddox, 1999). Philosopher John R. Searle, of the University of California, Berkeley: "At the present state of the investigation of consciousness we *don't know* how it works and we need to try all kinds of different ideas" (Searle, 1995).

In view of our ignorance about the essential nature of consciousness, and considering the experimental evidence we've reviewed, these "different ideas" should include the concept of nonlocal consciousness that is a central theme of this book. Opposition to this postmaterial perspective is not surprising and is predictable and even desirable. This is how science progresses. As Sir Edward Bullard, the distinguished geoscientist of Cambridge University said in 1975, in discussing the resistance in geology to the idea of plate tectonics and continental drift:

"There is always a strong inclination for a body of professionals to oppose an unorthodox view. Such a group has a considerable investment in orthodoxy: they have learned to interpret a large body of data in terms of the old view, and they have prepared lectures and perhaps written books with the old background. To think the whole subject through again when one is no longer young is not easy and involves admitting a partially misspent youth.   ... Clearly it is more prudent to keep quiet, to be a moderate defender of orthodoxy, or to maintain that all is doubtful, sit on the fence, and wait in statesmanlike ambiguity for more data..." (Bullard, 1975).

The heretical concepts of plate tectonics and continental drift eventually prevailed because of empirical evidence (Hellman, 1999). So, too, will the evolution of a form of medicine that honors *all* we are, the material and the postmaterial. Why? Because of that factor which, in science, makes all the difference: *evidence.*

Postmaterial science involves the recognition that we are intimately connected through nonlocal, unitary, fundamental consciousness. The realization of our intrinsic unity is our best hope to survive and thrive on this planet. *Yet it is more than hope.* It is a worldview already embraced by millions, including a growing cadre of scientists. The emerging icon is wholeness. Wholeness is related to terms such as "undiminished," "integral," "complete," and "unimpaired."

That is what healing has always been about.

Chapter Eleven

Supersynchronicity and Primacy of Consciousness: Bridging Science, Metaphysics and Spirituality

Gary E. Schwartz, PhD

These "coincidences" may be indicating the existence of some deep, underlying unity, a generalized non-locality beyond space and time, perhaps even involving all physical and even biological theories, manifested in the fundamental constants and linking the microcosm to the macrocosm.

Menas Kafatos

Synchronicity is an ever-present reality for those who have eyes to see.

Carl Jung

Introduction: Adding Universal and Intelligence to Consciousness

I want to begin by addressing some fundamental and far reaching follow up questions that are of paramount importance to human understanding and evolution.

Question 1: If consciousness is *primary* – the theme of this volume – does it have any specific *qualities*, and if the answer is yes, what are they?

Question 2: If consciousness has *qualities*, are its qualities *universal*, applying to all things at all levels, from the ultra-micro (e.g. subatomic particles and smaller) to the super-macro (e.g. superclusters of galaxies and larger), and everything in between?

Question 3: If consciousness is *universal*, does it consist of universal processes such as the capacity to *create and process information*?

Question 4: If consciousness can *create and process information*, are these processes an expression of a *universal* (and unified) primary *intelligence* whose capacities and potentials require our envisioning scales of the infinite (for an overview, see *The Mathematics of Infinity*, Faticoni, 2012)?

Question 5: If consciousness is *universal* and *intelligent*, do these *universal capacities* include creativity and inventiveness, intention and purpose, learning and growth, etc. – i.e. what psychologists call the *mind*?

Question 6: If a *universal intelligent consciousness* has such *universal capacities*, does it play an *active role in the functioning of the universe, including our personal lives*? and

Question 7: If this *universal intelligent consciousness plays an active role in the functioning of the universe, including our personal lives, how can we discover these fundamental roles and potentially improve our lives accordingly?*

In this chapter, I will outline how it is possible to use the methods of scientific reasoning and inference, observation, and statistical analysis, to reveal what Kafatos in this volume refers to as the "Living Presence," and what I am referring to as a Universal Intelligent Consciousness, not simply within the material world per se, but even more importantly, within the human mind as well.

Specifically, I will document and demonstrate how the careful observation and analysis of complex, serial coincidences or synchronicities in contemporary life can reveal the existence of this Living Presence and our capacity to interact / participate with It.

Following Kafatos, from this point onward I will sometimes capitalize words like Consciousness, Universal, Intelligence, Learning, Living Presence, and Laws to "indicate that they play a central role in the proposed paradigm" (Kafatos, 2018).

Also following Kafatos's example, and expanding it further, I have subtitled this final chapter "Bridging Science, Metaphysics and Spirituality." There are two primary reasons for adding spirituality to the subtitle.

The concept of a Universal Intelligent Consciousness, and science's ability to study It (just as science has the ability to study the human mind, animal minds, and ultimately the presence of mind at any level), *inherently addresses the same fundamental concepts and concerns as explored by mystics and gnostics throughout recorded history.* No matter what the words that are used – e.g. Yahweh, Great Spirit, Infinite Awareness, Creative Intelligence, Cosmic Consciousness, Allah, God, the Source – the truth is that these words all ultimately refer to some sort of an Ineffable Oneness whose vast potential includes abstract concepts like Omni (e.g. Omnipresent) and Infinite (e.g. Infinite Mind).

The majority of humanity's greatest and visionary scientists – including Newton, Maxwell, Einstein, Planck, Pauli, and I would include Bohm – *not only firmly believed in the existence of some sort of Universal Intelligent Consciousness, they saw science as a means of coming to know It.* As Einstein forthrightly stated it, his ultimate quest was to know *"The Mind of God."*

Here is not the place to address the complex and acrimonious history bridging science, metaphysics, religion, and spirituality. Nor is this the place to explore the controversy that exists, even among contemporary postmaterialist scientists, in terms of people's aversion to, or preference for concepts that bridge science and "spirit." Instead, our focus here is to freely explore opportunities for advancing the connections between science and spirituality. Since moving to the University of Arizona, I have explored these connections in multiple books, *The Living Energy Universe* (Schwartz and Russek, 1999), *The G.O.D. Experiments* (Schwartz, 2006), *Super Synchronicity* (2017), and *Greater Reality Living* (Pitstick and Schwartz, 2018).

My personal scientific journey has led me to the same conclusion as Kafatos (2018) when he says:

"Science and spirituality are converging: Both science and spirituality seek unity, one by exploring the outer world, the other by exploring the inner world."

Moreover, I have come to share Kafatos's sense of urgency when he writes:

"It is time to realize we are at crossroads and as planetary citizens make our choices. We can explore the meaning and practice of true involvement of ourselves in the environment as true citizens of the Earth. Either we move forward with the awareness of the sacredness of all life, the brotherhood/sisterhood for all humans on Earth, a higher spiritual purpose; or we go down the path of more of the same, the relentless rise of the ego, until perhaps we end up annihilating ourselves.

From the point of view of the Conscious Universe, the freedom to choose is ours if we are to fulfill our planetary and human destinies."

It is in this spirit (no pun intended) that I herein explicate how what Bernard Beitman (Beitman, 2009; 2016) terms "Coincidence Science," and I term "Supersynchronicity Science" (Schwartz, 2017), can reveal the Living Presence of the Universal Intelligent Consciousness in human life and show how this science can assist the process of human survival and evolution.

Understanding How Serial Coincidences Can Be Evidence for a Universal Intelligent Consciousness

The following fictionalized prototypic example is based upon real-life serial coincidences that point to the existence of a Universal Intelligent Consciousness. Real-life serial coincidences can be far more complex, sophisticated, meaningful, and evidential. I will later discuss exemplary published data (Schwarz, 2015a) in the chapter.

Imagine that you are an adult woman, age 47, trying to make

the decision about whether to undergo heart surgery, and you are concerned about whether the surgery will be successful. You have taken a leave of absence from your position as a vice-president of a medical device company. Your position requires that you pay close attention to details, and carefully weigh risks and benefits.

Though you are not a religious person, you do practice yoga and meditation. You decide to meditate and specifically "ask for guidance" to help you with this decision. You do not tell anyone, including your husband and two children, that you have asked for such guidance in your meditation.

Following your private request, you start noticing a flurry of instances involving bears showing up in your life. Below are sample of common coincidence possibilities with bears:

You turn on the TV and discover that there is a National Geographic program on bears living in Yellowstone National Park. Though you do not especially like bears, you are curious and decide to watch it. You learn that bears are interesting creatures that express courage and protection.

The next morning you receive a surprise email from a college friend telling you a funny story about a bear. You can't recall the last time someone spontaneously sent you an email about a bear story, funny or serious. At this point you assume this is "just a coincidence."

You go out for lunch to local restaurant and notice that a young boy sitting at a nearby table is wearing a tee shirt featuring a bear. It catches your attention because it reminds you of the National Geographic TV show plus the morning's unanticipated email from your friend. You can't recall the last time you sat near someone who was wearing a bear tee shirt.

You return home and resume reading your historical novel about the Korean War. To your amazement, one of the characters, a two-star general, is addressing his troops and uses the metaphor of a bear as a symbol of being courageous. You can't recall the last time you read about a bear, or bear symbolism, being featured in the type of historical novels you read. You begin to wonder, is the unfolding occurrence of bears in your life a possible sign or message about your surgery? How could you decide?

Later in the afternoon your thirteen-year old daughter comes home from school. She confesses that she has been worried about your possible heart surgery and decided to ask her soccer coach (a teacher she admires) for his opinion. Your daughter then quotes her coach / teacher as saying that "Sometimes it is necessary for us to grin and bear things." You are aware that the phrase "grin and bear things" is not a phrase that you or your daughter use. The choice of words from your daughter's coach strikes you as timely and weird. This reminds you of a clever phrase by Yogi Berra who said, "It's too coincidental to be a coincidence."

That night, you turn on the TV and discover that HBO is playing a rerun of a fantasy movie called *Ted* featuring a jumbo teddy bear. Normally you would never watch such a silly movie, but given the curious timing of it being scheduled at this moment, you decide to "grin and bear it" and watch the movie. You discover that the ending is not only positive, but the main character becomes healthy.

You then decide to learn something about the history of bears and their symbolism. You go to Google and type in "animal symbolism of bear." You learn that in Native American traditions the bear is often seen as being a symbol of courage. You read that the presence of a bear as a "totem animal" is for those who "appreciate the sweetness of life." You also read that one should "invoke" the Bear as a "Power Animal" when "protection is needed." You now see the potential connection to your question.

Being detail oriented, you review this series of coincidences involving bears that appeared within a 24-hour period, and you allow yourself to ask the question, "how could such a combination events have occurred"? You appreciate that the combination of seven bear related events involved more than seven different people, each living their lives seemingly independently of each other, at least concerning bears per se. You are certain that each of these events happened, and that to the best of your recollection (i.e. you appreciate that you cannot be certain about this), your sense is that you have never spontaneously experienced such a flurry of bear-related events in your normal, daily life.

Having rationally ruled out conventional explanations such as (1) misperception, (2) lack of prior attention, and (3) chance, as being credible explanations for what transpired, you wonder "how could this unique, meaningful collection of bear events have been orchestrated?"

Now that you understand that the bear and its symbolism are meaningfully related to your important personal question in a timely way, here is my question for you, the reader: Would you interpret the totality of the events as reflecting a "directed and intelligent answer" to your question?

Would you then logically infer that someone, or more likely, "Something," was aware of you and your personal needs, and that it had the Intelligence, Power, and Wisdom, to organize such a creative answer?

Now, what if instead of seven events, there had been seventeen events, or even seventy events? As mind-boggling as this may sound, and although I have not yet published these data, I have observed and kept careful records (including hundreds of photographs) of two specific occasions where more than one hundred and twenty serial coincidences, involving hundreds of different people, occurred within a few weeks period.

Finally, let's change the example slightly (yet as you will see, profoundly). The only elements we will modify is that (1) you do not meditate, and (2) you did not specifically "ask for guidance." Otherwise, virtually all the details are the same.

Here is the deep question: If you had *not* consciously asked for guidance, and yet *all the bears had spontaneously occurred,* would you entertain the possibility that some sort of Universal Intelligent Consciousness was aware of you and your needs, and that It was creatively giving you potential guidance *even though you were not aware of It?*

Though survey statistics on this question are not currently available, based on thirty years of tracking serial coincidences in myself and others, my estimate is that serial coincidences frequently occur in the *absence of people consciously requesting specific information or assistance.*

Now that you hopefully have some understanding of the relationship between (1) the occurrence of surprising sequences of coincidences in human life, and (2) the hypothesis of the presence of a Universal Intelligent Consciousness, we can (3) consider a brief history of the study of coincidence and synchronicity, (4) analyze exemplary contemporary serial coincidence evidence, and (5) examine how the FACT framework can be used to formally address the supersynchronicity / Universal Intelligent Consciousness connection.

But first, a brief comment about the distinction between laboratory versus observation science and its relevance to supersynchronicity science is in order.

Honoring Controlled Laboratory and Observational Science

Some fields in science, such as quantum physics, neuroscience, and cognitive psychology, can be performed in the laboratory under controlled conditions; parameters can be manipulated experimentally, and control conditions can be evaluated.

Other fields in science, such as astrophysics, environmental science, and anthropology, are limited to systematic observational methods and associated data analysis. Observing galaxies, hurricanes, and cultures, do not usually permit experimental manipulation.

Clearly, controlled laboratory science and observational science both belong in science, and they complement each other.

Supersynchronicity science – at least in humans – happens to be more like astrophysics than quantum physics. Though certain parameters can be investigated in the laboratory, such as individual differences in intuitiveness or training procedures for increasing awareness of synchronicities, most of the raw data requires the systematic chronicling of events in real life.

Careful observations from individual cases should therefore not be dismissed because they were collected in the field rather than in a controlled laboratory. The search for universal principles can be pursued by looking for replicability of patterns of observations across individuals.

Laboratory science can be very satisfying and even fun. I was formally trained in laboratory science, and I have directed multiple research laboratories at Harvard, Yale, and the University of Arizona. However, I have come to appreciate how observational science can also be satisfying and fun, and this is especially the case for supersynchronicity research.

A Brief History of Coincidence and Supersynchronicity

The concept of synchronicity was introduced to psychiatry, psychology, and the general public in the early twentieth century through the creative and sophisticated writings of Carl Jung, MD. Jung defined synchronicity as "the simultaneous occurrence of events that appear significantly related but have no discernible causal connection" (Jung, 1974).

However, the term "simultaneous" is somewhat of a misnomer in that the events do not typically occur "at the same time," but rather as a sequence of events over some period of time. Key to synchronicity is the process of timing.

Also, what is meant by "no discernible causal connection" refers to no discernible *mechanical or material* causes existing between the events, not to the absence of an inferred higher informational and intelligent arranging process (or co-arranging with our minds) of the improbably timed sequences of events observed.

I have found it useful to categorize Jung's synchronicities into the following three types (Schwartz, 2017):

Type I Synchronicities: Two events are significantly related over time (the type of synchronicities typically described by Jung),

Type II Synchronicities: Three to five events are significantly related over time, and

Type III Synchronicities: Six or more events are significantly related over time.

Because of their extremely high improbabilities and evidential nature, I refer to Type III Synchronicities as supersynchronicities.

The scientific term supersynchronicity was coined following the tradition of physics and astrophysics. Physicists often use the word super as a prefix. Well known examples include superconductivity, supercomputers, and superclusters of galaxies.

However, the word super was used as an adjective (i.e. *Super Synchronicity*) rather than a prefix (supersynchronicity) in the title of my book (Schwartz, 2017) for the purpose of familiarity and clarity of communication to a general audience. Common examples include super markets, super stars, and the super bowl.

Experiencing Coincidences and Synchronicities in Life: The Weird Coincidence Survey

Individuals in all walks of life have experienced and reported highly improbable synchronicities in their lives, what Bernard Beitman,

MD, refers to as meaningful coincidences. Beitman is a Visiting Professor at the University of Virginia and former Chairman of the Department of Psychiatry at the University of Missouri-Columbia.

In his book *Connecting with Coincidence: The New Science for Using Synchronicity and Serendipity in your Life* (Beitman, 2016), Beitman presents a wealth of evidence for the reality of meaningful coincidences (i.e. Type I synchronicities) in daily life. His book includes research using a paper and pencil scale he and his colleagues created called the Weird Coincidence Survey.

Table 1 lists key items in the Weird Coincidence Survey (from Coleman, Beitman and Celebi, 2009). Students (n=343) at the University of Missouri rated the items from 1 (strongly disagree), 2 (disagree), 3 (neither agree or disagree), 4 (disagree), to 5 (strongly agree). As would be expected (and the authors predicted). the students varied greatly in their reported experiences of coincidences. Some students scored very low while others scored very high.

Regardless of your past experiences with coincidences and synchronicities, to understand the breath and depth of this phenomenon, I strongly encourage you to read each of these items and consider how you would rate them. If you are interested, you can also fill out a version of the scale on a website created by Beitman that is devoted to coincidence science (www.coincider.com).

Table 1.
Categories and Items from the
Weird Coincidence Survey

Change and Direction
I am introduced to people who unexpectedly further my work/career/education.
In attempting to reach a goal, obstacle after obstacle prevented me from continuing on a path, which I later discovered was better for me.

I advance in my work/career/education through being at the "right place right time."
Meaningful coincidences change my life.
A series of coincidences points me toward taking a particular action in my personal life, career, or education.
Meaningful coincidence helps determine my educational path.
Meaningful coincidence validates my course of action.
Love Connection
I experience strong emotions or physical sensations that were simultaneously experienced at a distance by someone I love.
After a loved one died, I have received some indication that this person was communicating with me.
I am in the right place at the right time to rescue somebody.
I discover that I felt pains and/or anguish as someone I loved was dying in another place.
Think/emotion
I think of calling someone, only to have that person unexpectedly call me.
When my phone rings, I know who is calling (without checking the cell phone screen or using personalized ring tones).
I run into a friend in an out-of-the-way place.
I think about someone, and then that person unexpectedly drops by my house or office or passes me in the hall or street.
Dreams
I have dreams that predict future events.

I have dreams that supply me with specific information about my personal life, career, or education.
I have dreams, and later find out that events in my dreams actually happened around the same time that I had dreamt them.
I have dreams about unknown persons whom I then subsequently met.
Think/idea
I think about a song and then hear it on the radio.
The same name or word has appeared several times in close proximity in different contexts.
I think of an idea and hear or see it on radio, TV, or internet.
I think of a question only to have it answered by external media (ie, radio, TV, people) before I can ask it.
A certain number regularly appears in my life. And that number is_____
I experience a series of numerically-related coincidences (for example, buying something for $1.44 before taking flight #144 at 1:44 pm).
Analysis/interpretation
I believe God speaks to us through meaningful coincidences.
I believe fate works through meaningful coincidences.
I believe coincidences can be explained by the laws of probability or chance.
Meaningful coincidences help me grow spiritually.
I believe that human minds are interconnected.
I feel that meaningful coincidences point to a connection between my internal and external worlds.
After experiencing meaningful coincidence, I analyze my experience.

You will note that one of the items included above specifically addresses the Universal Intelligent Consciousness hypothesis.

> I believe God speaks to us through meaningful coincidences.

Beitman has edited two special issues of *Psychiatric Annals* that focus on coincidences (2009, 2011), and my colleagues and I have contributed a research paper to his series. We reported that in a sample of 123 undergraduate students from the University of Arizona, people who scored high on various personality scales that measure intuition typically scored high on the Weird Coincidence Survey as well (Attig, Schwartz, Figueredo, Jacobs, and Bryson, 2011).

Two Meanings of Coincidence

In general usage the term coincidence has two different meanings:

Definition 1: coincidence as in co-incidental (i.e. co-occurring). This definition simply *describes* the observed occurrence of two events; it does not consider (1) how the co-incidence occurred or (2) what the co-incidence might signify.

Definition 2: coincidence as in randomness or chance (i.e. the phrase "that was just a coincidence."). Here the definition involves a *specific interpretation or inference* about the observed co-occurrence (i.e. that it was a chance pairing and has no intended meaning or message).

When Beitman refers to what he terms "meaningful coincidences," he implies that the co-occurrences (Definition 1) are *not* random (Definition 2) and that they have informational significance for the persons' experiencing them. The concept of meaningful coincidence is comparable to the concept of synchronicity as developed by Jung and employed in clinical psychiatry and psychology.

Beitman (2011) has proposed that future coincidence science should address the following goals:

Develop a taxonomy of coincidences.

Clarify the importance of time intervals and degrees of similarity.

Define methods to judg e the strength and weakness of coincidences and the differing relevance.

Develop and clarify interpretation principles.

Expand the value and clarify the problems of coincidence use.

Further characterize coincidence prone people.

Address the positive correlation between intense affect and increased coincidence frequency.

Test viable theories, recognizing that we may be expanding our understanding of causation.

Develop methods for increasing the frequency of coincidence detection.

The goal I have placed in italics is the focus of the present chapter – evidence for the role of a Universal Intelligent Consciousness as a Universal Coincidence Creator spanning Quantum Physics and Astrophysics (Kafatos, 2018), and everything in between, including human life.

This is not to say that every co-incidence or co-occurrence that exists in the universe is necessarily consciously mediated, or that it has a specific meaning. What I am proposing is that a subset of all co-incidences (Definition 1) are not "just coincidences" (Definition 2) and involve the agency of consciousness as envisioned in postmaterialist science.

Some Personal Examples of Serial Coincidences And Supersynchronicities

Some individuals, myself included, are on the far right side of the bell-shaped curve in terms of witnessing what Beitman (2016) calls "serial coincidences," and I term supersynchroncities (Schwartz,

2017). Whereas Type I synchronicities are fairly common – for example, as measured in the Weird Coincidence Survey – Type III synchronicities are not widely recognized, either in the general public or in the scientific community.

Though formal data have not been collected, my experience is that even among people who consider themselves to be spiritual, relatively few (less than five percent) recall having experienced multiple Type III synchronicities. Supersynchronicities can be quite complex and seem extremely weird; they can be experienced as being mind-boggling if not downright unbelievable.

It turns out that Beitman and I have experienced a collection of curious co-occurrences that began *before* we formally met (e.g. historical connections between us at Yale and at Stanford, both of us independently writing book on coincidence and synchronicity). Being consummate coincidence observers, we began taking notice of our historical as well future coincidences after we formally met in 2010. I subsequently devoted a whole chapter to our complex Type III synchronicity in *Super Synchronicity*.

As a mainstream trained materialist scientist, I would have typically interpreted such coincidences as simply due to chance (the second definition of coincidence), and I would have not given them a second thought. However, after more than thirty years of tracking and analyzing highly improbable serial coincidences in my life and the lives of colleagues, students, and friends, I have learned to keep an open mind about coincidences, especially when they occur in flurries. Consequently, I consciously stay open to the possibility of making surprising and meaningful synchronicity discoveries, even when I am writing a chapter about supersynchronicity evidence for the presence of a Universal Intelligent Consciousness.

For example, literally while I was writing the introduction to this chapter (June 1, 2018), I discovered a surprising additional (and particularly meaningful) coincidence connecting Beitman and me.

In the process of examining the home page of Beitman's clinical website (www.drbeitman.com), and I had never visited it before (I had previously visited his coincidence science website mentioned above), I noticed that Beitman made a point of stating that his office's location was "On the corner of 11th St."

Why did this specific sentence surprise me, and how could a specific number be particularly meaningful? The answer is that my first introduction to the phenomenon of synchronicity involved a statistical anomaly concerning coincidences with the number 11.

As I explain in detail my book *Super Synchronicity*, my supersynchronicity journey at Yale University began with the unexpected discovery of the apparent presence of the number 11 (including sets of numbers and letters that added up to 11, calculated using a standardized set of procedures), in my life at the time. This statistical anomaly involving number 11 coincidences proved to be highly improbable and ultimately very meaningful in my both my professional and personal life (e.g. connection of the number 11 to the mystical tradition of the Kaballah, see below).

What is curious is that the original series of number 11 coincidences that I observed at Yale included at least six specific street numbers, associated street names, and locations involving the number 11 (see Schwartz, 2017 for details). Hence, you can appreciate my surprise in discovering Beitman's specific reference to 11th street in the process of my crafting the introduction to this chapter, and my reason for sharing this discovery process here.

As you will recall in Table 1, two of the items included in Beitman's Weird Coincidence Survey specifically address the question of numbers. They are:

A certain number regularly appears in my life. And that number is_____ .
I experience a series of numerically related coincidences (for example, buying something for $1.44 before taking flight #144 at 1:44 pm).

Had there been just two, or maybe a few, coincidences involving the number 11, I would have immediately interpreted them as due to chance and dismissed them as such. However, I ended up discovering that there were literally more than 11 of them (no joke). In fact, the calculated statistical combination of the coincidences (termed the conditional probability) resulted in a probability value that was so tiny (at least $p < 1^{-9}$) that it caused a science-minded, statistically savvy person like me to pause and ponder.

The question arises, was this highly improbable serial coincidence "just a coincidence" (i.e. the second definition of coincidence)?

Or, was it possible that this seemingly weird pattern of numbers had a specific meaning, either: for me personally (e.g. was there some specific significance, unknown to me at the time, concerning the number 11 per se) and / or scientifically for all of us (e.g. if the serial pattern of events expressed a specific message or meaning, what kind of inferred, seemingly universal and intelligent process could have known this and somehow directly, or indirectly, orchestrated the sequence)?

Range of Possible Explanations: From Material to Postmaterial

When I first noticed the apparent statistical anomaly with the repeated numbers related to 11 at Yale, *and after empirically determining that none of my family, friends or students experienced a similar 11 related anomalous series of coincidences in their respective lives* – what can be considered as a control group – I carefully considered a collection of possible explanations for how it could have occurred. I have listed the range of possible explanations below from the material (lower steps) to the postmaterial (higher steps), including the most challenging possibilities that bridge science and spirituality (the highest steps) (adopted from Schwartz, 2017).

Table 2
Staircase of Possible Explanations of Supersynchronicities

Explanation 12 Universal Intelligent Consciousness —Collective
Explanation 11 Universal Intelligent Consciousness —Personal
Explanation 10 Higher Spiritual Beings
Explanation 9 Human Spirits
Explanation 8 Human Intention and Energy
Explanation 7 Biophysical and Social Self-Organization
Explanation 6 Geophysical and Astrophysical Forces
Explanation 5 Psychological and Social Causes
Explanation 4 Beyond Probable Chance
Explanation 3 Chance Coincidences
Explanation 2 Selective Attention
Explanation 1 Deception—Self (misinformation) or Other (disinformation)

In my supersynchronicity book I had the freedom to devote a long chapter to discussing each of the 12 possible explanations in depth, plus I had the space to write a second chapter specifically focused on what I call quantum synchronicity theory.

Moreover, I had space to discuss how the number 11 turns out to have a historical meaning associated with ancient mystical traditions such as the Kaballah, and how this spiritual meaning directly connects the process of contemplation and intuition (Kaballah literally means "to receive") with the existence of Oneness / Unity and the Universal processes of Differentiation and Evolution.

Here we are limited to a few pages and therefore I must focus on a subset of explanations. Given the theme of this volume, I will contrast the most common materialist explanations (1-4) with the most controversial postmaterialist explanations (9-12).

Explanations 1 and 2 address the most obvious skeptical concerns. Was it possible that my observations reflected a case of careless, if not mistaken, perceptions as well as faulty pattern recognition on my part (e.g. perceiving illusory patterns in otherwise random information)? For the record, unless one is a careful observer and rigorous thinker, it is relatively easy to make such mistakes, and they must be considered.

Explanation 3 address the most obvious statistical concerns. If the observations were accurate, did they simply reflect a highly improbable chance event, for example explained in terms of large number probabilities?

Explanation 4 becomes important only if (a) Explanations 1-3 can be ruled out, and (b) strong evidence for Explanation 4, is obtained. We will consider a compelling example of such evidence in a subsequent section of this chapter.

By contrast, Explanations 9-12 addressed the possibility that postmaterial conscious processes, extending from the effects of postphysical individual human minds (Explanation 9, simply called Human Spirits) to some sort of invisible, potentially Super-Intelligent, Universal Conscious Process (Explanations 11 and 12, such as a Universal Intelligent Consciousness), were playing a role in mediating the complex sequence of synchronicities observed, in the process conveying intentional meaning, if not implicit guidance, to the people involved.

When I was at Yale (1976-1988), I assumed that Explanations 1-3 had to be true. Even if I allowed myself to accept the fact that the totality of the evidence for the number 11's provide support for Explanation 4 (beyond chance effects), I preferred to limit my considerations to possible higher order materialist explanations (e.g. Explanation 5, psychological and social causes such as the six degrees of separation explanation) rather than address the highest postmaterialist explanations (9-12).

The very idea of Explanations 9-12 flew in the face of my materialist education, they severely challenged my professional conceptual worldview, and they required that I seriously consider rejecting my essentially atheist upbringing and adopting a more consciousness focused (and spiritual) vision of the universe.

Rational and Rigorous Inference: The Common Requirement for the 12 Explanations

Before discussing how I ultimately was led (1) to reject Explanations 1-4 as being credible explanations for understanding the existence of complex serial coincidences, and (2) to accept a combination of Explanations 9-12 as being essential for understanding sophisticated supersynchronicities, it is important to address what is a common requirement underlying all 12 explanations. The common requirement is that they all involve degrees of *rational and rigorous inference* based on observation. Let's consider the initial four materialist explanations in terms of the inference process.

We must *infer* the process of self-deception (e.g. denial of evidence that challenge our beliefs) or other-deception (e.g. conscious lying in his or her reporting) from the behavior of the person we observe (Explanation 1).

We must *infer* the process of selective attention from the observations made (e.g. that the person selectively experiences, and reports seeing certain things and does not experience and report seeing other things) (Explanation 2).

We must *infer* the process of chance from a collection of data / events whose order we cannot describe or understand (e.g. the data "seem" to be random) (Explanation 3).

We must *infer* the process of some sort of causal connections, if not organizing process (s), from the patterns of data / events observed (e.g. through statistical conditional probability analyses revealing ultra-low probabilities of the observed sequences of events occurring by chance) (Explanation 4).

As we continue to move up the staircase of possible

explanations, the process of inference becomes ever more complex, abstract, and demanding of logic and rigor. By the time we reach the top four explanations, the inference process becomes especially sophisticated and challenging. As you will see, attempting to explain the documented sequence of 15 giraffe-Paris pairs of events requires a sophistication of inference concerning the level of intelligence and power that would be required to orchestrate (conceive and manifest) such an astronomically improbable and hyper-meaningful sequence events spanning people and time.

Even individuals who accept the reality of the improbability of such events (myself included) find it challenging to discern when a given coincidence or string of coincidences has potential agency and meaning, and when it does not. Here is how one anonymous reviewer of this chapter said it, paraphrasing his words slightly:

How do we actually know when something is coming from a Higher Power or when it is just that there happen to be ravens, etc. around and we notice them? I know that synchronicities are real. However, I also suspect that many times when I or others see things - giraffes, bears, Eiffel towers, etc, they are just beautiful images that we can appreciate, or some things that we are supposed to attend to in a different way....

It is like the question many spiritual seekers have about their meditations: how do we know whether something coming to us is from our own minds, or is from our Higher Selves?

My general response is that the first thing I do is attempt to estimate the degree of improbability of the serial events observed. The greater the number of events, the greater the improbability of their having occurred by chance, and the greater the justification for searching for potential causal explanations. In other words, we can scientifically infer that a set of events is most likely not random and represents some sort of causal, intelligently created set of events, and still remain "skeptical" (i.e. questioning) about what the organized sequence of events might mean.

The conceptual process of determining potential personal meanings from the patterns of observations is highly complex and beyond the scope of the present chapter. The reader is referred to Beitman (2016) for a detailed discussion of the question of inferring meaning from improbable coincidences.

How I Changed My Mind

I should explain that I seem to have a natural proclivity for mathematics and detecting patterns in numbers. For example, in high school I often earned 100's in math exams, and as absurd as this may sound, I received final grades of "100" (averaged up by the teachers or professors to fit their grading systems) in a math course (high school), a physics course (undergraduate), and a statistics course (graduate school). Also, I was fortunate to have received excellent scientific training in experimental psychology, psychophysiology, and clinical psychology at Cornell University, the University of Wisconsin, and Harvard University.

I share this personal history to help you understand that my fascination with, and ultimate acceptance of, non-random (Explanation 4) and meaningful serial coincidences in real life and their potential evidence for the existence of intelligent conscious processes in the universe (Explanations 9-12), was that I had the formal education and associated analytic skills required for carefully evaluating, and ultimately rejecting, Explanations 1-3 (and other materialist explanations 5-9) as sufficient to account for such anomalies.

Because potentially meaningful synchronicities are primarily observed in people's personal lives (though once one learns how to look for them, it is possible to discover meaningful synchronicities in other levels of nature and the cosmos as well), it is understandable why the study of synchronicities has historically been the province of clinical psychiatry and psychology.

In a series papers reported in the peer-reviewed journal

Spirituality in Clinical Practice (Schwartz 2014, 2015a-b) published by the American Psychological Association, I have reported multiple examples of extraordinarily improbable and highly meaningful supersynchronicities containing 10 to 18 synchronicities in a given sequence of time. The book *Super Synchronicity* (Schwartz, 2017) lists more than 100 supersynchronicities involving more than 100 credible individuals from all walks of life, including scientists, physicians, heads of companies, lawyers, teachers, artists, students, etc., and it provides detailed evidence of more than a dozen highly complex and sophisticated supersynchronicities.

After carefully evaluating the totality of the evidence, I have been "forced to the conclusion" that the simplest and most parsimonious explanation for the evidence, including the most controversial and mind-boggling of the evidence, is the probable existence of a Universal, Super-Intelligent, Holographic-Like consciousness – what Larry Dossey calls the One Mind, Marjorie Woollacott calls the Infinite Awareness, Menas Kafatos calls the Living Presence, and Sri Aurobindo calls the Super Mind. The pattern of coincidences is too sophisticated, it requires the simultaneous and sequential synchrony of too many people, and it requires too much knowledge of all the participants over time, to be organized and orchestrated by human intelligence per se.

Why do I say, "forced to the conclusion"? The reason is that I have adopted a rational and evidence-based process for drawing conclusions about the nature of reality, which for clarity of communication purposes, I simply refer to as the Five Additive Criteria Test (FACT).

The FACT framework was introduced in Chapter 2 of this volume. A summary of the five additive criteria was shown in Table 3 in Chapter 2 and is reprinted below:

TABLE 3
The Five Additive Criteria Comprising FACT

Criteria	Description
Criterion 1:	Reason and Scientific Theory
Criterion 2:	Scientific Evidence
Criterion 3:	Community of Credible and Trustworthy Believers
Criterion 4:	Direct Personal Experiences
Criterion 5:	Responsible Consideration of Skepticism about Criteria 1-4

As explained in Chapter 2, *in those instances where all five criteria have been clearly met, then logic dictates that the responsible (and ethical) course of action is for us to accept the conclusion as most likely true, no matter how novel, challenging, counter-intuitive, or even mind-boggling the conclusion may be.*

To illustrate the potential universality of the FACT framework, I will illustrate below how I have applied it to the phenomenon of supersynchronicity and its implications for inferring the existence not of the primacy of consciousness (as in awareness) per se, but more specifically for the existence of the primacy of *Intelligent* Consciousness as a Universal quality regarding the role of Consciousness in nature and the physical cosmos. As you will see, evidence for supersynchronicity can strain one's imagination and push it beyond its limits.

Before considering Criterion 1: Reason and Scientific Theory, that support Explanations 9-12, let's take a detailed look at the phenomenon of supersynchronicity and discuss Criterion 2: Scientific

Evidence, focusing on a compelling example published in a peer-reviewed journal.

Criterion 2: Scientific Evidence

The following supersynchronicity involving 15 pairsof replicated coincidences (i.e. a novel combination of two events that occurred 15 times over 13 days) was reported in detail in Schwartz (2015a). It illustrates the complexity of sophisticated patterns of serial coincidences that can be observed and documented in real life. It also complements and extends the topic of the survival of consciousness hypothesis discussed previously in Chapter 2.

I remind the reader that we typically establish the reality of this phenomenon from the perspective of observational science rather than laboratory science.

A brief history: On June 9, 2014, I was contacted by a prominent physician whom I will call Dr. G. (a pseudonym). Dr. G. was calling on behalf of a successful businessman and dear friend of his whom I will call Mr. D. Mr. D. was deeply grieving the death of his parents, and he desperately wanted to speak with a skilled research medium (a person who had been scientifically documented to be genuine – i.e. was not a professional magician or fraud – and could be trusted).

Having published three books describing compelling evidence of genuine mediumship documented in carefully scrutinized individuals using single blind, double blind, and triple-blind protocols (Schwartz 2002, 2005, 2011), I was in a good position not only to recommend highly responsible and skilled research mediums, but to potentially make the request that these mediums make an exception and provide Mr. D. with quickly scheduled readings.

I was able to speak with Mr. D. on June 14, 2014. Based on this conversation, I decided that I should try to pull out all the stops and see if I could arrange for Mr. D. to have long-distance phone readings with three gifted research mediums. Mr. D. is an open-minded yet skeptical person, and he is deeply interested in research in this area. We agreed that that if I could arrange for him to have private readings with three different mediums under blinded conditions, and if the readings were especially evidential, that these experiences might help him and his family with the grieving process.

Sometimes the seemingly impossible happens relatively effortlessly, and I managed to arrange for Mr. D. to have long-distance readings on June 17th, June 23rd, and June 24th. These dates are important because the combination of 15 synchronicity pairings began on June 18th, seemingly peaked on June 24th, and then continued through June 28th. The inspiration to write the article occurred on June 25th, a date which will become especially relevant.

As it so happened, I was scheduled to be in New York City on June 25th and 26th to serve as a Visiting Scholar in Lisa Miller's Spirituality Mind Body Institute, Summer Intensive Master's Degree Program at Columbia University. I was invited to spend a day and a half teaching the students about postmaterialist science and psychology and the emerging convergence of science and spirituality. This included theory and research concerning the existence of the living soul (e.g. contemporary mediumship research) and the existence of a greater spiritual reality (e.g. contemporary synchronicity research as related to the Universal Intelligent Consciousness hypothesis; Schwartz, 2006).

I decided that I would feature a discussion about God, synchronicity and postmaterialist psychology for these students, especially a previous article (Schwartz, 2014) that reported synchronicities, which included Lisa Miller, the director of the summer institute (and coincidentally the co-editor of the journal). Meanwhile, it just so happened that both Mr. D. and Dr. G. lived part of the time in NYC. In fact, it was possible for me to have the opportunity to meet with both Mr. D. and Dr. G. on June 27th following Mr. D.'s readings.

However, prior to coming to NYC, I had no idea that an extraordinary combination of fifteen giraffe-Paris *pairs* of synchronicities was about to unfold which connected the three of us, and that this collection of spiritually transformative synchronicities would serve as an ideal exemplar of real-life evidence of spirituality in practice for the Columbia masters students.

Table 3 briefly summarizes the 15 pairs of synchronicities, including their dates of occurrence. The Schwartz (2015a) article presented each pair in detail, placed it in context, and explained its significance. In this chapter I have space to present the first 5 in detail.

TABLE 3:
Summary Listing of 15 Giraffe-Paris Pairs

PAIR NUMBER	DATE	NATURE OF GIRAFFE – PARIS PAIR
1	6/16	Mr. D. secretly requests giraffe and Paris information from mediums
2	6/18	G. Schwartz notices giraffe and Eiffel Tower at Canyon Ranch
3	6/22	G. Schwartz reads giraffe and French in Davids and Schwartz book
4	6/22	R. Schwartz sees giraffe picture and reads Paris in My Friend Michael book
5	6/24	Dr. G. sends giraffe photo and Schwartz's watch two movies involving Paris
6	6/24	Bag displayed with 2 giraffes, two stores feature Paris name
7	6/	Novelty store has giraffe with French writing,

Is Consciousness Primary?

PAIR NUMBER	DATE	NATURE OF GIRAFFE – PARIS PAIR
	24	Paris store around corner
8, 9, 10, 11	6/26	Four Columbia students share recent giraffe - Paris coincidence
12	6/26	Drug store features giraffes and whole window of Paris products
13	6/27	Miller's son wears giraffe socks, Dr. Parisetti emails me a research proposal
14	6/28	NY Airport, CNN commercial shows giraffe, then shows Eiffel Tower
15	6/28	Atlanta Airport, store has miniature giraffe with French writing, Crepe store, woman with luggage that says Paris and purchased in Paris

It is important to understand that I was not informed about Mr. D.'s secret experiment (called #1 in Table 3) until Dr. G. had spontaneously emailed Mr. D. and me the giraffe photo (Synchronicity #5) and Mr. D. had finished all three readings. *Hence, I was not aware that pairs #1 – 5 were potential synchronicities until Mr. D. confessed his secret experiment.*

I invite you to consider the following question: what percentage of your family members and friends, if you asked them the question "What is your favorite animal?" and "What is your favorite city" do you think would say both "giraffe" and "Paris"? Is the giraffe your favorite animal and is Paris your favorite city?

As you read the evidence, think back to the last time that you experienced both a giraffe and Paris closely in time; it turns out that the base rate for experiencing such pairings is extremely small.

Pair #1: Mr. D. Initiates a Private Secret Experiment With Giraffe and Paris

Sometime between Mr. D.'s conversation with me on June 14th and his first long-distance phone reading on June 18th, Mr. D. decided to conduct a secret, private experiment. He requested (in his mind) that his deceased mother reveal herself by bringing up her favorite animal (the giraffe) and her favorite city (Paris). All of us – Dr. G., the three mediums, and me – were kept blind to this self-science experiment. I list this as Pair #1 because it occurred first. However, I was not informed about it until June 24th, the day after the three readings had been completed and Dr. G. had spontaneously texted us a photo of a giraffe (Event #5). This novel situation makes the emergence of the giraffe – Paris pairs even more meaningful. Since Mr. D.'s mediumship readings were strictly confidential they will not be discussed here.

Pair #2: G. Schwartz notices a giraffe and an Eiffel Tower at Canyon Ranch

On Wednesday, June 18th I had dinner with two guests in the main dining room at Canyon Ranch in Tucson (www.canyonranch.com). We selected this night because at that time I regularly lectured at Canyon Ranch on Wednesday nights. This couple is unusual in that the husband recently received a Master of Divinity degree from Yale University (he entered the Yale Divinity School after he had retired from a successful business career in his late 50's); also, his wife recently retired from a successful career as an investment banker.

The dining room has at least sixty tables. Four tables look directly out a window at beautifully landscaped area, which includes a gigantic statue of a giraffe (maybe 18 or so feet tall). Not only were we coincidently seated at this table, but I was seated in such a way that I looked directly out at this giraffe.

Since the giraffe has been there for at least a couple of years, my being seated looking at the giraffe that night, though it was rare for me (e.g. maybe once in a hundred meals), held no special meaning for me at the time.

Then two days later, on Friday, June 20th (I regularly gave a workshop at Canyon Ranch on Friday afternoons) – I noticed there was a three-foot tall statue of the Eiffel Tower (used to support a sign of special events for the day) just outside the dining room.

This Eiffel Tower stand had been placed there every Friday (French food day) for a least a couple of years, so it's being there per se was not novel. *What was special, however, was that I actually stopped and stared at it that Friday, and even considered taking a photograph of it! I had never experienced this inclination before.*

Though I thought it odd that the Eiffel Tower was capturing my attention that afternoon, since I had no context to place it in, I simply noted the urge and let it be. I had no idea at the time that this Canyon Ranch giraffe and Eiffel tower "awareness pairing" might become meaningful a few days later.

Pair #3: G. Schwartz reads giraffe and Paris in David's and Schwartz' book

On Sunday June 22nd, my wife Rhonda and I flew to New York City. I decided to read Part I of a book I was writing with Paul Davids, the producer of a documentary titled *The Life After Death Project* (www.lifeafterdeathproject.com). Part I was written by Davids; I was writing Part II at the time (see Davids and Schwartz, 2016).

In reading the section concerning a research mediumship reading I had arranged for Davids, I was reminded that this medium (1) had mentioned seeing an animal which looked like a giraffe, and (2) she had emphasized that France was importantly related to the deceased (actually Paris, though she did not say this).

Reading about the giraffe in this context reminded me how

very rare it was for a medium to mention a giraffe in a mediumship reading (I have witnessed over a thousand mediumship readings, and I could not recall a medium ever mentioning a giraffe). I had no idea that the timing of reading about this giraffe in a French context would become important in a few days.

Pair #4: R. Schwartz sees giraffe picture and reads Paris in *My Friend Michael* book

Meanwhile, Rhonda had spontaneously decided to bring along a book titled *My Friend Michael,* and she began reading it on the plane on June 22nd. She noticed that the book included a photo of three hedge-type bushes, each carved in the shape of a giraffe (which struck her as odd), and she read that the book was dedicated to someone named Paris (and others). It is important to understand that Rhonda only mentioned this giraffe – Paris pairing on June 24th, after I had shared with her my conversation with Mr. D that morning. She then showed it to me in her book.

Pair #5: Dr. G. sends giraffe photo and the Schwartz's watch two movies involving Paris

Seemingly out of the blue, on the morning of June 24th, Dr. G. texted Mr. D. and me a photo he had just taken of a giraffe at sunset. Dr. G. was in Africa at the time. Apparently, he happened to glance out his window and saw a real giraffe walking by. He thought the photo was beautiful (it was) and would make us smile (it did).

Meanwhile, the night before (June 23rd), Rhonda and I spontaneously watched two movies On Demand. The first movie took place in Paris, and included a scene involving the Eiffel Tower; the second movie took place in New York City but included a brief scene involving the Eiffel Tower.

It was only after (1) Mr. D. called later in the morning of June 24th, (2) he confessed his secret Giraffe – Paris experiment with the mediums, and (3) he mentioned how odd it was that Dr. G. had texted us with the photo of the giraffe, that I began to put two and two together, and in conversations with Rhonda and with Mr. D. envisioned the possible unfolding of the previous giraffe – Paris coincidence pair.

Pairs #6 - #15 Space precludes presenting the details for these additional 10 pairs here; they are available in the publication (Schwartz, 2015). What matters here is that you understand that four of the giraffe – Paris pairs involved students at the Spirituality Mind Body Institute at Columbia plus other individuals, including Lisa and her children.

When we attempt to envision what kind of intelligence could conceive and orchestrate such a sweeping assortment of meaningful and timely pairs, it seems incredulous to imagine that any single (or combination) of humans – in the physical and or postphysical (i.e. in spirit) could have conceived and arranged them. Hence, returning to Table 2, it seems unlikely that Explanations 9 and 10 would be sufficient to explain this supersynchronicity of pairs.

How Rare is This Combination of Giraffe – Paris Pairs?

In order to appreciate how rare is this combination of giraffe – Paris pairs, it is valuable to take a moment and ponder the likelihood of their replicated pairing in English speaking countries. Here is not the place to consider such calculations in great detail, only to highlight their astronomical improbability – and I mean this literally (see below).

The following analysis employs data on word frequency usage. Although this procedure is inherently limited and simplistic, word frequency usage provides a heuristic way to *estimate* the potential appearance of visual stimuli and events associated with specifiable occurrences. What we are doing is attempting to determine base rates of the probability of giraffes and Paris occurring, first individually, and then in pairs; this can be employed as an estimated control condition for comparison.

As an anonymous reviewer of the published article noted that although this methodology is "very limited," s/he concluded that "as an example and / or starting point it may still be adequate." As you will see, *when we use the most conservative estimates of the probability of their pairing – I call this super conservative – the estimates are clearly (if not excessively) adequate.*

According to www.wordcount.org (calculated from a British data base consisting of 100 million words taken from diverse sources), the word giraffe is ranked at 34,887. The word Paris is ranked at 1,681; the word Eiffel is ranked at 35,831.

The conditional (multiplied) probability of the paired rankings of giraffe *and* Paris is 1 out of 58,645,047. The conditional probability of the paired rankings of giraffe and Eiffel tower is even more improbable, 1 out of 1,250,036,097. Of course, to calculate their pairing in terms of total words in a given document (e.g. giraffe and Paris occurring in a document containing 250 words), the values would be adjusted upwards (i.e. their pairing would be more probable).

A more conservative (and probably more accurate) estimate of their pairing can be derived from http://www.wordcount.org/querycount.php. It calculates the rankings based upon the number of times people used www.wordcount.org to look up a given word. For queries about giraffe, the ranking is 2048. For queries about Paris the ranking is 596, and for Eiffel the ranking is 20,353.

The conditional probability of someone looking up giraffe, followed by looking up Paris, is 1 out of 1,220,608. For giraffe and Eiffel, it is 1 out of 41,682,944.

Let's be more conservative and say that the pairing of giraffe and Paris is 1 in a 100,000 rather than 1 in a 1,000,000. The question arises, what is the probability that giraffe – Paris pairings will replicate 15 times by chance alone in a relatively short period of time? The calculated value would be 10000015 which is 1E +75. This is 1 followed by 75 zero's!

Let's be very conservative and say that the pairing of giraffe and Paris is 1 in a 1000. The giraffe – Paris pairing value would be 100015 which is 1E + 45. This is 1 followed by 45 zero's, which is still an astronomically huge number.

Finally, *let's be "super" conservative and say that the pairing of giraffe and Paris is as frequent as 1 in a 100. This is clearly a gross overestimate of the pairing of giraffe and Paris events in normal daily life. The giraffe – Paris pairing value for 15 co-occurrences of their pairing would be 10015 which is 1 followed by 30 zero's.*

How can we understand such huge numbers – even just the super conservative one?

Consider the following. Let's say that it takes a minute for us to observe a giraffe reference / object / picture followed by a Paris reference / object / picture. Let's say that we are going to actively search for giraffe – Paris pairings every minute, 24 hours a day, every day, 365 days a year, for as long as takes for such a pairing to occur by chance. How long, in years, would it take to observe fifteen pairings?

The age of the universe is generally believed to be 13.7 billion years old. There are 525,600 minutes in a year. The total number of minutes in the age of the universe comes out to 7,200,720,000,000 which is less than 1 followed by 13 zero's. *Simply stated, the probability of 15 giraffe – Paris pairings occurring in a short period of time (e.g. 1 followed by 45 zero's) would take much (much) longer than the entire age of the universe (1 followed by 13 zero's) to occur by chance alone – hence the term astronomically improbable.*

Notice that even if we could speed up the real-life process and take only a second to observe a giraffe – Paris pairing rather than a minute, this would only increase the number of possible pairings we could detect nonstop over the entire age of the universe from 1 followed by 13 zero's to approximately 1 followed by 15 zero's.

And even if giraffe – Paris pairings occurred as frequently as 1 out of a 100 times, getting fifteen pairs in a row in a short span of time (i.e. thirteen days) would be in the neighborhood of 1 followed by 30 zero's. This is more that the age of the universe multiplied by the age of the universe.

Finally, what if every single person on the planet living today – approximately 7.5 billion people, from infants to the elderly – did this simultaneously. Conservatively rounding this number up, this would be 1 followed by 10 zeros. Going from 1 person to 10,000,000,000 people would only reduce the conditional probability from 1E-30 to 1E-20. In other words, it would still take longer that the age of the universe to see fifteen pairs occur by chance.

And this is just one example of a major supersynchronicity. Hence the justification of "mind boggling."

An Amusing Giraffe-Paris Pairing During the Editing of This Chapter?

It is curious that when Marjorie Woollacott was reading the first draft of this chapter, she spontaneously experienced a giraffe-Paris pairing. Given its potential significance to intended purpose of this chapter, it is appropriate for us to report (and honor?) it.

Concerning the giraffe, apparently Marjorie was ordering a new pair of hiking pants from www.moosejaw.com, and what came up on her screen was a picture of a baby giraffe. Marjorie thought this was odd since pictures of giraffes do not typically appear in the sites she visits. Below is a screen shot from Marjorie's computer.

Given the surprising appearance of the baby giraffe picture during the period she was reading about the giraffe-Paris supersynchronicity, I asked Marjorie if she had recently witnessed anything connected to Paris.

Upon reflection, she remembered that the night before, she had watched a movie, *Vincent Van Gogh: A New Way of Seeing*, and Van Gogh had spent time in Paris. In a subsequent email Marjorie wrote that "I think there were a few scenes that involved Paris, or at least the outskirts, as he went there to live with his brother Theo, shortly before he committed suicide."

As someone who pays close attention to coincidences in terms of both statistics and possible meanings, I could not help smiling for three reasons:

The subtitle of the movie, *"A new way of seeing"* complements Jung's quote that introduces this chapter: *Synchronicity is an ever present reality for those who have eyes to see."*

Vincent's brother's name happens to be Theo, which means God in Greek. Since this chapter addresses the Universal Intelligent Consciousness hypothesis, the coincidence of this name is humorous to say the least. And

Although this additional coincidence borders on the absurd, it is amusing (if nothing else) that Kafatos happens to be Greek. As Einstein said, "If at first the idea is not absurd, then there is no hope for it."

Being a careful scientist, Marjorie is cautious about drawing any conclusions about the timing of her surprising giraffe-Paris experience since she has never paid attention to the frequency of giraffe and Paris occurrences in her daily life. However, having investigated the spontaneous frequency of giraffe and Paris pairings in many people's lives for the past few years, my working hypothesis is that Marjorie may have just joined the giraffe-Paris Coincidence Club.

And if this instance causes you to wonder whether the Universal Intelligent Consciousness has a sense of humor, you are not alone. Sometimes sequences of coincidences do seem silly if not hilarious (e.g. I present evidence of a supersynchronicity involving 21 duck events in a 6 day period in Schwartz, 2017). Just because a given supersynchronicity may seem silly is not a reasonable or responsible reason to dismiss it; it may be telling us something important about the nature of the Universal Intelligent Consciousness, that is, if we have eyes to see....

Criterion 1: Reason and Scientific Theory

In light of the totality of the evidence described above, is it possible that some sort of "Guiding-Organizing-Designing," "One Mind," or "Super Mind" process might exist and be at least partly responsible for the emergence of such highly improbable, complex, and meaningful timed sequences of events in real life? (Explanations 11 and 12)?

The answer is yes. Various authors have reviewed the logic and theory (e.g. Chalmers, 1996; Haisch, 2010; Chopra, 2014). I will include one fundamental example here (from Schwartz, 2006) that illustrates the fallacy of using randomness as an overarching explanation for supersynchronicities.

Many scientists and laymen alike assume that "randomness" is a genuine process in nature, and that events can and do occur "by chance." The existence of randomness is a core assumption of Darwinian evolution, and it is a core assumption in certain interpretations of quantum physics as well. This assumption is so deeply ingrained in contemporary science that it is rarely questioned. However, logic and theory appropriately integrated lead to a different conclusion. (See also Spencer, 2012 for a critique of related common assumptions about quantum physics.)

First, statistical theory is very clear that two conditions are necessary in order for a random process to occur and result in the appearance of a random distribution of numbers. The first condition is that *each event must be independent of every other event over time*. In other words, the flipping of one coin, for example, cannot have an influence or carry any effect on the flipping of the next coin. Independence of events is essential for a random process to occur.

The second condition, which follows from the first, is that *the events cannot change over time*. In other words, the coins cannot wear out, the coin flipper cannot learn how to influence the inferred randomness of the process, etc.

It turns out that when both of these conditions are met—and they can never be completely met, even by computer algorithms—one will *always* observe a random distribution of numbers (e.g. the well-known bell-shaped curve). *With a suitable number of observations, this effect will be observed 100% of the time.*

For example, if we program a computer to (1) select 100 numbers "randomly" from 1 to 100 and then calculate the mean of these 100 numbers (the mean will be approximately 50), then (2) perform this operation 100 times, and (3) plot the distribution of the means, we will observe a "bell-shaped" curve with a peak around 50, and we will obtain this pattern 100% of the time! we will never get a straight line, or a V-shaped curve, or an inverted bell-shaped curve. In fact, being an experimental scientist, I have actually written such a program, tested it, and confirmed that these are the results.

The implications of this are quite profound. *First of all, randomness does not occur "by chance"—randomness occurs only when the precise conditions (of independence) are met. Second, when these conditions do occur—i.e. independence of events—the probability of observing a random distribution of numbers is 100%.*

Note that none of the above is controversial per se. However, it is unfortunately not widely known or appreciated, even by many distinguished scientists.

In sum, logic and theory leads to the following conclusion:

Creative / new patterns of events do not occur "by" chance. Rather, what "randomness" does (i.e. what the condition of independence does) is give creative / new events "the" chance (i.e. opportunity) to occur.

Now, the key question arises: does complete independence exist in nature as the statistics of randomness requires? *Logic and theory are very clear here; the answer is decidedly no.*

Both classical and contemporary theories in physics explain how all physical systems—from subatomic particles to superclusters of galaxies, and everything in between—are interconnected by forces and fields. For example, Newtonian theory states that every object that has mass has a gravitational field extending out in all directions, infinitely, in space. These universal gravitational fields are "mutually attractive" and hold the entire universe together. The existence of interconnecting fields includes electrical and magnetic fields, and physics now includes "dark energy" as an additional interconnecting process.

Moreover, classical and contemporary systems theories explain how all components in all levels of systems are interconnected via positive and negative feedback loops. These feedback loops not only influence the relationship between components but *alter the processes over time*. In fact, feedback loops are critical to learning in all systems, be they neural networks in the brain or neural network software in a computer.

In other words, the preponderance of theory indicates that systems in nature are not independent; on the contrary, they are *interdependent*. Basic logic points to the irrefutable conclusion that nature does not fit the conditions necessary for truly "random processes" to occur.

It follows that just because a given sequence of numbers may "appear" to be random does not necessarily mean that they reflect a "random process."

Consider the number pi (the circumference of a circle divided by its diameter). The number sequence in pi has been calculated to millions of digits, and no mathematician has yet discovered a repeating sequence (or explanation) for the resulting sequence. The sequence of numbers appears "random." And yet, the exact sequence of numbers is replicated 100% of the time, regardless of the size of the circle involved in the calculations.

If "randomness" does not occur "by chance" (instead requiring two specific conditions related to complete independence), then, for even stronger reasons, "order" cannot occur "by chance" either. If we cannot rationally and justifiably explain the existence and evolution of order in nature and the universe as due to an inferred "random process," then we must logically look to the existence of some sort of creative ordering / synchronizing process in nature and the universe. It is unscientific and illogical to assert anything other than something similar to this conclusion.

In addition, experiments in quantum physics using the double-slit paradigm indicate that not only does the act of measuring the behavior of a photon or electron alter the behavior and distributions of the photons and electrons, but some scientists even claim that the mind itself can alter the distributions. Radin and colleagues (summarized in Radin, 2018 and his chapter in this volume) have conducted a series of elegant experiments demonstrating how the human mind, when intentionally focused on the optical measurement system, appears to alter the behavior of the photons in replicable ways.

Moreover, years of experiments in psychokinesis have documented the effects of the human mind on "random number generators"—be they created via software, or by hardware tracking "noisy" electrical circuits—and these effects can be observed both locally and globally (e.g. Nelson et al, 2011).

Probably the most important thing to consider concerning the relevance of these basic science experiments to the phenomenon of supersynchronicity is the replicated observations made in double-slit experiments, where single photons or electrons are emitted and detected by CCD (charge-coupled device) cameras behind the two slits.

Even though the photons or electrons are being emitted as "individual" events—and they appear to occur "randomly" as "individual" dots, appearing one at a time (as registered by individual pixels on the CCD)—what emerges (i.e. *accumulates over time*) is the appearance of a non-random "interference" wave pattern, and under appropriately controlled experimental conditions, this emerging wave pattern replicates 100% of the time!

The individual dots only appear "random" in that we cannot predict where a given dot will appear on the CCD camera at any given moment in time. *However, this seemingly random interpretation belies the fact that some sort of invisible organizing process (which the famous physicist David Bohm called "pilot waves") leads the dots to emerge over time as a completely replicable wave pattern of dots, mathematically described as an interference wave function.*

I have suggested that synchronicities are like photons or electrons: individual synchronicity events appear like individual "dots" and may seem "random." However, over time non-random patterns can be observed; that is, if one is prepared to "connect the dots" and see the emerging bigger picture, which is the basis of what I call the Quantum Synchronicity Theory (Schwartz, 2017).

If you want to observe the behavior of electrons or photons, then you need to open your eyes and read the measurements. Similarly, as Jung said, "synchronicity is an ever-present reality for those who have eyes to see", which is especially the case with supersynchronicities.

Is Consciousness Primary?

Criterion 3: Community of Credible and Trustworthy Believers

As discussed in Chapter 2, the third criterion requires a community of credible and trustworthy people who support the possibility that a given belief is probably valid.

When it comes to novel beliefs, and especially highly controversial beliefs, discovering a community of credible and trustworthy people who have formed and adopted the belief provides additional justification for seriously considering the possibility that the belief may be accurate and responsible. I have found that discovering such people has played an important role in my coming to accept the conclusions provided by Criteria 1 and 2 above.

I have developed a simple yet comprehensive set of parameters for determining whether someone fits Criteria 3. For ease of learning and remembering, I call this set of seven parameters the "Seven S's". They are:

Successful,
Smart,
Skeptical,
Sophisticated,
Savvy,
Sane, and
Straight (as in, honest and trustworthy)

It is worth repeating these criteria here. Though one can debate the precise definitions of each of these seven S's, the fact is that it is relatively easy to find individuals who clearly meet all of these seven S's: People who are highly *successful* in their chosen professions (CEOs and executives in major companies, senior professors at major universities, directors of distinguished institutions and centers, winners of esteemed prizes and awards, etc.),
AND

They are very *smart* (they may have high IQ scores, have received high grades in college and graduate schools, are established problem solvers, etc.),
> AND

> They are demonstrably and genuinely *skeptical*, as in they are questioning, thoughtful, challenging of information and ideas, cautious about drawing conclusions, etc.,

> AND

> They show strong evidence of being *sophisticated* in complex thinking, are careful to consider multiple viewpoints and alternative sources of information and interpretation, are able to analyze and integrate divergent and even conflicting information and interpretations, etc.,

> AND

> They have a history of being *savvy*, as in they are experienced, knowledgeable, balanced, mature, clever, not easily fooled, etc.,

> AND

> They are described by their peers (as well as reliable health care professionals) as being *sane* (e.g. they do not show any evidence of neurosis, psychosis, delusions, psychopathy, personality disorder, extreme narcissism, cognitive impairments of information processing and memory, etc.),

> AND, MOST IMPORTANTLY

> They are *straight*, as in they are trustworthy, honest, ethical, focused on accuracy / truthfulness, humble, and aware of limitations or absence of important information or knowledge in a given circumstance, etc.

Now, when these types of "Seven S" people hold a belief in something, it is wise (i.e. rational and responsible) for us to give them the "benefit of the doubt" regarding the probable validity of the belief in question.

In the case of supersynchronicities, super-timing, and the orchestrating presence of some sort of universal mind (i.e. a Super Mind), I have met over a hundred "Seven S" people who have formed and hold this belief. They include scientists, professors, CEOs, lawyers, creative artists, physicians, and therapists (Schwartz, 2017).

Moreover, it is reasonable to conclude that the contributors to the present volume meet these seven criteria as well.

Note that I am not proposing that we accept their (or in the case of this volume, our) beliefs about the primacy of consciousness blindly and without reflection, but that we give these beliefs serious consideration, and not let our "emotional doubts" get in the way.

Also, I am not proposing that Criterion 3, by itself, is sufficient to justify adopting and holding a specific belief. What I am saying is that when Criteria 1 *and* 2 have been met, the *addition* of Criterion 3 adds further reason to support the idea that adopting and holding a given belief may be accurate and responsible.
Criterion 3 certainly has helped me come to finally accept the logic and evidence of supersynchronicity as being a real phenomenon that strongly supports the primacy of consciousness hypothesis.

Criterion 4: Direct Personal Experience

Unlike many phenomena in science, it is possible for people to have direct experiences of certain core phenomena related to postmaterialist consciousness research. Experiencing meaningful coincidences, and even supersynchronicities, can be enjoyed widely. Books like Beitman (2016) and Schwartz (2017) provide compelling evidence for this fact.

It turns out that every one of the contributors to this volume have experienced meaningful coincidences in their lives, and a subset are like me in terms of being on the far right side of the bell-shaped synchronicity experiencing curve.

However, one must be open to seeing synchronicities, for as Jung reminds us, "Synchronicity is an ever-present reality for those who have eyes to see." This requires that we develop the skills – including the discernment – to track and interpret them. Ascribing potential meaning and significance to supersynchronicities is one of the most difficult and challenging opportunities in the study of supersynchronicities and their applications to decision making in life. I have recommended taking a scientific approach to tracking and interpreting potential synchronicities, and I provide some guidelines for practicing self-science successfully (Schwartz, 2017).

Criterion 5: Responsible Consideration of Skepticism about Criteria 1-4

As discussed in Chapter 2, the fifth criterion refers to responsible consideration of skepticism about Criteria 1-4. Does responsible skepticism about Criteria 1-4 still support the possibility that supersynchronicities are real, and that the simplest and most parsimonious explanation of the totality of the evidence requires our serious consideration of Explanations 9-12? The key word here is "responsible".

By "responsible" I mean:
honest,
fair,
comprehensive,
unbiased,
open-minded,
critical,
discerning,
flexible, and accountable.

This kind of responsible skepticism is not only valid; it is essential. It is my belief (no pun intended) that the process of responsibly questioning everything for the purpose of seeking truth, whatever it may be, is a core quality not only of science, but of personal integrity in general. True / genuine skeptics are skeptical about everything, *including the process of skepticism itself*. If they are not, then they are pseudo-skeptics.

I added Criterion 5 to this evolving framework to remind me personally (and by extension, my scientist colleagues collectively) that the formal process of "taking stock" and "doing due diligence" concerning Criteria 1-4 is an essential fifth step in the truth-seeking process. Taking the time to step back and carefully re-evaluate (1) theory, (2) evidence, (3) people, and (4) personal experiences to ensure that they *all* pass muster increases the probability that a conclusion about a given belief is accurate and responsible.

I regularly include Criterion 5 in my research activities and have illustrated how it can be applied to controversial topics such as the belief in the survival of consciousness after death (see Chapter 2).

In the process of working through Criterion 5, I regularly consider the four most extreme skeptical criticisms that speak directly to Criteria 1-4:

> Criticism 1: "The professed belief is scientifically impossible." (Criterion 1).
>
> Analysis: This is clearly not the case. As the present volume attests, there are various credible theoretical perspectives and associated evidence that point to the viability of the primacy of consciousness hypothesis and the plausibility of Universal Intelligent Consciousness in the cosmos. Moreover, the content summarized in the present chapter regarding the criteria for the existence of randomness and the existence of fields are well established in statistics and physics.
>
> Criticism 2: "There is no credible research for the belief, and what research exists can be explained by conventional theories." (Criterion 2)

Analysis: Regarding research documenting serial coincidences / supersynchronicities per se, the evidence is relatively new and clearly requires replication and extension. However, enough credible individuals have personally experienced highly improbable serial sequences of events to justify having strong confidence that the phenomenon is real and should not be dismissed. Moreover, careful analysis of the complexity of the patterns clearly requires the inferred actions of some sort of super sophisticated Universal Intelligent Consciousness, just as highly intelligent consciousness (e.g. skilled writers and directors) are required to create and manifest, for example, the highly complex scripts expressed in contemporary documentaries and movies.

Criticism 3: "Anyone who holds this belief is not credible and cannot be trusted, e.g. the person is uneducated, or not very intelligent, or they are irrational, etc." (Criterion 3)

Analysis: This is clearly not the case concerning the primacy of consciousness hypothesis, as illustrated, for example, by the histories of the authors of this volume. And although the authors of this volume vary concerning their certainty about the primacy of consciousness and the role of consciousness in the cosmos as a whole, they vary not because of their level of education, intelligence, or rationality, but their genuine questioning about the nature of universal consciousness itself.

Criticism 4: "All personal experiences that support the belief are invalid, e.g. the experiences reflect misperceptions, misinterpretations, delusions, etc." (Criterion 4)

Analysis: Although this is likely the case for some individuals (e.g. person's suffering severe mental illness), it clearly does not apply to all individuals. In fact, some of the very best evidence for supersynchronicity comes from persons who are highly skilled in making and interpreting scientific evidence.

In sum, after carefully and critically re-evaluating Criteria 1-4 as applied to supersynchronicity, here is the conclusion I have reached:

Only the most ardent, biased, and closed-minded skeptic could read the logic and evidence presented in this chapter, in the context of this entire volume, and emphatically argue: (1) supersynchronicity does not exist, (2) complex serial coincidences can be completely accounted for using only Explanations 1-3, and (3) even if other higher order explanations are required, Explanations 9-12 are obviously impossible and therefore should be given no scientific credence whatsoever

Supersynchronicity and the Primacy of Universal Intelligent Consciousness

When one responsibly examines the patterns of synchronicities, and even patterns of supersynchronicities – which parallels examining patterns of stars within galaxies and then seeing patterns of galaxies in superclusters of galaxies - one discovers that supersynchronicities can extend over months, years, decades, and possibly much longer. Moreover, one can begin to discern more complex layers of meaning and "stories" as if the supersynchronicities were crafted by a super-creative, super-intelligent script writer.

It is important to understand that when I propose that patterns of synchronicities, and even patterns of supersynchronicities, appear to have an underlying sophisticated structure, I am not being anthropomorphic. I am not ascribing specific human characteristics to a hypothesized universal consciousness.

Instead, what I am doing is applying universal concepts of logic, mathematics, structure and function in the tradition of, for example, general systems theorists. Such theorists search for universal principles that apply to all systems, at all levels, from the subatomic (and smaller) to superclusters of galaxies (and larger), and everything in between.

For the reader interested in even more mind-boggling evidence implying the existence of some sort of super-intelligent consciousness process in human life. Before closing, I would like to mention a curious quality about supersynchronicity. In most areas of science, the more evidence one obtains that strongly supports a given idea, the more confident one feels that it is true.

However, because the evidence for supersynchronicity can seem so mind boggling at times, the more evidence one obtains that strongly supports the existence of an active conscious greater reality, the more incredulous one may sometimes feel. This, so to speak, comes with the supersynchronicity territory, and the challenge is for us to become peaceful with this.

If any area in empirical science points to the justification for advancing and bridging science and spirituality it is the emerging reality of supersynchronicity, especially when viewed through the lens of universal principles (e.g. Kafatos, 2018). My hope is that this chapter, in the context of this visionary volume, can contribute to the open minded, and open hearted, consideration of such far-reaching opportunities for science and society.

In closing, I would like to propose that paraphrasing Jung, *the Universal Intelligent Consciousness is an ever-present reality for those who have eyes to see.* And that *the future development of Universal Sciences can foster humanity's ability to see....*

Chapter Twelve

Scientism and Religion, Essential Science and Essential Spirituality

Charles T. Tart

In this chapter I intend to discuss the reasons I believe we need to widen science to include a postmaterialist phase, including research on what I call humans' spiritual nature. I will include both my personal experiences and my laboratory research that have contributed to my current view.

But several terms need clarification here as part of describing why I think we need to expand science to what we are calling a *postmaterial* phase, and my clarifications will act to some degree as micro-essays starting to outline my reasons for believing we need a postmaterialist science. I'll deal with terms like *essential science, "normal" or paradigmatic science, scientism, essential spirituality, religion, spirit, transpersonal,* and *total materialism.* These are used in widely varying ways in general, so here are the more specific, working meanings I use them with here.

Essential Science

Essential science (C. Tart, 1972) is a highly successful method for clarifying and advancing understanding in many areas. Four traditional methods people have used for gaining knowledge are constructively combined. I've often called these methods the *Way of Authority*, the *Way of Experience*, the *Way of Reasoning*, and the *Way of Revelation*. To learn something, you could (1) ask an authority – but they may be fallible. (2) Learn from appropriate experience – but we all know people who have had lots of experience with something, yet learn little from it. (3) Reason things out to their apparently logical conclusions – but we now know logics are based on semi-arbitrary assumptions.   Or (4) have some kind of revelation, usually in an altered state of consciousness (ASC) (C. Tart, 1969) so you feel you directly **know**, directly intuit The Truth – but many obviously True (to the experiencer)   and deep revelations of many people have turned out to be true only in limited contexts, or factually false.

Essential science, an ever continuing process, diagrammed in Figure 1, is, to put it simply, founded on detailed and accurate observation of what happens in a field of interest (Way of Experience), data collection.   This leads to theories about *why* things were observed to happen as they were observed to happen.   A scientific theory must make good sense of already observed data (Way of Reasoning) and, very importantly, should make *testable predictions* about things not yet observed.   If a theory makes no testable predictions, the theory may seem satisfying, obviously true, fashionable, philosophically profound, intellectually brilliant, etc., but it's not a scientific theory.   If a theory's predictions are confirmed, the theory continues to be worked with and extended.   If not confirmed, the theory needs modification, or rejection and replacement by some other theory.

While the fashion is to describe scientific theories as if they were always the result of precise observation and impeccable, logical reasoning, sometimes they are revealed in a flash of insight (Way of Revelation) and are later presented in a more logical seeming form to be more socially acceptable.   Allowing people to think that your theories come to you as a result of rigorous observations and subsequent logical analysis helps to get you tenure in academia, in the culture of science, but saying that you basically get them from flashes in your dreams or meditation practice won't.

All of the above stages are openly and honestly shared with relevant colleagues (Way of Authority) who can further develop and check observations and reasoning, test the theories, etc. This ongoing process thus starts with relatively crude knowledge about some area, develops more adequate theories, which in turn are further developed by colleagues, etc. Thus essential science is usually a long-term, evolutionary process, rather than a simple discovery of some eternal truth. *Observables always remain the primary source of authority in essential science* and theories, even though they may be quite good at predicting a wide range of phenomena, are always subject to improvement, modification, or rejection. The so called "laws" developed by scientific method are a psychological phenomenon where, craving certainty, we decide a highly useful theory is the ultimate discovery of the laws of the universe.

Normal or Paradigmatic Science

I focus on the essence of scientific method here. When a particular field has developed to the level Thomas Kuhn (Kuhn, 1962)

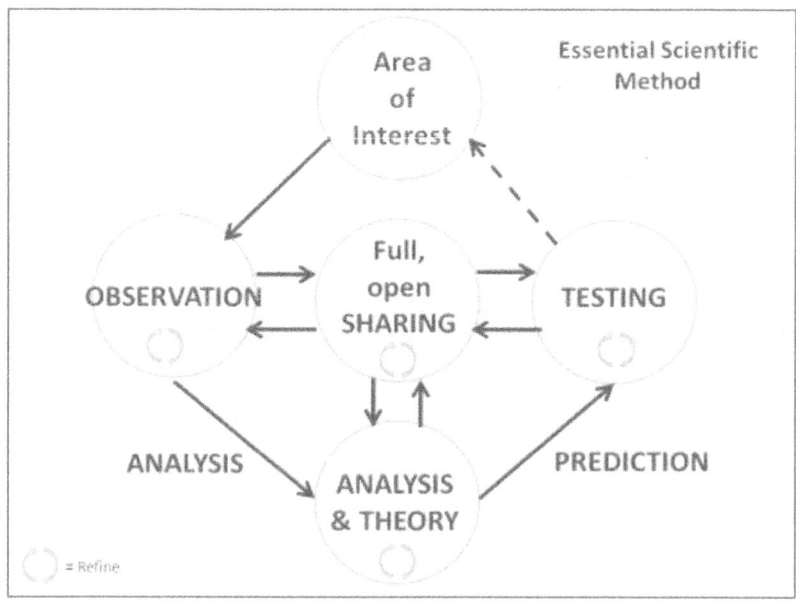

calls a paradigmatic science or "normal" science, much of its work can happen at and be stimulated by more theoretic levels, but all theories must eventually be tested back against observation. String theory, popular for some time in physics, e.g., showed great promise for wider ranging explanations, but to date has lacked empirical/testable predictions such that some physicists are wondering if it should still be called science, rather than a specialty in mathematics or philosophy.

This idealized version of essential science is, of course, practiced by us human beings, so reality gets more complicated, and often essential scientific method does not live up to its full potentialities. The Academy for the Advancement of Postmaterialist Science, AAPS, aims to identify and correct some of the unnecessary constrictions applied to scientific inquiry.

Scient*ism:*

*Scientism*is a term coined by sociologists (Hobbs, 1910; Wellmuth, 1944) more than a century ago to indicate that when a branch of science is perceived as very successful in explaining the world, its current theories of the nature of things start to become fixed beliefs, an automatic way of thinking and acting, rather than remaining *working hypotheses*, **always** subject to further expansion, testing, and possible rejection or replacement by more adequate theories, as called for by essential science. An "ism" is "A form of doctrine, theory, or practice having, or claiming to have, a distinctive character or relationship." (Shorter Oxford English Dictionary) So scientism is a recognition of our human nature wherein what should remain a testable theory or working hypothesis becomes a doctrine. Because of its large implicit or automatic biasing of thinking processes, scientism often results in ignoring observations that do not fit in with the prevailing paradigm, rather than an objective evaluation of them with essential science. Kuhn (Kuhn, 1962) points out that many major advances in science have come about as a revolution rather than a straightforward extension of knowledge; ignored data is finally recognized as important and new working theories are developed.

Spirit

I cannot adequately "define" *Spirit*, and all terms like it tend to carry multitudes of connotations and associations, implicit as well as explicit, that excite, anger, or confuse us. But in general, by Spirit I here mean the widespread human belief – often based on life-changing, transpersonal experiences – that there is another level of reality, usually seen as a higher, more important level than the everyday material level. People may call it God, angels, spirits, gods, mystical consciousness, etc. In this essay I use Spirit (deliberately capitalized to remind us of the great importance of such experiences to those who have them) to refer to such transpersonal experiences, rather than to the doctrinal modifications and distortions implicitly or explicitly created in the course of the development of religions. Uncapitalized "spirit" is the general, conversational usage.

Essential Spirituality

By *essential spirituality*, I refer to a wide range of hard-to-describe-in-ordinary language, indeed often ineffable experiences people have. Currently it is fashionable in psychology to term these *transpersonal experiences*, going way beyond, *trans*, the ordinary reality and capacities of a personal, embodied ego. My ordinary experience of myself right now, e.g., is that I am a physical body sitting in a physical location, taking in air and information from material events, and limited in my abilities by the principles of physics. As a human it's possible for me to have a far more intense and convincing experience that "I" really am something much beyond any concept I have of "I," and am an aspect of the whole universe.

Such experiences have been roughly designated by terms like mystical experiences, peak experiences, visions, etc., where the experiencers feel they have **direct** and deep understanding of such things as the Unity of all life, the pervasiveness of Intelligence and Love in the universe, the inherent Meaningfulness of life, the direction life and personal development should take in developing Wisdom and Compassion, etc. I capitalize these terms here as a reminder of the deep emotional, as well as cognitive impact transpersonal experiences typically have on the experiencers; they are not intellectual abstractions. Almost all people who have near-death experiences (NDEs) or out-of-the-body experiences (OBEs) (Tart, 1998), e.g., do not report that they have intellectually deduced there is some kind of survival of death, they **know** it, and now strive to live their lives in terms of consequences for long-term development, beyond a single lifetime.

Transpersonal experiences usually feel more real than ordinary experiences in the physical world, and seem to directly show the experiencer that there is a spiritual reality to the universe.

Essential spirituality, in parallel with essential science, is a term I have coined that emphasizes having, observing, thinking about spiritual *experiences* rather than intellectual or emotional responses to *beliefs* about the spiritual. It is a term for an idealized process, a relatively "objective" investigation of the spiritual, implying an investigator could induce altered states of consciousness (ASCs) or the like to explore spiritual experiences without having her or his experiences being too shaped by previous spiritual and religious beliefs and conditionings. But we can imagine a continuum. At one end, the investigator has few or no relevant prior beliefs and conditionings, and/or can compensate for them. NDErs, e.g., often report meeting a numinous being, roughly described as made of light, telepathically in contact with them, accepting of and loving them. Some NDErs with strong Christian backgrounds immediately start naming this aspect of the experience a meeting with Jesus, which may bias other aspects of description. Some more neutrally stay close to describing the direct experience and talk of a numinous Being of Light.

Our needs for understanding and happiness may strongly bias our perception of even our own experiences, as well as of external events. Many people who have told me about their transpersonal experiences (Tart, 1999) over the years, e.g., have had an unsatisfactory life in terms of overall meaning, a condition common with a totally materialistic outlook (see below), and when they have an experience that is so different and more intense than everyday experience, and represents what they have been looking for, they tend to almost automatically decide that now they know Absolute Truth. But the ability to have a more "objective" (tricky word in this context!) and scientific (at least partially) knowledge of the spiritual will depend on collecting as clear and accurate a description, the data, of transpersonal experiences as possible. Thus someone with fewer a priori beliefs, or the ability to compensate for them and put them aside in reporting, may make a better investigator for essential spirituality. We need a motto on the order of

"It's wonderful to have a vivid, obviously true, perception of The Truth in line with what we deeply want. Those feelings are part of the data of what was experienced and observed, and should be respected, but are not necessarily the Final Truth...."

Religion

By *religion* I refer to organized bodies of ideas/beliefs about the nature of reality, of the spiritual forces behind reality, and consequent standards of how to act and live, ideas and concepts that have become *doctrines*. A religion may have begun from essential spirituality, the transpersonal "raw data" of spirituality, as it were, as a result of powerful, "mystical" experiences by one or more individual founders and developers. But the insights these founders attempted to convey or their theories about them have been worked over, to various degrees, to become socialized, acceptable to and compatible with social realities of the time, often to various degrees to support and legitimatize the then governing elite. Generally, in religion people are not encouraged to have direct, individual transpersonal experiences and may, indeed, be punished if they have or report them. The developed doctrines are enshrined as the Highest Truth available, are not to be questioned and, indeed, questioning may be considered heresy and punished when religions have strong social and political powers.

Total Materialism:

By *Total Materialism*, I mean the belief that *all* the phenomena of reality, including those mental experiences of the kind mentioned above, will ultimately (if we are smart enough) be fully explained by the operation of physical, material objects acted upon by physical, material forces. The real "meaning" (insofar as matter can have any kind of inherent meaning) of everything I write here, from the perspective of Total Materialism, isn't really fundamentally explained by my intentions or other operations of my "mind," but by electrochemical patterns affecting neurons and neurochemicals in my physical brain, which in turn affect molecules and atoms, etc., etc., down to whatever level of sub-microscopic reality is considered as the final divisible material state at any historical period. Atoms were once considered ultimate, now we have multitudes of subatomic particles.

I find materialism a really useful cognitive approach, a mental tool, for working with all sorts of material problems, even for partially explaining the operation of what I normally consider my "mind." Indeed, I love material science, was a radio engineer before becoming a psychologist, and am more skilled with using tools and handling practical, material problems than many people...but evidence forces me to postulate that there's more to reality than that, a really important more... William James (James, 1925) characterized it as The More...

Personal Factors Making Postmaterialist Science Important to Me

The above is straightforward scientific/scholarly writing and reasoning, but an important point of this book is illustrating how real people got involved in and are working with The More, phenomena we think are important but not likely to be understood or usefully applied with only the tool of Total Materialism. So let me humanize my concerns with information on my own background and the research and experiences that led me to believe that materialism was not sufficient to explain phenomenal reality, and convinced me that a postmaterialist perspective that included consciousness, better fits the data from many laboratory experiments on psi phenomena.

Educational/Belief Background

I was never a Total Materialist, except in so far as when, e.g., my car needed repair (way too often in my impoverished student days!), I wanted a good materialist mechanic to work on it, one who knew, e.g., which cam should push on which piston rod and at exactly what time, not somebody who prayed over my car. I wouldn't *totally* rule out the possibility that someone praying over my car might help it run better, and know how to design experiments to objectively test such a claimed skill, but practically, material science is excellent for dealing with most material things and, given current knowledge, the likelihood of prayers fixing my car seems awfully low...

By the time I was a teenager, I had already become what I would call a *pragmatic dualist*, believing there were (at least) two domains of reality, loosely characterized as "material" and "spiritual," that needed to be understood. I was very much in love with all things scientific, often reading, on my own initiative, several books a week on various aspects of science. The unusual aspects compared to most people was that as part of my thirst for knowledge, I came across old books on *psychical research,* and then more contemporary literature on experimental *parapsychology**. I always add "pragmatic" to "dualist" as I'm not interested in abstract speculation, but in ideas which have observable/experienceable consequences. Besides just being generally curious about this psychic material, it was highly relevant to dealing with my personal crisis of faith in the religion, Lutheranism, I was raised in.

Psychical research was started in the late 1800s by some highly educated men and women who were going through similar crises of faith. Science had "proven" that all religion was nonsense, hadn't it? But wasn't religion the source of the most important human values and morality? Wouldn't we be much more "red in tooth and claw" without the guidance of religion?

The founders of the Society for Psychical Research (SPR) (https://www.spr.ac.uk) proposed the application of scientific *method* to refine knowledge of the religious and spiritual. The emphasis was on essential science, science as *method,* as described above – careful observation, logical theorizing, leading to predictable, testable

---

* *Some people uses "psychical research" and "parapsychology" synonymously, but the traditional distinction is that psychical research is a wider term, looking at unusual events apparently defying materialistic explanation that happen in people's lives, while parapsychology now generally refers to laboratory experiments on such events.*

consequences of theories as the main way of assessing their value, and honest and open sharing and cooperation with other investigators – as opposed to taking the then current *theories* of science as the final truth about things, scientism.

I found this proposal brilliant! Instead of endless abstract debates about faith, God's Will, the irrationality of religion, etc., use this highly productive method of essential science for refining knowledge!

A few investigators had been applying the methods of essential science for decades by the time I came across this material, and it became clear to me, after reading lots of books on the results, that the evidence for the existence of phenomena like telepathy and clairvoyance, forms of extrasensory perception (ESP), was just overwhelming. They happened sometimes, even if not (yet) reliably or understandably. This didn't mean that the Lutherans or the Catholics or the Buddhists or whoever were right about everything, or that religions were filled with ideas that were factually incorrect and sometimes crazy-making, but experimental results by the 1940s certainly indicated there was something important going on, and that forms of ESP had some qualities like those generally considered spiritual. I decided I wanted to devote my life to working on clarifying what was real and useful and what wasn't in spirituality as my prime scientific focus, and that's been the theme that's run through all my work. "Spirituality" here, as I and many others use the term and clarified earlier, refers to the basic human observations and experiences underlying religion, the basic *data*, rather than to the doctrines and beliefs that then accumulate, as basic experiential knowledge is often distorted to fit into upholding social norms, religion.

I'll give one small (?) example of scientific methods showing that something real and important did sometimes happen. From a Total Materialist view, solitary praying is nothing but talking to yourself, but if, as I decided was long ago proven, there is a form of ESP we crudely call "telepathy," then perhaps your prayers may be going "somewhere," rather than being nothing but talking to yourself. Still a million questions, but a start on clarification... And perhaps an incentive to research the question of what tends to make prayer more effective in terms of getting results?

Evidence for a Perspective Beyond Total Materialism

As to the scientific evidence that convinced me to change my mind about materialism, it was mainly books on parapsychological research by people like Duke University's J. B. Rhine, as well as lots of field reports on spontaneous experiences, the latter better grouped under the heading of psychical research. I have always felt that both were important: laboratory research can be oh so rigorous, but so easily can be quite sterile and leave out the meaning and emotional dimensions that are essential to making psychic and spiritual things happen. If you look at spontaneous psychic experiences, e.g., there are huge numbers of reports of a person suddenly having a negative vision or dream, or feeling about a distant loved one when there were no material reasons for such events, and then finding out shortly afterward that the loved one had died or been badly wounded right at that time. The emotional levels involved are not the same as a student guessing the order of a deck of cards in the laboratory! One of my first formal experiments tried to bridge this gap by measuring bodily responses (EEG, GSR, heart rate) when an agent, sensorially shielded from the percipient, received very painful electric shocks at random intervals (Tart, 1963).

This is not at the intensity level of a loved one dying but speaking as the agent who received the shocks (no one else volunteered for this role), it was far more intense than a mere cognitive event! Significant physiological responses in the percipient, correlated with the agent being shocked, were found, while the percipients' conscious responses that something had happened were uncorrelated.

The study showed that physiological response might be a useful indicator of sensitivity to ESP, but much more research needs to be done.

As a transpersonal psychologist, I'm also interesting in studying the meanings psychic and spiritual experiences have for people (they can be enormous, a major life change from a 5-minute experience), regardless of of whether a particular experience had adequate evidence for parapsychological functioning being part of it, or that it might indeed have been "all in the mind." Note I said all in the "mind," not all in the "head."

I have discussed and summarized much of the basic research of parapsychology in various books of mine, such as (Tart, 1977a,b and Tart, 2017), and, I have included references to a sampling of some excellent books (Dossey, 1993; Kelly, 2015; Feather, 2005; Kelly, 2007; Mitchell & White, 1974; Radin, 1997, 2006; Schwartz & Simon, 2002; Schwartz, 2007; Targ & Puthoff, 1977; Tart, Puthoff, & Targ, 1979).

Personal Experience Beyond the Material

As to direct personal experiences calling for a postmaterialist interpretation, I simply had not had any in my early life, maybe up into my 20s or so. I had had some interesting psychological experiences, such as interesting dreams, which helped make me very curious about how my mind worked, and I would've liked to have had some psychic experiences, to get a more direct feel for the "inside" of such experiences, but no luck. I particularly thought it would be really neat to have an out of body experience (OBE), and I read Muldoon and Carrington's fascinating book (Muldoon & Carrington, 1956) on how to have "astral projections," the old term for OBEs. Sylvan Muldoon (1903-1969) was an American writer who began spontaneously have OBEs and experimented with them. He took the quite sane attitude that most people would think he was insane for claiming to have such experiences, but he described what had happened to him and techniques he had found make them more likely to happen. If you were really interested, you could try the techniques. If they worked for you, you would know he was reporting accurately, if they didn't work Muldoon understood if you still believed him to be crazy. Many times I tried getting into a state of *extreme* relaxation, as recommended by Muldoon, as I went to sleep, while holding an intention to leave my body, while still a teenager --- but it didn't work; no obvious OBEs resulted.

Although maybe --- once I did have an interesting dream. This was during my sophomore year at MIT. I was trying the technique, when suddenly I found myself in a dream where I was sitting on top of a house. Then some kids in the street threw snowballs at me. One of the snowballs hit me in the face and woke me up very suddenly, with a huge, physical body shock sensation! I wondered if, while not being completely awake, I was beginning to have an out of body experience, and this was what Muldoon called a *repercussion* from the "astral body" slamming too suddenly back into the physical. But I knew I could well be rationalizing, wanting to believe my efforts had gotten me something... I am generally careful to remain open about interpreting my own experiences and not looking at all the possibilities.   One of
the things I personally like about being a scientist is the insistence that clever ideas/theories are not enough, our minds are brilliant at constructing patterns where there may not be any in reality; theories must be tested back against observables.

Later on in life I've had various kinds of psychic experiences. Many were what I came to think of as garden-variety psychic events, not worth making a fuss about once you had accepted the reality of some psychic events anyway. A few gave me interesting ideas about possible processes involved, such as one where I, quite uncharacteristically, started speaking aloud an unusual word that was not part of my working vocabulary and then finding a letter from a person named that at my office the next day (Tart, 1989).

One that I'm 99+% sure was ESP was pretty spectacular though.

I was driving to meet someone one evening in Berkeley, California. I was to go to the back door of the private house he was staying at so as to not disturb a meeting taking place in the front room. While driving there I suddenly had strong visions/images/feelings of being shot at, beaten up and otherwise attacked! These images were so strong that several times I almost pulled my car over to turn around! This was not me, my mind didn't work like that, I'd never felt like that before (or since), I wasn't a coward, I was ashamed!

I quickly diagnosed myself then as having passed for normal all my life, but clearly I was crazy as a loon underneath, and damned ashamed of it! But I was also stubborn, and would not let these overwhelming convictions of danger stop me!

I went and met my new friend anyway. I certainly didn't tell him I'd had a crazy episode on the way over, and I tried not to think about this disgraceful lapse --- until I had a letter from him a week or so later, saying that while he was waiting for me out in front of the house, rather than in the kitchen, he got caught up in all sorts of vivid worries and feelings about being shot at or beaten up, and was glad I came and we went away! This was a quiet, residential neighborhood, not an area where things like that happened. And did I know that the Symbionese Liberation Army kidnapped heiress and then UC Berkeley student Patty Hearst one block down the street, a little after we left to go off to the coffee shop?

I wasn't crazy! Some part of me knew of a bunch of violent people with guns, loaded with cyanide tipped bullets, who did shoot at people and beat people up, were either coming very quickly or maybe were already sitting there in their parked cars, maybe I walked right by them

Working Hypotheses Dealing with a Postmaterialist Perspective

What are my current working hypotheses? Wow! Hardly a simple question! I've spelled out aspects of my beliefs in various books (Lee, Ornstein, Galin, Deikman, & Tart, 1975; Tart, 1969, 1971, 1975a, 1975b, 1986, 1994, 2001, 2009; Tart et al., 1979; Tart, 1997), but I'll try to cut to the essence here.

In some sense, I assume consciousness is as primary as matter. Whether it's more or less primary than matter, I have no idea. But it's just as fundamental. No matter how much you understand matter, if you don't understand consciousness, your knowledge is far from complete. I don't think consciousness or mind is going to be explained "away" as an epiphenomenon of matter.

I don't know what the above statements mean in any absolute sense, but they are the best sense I can make of things at present.

I accept the extensive evidence that is easily interpreted to mean that human life is probably very much the result of biological evolution over a very long time. I doubt that is all the evidence and theory you need to fully explain us though. So I tend to hypothesize (I stress working hypothesis, not any absolute truth) that when our nervous systems got complex enough to "host/attract/meld with" (feeling funny about using words like these) the "something else" we grossly refer to as *mind*, our full human consciousness evolved. My, and your, ordinary, experienced consciousness/mind is then usefully understood as a combination of primary consciousness that's *extremely* involved with a very sophisticated bio-computer. It's a *systems emergent* (Tart, 1973), with properties more than linear sums of its components. It's like when you're driving your car for the thousandth time, if you want to go left you don't have to think about how it's done, you just do it, turning the wheel is part of the automatic operating system of your current mental state. Your body image, going from your insides to the surface of your skin when you're walking, is reprogramed to run from fender to fender, bumper to bumper.

My working hypothesis goes on to think that some aspect of "me", my more mindlike, less material consciousness, may survive death. For a while after death though, through force of habit, I will probably feel a lot like my ordinary self. But without the constant shaping of experienced consciousness per se by my physical body and nervous system, the quality of my consciousness will probably change and become like... Who knows? Interestingly people who spontaneously have OBEs usually perceive that they have a "body" like their ordinary physical body, although they know or perceive that physical body is back in a bed somewhere, but with prolonged or oft repeated OBEs the "self," the center of consciousness, may be more abstract...

People who have had various kinds of mystical experiences may have had previews of this future state, but the attempts to explain them in ordinary language are very frustrating and inadequate... Whether we will ever adequately understand this in our ordinary, embodied, alive state, I don't know, but I do believe that clever research can help us understand a lot more than we do now. My 1972 proposal for the creation of state-specific sciences may be a step in the direction of being able to use our minds in wider ways than we normally do (Tart, 1972). As much as possible, for me it's not a matter of "believing in" something beyond the physical, although believing anything has important psychological effects, it's a matter of researching and learning as much as we can.

Researching the Basic Importance of Consciousness

I'm going to focus on one important question that I gave in my methodological paper about at our founding AAPS meeting in 2017 (Tart, 2017), namely:

"How in the world do we do science when consciousness becomes primary and you have psychic connections all over the place? When you can't assume the total shielding of experiments from all other influences as we normally do today?"

I'm going to be very interested in getting's people's responses to the understanding I lay out. And I should put "understanding" in quotes, because it's not as if I have the answers, but I see some major problems. Not so major that we should give up, but we sure shouldn't ignore them, or they will really come back to bite us at some point.

Can We Progress?

Note that I've used the terms "Essential Science" and "Essential Spirituality" in the title of this chapter. The hopes and expectations I have for a deeper understanding and good application of research are about two essential forms of science and spirituality, forms in which a deep and genuine curiosity *and* a willingness to admit ignorance and error, to stay open-minded and be willing to question current understandings even when they are widely accepted, are primary aspects of practice. It's an idealization, and we humans seldom get close to ideal openness, curiosity and humility. But much of what is conventionally called science and spirituality is only partially driven by those kinds of motivations, and other motivations, such as being attached to feelings of superiority or safety as a result of one's greater knowledge and power distorts possible research.

In mild form, there can be useful limitations in science, it's what Thomas Kuhn (Kuhn, 1962) called *normal science*. It occurs and persists when a field has developed a very useful theory that has become a *paradigm*, an overarching framework to decide what's important to observe and think about, what's important to understand better and what can be ignored, rather than the full openness of essential science. Paradigmatic research is very useful, a productive way of thinking, observing, experimenting in great depth, but it tends to blind us to the full range of reality. Observations which don't make sense in terms of the prevailing paradigm tend to be ignored without closer inspection.

In its worst form, what's labeled "science" becomes scient*ism*, there is such automatic and habitual cognitive and emotional overattachment to the prevailing paradigm that it leads to serious distortions of observation and thinking. The kinds of empirical observations, primarily for me the study of altered states of consciousness and the results of scientific parapsychology, which led me to the conviction that we need a postmaterialist science (not a rejection of the usefulness of material explanations and research but an opening and expansion to the whole range of reality), have so often been scientistically rejected that, if acknowledged, it would constitute an enormous embarrassment to those who've engaged in them. The acceptance in scientific journals of "skeptical" arguments against the reality of ESP, e.g., that routinely involve the assertion that significant results must be due to experimental error, *even though there is usually no actual proof of such error*, is disgraceful. It embarrasses me, as a scientist, that otherwise brilliant colleagues can become pseudo-skeptics, practitioners of scient*ism* rather than science.

Similarly, I think of Essential Spirituality as a desire to deeply know higher spiritual truths†. If there is too much attachment, intellectual or emotional, to one's existing spiritual practices and beliefs, especially if based on powerful transpersonal experiences, though, this inhibits the chances of examining current spiritual beliefs to see which might need development, changing, or rejection. When this is combined with secular authority and rewards that often

---

†*I know I am oversimplifying here, but it would take us too far afield to get into the incredible emotional allure of various spiritual experiences.*

come from being a religious/spiritual authority, openness to the spiritual becomes a matter of only being interested in and accepting what agrees with one's previous beliefs.

So Where Does All This Leave Me, And Our Human Quest for Knowledge?

I stress that I'm very much a *pragmatic* materialist. This assumption about reality being made up of very basic units, and the understanding that can arise from straightforward, additive properties of these units, has led to excellent progress in understanding and controlling the material world. Add in our growing appreciation for emergent, system properties, and our understanding and application get better. I would like to see far more resources devoted to materialistic science than happens now, and expect big payoffs in terms of human welfare. I may hypothesize that I'm a "non-material" mind of some sort interacting with my brain, but the more I know about how brains operate, the better the results. It's possible to drive a car well while knowing nothing about how it works, but I prefer having good driving skills *and* knowing the properties and limits of my car.

I'm also a psychologist, particularly a transpersonal psychologist, fascinated by how the mind works, and I'm as or more interested in studying it from the "inside," experientially, as from the "outside," through behaviorism and brain science. I'm very aware of the many negative effects on human happiness that have occurred because of the narrowing of curiosity and understanding that has occurred because, among other things, materialistic science has been so successful and often becomes scientism. I've spoken with many people, scientists as well as non-scientists, who had some sense of a sacred, higher purpose to life than physical pleasure, but who've become rather depressed because they think science has somehow *proven* that all spiritual ideas are nonsense.

I can recall from my childhood, e.g., that there were many people who were "poor" by materialist standards, with no hope of becoming well off, much less rich, yet who felt that their lives were great successes because they had managed to live in accordance with what they believed were higher, religious or spiritual values. I suspect there are many fewer people like that now. How much energy can you put into a system for guiding your life that you are told has been scientifically proven to be meaningless, just a consequence of survival of the fittest in a universe with no inherent higher meaning‡? Yet any intelligent person knows that the billions of people on the earth cannot live at the material richness standards of the current elite, and ecological disaster is looming. So the (mis-)interpretation of science as showing that all spiritual ideas are nonsense has had, and continues to have, disastrous consequences.

One understandable reaction is a desperate over-attachment to some religion or spiritual system, indeed any comprehensive belief system, which too easily turns into something like "My God, the only One, wants me to kill you heathens!" or "It's good I'm a person of superior intelligence, not taken in by all that spiritual crap, able to insulate myself from the worst…"

I am definitely not arguing that we must accept anything and everything labeled "spiritual" or "religious" as true! One reason the scientific interpretation of all spirituality and religion as nonsense has become so prevalent is that these fields are full of human twists, distortions and perversions of whatever the transpersonal

---

‡ *Some years ago I devised a psychological group exercise to help people realize how much the picture of Total Materialism and its apparent demonstration that all religion and spirituality are nonsense affects them. It is an unpleasant exercise for most people, but valued for what they learned. A web version can be found at —http://www.westerncreed.com/Tart_ITP.html.*

reality is – but this is true of all fields of human endeavor. The need is to study and understand the postmaterial, the transpersonal, its applications, good and bad, and slowly refine human spirituality to truer and healthier forms.

Can we figure out everything about reality and our human selves? Darned if I know, but I'm sure that by expanding our research horizons to develop a postmaterialist science, we can learn a lot more that promises to improve our human condition! I could be wrong; maybe we aren't smart enough to go further, but thinking we can provides motivation to try, whereas thinking we can't stops us. As Henry Ford is reputed to have said, "Those who think they can and those who think they can't are both right." I am thankful to have made some small contributions in this direction of expansion…and am very pleased with the young, bright minds getting interested in postmaterial science!

About the Authors

MARIO BEAUREGARD, PH.D., is a neuroscientist currently affiliated with the Department of Psychology, University of Arizona. He received a bachelor's degree in psychology and a doctorate degree in neuroscience from the University of Montreal. Upon completing his B.Sc. in psychology and his Ph.D. in neuroscience from University of Montreal, Mario earned two postdoctoral fellowships in experimental neuropsychology, the first at the University of Texas in Houston (1992-94), and the second at the Montreal Neurological Institute at the McConnell Brain Imaging Centre at McGill University (1994-96). He was also an Associate Researcher at the University of Montreal in the Departments of Psychology and Radiology, as well as the Neuroscience Research Center.

The author of over 100 publications in neuroscience, psychology, and psychiatry, Mario has been selected by the World Media Net to be among the "One Hundred Pioneers of the 21st Century" due to his considerable research into the neuroscience of consciousness. In 2013, he participated in a dialogue with the Dalai Lama regarding the science of mind (Melbourne, Australia). In September 2007 Mario published the book, *The Spiritual Brain: A Neuroscientist's Case for the Existence of the Soul* (HarperCollins), in collaboration with science writer Denyse O'Leary. He more recently published *Brain Wars*, (Harper Collins, 2012). In these books, he demonstrates that mind and consciousness are much more than the activity of nerve cells in our brains. He is also co-author of the Manifesto for a Postmaterialist Science , the author of the *Theory of Psychelementarity* and one of the founders of the Campaign for Open Science.

Dr. Beauregard's groundbreaking work on the neurobiology of emotion and mystical experience while he was at the University of Montreal has received extensive international media coverage.

More recently, the National Film Board of Canada has produced a documentary film about his work titled, The Mystical Brain. Dr. Beauregard is also a distinguished member of the Institute for Research on Extraordinary Experiences in France and the Lifeboat Foundation in the United States.

Dr. Beauregard has appeared over several radio programs in the U.S.A., Canada, and Europe, Asia, and Australia. His research has been featured on TV (Discovery Channel) and in many newspapers and magazines, including *Nature, Science, The New Scientist, Scientific American Mind,* and *The Economist*. He has received a number of distinctions, including the Joel F. Lubar Award (International Society For Neuronal Regulation, USA) and the Spectrum Award (The Institutes For The Achievement of Human Potential, USA).

《》

EDWARD R. CLOSE, PH.D. has been involved in pursuing an understanding of the interaction of consciousness and quantum reality since 1977. He is currently research consultant to the Pacific Neuropsychiatric Institute in Seattle, and Principle Environmental Scientist at EJC Advantage, LLC, in Missouri. His academic background and experience have uniquely prepared him for involvement in post-materialism scientific research.

Studying physics, mathematics, logic, and philosophy as an undergraduate, he was elected to Kappa Mu Epsilon, National Mathematics Honor Society, and in 1958, he was involved in experiments in parapsychology, corresponding with Dr. J.B. Rhine of Duke University. Ed received initiations in Kriya Yoga from Self-Realization Fellowship (SRF) in 1960. He earned a degree in mathematics and physics from Central Methodist College (now Central Methodist University) in Fayette, Missouri in 1962. Ed studied quantum physics, electronics, computer programming, mathematical modeling, hydrology, geology, geophysics, environmental engineering, and systems analysis in graduate programs at several major universities including: Rolla School of mines and metallurgy (now the University of Missouri at Rolla), The University of Iowa in Iowa City, the University of Missouri in Columbia, the University of Arizona at Flagstaff, Case Western Reserve, UCLA, and UC Davis, and he completed one year in residence in a PhD program at Johns Hopkins University in 1972. In addition to course work, he pursued independent research at the universities listed above, and at UC Berkeley, Cal-Tech, and the University of Puerto Rico, Rio Piedras Campus.

Ed was one of the seven charter members of the Department of Interior Systems Analysis Group from 1969 to 1972, working with PhDs from Harvard, Stanford, the University of Maryland, and Johns Hopkins. He was USGS Engineer on the USGS/USCOE Hydrologic Engineering Center Worth of Streamflow Data Study, and project engineer of the USGS Puerto Rico Island-Wide Water Resources Management study. Ed published a number of research papers and in 1977, his first book on consciousness expansion was published. In 1980, he was project hydrologist on the Mx-Missile Prototype Project at Vandenburg AFB, and in 1981, he went to Yanbu Industrial City in Saudi Arabia as environmental planner.

Ed has also carried out significant research in alternative health modalities and developed "The Close Protocol" for dealing with toxic mold. He was a charter member of the International Integrated Health Professionals Council from 2009 until 2013. From 1985 until 1989, working as supervisory hydrogeologist in the Middle East, and for an engineering firm in California, he completed his thesis and received his PhD in environmental engineering in 1989.

Besides being an experienced teacher of mathematics, physics and earth sciences, Ed has taught classes in meditation techniques in Denver, Colorado, San Juan, Puerto Rico, Tampa Florida, and Cape Girardeau, Missouri. He also served as Group Leader for SRF

Meditation Groups in Sacramento, CA and Washington, DC from 1967 until 1972.

Ed has been called a polymath. He has been an active member of MENSA, the International Society for Philosophical Enquiry (ISPE), the Exceptional Creative Achievement Organization, ISI (151) High-IQ Society, and the Young Geniuses Society. He is recognized as exceptionally and profoundly gifted. In 2016, he attained the level of *Diplomate*, the highest public rank in ISPE, and is a Distinguished Fellow of the ECAO.

Ed has received a number of recognitions and awards, including the Gabino Barreda Award, from the government of Mexico in 2013, *"for his history of service and contribution to the strengthening of the educational system"*, presented at the first Science and Spirituality Conference in Puebla Mexico, where he was a guest speaker. He also received special recognition in 2016, along with Dr. Vernon Neppe, from the ISPE, receiving the worldwide, interdisciplinary, seldom awarded, Whiting Memorial Prize.

Ed has been on several TV and radio talk shows, including *the Power Hour* with Joyce Riley, *Signs of Life* with Bob and Phran Ginsberg, *Coast to Coast* with George Noory, and *the Independent Expression Talk Show* with Shirley Mc Laine. He is author of seven books, co-author of three, and author of more than 500 papers, articles and written discussions. A sought-after speaker, he has been guest speaker at conferences across the US and internationally.

In 2010, Ed participated an expedition filming "The Frankincense Trail" a documentary shot on location in the Sahara Desert, south of Giza in Egypt, and in the Ancient City of Petra. He served as a consultant to the director of the film on Pre-Mohammedan Culture and the Semitic languages. He was also cast as the Chief Physician-Priest in the 75-member cast portraying a Frankincense Trail caravan carrying frankincense and myrrh resins from Southern Arabia to Damascus, Jerusalem and Egypt.

Dr. Close is currently focused on helping others improve their physical, mental and spiritual health, and is honored to be a member of the Academy for the Advancement of Postmaterialist Sciences.

⟨◊⟩

LARRY DOSSEY, M.D. is a physician of internal medicine. He is currently the executive editor of the peer-reviewed journal Explore: The Journal of Science and Healing. He was a co-founder of the Dallas Diagnostic Association and is former Chief of Staff of Medical City Dallas Hospital. Larry is also past president of The Isthmus Institute of Dallas, an organization dedicated to exploring the possible convergences of science and religious thought.

Larry is the former co-chairman of the Panel on Mind/Body Interventions, National Center for Complementary and Alternative Medicine, National Institutes of Health. He was a founder and executive editor of the journal Alternative Therapies in Health and Medicine, 1995 to 2004.

Upon graduating with honors from the University of Texas at Austin, Larry worked as a pharmacist while earning his M.D. degree from Southwestern Medical School in Dallas, 1967. Before completing his residency in internal medicine, he served as a battalion surgeon in Vietnam, where he was decorated for valor. He helped establish the Dallas Diagnostic Association, the largest group of internal medicine practitioners in that city and was Chief of Staff of Medical City Dallas Hospital in 1982.

Larry has published approximately 200 articles, editorials, and contributed chapters and is the author of thirteen books, including Space, Time & Medicine (1982), Beyond Illness (1984), Recovering the Soul (1989), Meaning & Medicine (1991), Healing Words (1993; a New York Times bestseller), Prayer Is Good Medicine (1996), Be Careful What You Pray For (1997), Reinventing Medicine (1999),

Healing Beyond the Body (2001), The Extraordinary Healing Power of Ordinary Things (2006), The Power of Premonitions (2009), and One Mind: How Our Individual Mind Is Part of a Greater Mind and Why It Matters (2013). He is also co-author of What Is Consciousness? (2016).

Larry's books have been translated into languages around the world. His goal in all his books is to anchor the so-called holistic health movement in a model that is scientifically respectable and which, at the same time, answers humankind's inner spiritual needs.

The impact of Larry's work has been remarkable. Before his book Healing Words was published in 1993, only three U.S. medical schools had courses devoted to exploring the role of religious practice and prayer in health; currently, nearly 80 medical schools have instituted such courses, many of which utilize his works as textbooks. In his 1989 book Recovering the Soul, he introduced the concept of "nonlocal mind" -- mind unconfined to the brain and body, mind spread infinitely throughout space and time. Since then, "nonlocal mind" has been adopted by many leading scientists as an emerging image of consciousness. Larry's ever-deepening explication of nonlocal mind provides a legitimate foundation for the merging of spirit and medicine. The ramifications of such a union are radical and call for no less than the reinvention of medicine.

In 2013, Larry Dossey received the prestigious Visionary Award that honors a pioneer whose visionary ideas have shaped integrative healthcare and the medical profession.

«◊»

MENAS C. KAFATOS, PH.D. is The Fletcher Jones Endowed Chair Professor of Computational Physics at Chapman University, Orange, CA. He received his B.A. in Physics from Cornell University in 1967 and his Ph.D. in Physics from the Massachusetts Institute of

Technology in 1972, under the direction of the renowned Professor Philip Morrison, who studied under J. Robert Oppenheimer. After postdoctoral work at NASA Goddard Space Flight Center, he joined George Mason University (GMU) in Fairfax, VA, and was University Professor of Interdisciplinary Sciences from 1984-2008, where he also served as Dean of the School of Computational Sciences and Director of the Center for Earth Observing and Space Research. He and a team of computational scientists joined Chapman University in fall, 2008. He served as Founding Dean of the Schmid College of Science and Technology and Vice Chancellor at Chapman University (2009-2012). He directs the Center of Excellence in Earth Systems Modeling and Observations.

Overall, he has received more than 70 grants and contracts from a variety of sources including the Office of Naval Research (ONR), NASA, National Science Foundation (NSF), Naval Research Laboratory and USDA. He was the Director of the largest GMU research center, Center for Earth Observing and Space Research (CEOSR) with $8.5M in expenditures in Fiscal Year (FY) 04, and $8.6M in FY05. As P.I. he brought total funding in excess of $40M to GMU between 2000 – 2007 and more over 18 years. He was the top funded PI in federal sponsor expenditures at Chapman University for 2010-2011. His total Chapman University grants and contracts exceed $1M to date.

He is Outstanding Visiting Scientist, Division of Environmental Science & Ecological Engineering, Advisor Brain Korea 21 Plus Eco-Leader Education Center, Korea University; Affiliated Researcher, National Observatory of Athens, Hellas; Executive Director of the Nalanda Consciousness Network. He is a quantum physicist, cosmologist, natural hazards and climate change researcher and works extensively on the quantum physics and the nature of the mind, cosmic Awareness and topics bridging science to philosophy and religion, particularly Orthodox Christianity and Zen Buddhism. He has 44 years of experience in undergraduate and graduate teaching and research, in Earth systems science, natural hazards and climate change, remote sensing and data information systems, physics, computational and theoretical astrophysics, astronomy, foundations of quantum theory, and most importantly, consciousness and the nature of reality. He gives workshops in science and spirituality as well as Natural Laws for business leaders and corporations.

He has published or co-authored 19 books including The Conscious Universe (Springer-Verlag, 1990, 2000), The Non-local Universe (Oxford University Press (1999), Principles of Integrative Science (Romanian Academy of Sciences Press, 2000); Looking In, Seeing Out (Theosophical Publishing House, 1991). He is co-author with Deepak Chopra of the New York Times best seller book You Are the Universe (Penguin/Harmony/Random House, 2017), and Living the Living Presence (in Korean, Miroksa Press, Seoul, 2016; and in Greek, Melissa Publishing, 2017). He has published more than 320 per-reviewed journal articles, refereed published proceedings and book chapters. Total Citations: 5,370+ (from Research Gate, 2016). Average citations per work 22.32 (for 173 publications). Highest Citation of single article: 500 (from all database sources). In the last several years, he has been publishing at the rate of 5 - 10 papers per year, with h-index: 38 (very high). Research Gate score: 42.81.

He is co-author of several blogs in Huffington Post and San Francisco Chronicle, with Deepak Chopra and others; and has his own blog in Huffington Post, writing as a "wandering scientist". He is recipient of the Rustum Roy Award from the Chopra Foundation, February 2011, which "honors individuals whose devotion and commitment to their passion for finding answers in their field is matched only by their commitment to humanity"; honorary member of the Romanian Academy of Sciences; Member, Board of Trustees, Universities Space Research Association (USRA), 2006-2008;

Member, OCTANe Board, 2010 - 2013; Chairman of the Board of the American Hellenic Council; IEEE Orange County Chapter - Outstanding Leadership and Professional Service Award, October, 2011, etc. He has been interviewed numerous times by: U.S. national TV networks (ABC, KCBS, Voice of America), Korean and Greek TV networks (KBS1 in Korea; ERT, SKAI-Eco, in Greece; PIT in Cyprus; TV and radio stations in Crete, cretalive, tv CRETA, Krete tv), national and regional newspapers and radios in Korea, (Hankook), Greece (Kathimerini, Eleutherotypia, Ethnos, Patris), and the United States (National Herald, OC Register, L.A. Times, Washington Post, Atlanta Journal, Korea Times).

In February 2018, he was elected Foreign Member of the Korean Academy of Science and Technology. Membership in KAST is prestigious and an extremely small percentage of all researchers in the fields represented. KAST areas include natural sciences, engineering, policy studies, agriculture and fisheries sciences, and medicine. KAST has a total of about 600 members. There are a total of 67 KAST foreign members, of which half are Nobel Laureates. He delivered keynote address to the KAST General Assembly on February 26, 2018 on the New Interdisciplinary Science Paradigm in which he outlined where the new science paradigm is heading.

«◊»

JULIA MOSSBRIDGE, PH.D. is the Director of the Innovation Lab at the Institute of Noetic Sciences, the Lead Robot Psychologist and Executive Coach at Hanson Robotics, a Visiting Scholar in the Psychology Department at Northwestern University, the Science Director at Focus@Will Labs, and an Associate Professor in Integral and Transpersonal Psychology at the California Institute of Integral Studies. She received her Ph.D. in Communication Sciences and Disorders from Northwestern University, her M.A. in Neuroscience from the University of California at San Francisco, and her B.A.

with highest honors in neuroscience from Oberlin College.

Julia's interest in how time is perceived by unconscious and conscious processes has led her to examine aspects of both cognitive and perceptual timing (e.g., order effects on reading comprehension, perceptual integration across senses) as well as controversial reverse-temporal effects (covered in ABC News 20/20, Wall Street Journal Ideas Market, Fox News and other mainstream media outlets). She is also the 2014 winner of the Charles Honorton Integrative Contributions award for this work. She is currently working on a book related to this work, The Premonition Code, to be released in October 2018 from Watkins Media.

She is also currently engaged in four love-centered projects: 1) LOVING AIs, a project designed to bring unconditional love into artificial intelligence (especially artificial general intelligence), 2) a project in which she is examining whether hypnosis can be used to induce a state of unconditional love, 3) The Calling, her current book project about how love gets translated into life purpose, and 4) consciously bringing unconditional love into the lives of the tech workers and executives she coaches.

Julia received funding from the National Institutes of Health in her role as post-doctoral member of the Psychology Department at Northwestern University in Evanston, IL. She is a peer reviewer for Brain Research, Perception, Cognition, PLoS One, Explore, and Journal of the Acoustical Society of America. She also invented and patented Choice Compass, a physiologically based decision-making app.

Julia is the author of *Unfolding: The Perpetual Science of Your Soul's Work* (New World Library, 2002) and *The Garden: An Inside Experiment*. She is the co-author, with Imants Baruss, of *Transcendent Mind: Re-Thinking the Science of Consciousness*, Published in 2017 by the American Psychological Association.

DIANE HENNACY POWELL, M.D. is an award-winning clinician and internationally recognized expert on autism and savant syndrome. She is an independent researcher with a private neuropsychiatry practice in Medford, Oregon. Dr. Powell graduated *Summa cum laude* from Ohio State University, where she trained in neuroscience. She was granted a full scholarship to Johns Hopkins School of Medicine (1979-1983), where she stayed for her residency training in psychiatry (1983-1987). She was on faculty at Harvard Medical School (1987-1989) before her Post-Doctoral Fellowship in the Genetics of Inborn Metabolism at the University of California, San Diego (1989-1990).

In 1991, Dr. Powell was invited by the Chairman the Women's Studies Department at the University of California, San Diego to teach an upper division course on cultural and biological contributions to gender differences in behavior. She became one of nine co-founders of the International Association of Women for Change and was voted to be one of the fifty-five most influential people in San Diego in 1992 by *First Thursday*. While in San Diego she created treatment programs for Survivors of Torture, Inc. and the McCandless Women's Center.

Dr. Powell came to the conclusion that our model in neuroscience is not only incomplete, it is based upon false assumptions. She became the Director of Research for the John E. Mack Institute in 2005 and was the Project Director for the *Annual Transformation of Consciousness Report* for the Institute of Noetic Sciences, which resulted in the widely-acclaimed *2007 Shift Report*. She has contributed chapters to five academic books, including the 2012 *Seriously Strange: Thinking Anew about Psychical Experiences* (Kakar, S. and Kripal, J.), and is the first author on five peer-reviewed scientific publications. Her 2008 book *The ESP Enigma* (Walker) received an award from the LA Festival of Books and has been translated into German, Portuguese, and Finnish.

Dr. Powell has presented her research on autistic children at scientific conferences in the U.S. and abroad, and appeared in numerous podcasts, and radio and television shows, including Dr. Phil. She has been an invited member of multiple think tanks, including the La Jolla Group for Understanding the Origin of Humans, and has served on the Board of the Jean Houston Foundation since 2010, the Scientific Advisory Board of the Forever Family Foundation since 2013, and on the Parapsychological Association's Book Award Committee since 2016.

《◊》

DEAN RADIN, PH.D. is Chief Scientist at the Institute of Noetic Sciences and Associated Distinguished Professor of Integral and Transpersonal Psychology at the California Institute of Integral Studies. Dean earned a BSEE degree in electrical engineering, magna cum laude and with honors in physics, from the University of Massachusetts, Amherst, and then an MS in electrical engineering and a PhD in psychology from the University of Illinois, Urbana-Champaign in 1979. Prior to joining the IONS research staff in 2001, he held appointments at AT&T Bell Labs, Princeton University, SRI International, and several other academic and industrial research facilities.

Since 1990, he has received over $2 million dollars in grants from numerous private foundations, professional organizations, and donors. He is author or coauthor of hundreds of scientific, technical, and popular articles, four dozen book chapters, and three bestselling popular books including *The Conscious Universe* (HarperOne, 1997), which received the Scientific and Medical Network's 1997 book award, *Entangled Minds* (Simon & Schuster, 2006), and *Supernormal* (Random House, 2013), which received a 2014 Silver Nautilus Book

Award. His fourth book, *Real Magic*, will be released in April 2018 (Penguin Random House). *Supernormal* and *Real Magic* are available as audio books, and the print books have been translated into French, German, Italian, Polish, Portuguese, Russian, Bulgarian, Latvian, Turkish, Czech, Japanese, Chinese, Korean, and Arabic.

His academic articles have appeared in journals ranging from Foundations of Physics and Physics Essays to Psychological Bulletin and the Journal of Consciousness Studies; he has been Co-Editor-in-Chief of the Elsevier journal Explore since 2009; he was featured in a New York Times Magazine article in 1996; and he has appeared on dozens of television programs throughout the world. He has given over 400 interviews and talks, including presentations at Harvard (medical), Stanford (statistics), Cambridge (England, physics), Princeton (psychology), the Sorbonne (Paris, yoga), and the University of Allahabad (India, neuroscience); for industries including Google, Johnson & Johnson, and Rabobank; and for government organizations including the US Navy CNO's Strategic Studies Group, US Army Special Operations Command, the Naval Postgraduate School, DARPA, the National Academy of Sciences, the Indian Council of Philosophical Research (India), the International Center for Leadership and Governance (Malaysia), and the Australian Leadership Retreat (Australia).

Dean was elected President of the AAAS-affiliated Parapsychological Association five times. In 2017 he was named one of the 100 most inspiring people in the world by the German magazine OOOM. He received special merit awards from Bell Laboratories and GTE Laboratories in 1984, 1989, and 1992; an Outstanding Contributions Award and the Charles Honorton Integrative Contributions Award from the Parapsychological Association in 1996 and 2015, respectively; the Nascent Systems Innovative Research Prize in 2017; the Silver Nautilus Book Award in 2014 for his book, Supernormal; and the Alexander Imich Award from the Rhine Research Center in 1996. He was an invited speaker for the Chief of

Naval Operations Strategic Studies Group in 2010, 2011 and 2012, the National Visiting Professor of the Indian Council of Philosophical Research in 2010, invited speaker for the International Center for Leadership and Governance in Kuala Lumpur in 2013 and 2014, and invited speaker for the Australian Davos Connection in Hayman Island, in 2015.

Dean has been interviewed by over a hundred television, radio, and podcast programs worldwide, and some two dozen documentaries and feature films.

‹◊›

GARY E. SCHWARTZ, PH.D. is Professor of Psychology, Medicine, Neurology, Psychiatry, and Surgery at the University of Arizona, at the main campus in Tucson. In addition to teaching courses on health and spiritual psychology, he is the Director of the Laboratory for Advances in Consciousness and Health. Gary received his Ph.D. in psychology from Harvard University in 1971 and was an assistant professor at Harvard for five years. He later served as a professor of psychology and psychiatry at Yale University, was director of the Yale Psychophysiology Center, and co-director of the Yale Behavioral Medicine Clinic, before moving to Arizona in 1988.

In September 2002, he received a $1.8 million dollars award from the National Center on Complementary and Alternative Medicine of the National Institutes of Health to create a Center for Frontier Medicine in Biofield Science at the University of Arizona, which he directed for four years. Gary collaborated with Canyon Ranch on biofield science and energy healing research and served as the Corporate Director of Development of Energy Healing.

Gary has published more than four hundred and fifty scientific papers, including six papers in the journal Science. Gary has also co-edited eleven academic books and is the author of The Sacred Promise (2011), The Energy Healing Experiments (2007), The

G.O.D. Experiments (2006), The Afterlife Experiments (2002), The Truth about Medium (2005), and The Living Energy Universe (1999). The Energy Healing Experiments (2007) received the Gold Medal from the Nautilus Book Awards. His new books are An Atheist in Heaven (2016), written with Paul Davids, and Super Synchronicity (2017).

Gary is a Fellow of the American Psychological Association, the American Psychological Society, and the Academy for Behavioral Medicine Research. He received a Young Psychologist Award and an Early Career Award for Distinguished Research from the American Psychological Association. He served as President of the Biofeedback Society of America and the Health Psychology Division of the American Psychological Association. In 2004 he received a Distinguished Scientist Award for Energy Psychology from the Association for Comprehensive Energy Psychology, and in 2006 a Distinguished Scientist Award from the United States Psychotronic Association. In 2012, he received the Distinguished Contribution to the Science of Psychology from the Arizona Psychological Association. Gary is highly experienced in speaking publicly about health psychology, energy healing, and spiritual research, and is in high demand. He has been interviewed on major network television shows including Dateline and Good Morning America, as well as on MSNBC, Nightline, Anderson Cooper 360, and The O'Reilly Factor. His work has been the subject of documentaries and profiles on Discovery, HBO, Arts & Entertainment, Fox, History and the SciFi Channel, among others. Gary has been interviewed on hundreds of radio shows, including four evenings on Art Bell's Coast to Coast AM, and on PBS, CBC and BBC. His work has been described in various magazines and newspapers including USA Today, the London Times, The New York Times, and The LA Times, as well as a feature profile in Biography magazine.

《〉》

STEPHAN A. SCHWARTZ has spent his life studying the nature of consciousness at both the individual and social level. He is an experimentalist, historian, futurist, and award-winning author, a Distinguished Consulting Faculty of Saybrook University, and a BIAL fellow. He writes both fiction and non-fiction, is a columnist for the journal *Explore,* and editor of the daily web publication *Schwartzreport.net.* In both he covers trends that are affecting the future from a perspective that incorporates consciousness as a factor. His other academic and research appointments include: Senior Samueli Fellow for Brain, Mind and Healing of the Samueli Institute; founder and Research Director for over 20 years of the Mobius Society laboratory, recipient of over $14.5 million in government and private individual and institutional funding; Executive Director of the Rhine Research Center; Adjunct Professor John F. Kennedy University; Scholar-in-Residence, Atlantic University; and Senior Fellow of The Philosophical Research Society.

Government appointments include: Special Assistant for Research and Analysis to the Chief of Naval Operations, consultant to the Oceanographer of the Navy.

He has also been editorial staff member of *National Geographic Magazine,* an editor of *Sea Power,* and staff reporter and feature writer for *The Daily Press* and *The Times Herald.*

For 50 years he has been studying the nature of consciousness, particularly that aspect independent of space and time. Schwartz is part of the small group that founded modern Remote Viewing research, and is the principal researcher studying the use of Remote Viewing in archaeology. Using Remote Viewing he discovered Cleopatra's Palace, Marc Antony's Timonium, ruins of the Lighthouse of Pharos, and sunken ships along the California coast, and in the Caribbean, as well as using nonlocal consciousness to solve crimes, including murder.

He also uses remote viewing to examine the future. Since 1978, he has been getting people to remote view the year 2050, and out of that has come a complex trend analysis that has demonstrated and continues to demonstrate high accuracy. His submarine experiment, Deep Quest, using Remote Viewing helped determine that nonlocal consciousness is not an electromagnetic phenomenon.

Other areas of experimental study include research into the role of nonlocal consciousness in creativity, genius, and spiritual epiphany; meditation, and focused intention at both the individual and group level; Therapeutic Intent/Healing, and the role of nonlocal consciousness in the anthropology of religions and spiritual practices. For the past 25 years he has also been doing research extending insights from the laboratory to the study of social change. How collective consciousness and shared intent has the power to create nonviolent social transitions.

Schwartz is the author of more than 200 technical reports and papers published over a wide range of disciplines and journals. He also has written numerous magazine articles for *Smithsonian, OMNI, American History, American Heritage, The Washington Post, The New York Times, The Huffington Post* as well as other magazines and newspapers.

He has also written and produced television documentaries, for USIA, ABC, NBC, and Nemoseen Media, and is the author of four non-fiction books: *The Secret Vaults of Time, The Alexandria Project, Mind Rover, Opening to the Infinite,* and his latest, The *8 Laws of Change,* winner of the 2016 Nautilus Book Award for Social Change. Also three novels, *Awakening – A Novel of Aliens and Consciousness,* 2018 Winner of the Book Excellence Award for Literary Excellence, *The Vision – A Novel of Time and Consciousness,* and *The Amish Girl – A Novel of Death and Consciousness.* Additionally, he has contributed chapters to over two dozen books edited by others.

Schwartz's research has been covered in the major papers, and magazines around the world, and presented in documentaries in many languages. For decades he has been a guest on nationally syndicated and network shows in Europe, Asia, and the Americas.

He is the recipient of a Certificate of Commendation from the Department of the Navy, the Parapsychological Association 2017 Outstanding Contribution Award, OOOM Magazine (Germany) 100 Most Inspiring People in the World award, and the 2018 Albert Nelson Marquis Award for Outstanding Contributions. He is listed in: Who's Who in the World, Who's Who in America, Who's Who in the West, Who's Who in Healthcare and Medicine.

His papers can be found on Academia.edu and Researchgate.com. Numerous news videos and documentaries about him and his research, as well as video and audio interviews with him, are to be found on YouTube. His personal website is: www.stephanaschwartz.com, and his daily web publication is: www.schwartzreport.net.

«◊»

CHARLES T. TART, PH.D. is an Emeritus Professor of Psychology at the Davis campus of the University of California and at the Institute of Transpersonal Psychology, (now renamed Sofia University), Palo Alto, and was one of the founders of the field of Transpersonal Psychology. He has been a Distinguished Visiting Professor at the Las Vegas campus of the University of Nevada, a consultant on US government sponsored research on the application of remote viewing to intelligence gathering at the Stanford Research Institute (now SRI International), and a Senior Fellow of the Institute of Noetic Sciences.

With wide-ranging interests, besides fourteen books, Professor Tart has published more than 250 scientific papers and articles, including major articles in *Science* and *Nature*. His two classic books, the best-selling *Altered States of Consciousness* (1969) and *Transpersonal Psychologies* (1975), were widely used texts that were instrumental in allowing these areas to become part of modern psychology. Books are pictured below, as well as a selected list of some journal publications. Many of his articles are archived online at www.paradigm-sys.com. Several hundred informal essays intended to stimulate students and younger researchers are available on his blog, blog.paradigm-sys.com. His classified and unclassified consulting work on the original remote viewing research at SRI, helped lead to more sensitive analysis techniques, and the success of operational remote viewing and some of Tart's work in selecting and training people talented on psi skills was important in influencing government policy makers against the further development and deployment of the multi-billion dollar MX Strategic Defense Initiative missile system, as then-current remote viewing levels of accuracy could have undermined the effectiveness of the plan to hide retaliatory missiles in many silos.

With many practical as well as theoretical interests, Professor Tart has been not only a laboratory researcher but a student of the Japanese martial art of Aikido (in which he holds a black belt), of various forms of meditation, of the psychology of Gurdjieff's Fourth Way mindfulness work, and of contemporary Buddhism. His primary goal is to build bridges between the best of the scientific and spiritual communities, and to help stimulate an expansion, refinement and integration of Western and Eastern approaches for knowing the world, both as generally useful knowledge and for personal and social growth.

He has been a popular speaker at many scientific and professional meetings, and although not limiting himself to mainstream foci, has received various awards for his research. One was the Distinguished Contributions to Scientific Hypnosis award from the American Psychological Association, Division 30, another the Science Social Innovations Award for 2000 for his The Archives of Scientists' Transcendent Experiences (TASTE) (http://www.issc-taste.org) project from The Institute for Social Inventions, providing a place for scientists to share their personal transcendent experiences. He also received the Abraham H. Maslow Award for outstanding contributions to the profession and practice of Humanistic Psychology, from Division 32 of the American Psychological Association.

Now semi-retired, he writes on many topics and is particularly interested in raising questions about how we develop a sufficiently objective science when issues of experimenter bias and psi connections are factored in, disrupting what he has named the "Newtonian shield" implicitly assumed in almost all current research.

《◊》

MARJORIE WOOLLACOTT, PH.D. is an Emeritus Professor of Human Physiology, and a member of the Institute of Neuroscience, at the University of Oregon. She was chair of the Human Physiology Department for seven years. In addition to teaching courses on neuroscience and rehabilitation, she taught courses on complementary and alternative medicine and meditation. She has recently (2017) accepted the position of Research Director for the International Association of Near Death Studies (IANDS). Marjorie graduated magna cum laude from the University of Southern California in 1968 and was elected to membership in Phi Beta Kappa. She received her Ph.D. in Neuroscience from the University of Southern California in 1973 and her M.A. from the University of Oregon in Asian Studies in 2005. She was also a research professor in the Department of Psychology at the University of Umea in Umea, Sweden, and in the National Center for Scientific Research in Marseille, France.

Marjorie has received over 7.2 million dollars in research funding from the National Institutes of Health and other research agencies for the past 35 years for her research in child development, aging, rehabilitation medicine and most recently, in meditation. Her areas of expertise include: 1) changes in attentional performance skills and underlying neural networks associated with the mental training of meditation and tai chi; 2) the development of balance and attentional abilities in normal children and in children with motor problems such as cerebral palsy and Down Syndrome; 3) factors leading to loss of balance function in the older adult, and in patients with motor disorders such as stroke and Parkinson's disease, in order to improve the quality of life and independence of adults well into old age; 4) the design of new assessment and treatment strategies to improve balance and attentional abilities. These include testing the efficacy of alternative forms of therapy such as tai chi and meditation for improving both attention and balance and gait abilities in patient populations; and 5) the development of musical performance skills in musicians.

Marjorie has published more than 200 scientific articles and written or co-edited eight books. She is the co-author, with Dr. Anne Shumway-Cook of the textbook for health care professionals, titled: Motor Control: Translating Research into Clinical Practice, which is in its 5th edition (2017). Her latest book, Infinite Awareness (2015) (winner of eight awards, including the 2017 Parapsychological Association Book Award, Eric Hoffer Book Award and the Nautilus Book Award) pairs Woollacott's research as a neuroscientist with her self-revelations about the mind's spiritual power. Between the scientific and spiritual worlds, she breaks open the definition of human consciousness to investigate the existence of a non-physical and infinitely powerful mind.

Marjorie was given the Oen Fellow Award in 2017 from Luther College, in Decorah, Iowa where she was invited to present a public lecture and lead class discussions on her book Infinite Awareness: The Awakening of a Scientific Mind. She was also given the Senior Scholar in Motor Development award from NASPSA in 2005 and the Distinguished Lecturer Award from the Department of Health

Professions at the University of Wisconsin, La Crosse in 2009. She was Invited to be Senior Scientist at the Max Planck Institute for Human Development, in Berlin Germany in 2009, and is a past President of the International Society for Posture and Gait Research.

Marjorie has been the keynote speaker at conferences in North and South America, Europe, Australia and Asia on topics including child development, aging, rehabilitation medicine, meditation, and near-death experiences. She has been interviewed on radio and television shows including AM Northwest, Buddha at the Gas Pump, and the Marie Manucherie show.

Acknowledgments

The editors would like to express their deepest appreciation to Sandy Bleaman, Shelby James, and Deborah Erickson for their help in the preparation of this volume, and Susan Klefstad for creating the index. And most importantly, we convey our special gratitude to the visionary contributors of this volume; collectively they demonstrate how science can continue to grow and evolve in its service to humanity and the planet. Finally, we acknowledge the loving support and collaboration of our spouses, Ronlyn, Paul and Rhonda.

Bibliography

Abe, K., Ichinomya, R., Kanai, T., & Yamamoto, K. (2012). Effect of a Japanese energy healing method known as *Johrei* on viability and proliferation of cultured cancer cells *in vitro*. *Journal of Alternative and Complementary Medicine*, 18(3), 221-228.

Achterberg, J. (2001). *Imagery in Healing: Shamanism and Modern Medicine*. Boston, MA: Shambhala.

Achterberg, J., & Dossey, B. M. (1994). *Rituals of Healing: Using Imagery for Health and Wellness*. New York, NY: Bantam.

Achterberg, J., Cooke, K., Richards, T., Standish, L., Kozak, L., & Lake, J. (2005). Evidence for correlations between distant intentionality and brain function in recipients: A functional magnetic resonance imaging analysis. *Journal of Alternative and Complementary Medicine*, 11(6), 965-971.

Ader, R., & Cohen, N. (1982). Behaviorally conditioned immunosuppression and murine systemic lupus erythematosus. *Science*, 215(4539), 1534-36.

Aminoff, M. J., Scheinman, M. M., Griffin, J. C., Herre, J. M. (1988). Electrocerebral accompaniments of syncope associated with malignant ventricular arrhythmias. *Ann Intern Med.*, 108, 791–796.

Aspect, A. (1982) *Experimental Test of Bell's Inequalities Using Time-varying Analyzers* Physical Review Letters, 49(25), 1804-1807.

Aspect, A., Grangier, P. & Roger, G (1982). *Phys. Rev. Lett.* 49, 91.

Auden, W. H. (1977). *The English Auden: Poems, Essays and Dramatic Writings, 1927-1939* (p. 246, Line 88). London: Faber and Faber.

Baker, R.R. (1980). Goal orientation by blindfolded humans after long-distance displacement: possible involvement of a magnetic sense. *Science, 210* (4469), 555-7.

Ball, P. (2016). We might live in a computer program, but it may not matter. . *BBC Earth.*

Baluška, F., Mancuso, S. (2009). Deep evolutionary origins of neurobiology. *Commun Integrat Biol.*, 2:1-6.

Bandura, A. (2001). Social cognitive theory: An agentic perspective, *Ann Rev Psychol.*, 52, 1–26.

Baron-Cohen, S. (1989). The autistic child's theory of mind: a case of specific developmental delay. *Journal of Child Psychology and Psychiatry, and Allied Disciplines, 30*(2), 28.

Baron-Cohen, S., Leslie, A. M. & Frith, U. (1985). Does the autistic child have a 'theory of mind'? *Cognition, 21*(1), 37–4.

Barušs, I., & Mossbridge, J. (2017). *Transcendent Mind: Rethinking the Science of Consciousness.* (pp. 3, 81, 171). Washington, DC: American Psychological Association.

Baumeister, R.F., Masicampo, E.J., Vohs, K.D. (2011). Do conscious thoughts cause behavior? *Ann Rev Psychol.*, 62, 331–361.

Beauregard, M. (2007). Mind does really matter: Evidence from neuroimaging studies of emotional self-regulation, psychotherapy, and placebo effect. *Prog Neurobiol.* 81, 218-236.

Beauregard, M. (2012). *Brain Wars*, New York, NY: Harper Collins.

Beauregard, M. (2014). The Primordial Psyche. *JCS*,21, 132-157.

Beauregard, M., O'Leary, D. (2007). *The Spiritual Brain.* New York: Harper Collins Publishers.

Beauregard, M., Schwartz, G.E., Miller, L., Dossey, L., Moreira-Almeida, A., Schlitz, M., Sheldrake, R., Tart, C. (2014). *Manifesto for a Postmaterialist Science. EXPLORE: The Journal of Science & Healing*, 10, 272-274.

Beauregard, M., Schwartz, G.E. R, Trent, N. (in press). *Expanding Science: Visions of a Postmaterialist Paradigm.* Vancouver: Param Media.

Beilock, S. (2012). How humans learn: lessons from the sea squirt, *Psychology Today*.

Beischel, J., Boccuzzi, M., Biuso, M., & Rock, A.J. (2015). Anomalous information reception by research mediums under blinded conditions II: Replication and extension. *Explore: The Journal of Science and Healing,* 11(2), 136-142.

Beischel, J., Schwartz, G. E. R. (2007). Anomalous information reception by research mediums demonstrated using a novel triple-blind protocol. *EXPLORE: The Journal of Science & Healing,* 3, 23–27.

Beitman, B.D. (2011a). Coincidence studies: A manifesto. *Edgescience,* 9, 11-17.

Beitman, B.D. (2011b). Coincidence Studies. *Psychiatric Annals,* Vol 41, Issue 12, 561-571

Beitman, B.D. (2016). *Connecting with Coincidence: The New Science for Using Synchronicity and Serendipity in Your Life.* Deerfield Beach, FL: HCI Books.

Bell, J.S. (1964) *On the Einstein-Podolsky-Rosen Paradox*, Physics, 1:195-200.

Bender, H. (1938). The case of Ilga K.: Report of a phenomenon of unusual perception, *Journal of Parapsychology*, 2, 5–22.

Bengston, W. (2010). *The Energy Cure: Unraveling the Mystery of Hands-on Healing.* Louisville, CO: Sounds True Publishing.

Bengston, W. F. (2012). Spirituality, connection, and healing with intent: reflections on cancer experiments on laboratory mice. *The Oxford Handbook of Psychology and Spirituality.* (Lisa J. Miller, ed.). (pp. 548-577). New York, NY: Oxford University Press; 2012.

Bengston, W. F., & Krinsley, D. (2000). The effect of the "laying on of hands" on transplanted breast cancer in mice. *Journal of Scientific Exploration,* 14(3), 353-364.

Bengston, W. F., & Moga, M. (2007). Resonance, placebo effects, and type II errors: some implications from healing research for experimental methods. *Journal of Alternative and Complementary Medicine,* 13(3), 317-327.

Bennett, C.L., *et al.* (2012). Nine-Year Wilkinson Microwave Anisotropy Probe (WMAP) Observations: Final Maps and Results. arcXiv:1212.5225 [astro-ph.CO].

Benor, D. J. (2002). *Healing Research.* Vol. 1. Southfield, MI: Vision.

Bergson, H. (1911). *Matter and Memory,* trans. N. M. Paul and W. Scott Palmer. London: George Allen.

Bernroider, G. (2003). Dimensional Analysis of Neurophysical Processes Related to Mentation.

Bernroider, G., & Roy, S. (2005), Quantum entanglement of K ions, multiple channel states and the role of noise in the brain, *SPIE* 5841-29, 205–14.

Blackie, A. & Spencer, J.H., Eds. (2015). *The Beacon of Mind: Reason and Intuition in the Ancient and Modern World.* Vancouver, BC: Param Media.

Blackmore, S.J. (1993). *Dying to Live: Science and the Near-Death Experience.* London: Grafton.

Blake, W. (1992). From: Augeries of innocence. In: Bartlett, John. *Bartlett's Familiar Quotations* (Justin Kaplan, general ed.). Sixteenth Edition. (p. 359). Boston: Little, Brown and Company.

Blanke O., Landis T., Seeck M. (2004). Out-of-body experience and autoscopy of neurological origin. *Brain. 127,* 243–258.

Bohm, D., & Hiley, B. J. (1995). *The Undivided Universe* (p. 389). London, UK: Routledge.

Bohm, D. (1986). In: Renée Weber. *Dialogues with Scientists and Sages* (p. 41). New York, NY: Routledge & Kegan Paul.

Bohm, D. In: Swami Ranganathananda (1991). *Human Being in Depth: A Scientific Approach to Religion.* (p. 87). Albany, NY: SUNY Press.

Bohr, N. (1958). *Atomic Physics and Human Knowledge.* New York, NY: Wiley.

Bohr, N. (1961). *Atomic Theory and the Description of Nature*, 4, 34, Cambridge: Cambridge University Press.

Bohr, N. (1987) *The Philosophical Writings of Niels Bohr.* Woodbridge, CT: Ox Bow Press.

Bourey, A.D., Schwartz, G.E. (2019 under review). *The Case for Truth.*

Broadbent, D. (1958). *Perception and Communication.* London: Pergamon Press.

Brandin, V. (2003) *Elements of Mathematical Theory of Intellect*, Interphysics Lab, Moscow.

Brandt, J. (2017). Personal communication.

Braud, W.G., Schlitz, M.J. (1991). Consciousness interactions with remote biological systems: Anomalous intentionality effects. *Subtle Energies,* 2, 1-46.

Brown, G.S, (1977) *Laws of form.* New York, NY: Julian Press, 1977.

Bullard, E. C. (1975). The emergence of plate tectonics: A personal view.*Annual Review of Earth and Planetary Sciences*, 3, 5.

Burgos, P.I., Hawkes, T., Cruz, G., Rojas-Sepulveda, I., &

Woollacott, M. (submitted). Effects of long term mental and physical practice on executive function: Are there differential effects of training type on EEG sources during a demanding task switch test?

Burtt, E.A. (1949). *The Metaphysical Foundations of Modern Science*. London: Routledge.

Carey, B. (2005, October 19). Scientists Bridle at Lecture Plan for Dalai Lama.

Carpenter, E. (1912). *The Drama of Love and Death*. New York, N.Y.: Allen.

Chaban, V. V., Cho, T., Reid, C. B., & Norris, K. C. (2013). Physically disconnected non-diffusable cell-to-cell communication between neuroblastoma SH-SY5Y and DRG sensory neurons.*Am. J. Translational Research*, 5(1), 69-79.

Chalmers, D. (1995). Facing up to the problem of consciousness. *Journal of Consciousness Studies*, 2 3), 200-219.

Chalmers, D. J. (1995). The puzzle of conscious experience. *Scientific American*, 273(6), 80-6.

Chalmers, D.J. (1996). *The Conscious Mind*. New York, NY: Oxford University Press.

Chidvilasananda, Sw. (1995). *The Yoga of Discipline*. Introduction. S. Fallsburg, NY, SYDA Foundation.

Chopra, D., & Kafatos, M.C. (2017). *You Are the Universe* Harmony, New York, NY: Random House.

Close, E.R. (1990)*Infinite continuity: a theory integrating relativity and quantum physics*. Los Angeles, CA: Paradigm Press.

Close, E.R. (2000) *Transcendental Physics*. Lincoln NE: I-Universe.

Close, E.R. Neppe, V.M. (2013) *Mathematical and theoretical physics feasibility demonstration of the finite nine dimensional vortical model in fermions*.

Seattle: *Dynamic Journal of Exceptional Creative Achievement* 1301:1301; 1-55.

Clute, H.L., Levy, W.J. (1990). Electroencephalographic changes during brief cardiac arrest in humans, *Anesthesiol.*, 73, 821–825.

Cohen, P. (1997, April 26). Can Protein Spring into Life?. *New Scientist*.

Coleridge, S. T. (1971). *The Statesman's Manual: Critical Theory Since Plato*. (Hazard Adams, Ed.) (p. 476). New York, NY: Harcourt Brace Jovanovich.

Cornell-Bell, A. H., Finkbeiner, S., Cooper, M.S. & Smith, S.J. (1990). Glutamate induces calcium waves in cultured astrocytes: long range glial signaling. *Science, 247* (4941), 470-473.

Cox, W.E. (1956). Precognition: An analysis II. *Journal of the American Society for Psychical Research*, 50 (1), 99-109.

Crick, F. & Koch, C. (2005). What is the function of the claustrum?*Philosophical Transactions of the Royal Society B: Biological Sciences. 360* (1458), 1271–9.

Currivan, J. (2017). *The Cosmic Holograph: In-formation at the Center of Creation*. Rochester, VA: Inner Traditions.

Dahle. P. (1940). Experimentelle untersuchungen über das gedankenslesen des lettischen mädchens Ilga K. *Zeitschrift für angewandte Psychologie und Charakterkunde, 58*, 273 – 316.

Damasio, A. (1999). The brain behind the mind. In Neuroscience: A New Era of Discovery. Retrieved November 16, 2001.

Darwin, C. (1897). In: *The Life and Letters of Charles Darwin* (F. Darwin, Ed.), 1, 81-82. New York, NY: D. Appleton & Co.

Davids, P.J., Schwartz, G.E. (2016). *An Atheist in Heaven: The Ultimate Evidence for Life After Death?* Los Angeles, CA: Yellow Hats Publishing.

Davidson, R.J., Kabat-Zinn, J., Schumacher, J., Rosenkranz, M., Muller, D., Santorelli, S.F., Urbanowski, F., Harrington, A., Bonus, K., & Sheridan, J.F. (2003). Alterations in brain and immune function produced by mindfulness meditation. Psychosom Med., 65(4), 564-70.

Dennis, K. L. (2012). New Revolutions for a Small Planet. London, UK: Watkins.

Dirac, P.A.M. (1937). *Nature* 139, 323.

Doran, C. and Lasenby, A. (2003) *Geometric Algebra for Physicists*, Cambridge University Press.

Dossey, L. (1989). Era III Medicine. In: *Meaning & Medicine* (pp. 189-193). New York, NY: Bantam.

Dossey, L. (1991). *Meaning &* Medicine (pp. 248-252). New York, NY: Bantam.

Dossey, L. (1993). *Healing Words: The Power of Prayer and the Practice of Medicine.* San Francisco, CA: HarperSanFranciso.

Dossey, L. (1997). *Be Careful What You Pray For.* San Francisco, CA: HarperSanFrancisco.

Dossey, L. (1999) Eternity Medicine. In: *Reinventing Medicine* (pp. 203-226). San Francisco, CA: HarperSanFrancisco.

Dossey, L. (1999). *Reinventing Medicine* (pp. 37-84). San Francisco, CA: HarperSanFrancisco.

Dossey, L. (2009). *The Power of Premonitions* (pp. 30-37). New York, NY: Dutton.

Dossey, L. (2013). *One Mind: How Our Individual Mind is Part of a Greater Reality.* Carlsbad, CA: Hay House.

Dossey, L. (2013). Unbroken wholeness: the emerging view of human interconnection. *Explore,* 9(1), 1-8.

Dossey, L. (2015). Consciousness: why materialism fails. *Open Sciences*.

Dossey, L. (2015). Telecebo: Beyond placebo to an expanded concept of healing. *Explore (NY)*, 12 (1), 1-12.

Drake, R.M. (1938). An unusual case of extra-sensory perception. *Journal of Parapsychology*, 2, 184–198.

Duane, T. D., & Behrendt, T. (1965). Extrasensory electroencephalographic induction between identical twins. *Science*, 150(3694), 367.

Dyer, W. (2010). *The Shift: Taking Your Life from Ambition to Meaning* (p. 50). Carlsbad, CA: Hay House.

Dyson, F. (1988). *Infinite in All Directions*. New York, NY: Harper & Row.

Dyson, F. (2011). How we know. *The New York Review of Books*, LVIII (4), 8-12.

Eccles, J., Robinson, D. N. (1985). *The Wonder of Being Human* (pp. 36, 53). Boston, MA: Shambhala.

Echeverria, F., Klinkhammer, G., & Thorne, K. S. (1991). Billiard balls in wormhole spacetimes with closed timelike curves: Classical theory. *Physical Review D*, 44(4), 1077.

Eddington, A. (1928). *The Nature of the Physical World* (p. 338). New York, NY: MacMillan.

Eddington, A.S. (1939). *The Philosophy of Physical Science*, Cambridge: Cambridge University Press.

Ehrenwald, H. (1940-1). Psychopathological aspects of telepathy. *Proceedings of the Society for Psychical Research*, 46, 224–244.

Einstein, A. (1905) *On a Heuristic Viewpoint Concerning the production and*

Transformation of Light. Berlin:*Annalen der Physik*, 17(6), 132–148.

Einstein. A. (1920) *Fundamental Ideas and Methods of the theory of Relativity, Presented in Their Development.* Princeton: *Collected Papers of Albert Einstein:* 7:31.

Einstein, A. (1926) In a letter to Max Born, 4, December 1926. *The Born-Einstein Letters*: New York, NY: Walker & Company, 1971.

Einstein, A. (1952) *Relativity, the special and the general theory*, 15th Edition, Appendix V, pp. 155. New York, NY: Crown Publishers.

Einstein, A. (1953) *A-Z Quotes.*

Einstein, A., Podolsky, B. & Rosen, R. (1935) *Can Quantum Mechanical Description of Physical Reality Be Considered Complete?* College Park MD: American Physical Society, Physical Review, 47:777-780.

Evans, D. (1993). *Spirituality and Human Nature* (pp. 147-151). Albany, NY: SUNY Press.

Falk, D., Lepore, F.E, & Noe, A. (2013). *Brain, 136*(4), 1304-1327.

Farhadi, A., Forsyth, C., Banan, A., Shaikh, M., Engen, P., Fields, J. Z., & Keshavarzian, A. (2007). Evidence for non-chemical, non-electrical intercellular signaling in intestinal epithelial cells. *Bioelectrochemistry*, 71(2), 142-148.

Feather, S. R., & Schmickler, M. (2005). *The Gift: ESP, the Extraordinary Experiences of Ordinary People* (p. 2). New York, NY: St. Martin's Press.

Fenwick, P., Lovelace, H., Brayne, S. (2010). Comfort for the dying: five-year retrospective and one-year prospective studies of end of life experiences. *Arch Gerontol Geriatr.*, 51, 173-179.

Ferlinghetti, L. (1960). *Her.* (p. 136). New York, NY: New Directions.

Fincke, J. (2003). The Babylonian Texts of Nineveh. Retrieved from http://oracc.museum.upenn.edu/saao/knpp/downloads/fincke_afo50.pdf

Fjell, A.M., Walhovd, K., Brown, T., Kuperman, J., Chung, Y., Hagler, D., et al. (2012). Multi-modal imaging of the self-regulating brain. *Proceedings of the National Academy of Sciences USA,109*, 19620–19625.

Fodor, J. (1992). The big idea: Can there be a science of mind? *Times Literary Supplement,* 5-7.

Foley, L.E., Gegear, R.L. & Reppert, M.R. (2011). Human cryptochrome exhibits light-dependent magnetosensitivity. *Nature Communications, 2.* doi:10.1038/ncomms1364.

Gauld, A. (1983). *Mediumship and Survival: A Century of Investigations.* Chicago, IL: Academy Chicago Publishers.

Gard, T., Taquet, M., Dixit, R., Hölzel, B.K., Dickerson, B.C., & Lazar, S.W. (2015). Greater widespread functional connectivity of the caudate in older adults who practice kripalu yoga and vipassana meditation than in controls. *Front Hum Neurosci. 16,* 137. doi:10.3389/fnhum.2015.00137. eCollection 2015.

Gödel, K. (1931)Über formal unentscheidbare Sätze der Principia Mathematica und *verwandter Systeme, Monatshefte für Mathematik und Physik,* 38 (1), 173–198.

Goff, P. (2017). Panpsychism is crazy, but it's also most probably true. *Aeon.*

Goldberg, P. (2010). *American Veda.* (p. 346). New York, NY: Harmony.

Goldberg, P. (2010). *American Veda.* (p. 270). New York, NY: Harmony.

Goodman, M. (2015). A quantum theory of consciousness may

require a paradigm shift in biology. *Journal of Consciousness Exploration & Research*, 6(1), 1-9.

Grandin, T. (2014) *The Autistic Brain: Helping Different Kinds of Minds Succeed.* New York, NY: Mariner Books.

Grant, J.A., Duerden, E.G., Courtemanche, J., Cherkasova, M., Duncan, G.H., & Rainville, P. (2013). Cortical thickness, mental absorption and meditative practice: possible implications for disorders of attention. *Biol Psychol.*,92(2), 275-81. doi:10.1016/j.biopsycho.2012.09.007

Greyson, B. (1993). Near-Death Experiences and the Physio-Kundalini Syndrome. *Journal of Religion and Health*,32, 277-290.

Greyson, B. (1993) The physio-kundalini syndrome and mental illness. *Journal of Transpersonal Psychology*, 25, 43-58.

Greyson, B. (2003). Incidence and correlates of near-death experiences in a cardiac care unit, *Gen Hosp Psychiatr.*, 25, 269-276.

Greyson, B. (2009). Near-death experiences and the physio-kundalini syndrome. *Kundalini Rising: Exploring the Energy of Awakening* (pp. 173-184). G.K. Khalsa, K. Wilber, Sw. Radha, G. Krishna, J. White, Eds. Boulder, CO: Sounds True.

Greyson, B. (2010). Seeing Dead People Not Known to Have Died: "Peak in Darien" Experiences. *Anthropol Humanism*, 35, 159-171.

Greyson, B. (2011). Cosmological implications of near-death experiences, *J Cosmol*, 14, 4684-4696.

Griffin, D. R. (1997). *Parapsychology, Philosopohy, and Spirituality: A Postmodern Exploration.* (p. 264). Albany, NY: SUNY Press.

Grinberg-Zylberbaum, J., Delaflor, M., & Attie, L. (1994). The Einstein-Podolsky-Rosen paradox in the brain: The transferred potential. *Physics Essays*, 7, 422–428.

Grinberg-Zylberbaum, J., Delaflor, M., Sanchez, M. E., & Guevara, M. A. (1993). Human communication and the electrophysiological activity of the brain. *Subtle Energies and Energy Medicine*, 3, 25-43.

Grinberg-Zylberbaum, J., & Ramos, J. (1987). Patterns of interhemispheric correlation during human communication. *International Journal of Neuroscience*, 36, 41-53.

Groblacher, S., Paterek, T., & Kaltenbaek, R. (2007). An experimental test of non-local realism. *Nature, 446.*

Gronowicz, G. A., Jhaveri, A., Clarke, L.W., Aronow, M.S., & Smith, T.H. (2008). Therapeutic Touch stimulates the proliferation of human cells in culture. *The Journal of Alternative and Complementary Medicine.*,14(3), 233-239. doi:10.1089/acm.2007.7163.

Gross, J.J. (1999). Emotion regulation: past, present, future, *Cognition and Emotion*, 13, 551-573.

Grosso, M. (2017) *The Final Choice: Death or Transcendence?* Hove, UK: White Crow Books.

Guggenheim, B., Guggenheim, J. (1997). *Hello from Heaven: A New Fiend of Research – After-Death Communication – confirms that life and love are eternal.* New York, NY: Random House.

Guilini, D. (2008) *Concepts of Symmetry in the Works of Wolfgang Pauli.* Albert Einstein Institute, Golm Germany.

Gurney, E., Myers, F. W. H., & Podmore, F. (1886). *Phantasms of the Living.* Volume 1. (pp. 188-189). London: Trübner.

Guth A. (1981). *Phys. Rev. D.*, 23, 347.

Haldane, J. B. S. (1927). When I am dead. In: *Possible Worlds and Other Essays* (pp. 209). (London, UK: Chatto and Windus. Quoted in: C. S. Lewis (1947). *Miracles* (pp. 19). London, UK: Fontana).

Haisch, B. (2007). Reductionism and consciousness. In T. Pfeiffer,

J.E. Mack, & P. Devereux (Eds.), *Mind before matter: Visions of a new science of consciousness* (pp. 51-63). Ropley, Hampshire, England, O Books.

Hameroff, S. (1998). Quantum computation in brain microtubules? The Penrose–Hameroff 'Orch OR' model of consciousness. *Philosophical Transactions of the Royal Society of London A, 356,* 1869-1896.

Haraldsson, E. (2003). Children who speak of past-life experiences: Is there a psychological explanation? *Psychology and Psychotherapy: Theory, Research and Practice, 76,* 55-67.

Haraldsson, E. (2012). Cases of the reincarnation type and the mind–brain relationship. In A. Moreira- Almeida, & F. Santana Santos (Eds.), *Exploring Frontiers of the Mind-Brain Relationship* (pp. 215-231). New York, NY: Springer.

Hawkes, T.D., Manselle, W., & Woollacott, M.H. (2014a). Cross-Sectional Comparison of Executive Attention Function in Normally Aging Long-Term T'ai Chi, Meditation, and Aerobic Fitness Practitioners versus Sedentary Adults," *Journal of Alternative and Complementary Medicine, 20,* 178–84.

Hawkes, T.D., Manselle, W., & Woollacott, M. (2014b). Tai Chi and Meditation-Plus-Exercise Benefit Neural Substrates of Executive Function: A Cross-Sectional, Controlled Study," *Journal of Complementary and Integrative Medicine 11,* 279–88.

Hearne, K. (1977) Visually evoked responses and ESP. *Journal of the Society for Psychical Research.* 49, 648-657.

Hearne, K. (1981). Visually evoked responses and ESP: Failure to replicate previous findings. *Journal of the Society for Psychical Research,* 51, 145-147.

Heisenberg, W. (1976). *Physics and Philosophy: The Revolution in Modern Science.* New York, NY: Harper and Row.

Hellman, H. (1999). *Great Feuds in Science.* (pp. 141-158). Hoboken,

NJ: Wiley.

Henry, R. C. (2005). The mental universe. *Nature, 436*, 29.

Herbert, N. (1987). *Quantum Reality* (p. 214, p 249). Garden City, NY: Anchor/Doubleday.

Hestenes. D and Sobczyk, G (1984) *Clifford Algebra to Geometric Calculus*, Kluwer Academic Publishers.

Hinterberger, T., Schmidt, S., Kamei, T., & Walach, H. (2014). Decreased electrophysiological activity represents the conscious state of emptiness in meditation. *Front Psychol.*, 17, 5:99.

Hobbs, A. (1910). Social Problems and Scientism. Harrisburg, PA: Stackpole.

Hobson, A. (2008). In: Steven Laureys and Giulio Tononi (eds.). *The Neurology of Consciousness: Cognitive Neuroscience and Neuropathology.* (p. xi). Salt Lake City, UT: Academic Press.

Hoffman, D. (2008). Consciousness and the mind-body problem. *Mind & Matter*, 6(1), 87-121.

Holden, J. M. (2009). Veridical Perception in Near-Death Experiences. In Holden, J.M., Greyson, B., & James, D. (Eds.) *The Handbook of Near-Death Experiences: Thirty Years of Investigation*, (pp. 185-211). Santa Barbara, CA: Praeger/ABC-CLIO.

Hou, C., Miller, B. L., Cummings, J. L., Goldberg, M., Mychack, P., Bottino, V., & Benson, D. F. (2000). Autistic savants. *Neuropsychiatry, neuropsychology, and behavioral neurology*, *13*(1), 29.

Huxley, A. (1945). *The Perennial Philosophy*. New York, NY: Harper Colophon Books.

Huxley, A. (1954/1991). *The Doors of Perception*, New York, NY: Perennial Library.

Jacobus, H. (2012). The Zodiac Sign Names in the Dead Sea Scrolls (4Q318) Features and Questions. ARAM, 24, 311-331. doi: 10.2143/ARAM.24.0.3009279.

Jahn, R.G. and Dunne, B.J. (2011). *Consciousness and the Source of Reality,* Princeton, NJ: ICRL Press.

Jahn, R.G. & Dunne, B.J. (2005) *The PEAR Proposition.* Princeton Engineering Anomalies Research Lab, Princeton University: *Journal of Scientific Exploration, 19(2), 195-245.*

James, W. (1898). Human immortality: Two supposed objections to the doctrine. In Murphy, G., & Ballou, R.O. (Eds.). *William James on psychical research* (pp. 279-308). New York, NY: Viking.

James, W. (1904). A world of pure experience. *The Journal of Philosophy, Psychology and Scientific Methods*, 1, 533-543.

James, W. (1925). *The Varieties of Religious Experience.* New York, NY: Longmans Green & Company.

James, W. (1977). Final impressions of a psychical researcher. In J. McDermott (Ed.), *The writings of William James: A comprehensive edition* (pp. 798-799).Chicago, IL: University of Chicago Press.

Jeans, J. (2001). In the Mind of Some Eternal Spirit, *Quantum Questions: Mystical Writings of the World's Great Physicists,* ed.K. Wilber. Boston, MA: Shambhala.

Johnson, S. In: Boswell, J. (1866). *The Life of Samuel Johnson.* Volume 3. (p. 112). London, UK: Routledge, Warne, and Routledge

Johnson, S. (2000). *The History of Rasselas* (p. 76). Ware, Hertfordshire, UK: Wordsworth editions.

Jonas, W. B., & Crawford, C. C. (2003). *Healing, Intention and Energy Medicine* (pp. xv-xix). New York, NY: Churchill Livingstone.

Jones, T. (3 April, 1994) The saint and Ann O'Neill.

Jung, C. (1972). *Synchronicity – An Acausal Connecting Principle*. Routledge and Kegan Paul.

Jung, C. G.(1975). *Psychology and Religion: West and East.* Volume 11 of *The Collected Works of C. G. Jung.* Sir Herbert Read and Gerhard Adler (Eds.); R.F.C. Hull (trans.) Second edition. (p. 12). Princeton, NJ: Princeton University Press.

Kafatos, M. (1986). In *Astrophysics of Brown Dwarfs*, ed. M. Kafatos R.S. Harring- ton, and S.P. Maran (1982), Cambridge: Cambridge University Press.

Kafatos, M. (1989). In *Bell's Theorem, Quantum Theory and Conceptions of the Universe*, ed. M. Kafatos, 195, Dordrecht: Kluwer Academic Publishers.

Kafatos, M. (1998). In *Causality and Locality in Modern Physics*, ed. G. Hunter et al.,29, Dordrecht: Kluwer Academic Publishers.

Kafatos, M. (2011). The Science of Wholeness, in *Analecta Husserliana*, T. Tymieniecka, A. Grandpierre (ed.), Springer Science, Business Media, B.V.

Kafatos, M.C. (2014). The Conscious Universe, in *Brain, Mind, Cosmos: The Nature of Our Existence and the Universe*, D. Chopra (ed.), New York, NY: eBook, Deepak Chopra, Publisher / Trident Media Group LLC.

Kafatos, M.C. (2015a). Fundamental Mathematics of Consciousness *Cosmos and History: The Journal of Natural and Social Philosophy*, 11(2):175-188.

Kafatos, M.C. (2015b). *Meditation: If You're Doing It, You're Doing It Right*, Alisson Tinsley and Chris Fields, Edit., Meditation is the effortless stilling of the mind: It is being with yourself, 153-158 (book chapter).

Kafatos, M.C. (2016) *Living the Living Presence* (in Korean) Seoul,

Korea: Miruksa Press.

Kafatos, M.C. (2017). *Living the Living Presence* (Βιώνοντας την Ζωντανή Παρουσία, in Greek), Athens: Μέλισσα Publishers.

Kafatos, M., & Kafatou, Th. (1991). *Looking In, Seeing Out: Consciousness and Cosmos*, Wheaton, IL: Quest Books/The Theosophical Publishing House.

Kafatos, M.C., & Kak, S. (2015). Veiled Nonlocality and Cosmic Censorship, *Physics Essays*, 28,182-187.

Kafatos, M.C., & Kato, G.C. (2017). Sheaf theoretic formulation for consciousness and qualia and relationship to the idealism of non-dual philosophies in Simeonov, P.L., Gare, A., Matsuno, K., Igamberdiev, A., Hankey, A. (Eds.), *The Necessary Conjunction of The Western and Eastern Thought Traditions for Exploring the Nature of Mind and Life*. Special Theme Issue Integral Biomathics. *Prog. Biophy. Mol. Biol.* 131: 242-250 Elsevier, ISSN: 00796107.

Kafatos, M.C., Lee, H., & Yang, K.-H. S. (2014). The Non-Local Universe is the Conscious Universe. In: *The Mysteries of Consciousness: Essays on Spacetime, Evolution and Well-Being*, Ingrid Fredriksson (Edit.) Print ISBN: 978-0-7864-7768-5 Ebook ISBN: 978-1-4766-1690-2.

Kafatos, M.,. & Nadeau, R. (2000). *The Conscious Universe: Parts and Wholes in Physical Reality*, New York, Springer-Verlag, ISBN: 978-0387988658, translated also in German, Dutch, etc.

Kafatos, M., Roy, S., & Roy, M. (2005). "Variation of Physical Constants, Redshift and the Arrow of Time", *Acta Physica Polonica*, 36, 3139-3161.

Kafatos, M.C., & Yang, K-H. S. (2018). The Participating Mind in the Quantum Universe. *Cosmos and History: The Journal of Natural and Social Philosophy, 14(1)*, 40-55.

Kastner, R. E. (2012). *The transactional interpretation of quantum mechanics: The reality of possibility*. Cambridge: Cambridge University Press.

Kastrup, B. (2014). *Why Materialism Is Baloney: How True Skeptics Know There Is No Death and Fathom Answers to life, the Universe, and Everything* (Kindle Edition ed.): John Hunt Publishing.

Kastrup, B. (2018). *The Idea of the World* (in press).

Kauffman, S. (2008). God enough. Interview of Stuart Kauffman by Steve Paulson.

Kauffman, S. A. (2016). *Humanity in a Creative Universe* (K. Edition Ed.): Oxford University Press.

Kennedy, J. B. (1995). On the empirical foundations of the quantum no-signalling proofs. *Philosophy of Science, 62*(4), 543-560.

Kelly, E. F., Crabtree, A., & Marshall, P. (Eds.). (2015). *Beyond Physicalism: Toward Reconciliation of Science and Spirituality*. Lanham, MD: Rowman & Littlefield.

Kelly, E. F., Kelly, E. W., Crabtree, A., Gauld, A., Grosso, M., & Greyson, B. (2007). *Irreducible Mind: Toward a Psychology for the 21st Century*. Lanham, MD: Rowman and Littlefield.

Kelly, E. F. (2015). Toward a Worldview Grounded in Science and Spirituality, In: *Beyond Physicalism: Toward Reconciliation of Science and Spirituality*, ed. E.F. Kelly, A. Crabtree, & P. Marshall. Lanham, MD: Rowman & Littlefield.

Kelly, E.W., & Archangel, D. (2011). An Investigation of Mediums who Claim to Give Information About Deceased Persons. *The Journal of Nervous and Mental Disease, 199*(1), 11-17.

Kelly, E. F., & Lenz, J. (1975). EEG changes correlated with a remote stroboscopic stimulus: A preliminary study. In: Morris, J., Roll, W., Morris, R. (Eds.). *Research in Parapsychology 1975*. (pp. 58-63). Metuchen, NJ: Scarecrow Press. (Abstracted in: (1975). *Journal of Parapsychology*, 39, 25.

Kelly, E. F., & Presti, D. (2015). A Psychobiological Perspective on 'Transmission' Models, in: *Beyond Physicalism: Toward Reconciliation of Science and Spirituality*, ed. E. F. Kelly, A. Crabtree, and P. Marshall. Lanham, MD: Rowman & Littlefield.

Kirschvink, J.L, Kobayashi-Kirschvink, A, Diaz-Ricci, J.C. & Kirschvink, S.J. (1992). Magnetite in human tissues: a mechanism for the biological effects of weak ELF magnetic fields. *Bioeletromagnetics*. Suppl 1: 101-13. PMID 1285705.

Kittenis, M., Caryl, P., & Stevens, P. (2004). Distant psychophysiological interaction effects between related and unrelated participants. *Proceedings of the Parapsychological Association Convention 2004*: 67-76. Meeting held in Vienna, Austria, August 5-8, 2004.

Kobayashi, M., Kikuchi, D. & Okamura, H. (2009). Imaging of ultraweak spontaneous photon emission from human body displaying diurnal rhythm. PLoS ONE, *4*(7), e6256 doi:10.1371/journal.pone.0006256.

Koch, C. (2012). *Consciousness: Confessions of a Romantic Reductionist.* (p. 119). Cambridge, MA: MIT Press.

Koch, C. (2014). Is consciousness universal?. *Scientific American*.

Koestler, A. (1972). *The Roots of Coincidence,* New York, NY: Random House.

Kolbaba, S. J. (2016). *Physicians' Untold Stories* (pp. 115-122). North Charleston, SC: CreateSpace IndependentPublishing Platform.

Koob, A. (2009). *The Root of Thought: Unlocking Glia-The Brain Cell That Will Help Us Sharpen Our Wits, Heal Injury, and Treat Brain Disease*. Upper Saddle River, NJ: FT Press.

Koons, R. C., & Bealer, G. (2010). *The Waning of Materialism* (Kindle Locations ed.). Oxford: Oxford University Press.

Kramer, P. D. (1993). *Listening to Prozac: A Psychiatrist Explores*

Antidepressant Drugs and the Remaking of the Self. New York, NY: Penguin Books.

Kugel, W. (2010). A faulty PK meta-analysis. *JSE,* 25, 47–62.

Kuhn, T. (1962). *The structure of scientific revolutions.* Chicago, IL: University of Chicago Press.

Kuhn, T. S. (1970). *The Structure of Scientific Revolutions.* Chicago: University of Chicago Press.

Lallier, F., Velly, G., Leon, A. (2015). Near-death experiences in survivors of cardiac arrest: a study about demographic, medical, pharmacological and psychological context. *Critical Care,* 19 (Suppl 1), pp.421.

Laszlo, E. (2006). *Science and the Reenchantment of the Cosmos: The Rise of the Integral Vision of Reality.* Rochester, Vermont: Inner Traditions.

Lawrence, D. H.(1992). In: Michael Bell, *D. H. Lawrence: Language and Being.*(p. 51). New York, NY: Cambridge University Press.

Lawrence, M., Repede, E. (2012). The incidence of deathbed communications and their impact on the dying process. *AJHPM,* 30, 632-639.

Lee, P., Ornstein, R. , Galin, D., Deikman, A., & Tart, C. (1975). *Symposium on Consciousness.* New York, NY: Viking Press.

Leibniz, G.W. (1697) *On the Ultimate Origination of Things.* Hanover, Germany: G.W. Leibniz Bibliothek, Shelfmark LH 4, 1, 10 Bl. 2-4.

Leibniz, G. W. In: Garber, D. (2009). *Leibniz: Body, Substance, Monad.* (p. 51). Oxford, UK: Oxford University Press.

Levin, J. (2000). A prolegomenon to an epidemiology of love: Theory, measurement, and health outcomes." *Journal of Social and Clinical Psychology,* 19, 117-136.

Levin, J. (2008). Esoteric healing traditions: A conceptual overview. *Explore*, *4*(2).

Levin, J. (1999). The power of love. [Interview]. *Alternative Therapies in Health and Medicine*, 5(4), 78-86.

Lewin, R. (1980). Is your brain really necessary? *Science*, *210*(4475), 1232-1234.

Lhermitte, F., Pilon, B. & Serdaru, M. (1986). Human autonomy and the frontal lobes. Part I: Iimitation and utilization behavior: A neuropsychological study of 75 patients. *Annals of Neurology*. *19*(4), 326–34.

Lhermitte, F. (1986). Human autonomy and the frontal lobes. Part II: Patient behavior in complex and social situations: The 'environmental dependency syndrome. *Annals of Neurology*. *19*(4), 335–43.

Lloyd, D. H. (1973). Objective events in the brain correlating with psychic phenomena. *New Horizons*, 1, 69-75.

Lombardo, M.V., Chakrabarti, B, Bullmore, E.T., MRC AIMS Consortium, & Baron-Cohen, S. (2011). Specialization of right temporo-parietal junction for mentalizing and its relation to social impairments in autism. *Neuroimage*, *56*(3), 1832-8.

Lommel, P., Van. Wees, R., Van, Meyers, V., & Elfferich, I. (2001). Near-Death Experience in Survivors of Cardiac Arrest: A Prospective Study in the Netherlands, *Lancet 358* (9298), 2039–45.

Lorimer, D. (1990). *Whole in One.* (pp. 72-105). London: Arkana/Penguin.

Lutz, A., Slagter, H.A., Rawlings, N.B., Francis, A.D., Greischar, L.L., & Davidson, R.J. (2009). Mental training enhances attentional stability: neural and behavioral evidence. J Neurosci., 21;29(42), 13418-27.

Macy, M. (2001). *Miracles in the Storm: Talking to the Other Side with the*

New Technology of Spiritual Contact. New York, NY: Penguin / Berkley /NAL.

Maddox, J. (1999). The unexpected science to come. *Scientific American,* 281(6), 62-7.

Marshall, P. (2005). *Mystical Encounters with the Natural World.* Oxford: Oxford University Press.

Mason, S. (2008). Flavius Josephus: translation and commentary, vol. 1b: Judean War. Leiden: Brill.

May, E. C., Targ, R., & Puthoff, H. E. (1979). EEG correlates to remote light flashes under conditions of sensory shielding. In: Charles Tart, Hal E. Puthoff, Russell Targ (Eds.). *Mind at Large: IEEE Symposia on the Nature of Extrasensory Perception.* Charlottesville, VA: Hampton Roads Publishing Company.

McDaniel, S. V. (2012). Book review of Matthew Colborn, *Pluralism and the Mind: Consciousness, Worldviews, and the Limits of Science Journal of Scientific Exploration.* 26(3), 657-661.

McFadden, J. (2002). The conscious electromagnetic information (CEMI) field theory: the hard problem made easy? *Journal of Consciousness Studies,* 9(8), 45-60.

McMillan, F. D. (1999). The placebo effect in animals. *J Am Vet Med Assoc,* 215(7), 992-9.

Millar, B. (1975). An attempted validation of the "Lloyd effect." In: J. D. Morris, W. G. Roll, R. L. Morris (Eds.). *Research in Parapsychology 1975.* (pp. 25-27). Metuchen, NJ: Scarecrow Press; 1975.

Millay, J.(2000). *Multidimensional Mind: Remote Viewing in Hyperspace.* Berkeley, CA: North Atlantic Books.

Miller, B.L., Boone, K., Cummings, J.L., Read, S.L. & Mishkin, F. (2000). Functional correlates of musical and visual ability in frontotemporal dementia. *British Journal of Psychiatry. 176*, 458–463. doi:10.1192/bjp.176.5.458.

Mills, A., Lynn, S.J. (2000). Past-life experiences. In Cardeña, E., Lynn, S.J., & Krippner, S. (Eds.). *Varieties of anomalous experience: Examining the scientific evidence* (pp. 283-313). Washington, DC, US: American Psychological Association.

Mitchell, E., & White, J. (1974). Psychic Exploration: A Challenge for Science. New York, NY: Putnams.

Moffitt, T.E., Arseneault, L., Belsky, D., et al. (2011). A gradient of childhood self-control predicts health, wealth and publicsafety. *Proceedings of the National Academy of Sciences USA, 108*, 72693–72698.

Moody, R. (1976). *Life After Life: The Investigation of a Phenomenon – Survival of Bodily Death.* Harris, PA: Stackpole Books.

Mossbridge, J. (2015). Time and the unconscious mind. *arXiv preprint arXiv:1503.01368.*

Mossbridge, J. & Radin, D. (2018a). Precognition as a form of prospection: A review of the evidence. *Psychology of Consciousness: Theory, Research and Practice, 5*(1):78-93.

Mossbridge, J. & Radin, D. (2018b). Plausibility, statistical interpretations, physical mechanisms and a new outlook: Response to commentaries on a precognition review. *Psychology of Consciousness: Theory, Research and Practice, 5*(1):110-116.

Mossbridge, J., Tressoldi, P. E., & Utts, J. (2012). Predictive physiological anticipation preceding seemingly unpredictable stimuli: a meta-analysis. *Frontiers in Psychology*, 3, 390.

Mossbridge, J., Tressoldi, P., Utts, J., Ives, J. A., Radin, D., & Jonas, W. B. (2015). We Did See This Coming: Response to, We Should Have Seen This Coming, by D. Sam Schwarzkopf. *arXiv preprint arXiv:1501.03179.*

Muldoon, S., & Carrington, H. (1956). The Projection of the Astral Body. London: Rider.

Nadeau, R., & Kafatos, M. (1999). *The Non-Local Universe: The New Physics and Matters of the Mind.* New York, NY: Oxford University Press.

Nagel, T. (2012). *Mind and Cosmos: WhytThe Materialist Neo-Darwinian Conception of Nature Is Almost Certainly False* (Kindle Edition Ed.): Oxford University Press.

Nelson, R. (2018, February 2). The Global Consciousness Project. Meaningful Correlations In Random Data.

Neppe, V.M. Close, E.R. (2012) *Reality begins with consciousness: a paradigm shift that works.*Seattle, WA: Brainvoyage.com.

Nineveh Tablet Collection. (n.d.). *British Museum Ashurbanipal Library Project.* Project Director J. C. Fincke. Retrieved December 3, 2017.

Nishida, K., Razavi, N., Jann, K., Yoshimura, M., Dierks, T., Kinoshita, T., & Koenig, T. (2015). Integrating Different Aspects of Resting Brain Activity: A Review of Electroencephalographic Signatures in Resting State Networks Derived from Functional Magnetic Resonance Imaging. *Neuropsychobiology, 71*(1), 6-16.

Oizumi, M., Albantakis, L., & Tononi, G. (2014). From the phenomenology to the mechanisms of consciousness: integrated information theory 3.0. *PLoS computational biology, 10*(5), e1003588.

Orme-Johnson, D., Dillbeck, M. C., Wallace, K., & Landrith, G. S (1982). Intersubject EEG coherence: Is consciousness a field? *International Journal of Neuroscience,* 16, 203-209.

Parker, A.L., Kavallaris, M. & McCarroll, J.A. (2014). Microtubules and their role in cellular stress in cancer. *Frontiers in Oncology, 4,* 153. doi: 10.3389/fonc.2014.00153.

Parnia, S., Fenwick, P. (2002). Near death experiences in cardiac arrest. *Resuscit.*, 52, 5–11.

Parnia, S., Waller, D.G., Yeates, R., Fenwick, P. (2001). A qualitative and quantitative study of the incidence, features, and aetiology of near death experiences in cardiac arrest survivors. *Resuscit.*, 48, 149–156.

Parnia, S., Spearpoint, K., De Vos, G., Fenwick, P., Goldberg, H., Yang, J., Zhu, J. et al., (2014). Aware-Awareness During Resuscitation—A Prospective Study. *Resuscitation*, 85, no. 12, 1799.

Paulson, S. (2017). The spiritual, reductionist consciousness of Christof Koch.

Penfield, W. (1975). *The Mystery of the Mind* (pp. xiii, 79). Princeton, NJ: Princeton University Press.

Penrose, R. (2009). What is reality? *New Scientist*.

Persinger, M.A., & Valliant P.M. (1985). Temporal lobe signs and reports of subjective paranormal experiences in a normal population: a replication. *Perceptual Motor Skills*, 60(3), 903-9.

Pinker, S. (1997). *How the Mind Works.* (p. 146). New York, NY: W. W. Norton.

Poerio, G.L., Sormaz, M., Wang, H.T., Margulies, D., Jefferies, E., & Smallwood, J. (2017, March 21). The role of the default mode network in component processes underlying the wandering mind. *Soc Cogn Affect Neurosci.* Advance online publication. doi:10.1093/scan/nsx041

Pizzi, R., Fantasia, A., Gelain, F., Rossetti, D., & Vescovi, A. (2004). Non-local correlation between separated human neural networks. In: Donkor, E., Pirick, A. R., Brandt, H. E. (Eds.) *Quantum Information and Computation II*. Proceedings of SPIE5436. pp. 107-117.

Planck, M. (1899) *Über irreversible Strahlungsvorgänge. Sitzungsberichte der*

Königlich Preußischen Akademie der Wissenschaften zu Berlin. 5: 440–480. Planck units: pp. 478–80.

Planck, M. (1914). *The Theory of Heat Radiation*. Masius, M. (transl.) (2nd ed.). P. Blakiston's Son & Co.

Planck, M. (1931). *The Observer*. London, UK; January 29.

Playfair, G. L. (2002a). *Twin Telepathy: The Psychic Connection*. London, UK: Vega.

Playfair, G. L. (2002b). *Twin Telepathy: The Psychic Connection* (pp. 12). London, UK: Vega.

Playfair, G. L. (2002c). *Twin Telepathy: The Psychic Connection*. (pp. 16). London, UK: Vega.

Playfair, G. L. (2002d). *Twin Telepathy: The Psychic Connection*. (pp. 51). London, UK: Vega.

Pockett, S. (2012). The electromagnetic field theory of consciousness: a testable hypothesis about the characteristics of conscious as opposed to the unconscious fields. *Journal of Consciousness Studies, 19*(11-12), 191-223.

Powell, D. H. (2008). *The ESP Enigma: The Scientific Case for Psychic Phenomena*. New York, NY: Walker Books.

Powell, D.H. (2012). Psi and psychiatry: The quest for a new scientific paradigm, *Seriously Strange: Thinking Anew about Psychical Experiences*, Kakar, S. & Kripal, J. (eds.) New York, NY: Penguin.

Powell, DH, (2015a). Evidence for telepathy in a nonverbal autistic child. *Mindfield, 8*(1), 30-32.

Powell, D.H. (2015b). Autistics, savants, and psi: A radical theory of mind. *Edgescience, 23*, 12-18.

Pribram K. (1991). *Brain and Perception- Holonomy and structure in Figural*

Processing, NJ: Lawrence Erlbaum Associates Publishers.

Price, H., & Wharton, K. (2015). Disentangling the quantum world. *Entropy, 17*(11), 7752-7767.

Radin, D. (1997). *The Conscious Universe: The Scientific Truth of Psychic Phenomena.* New York, NY: HarperEdge.

Radin, D. (2004). Event-related electroencephalographic correlations between isolated human subjects. *Journal of Alternative and Complementary Medicine,* 10, 315–323.

Radin, D. (2006). *Entangled Minds.* New York, NY: Paraview/Simon & Schuster.

Radin, D., Michel, L., Galdamez, K., Wendland, P., Rickenbach, R. & Delorme, A. (2012). Consciousness and the double-slit interference pattern: Six experiments. *Physics Essays, 25*(2), 157- 171.

Radin, D., Michel, L. & Delorme, A. (2015) *Reassessment of an independent verification of psychophysical interactions with a double-slit interference pattern.* Physics Essays, 28 (4), 415-416.

Radin, D., Nelson, R. (2003). Research on mind–matter interactions (MMI): Individual intention. In W. B. Jonas & C. C. Crawford, (Eds.), *Healing, Intention and Energy Medicine: Research and Clinical Implications* (pp. 39-48). Edinburgh: Churchill Living-stone.

Ramachandran, V.S. & Hubbard, E.M. (2001). Synaesthesia: a window into perception, thought and language. *Journal of Consciousness Studies, 8*(12), 3-34.

Ray, O. (2004). The revolutionary health science of psychoendoneuroimmunology. *Ann NY Acad Sci.*, 1032, 35–51.

Rebert, C. S., & Turner, A. (1974). EEG spectrum analysis techniques applied to the problem of psi phenomena. *Behavioral Neuropsychiatry,* 6, 18–24.

Recordon, E.G., Stratton, F.J.M., & Peters, R.A. (1968). Some trials in a case of alleged telepathy. *Journal of the Society for Psychical Research, 44*(738), 390–399.

Rhine, L. E. (1962). Psychological processes in ESP experiences. Part I. Waking experiences. *Journal of Parapsychology,* 29, 88-111.

Ricard, M., Lutz, A., & Davidson, R.J. (2014). Mind of the meditator. Sci Am., 311(5), 38-45.

Rilke, R.M. (1954). *Letters to a Young Poet,* M.D. Herter Norton (Trans.) (pp. 69-70) New York, NY: W.W. Norton.

Rimland, B. (1978). Savant capabilities of autistic children and their cognitive implications. *Cognitive Defects in the Development of Mental Illness,* Serban, G. (ed), New York, NY: Brunner/Mazel.

Ritchie, G. (n.d.). Retrieved February 11, 2018.

Roe, C. A., Sonnex, C., & Roxburgh, E. (2014). Two meta-analyses of noncontact healing studies. *Explore (NY),* 11(1),11-23. doi: http://dx.doi.org/10.1016/j.explore.2014.10.001.

Roy S., & Kafatos M. (1999). Complementarity Principle and Cognition Process, *Physics Essays,* 12, 662-668.

Roy, A.E., Robertson, T.J. (2001). A Double-Blind Procedure for Assessing the Relevance of a Medium's Statements to a Recipient. *Journal of the Society for Psychical Research,* 65, 161–174

Rush, J. H. (1964). New directions in parapsychological research. *Parapsychological Monographs No. 4* (pp. 18-19). New York, NY: Parapsychological Foundation.

Rutherford. E. (1911) *The Scattering of α and β Particles by Matter and the Structure of the Atom.* University of Manchester: *Philosophical Magazine.* Series 6. 21: 669–688.

Saavedra-Aguilar, J.C., Gómez-Jeria, J.S. (1989). A neurobiological model for near-death experiences. *JNDS*, 7, 205-222.

Sabell, A., Clarke, C., &Fenwick, P. (2001). Inter-Subject EEG correlations at a distance — the transferred potential. *Proceedings of the 44th Annual Convention of the Parapsychological Association* (pp. 419-422). New York, NY: Parapsychological Association.

Sacks, O. (1995). *An Anthropologist on Mars*. New York, NY: Alfred A. Knopf.

Sacks, O. (1998). *The Man Who Mistook His Wife for a Hat: and Other Clinical Tales*. New York, NY: Touchstone Books.

Sacks O. (2007). *Musicophilia: Tales of Music and the Brain*. New York, NY: Knopf Publishing Group.

Samson, D., Apperly, I.A., Chiavarino, C. & Humphrey, G.W. (2004). Left temporo-parietal junction is necessary for representing someone else's belief. *Nature Neuroscience*, 7(5), 499–500.

Schilpp, P. (1951) *Albert Einstein -Philosopher Scientist* 2nd Edition, pp 671-672. New York, NY: Tudor Publishing,

Schrödinger, E. (1960). *My View of the World*. (p. 62). Cambridge: Cambridge University Press.

Schrödinger, E. (1969). *What is Life? and Mind and Matter* pp. 139, 145). London, UK: Cambridge University Press.

Schrödinger, E. (1982). In: Ken Wilber (Ed.) *Quantum Questions* (p. 81). Boulder, CO: New Science Library.

Schrödinger, E. (1983). *My View of the World* (pp. 31-34). Woodbridge, CT: Ox Bow Press.

Schrödinger, E. (1994). In: Walter Moore. *A Life of Erwin Schrödinger*. Canto edition. (p. 181). Cambridge, UK: Cambridge University Press.

Schwaninger, J., Eisenberg, P.R., Schechtman, K.B., Weiss, A.N.

(2002). A prospective analysis of near-death experiences in cardiac arrest patients. *JNDS*, 20, 215–232.

Schwartz, G. & Simon, W. (2002). *The Afterlife Experiments: Breakthrough Scientific Evidence of Life After Death*. New York, NY: Pocket Books.

Schwartz, G.E. (2005). *The Truth about Medium: Extraordinary Experiments with the Real Allison DuBois of NBC's Medium and Other Remarkable Psychics*. Newburyport, MA: Hampton Roads Publishing.

Schwartz, G.E. (2006). *The G.O.D. Experiments: How Science is Discovering God in Everything, Including Us*. New York, NY: Simon & Schuster.

Schwartz, G.E. (2007). *The Energy Healing Experiments: Science Reveals Our Natural Power to Heal*. New York, NY: Simon & Schuster.

Schwartz, G.E. (2010). Possible Application of Silicon Photomultiplier Technology to Detect the Presence of Discarnate and Intention: Three Proof-of-Concept Experiments. Explore *6(3)*, 166-171.

Schwartz, G.E. (2011a). *The Sacred Promise: How Science is Discovering Spirits Collaboration with Us in our Daily Lives*. Hillsboro, OR: Beyond Words / Simon & Schuster.

Schwartz, G.E. (2011b) Photonic Measurement of Apparent Presence of Discarnate Using a Computer Automated System. Explore, *7(2)*,100-109.

Schwartz, G.E. (2012). Consciousness, Spirituality, and Postmaterialist Science: An Empirical and Experiential Approach. In LJ Miller (Editor). *The Oxford Handbook of Psychology and Spirituality*. New York City, NY: Oxford University Press, 584-597.

Schwartz, G.E. (2014). God, Synchronicity, and Postmaterialist Psychology I: Proof-of-Concept Real-Life Evidence. *Spirituality in Clinical Practice, 1(2)*, 153-162.

Schwartz, G.E. (2015a). God, Synchronicity, and Postmaterialist Psychology II: Replication and extension of real life evidence. *Spirituality in Clinical Practice, 2(1)*, 86–95.

Schwartz, G.E. (2015b). God, Synchronicity, and Postmaterialist Psychology III: Additional Real-Life Evidence and the Higher Power Healing Hypothesis. *Spirituality in Clinical Practice, 2(4)*, 289-302.

Schwartz, G.E. (2015c). Science and the Process of Responsible Belief: The Five Additive Criteria Test (FACT). In Blackie A, Spencer JH (Eds). *The Beacon of Mind: Reason and Intuition in the Ancient and Modern World.* Vancouver, BC: Param Media.

Schwartz, G.E. (2016a). Science and the process of responsible belief: The Five Additive Criteria Test (FACT). In A. Blackie and J.H. Spencer (eds.). *The Beacon of Mind: Reason and intuition in the ancient and modern world.* Vancouver, BC, Canada: Param Media, in press.

Schwartz, G. (2016b). What is the nature of a post-materialist paradigm? Three types of theories. *Explore, 12(2)*, 123-127.

Schwartz, G.E. (2017). *Super Synchronicity: Where Science and Spirit Meet.* Vancouver, BC: Param Media.

Schwartz, G.E. (2018 in preparation). *The Case for the SoulPhone.*

Schwartz, G.E.R., Russek, L.G.S. (2001). Evidence of anomalous information retrieval between two mediums: Telepathy, network memory resonance, and continuance of consciousness. *JSPR, 65*, 257–275.

Schwartz, G.E.R., Russek, L.G.S., Nelson, L.A., Barentsen, C. (2001). Accuracy and replicability of anomalous after-death communication across highly skilled mediums. *JSPR, 65*, 1–25.

Schwartz, G.E.R., Russek, L.G.S., Barentsen, C. (2002). Accuracy and replicability of anomalous information retrieval: Replication and extension. *JSPR, 66*, 144–156.

Schwartz, G.E.R., (2018, in preparation). *The SoulPhone Experiments.*

Schwartz, S.A. (1978). Two Application-Oriented Experiments Employing a Submarine Involving Novel Remote viewing Protocols, One Testing the ELF Hypothesis, Invited Paper *ASPR*, New York, NY.

Schwartz S.A. (1978). *The Secret Vaults of Time.* New York, NY: Grosset & Dunlap.

Schwartz, S.A. (1979, April). Associated Remote Viewing: A Protocol for Using Remote Viewing for Event Prediction. *Annual Meetings of the Southwestern Anthropology Association/ Association for Transpersonal Anthropology.*

Schwartz, S.A. (1997). The Eastern Harbor of Alexandria, Egypt: A 16 Year Case Study in Science, the Media, and the Anomalous. Invited paper. *16th Annual Meeting of the Society for Scientific Exploration. Journal of Scientific Exploration. (In press 2020).*

Schwartz, S. A. (2007). *Opening to the Infinite: The Art and Science of Nonlocal Awareness.* (p. 38). Buda, Texas: Nemoseen.

Schwartz, S.A. (1980, March 10). The Use of Intuitively Derived Data in Archaeological Fieldwork. *Annual Meeting of the Southwestern Anthropological Association/Association for Transpersonal Anthropology.*

Schwartz, S.A. with Side-scan Sonar Survey by Harold E. Edgerton. (1980, January 11). A Preliminary Survey of the Eastern Harbour, Alexandria, Egypt Combining Both Technological and Extended Sensing Exploration. *Proceedings Annual Meetings of the Society for Underwater Archaeology.* Journal of Scientific Exploration 2020, Vol 34. (in press).

Schwartz, S.A. (1980). The Ecuador Project: Remote Viewing in the Location and Reconstruction of a Pre-Columbian Site in Ecuador. *Mobius Technical Report.*

Schwartz, S.A. (1982). Preliminary Report on a Prototype Applied Parapsychological Methodology for Utilization in Archaeology, with a Case Report. *Research in Parapsychology 1981*, Eds. W. G. Roll, R. L. Morris, & R. White (Scarecrow: Metuchen, N.J. & London, pp. 25-27.

Schwartz, S.A. (1983, November 30-December 1). First Steps in Application Methodologies for Parapsychology. Invited Paper. *Proceedings: Symposium on Applications of Anomalous Phenomena.*

Schwartz, S.A. (2010). Nonlocality and Exceptional Experiences: A Study of Genius, Religious Epiphany, and the Psychic. In *Advances in Parapsychological Research Vol. 9*, ed. S. Krippner. New York, NY: Plenum Press.

Schwartz, S.A. (2010). Nonlocality and exceptional experiences: a study of genius, religious epiphany, and the psychic. *Explore, 6(4)*, 227-36. PMID: 20633837.

Schwartz S.A. (2015). *The 8 Laws of Change*. Rochester, VT: Park Street Press.

Schwartz, S.A. & De Mattei, R.J. (1983). The Mobius Psi-Q Test: Preliminary Findings." *Research in Parapsychology 1982*, Eds. W. G. Roll, J. Beloff, & R. White Scarecrow: Metuchen, N.J. & London, pp. 103-105.

Schwartz, S.A., De Mattei, R., & Schlitz, M. (1984). The Pecos Project: Reconstruction of Life in a Southwestern Indian Village Along the Lower Pecos River, Circa 8th Century A.D. American Anthropology Association Annual Meetings.

Schwartz, S.A. & De Mattei, R. with independent archaeological evaluation by Roger Smith, (Institute for Nautical Archaeology). (1987). Remote Viewing and the Search for Columbus' Lost Caravels. *Conference on Underwater Archaeology/Society of Historic Archaeology Annual Meetings. Research in Parapsychology 1987*, Eds.Debra H. Weiner and Roger D. Nelson. (Scarecrow: Metuchen, N.J. &

London, 1988). pp.100-101. The Location, Description, and Reconstruction of Marine Sites Through Remote Viewing, Including Comparison With Aerial Photography, Geological Coring, and Electronic Remote Sensing. Zeitschrift für Anomalistik. Volume 19 (2019), pp. 113–139.

Schwartz, S.A. & De Mattei, R. (1989). The Discovery of an American Brig: Fieldwork Involving Applied Archaeological Remote Viewing, Including a Comparison with Side Scan Sonar and Satellite Imagery. *Proceedings.* Conference on Underwater Archaeology/Society of Historic Archaeology Annual Meetings. The Discovery of an American Brig: Fieldwork Involving Applied Remote Viewing Including a Comparison with Electronic Remote Sensing. Journal of Scientific Exploration, Vol. 34, No. 1, pp. 62–92, 2020.

Schwartz, S.A. De Mattei, R., Brame, E., & Spottiswoode, J. (2015). Infrared Spectra Alteration in Water Proximate to the Palms of Therapeutic Practitioners. Explore, 11, 143-53.

Schwartz, S.A, & Dossey, L. (2010). Nonlocality, intention, and observer effects in healing studies: laying a foundation for the future. *Explore (NY), 6(5).* 295-307.

Schweitzer, A. (1934). *Indian Thought and Its Development.* (Mrs. Charles E. B. Russell, Trans.) (p. 260). New York, NY: Beacon Press.

Schweitzer, A. (2017). Walt Martin, Magda Ott. *Albert Schweitzer's Reverence for Life.* (p. 178). Morrisville, NC: Lulu Publishing.

Scully, M., & Drühl, K. (1982) *Quantum eraser: A Proposed photon correlation experiment Concerning observation and delayed choice in quantum mechanics.* Physics Review A25, 2208-2213.

Searle, J. (1995). *Journal of Consciousness Studies*, 2(1), Quotation on front cover.

Seevinck, M. P. (2010). Can quantum theory and special relativity peacefully coexist?. *arXiv preprint arXiv:1010.3714.*

Seife, C. (2007). *Decoding the Universe: How the New Science of Information Is Explaining Everything in the Cosmos, from Our Brains to Black Holes* (Kindle Edition ed.): Penguin Publishing Group.

Segal, N.L. (1999). *Entwined Lives: Twins and What They Tell Us About Human Behavior.* New York, NY: Penguin Putnam.

Selfe, L. (1977). *Nadia: A Case of Extraordinary Drawing Ability in an Autistic Child.* London: Academic Press.

The Royal Society Biological Sciences, 364 (1522), 1399–1405. doi:10.1098/ rstb.2008.0290.

Shapiro, A.K., Shapiro, E. (1997). *The Powerful Placebo: From Ancient Priest to Modern Physician,* Baltimore, MD: Johns Hopkins University Press.

Sheldrake, R. (1999). *Dogs That Know When Their Owners Are Coming Home: And Other Unexplained Powers of Animals.* New York, NY: Crown.

Sheldrake, R. (2012). *Science Set Free: 10 Paths to New Discovery.* New York, NY: Random House.

Shelley, P. B. (1992). From: Adonais. In: Bartlett, John. *Bartlett's Familiar Quotations* (Justin Kaplan, general ed.). Sixteenth Edition. Ip. 209). Boston: Little, Brown and Company.

Siegel, D. J. (2016). *Mind: A Journey to the Heart of Being Human,* New York, NY: Norton Series on Interpersonal Neurobiology.

Siegel, S. (2002). Explanatory mechanisms for placebo effects: Pavlovian conditioning. In: *The Science of the Placebo: Toward an Interdisciplinary Research Agenda.* (H.A. Guess, Ed.) (pp. 133-157). London, UK: BMJ Books.

Silk, J. (1989). *The Big Bang,* New York, NY: W. H. Freeman.

Sinclair, U. (2001). *Mental Radio.* Charlottesville, VA Hampton Roads.

Singh, S. (2002) *Fermat's Last Theorem*. Notting Hill, UK: Fourth Estate, Ltd.

Smallwood, J., Beach, E., Schooler, J.W., & Handy, T.C. (2008). Going AWOL in the brain: mind wandering reduces cortical analysis of external events. J Cogn Neurosci., 20(3), 458-69.

Smartt, L. (2017). *Words at the Threshold: What We Say as We're Nearing Death*. Novato, CA: New World Library.

Society for Neuroscience. (2005, Nov. 12). Dalai Lama Urges That Ethics Be a Guide in the Application of New Scientific Knowledge," NR-05-08 (11/12/05).

Sperry, R. (1995). In: Brian, D. *Genius Talk: Conversations with Nobel Scientists and Other Luminaries*. (p. 367). Amsterdam, Netherlands: Kluwer Academic Publishers.

Standish, L., Johnson, L. C., Richards, T., & Kozak, L. (2003). Evidence of correlated functional MRI signals between distant human brains. *Alternative Therapies in Health and Medicine*, 9, 122-128.

Standish, L., Kozak, L., Johnson, L. C., & Richards, T. (2004). Electroencephalographic evidence of correlated event-related signals between the brains of spatially and sensory isolated human subjects. *Journal of Alternative and Complementary Medicine*, 10(2), 307-314.

Stapp, H. (2007). *Mindful Universe: Quantum Mechanics and the Participating Observer*. New York, NY: Springer-Verlag.

Stapp, H.P. (2015). A quantum mechanical theory of the mind/brain connection. In: *Beyond Physicalism: Toward a Reconciliation of Science and Spirituality*. E.F. Kelly, A. Crabtree, and P. Marshall, Eds. Lanham, MD: Rowman & Littlefield.

Stapp, H.P. (2017). *Quantum Theory and Free Will: How Mental Intentions Translate into Bodily Actions.* Berlin, Heidelberg: Springer Verlag.

Stevenson, I. (1966). *Twenty Cases Suggestive of Reincarnation.* Charlottesville, VA: University of Virginia Press.

Stevenson, I. (1970).*Telepathic Impressions: A Review of 35 New Cases.* Charlottesville, VA: University Press of Virginia.

Stevenson, I. (1976). A preliminary report of a new case of responsive xenoglossy: the case of Gretchen. *JASPR,* 70, 65-77.

Stevenson, I. (1987) *Children who remember previous lives.* Charlottesville, VA: University Press of Virginia.

Stevenson, I. (2001). *Children Who Remember Previous Lives.* Jefferson, NC: McFarland & Company.

Stoeber, M., & Meynell, H. (Eds.). (1996). *Critical Reflections on the Paranormal.* Albany, NY: SUNY Press.

Stokes, D. (1997). *Advances in parapsychological research 8* (Stanley Krippner, Ed.) (p. 38). Jefferson, NC: McFarland.

Swāmī Lakṣmanjoo. (2003, 2017). *Kashmir Shaivism: The Secret Supreme.* Culver City: Universal Shaiva Fellowship.

Swaminathan, N. (2008). Brain-scan cell mystery solved. *Scientific American Mind.*

Swāmī Shāntānanda. (2003). *The Splendor of Recognition,* South Fallsburg, NY: Siddha Yoga, South Fallsburg.

Tammet, D. (2007). *Born on a Blue Day: Inside the Extradorinary Mind of an Autistic Savant: A Memoir,* New York, NY: Free Press.

Tang, Y.Y., Hölzel, B.K., & Posner, M.I. (2015). The neuroscience of mindfulness meditation. *Nat Rev Neurosci. 16(*4), 213-25. doi:10.1038/nrn3916. Epub 2015 Mar 18. Review.

Tang, Y.Y., Ma, Y., Wang, J., Fan, Y., Feng, S., Lu, Q., Yu, Q., Sui, D., Rothbart, M.K., Fan, M., & Posner, M.I. (2007). Short-term meditation training improves attention and self-regulation.

Proc Natl Acad Sci U S A. 104(43):17152-6. Epub 2007 Oct 11.

Targ, R., & Puthoff, H. (1974). Information transmission under conditions of sensory shielding. *Nature,* 252, 602-607.

Targ, R., & Puthoff, H. E. (1977). *Mind Reach: Scientists Look at Psychic Ability.* New York, NY: Delacorte Press/Eleanor Friede.

Tart, C. (1963). Physiological correlates of psi cognition. *International Journal of Parapsychology,* 5, 375-386.

Tart, C. (1969). *Altered States of Consciousness: A Book of Readings.* New York, NY: John Wiley & Sons.

Tart, C. (1971). *On Being Stoned: A Psychological Study of Marijuana Intoxication.* Palo Alto, California: Science and Behavior Books.

Tart, C. (1972). States of consciousness and state-specific sciences. *Science,* 176, 1203-1210.

Tart, C. (1973). States of consciousness. In L. Bourne & B. Ekstrand (Eds.), Human Action: An Introduction to Psychology (pp. 247-279). New York, NY: Dryden Press.

Tart, C. (1975a). *States of Consciousness.* New York, NY: E. P. Dutton.

Tart, C. (1975b). *Transpersonal Psychologies.* New York, NY: Harper & Row.

Tart, C. (1977). *Psi: Scientific Studies of the Psychic Realm.* New York, NY: E. P. Dutton.

Tart, C. (1986). *Waking Up: Overcoming the Obstacles to Human Potential.* Boston, MA: New Science Library.

Tart, C. (1989). A case of predictive psi, with comments on analytical, associative and theoretical overlay. *Journal of the Society for Psychical Research,* 55, 263-270.

Tart, C. (1994). Living the Mindful Life. Boston, MA: Shambhala.

Tart, C. T. (1997). *Body, Mind, Spirit: Exploring the Parapsychology of Spirituality.* Charlottesville, VA: Hampton Roads.

Tart, C. (1998). Six studies of out-of-body experiences. *Journal of Near-Death Studies, 17*(2), 73-99.

Tart, C. (1999). The Archives of Scientists' Transcendent Experiences. *Journal of Consciousness Studies Online, Letters-to-the-Editor*(July 7).

Tart, C. (2001). *Mind Science: Meditation Training for Practical People.* Novato, California: Wisdom Editions.

Tart, C. (2009). *The End of Materialism: How Evidence of the Paranormal is Bringing Science and Spirit Together* Oakland, CA: New Harbinger.

Tart, C. (2017a). *The Secret Science of the Soul: How Evidence of the Paranormal is Bringing Science and Spirit Together.* Napa, California: Fearless Books.

Tart, C. (2017b). *Who is the Experimenter? Methodology Issues for a Science Beyond Total Materialism.* Founding meeting of the Association for the Advancement of Postmaterialist Science, Tucson, August 25, 2017.

Tart, C., Puthoff, H., & Targ, R. (Eds.). (1979). *Mind at Large: Institute of Electrical and Electronic Engineers Symposia on the Nature of Extrasensory Perception.* New York, NY: Praeger.

Tegmark, M. (2014). *Our Mathematical Universe: My Quest for the Ultimate Nature of Reality*: Random House/Knopf.

Tegmark, M. (2003). Parallel universes. Not just a staple of science fiction, other universes are a direct implication of cosmological observations, *Scient. Am.* 288(5), 40–51.

Tesla, N. (1995) *Inventions, Researches and Writings of Nikola Tesla.* New York, NY: Dorset Press.

Thaler, L, Arnott, S.R. & Goodale, M.A. (2011). Neural correlates of natural human echolocation in early and late blind echolocation experts. doi: 10.1371/journal.pone.0020162.

Theise, N.D., & Kafatos, M. (2013a). Complementarity in biological systems: a complexity view. *Complexity*, 18(6):11-20.

Theise, N. D., & Kafatos, M. (2013b). Sentience Everywhere: Complexity Theory, Panpsychism & the Role of Sentience in Self-Organization of the Universe, *Journal of Consciousness Exploration & Research*, 4(4):378-390.

Theise, N.D., & Kafatos, M.C. (2016). Fundamental awareness: A framework for integrating science, philosophy and metaphysics. *Communicative & Integrative Biology, 9*(3).

Thomson Reuters. (2014). 2013 Journal Citation Reports®.

Thoreau, H. D. In: Kronenberger, L., Auden, W. H. (1993). *The Viking Book of Aphorisms* (p. 212). New York, NY: Barnes & Noble Books.

Tononi, G., & Koch, C. (2015). Consciousness: here, there and everywhere? *Philos Trans R Soc Lond B Biol Sci. 370*:1668.

Tononi, G., Boly, M., Massimini, M., & Koch, C. (2016). Integrated information theory: from consciousness to its physical substrate. *Nature Reviews Neuroscience, 17*(7), 450.

Trakhtenberg, E.C. (2008). The effects of guided imagery on the immune system: A critical review, *Int J Neurosci.*, 118, 839-855.

Treffert, D. (1989). *Understanding Savant Syndrome*. New York, NY: Ballantine Books.

Tucker, J.B. (2013). *Return to Life: Extraordinary Cases of Children Who Remember Past Lives*. New York, NY: St. Martin's Press.

Vedral, V. (2011) Living in a quantum world. *Scientific American*, 304(6), 38-43.

Vedral, V. (2012). *Decoding Reality: The Universe as Quantum Information* (Kindle Edition ed.). Oxford: Oxford University Press.

Wackerman, J., Seiter, C., Keibel, H., & Walach, H. (2003). Correlations be tween brain electrical activities of two spatially separated human subjects. *Neuroscience Letters*, 336, 60-64.

Walker, A. (2012). *Anything We Love Can Be Saved: A Writer's Activism.* New York, NY: Random House.

Walker, S.I., & Davies, P.C.W. (2016). The "hard problem" of life. Retrieved from arXiv:1606.07184v1 [q-bio.OT]

Wallace, B.A. (2012) Meditations of a Buddhist Skeptic, New York, NY: Columbia University Press.

Warcollier, R. (2001). *Mind to Mind.* Charlottesville, VA: Hampton Road.

Wellmuth, J. (1944). *The Nature and Origins of Scientism.* Milwaukee, WI: Marquette University Press.

Wheeler, J. (1978) *Mathematical Foundations of Quantum Theory. The past and the delayed-choice double-slit experiment*; pp. 9–48. New York, NY: Academic.

Wheeler, J.A. (1981). In *Some Strangeness in the Proportion*, ed. H. Woolf, Reading, Addison-Wesley Publishing Co.

Wheeler, J. (1994) *At Home in the Universe*, pp. 288-290. Woodbury, NY: *American Institute of Physics, AIP Press.*

White, F. (1998). *The Overview Effect: Space Exploration and Human Evolution.* Reston, VA: American Institute of Aeronautics and Astronautics.

Wigner, E. P. (1969). Are We Machines? *Proceedings of the American Philosophical Society*, 113 (2), 95-101.

Wilkins, H. & Sherman, H. (2004). *Thoughts Through Space.*

Charlottesville, VA: Hampton Roads.

Williams, B.J. (2011). Revisiting the Ganzfeld ESP debate: A basic review and assessment. *JSE*, 25, 639–661.

Williams, D. (1992). *Nobody Nowhere: The Extraordinary Autobiography of an Autistic Girl*, New York, NY: Random House.

Woerlee, G.M. (2004). Cardiac arrest and near-death experiences. *JNDS*, 22, 235-249.

Woollacott, M. (2015). *Infinite Awareness: The Awakening of a Scientific Mind.* Lanham, Md: Rowman and Littlefield.

Wordsworth, W. (1992). From: Tintern Abbey. In: Bartlett, John. *Bartlett's Familiar Quotations* (Justin Kaplan, general ed.). Sixteenth Edition. (p. 373). Boston: Little, Brown and Company.

Van Lommel, P. (2010). *Consciousness Beyond Life: The Science of Near-Death Experience.* San Francisco, CA: Harper One.

Van Lommel, P., Van Wees, R., Meyers, V., Elfferich, I. (2001). Near-death experience in survivors of cardiac arrest: A prospective study in the Netherlands. *Lancet*, 358, 2039–2045.

Vitetta, L., Anton, B., Cortizo, F., Sali, A. (2005). Mind–body medicine: Stress and its impact on overall health and longevity. *Ann NY Acad Sci.*, 1057, 492–505.

Von Neumann, J. (1955). *Mathematical Foundations of Quantum Mechanics*, translated by Robert T. Beyer, Princeton, NJ: Princeton University Press.

Zbinden, H., Brendle, J., Tittel, W., & Gisin, N. (2001). *Phys. Rev. A*, 63, 022111/1-20.

Zeilinger, A. (n.d.). What do you believe is true even though you cannot prove it? *Edge*.

Index

Academy for the Advancement of Postmaterialist Sciences (AAPS)
  about, i
  future history of postmaterialism, 193
  inspiration for this volume, ii
  scientific inquiry constrictions, 377
Achterberg, Jeanne, 319–20
acquired savant syndrome, 258–60, 275
"Adonais" (Shelley), 323
Adrian, Edgar Douglas, 271
AE. *See* anomalous experiences
after-death communications as evidence, 14
Afterlife Experiments, The (G. E. Schwartz), 15
Alexandria Project nonlocal perception, 231–40
Alexandria Project, The (S. A. Schwartz), 238
alien hand syndrome, 253
American Prophet, An (Kirkpatrick), 214
American Psychological Association postmaterialism, 39–40
American Veda (Goldberg), 323, 325
anecdote label of personal experiences, 308
anesthesia and microtubules, 279
anesthesiologist father, 204–7
anomalous experiences (AEs)
  acquired savant syndrome, 258–60, 275
  beliefs changed, 244–45, 255–58
  brain reverse engineered, 268–73
  description, 244
  dissociative identity disorder, 282
  double-slit experiment. *See* double-slit experiment
  focused attention by many people, 241–42, 283
  glial cells in brain, 262–65, 276, 287–88
  headache and brother's gunshot wound, 308
  holograms and reality construction, 276–80
  magnetite lining of skulls and, 275
  materialism and savant syndrome, 246, 260
  materialism persisting, 253–55
  nonlocal communication. *See* nonlocal communication
  placebos, 282
  postmaterialist paradigm, 252–53
  prayer power. *See* prayer power
  psi phenomena. *See* psychic (psi) phenomena
  psychiatric skepticism, 244–46
  scientific acceptance of, 250–53
  scientists failing to elucidate, 143
  sheep-goat effect in psi research, 282
  super-synchronicities, 284–87
  telepathy in autistic savants, 265–68
  terminal lucidity, 254
  work of the Devil, 251
  Zeno effect on radioactive decay, 283, 284
anthropology of consciousness
  Cayce trances, 215
  development of researcher, 215–28
  rituals as protocols of empirical science, 216, 227–28
  archaeology and nonlocal perception, 227–30, 228
  Alexandria Project, 231–40
  numinous sites increase success, 239
Association for Research and Enlightenment (ARE), 212–14, 218
astral projections, 386
astrocytes in brain, 263–64, 265, 274, 288
Atheist in Heaven, An (Davids and G. E. Schwartz), 14, 15
atom quantum equivalence units, 74–114
  triadic nature of reality, 90–91

Triadic Rotational Units of Equivalence, 85–86
unification of quantum physics and relativity, 89–90
atomic-level choice, 155
attention
   brain as filter, 184–85
   focus and meditation, 164–67
"Augeries of Innocence" (Blake), 323
auras and synesthesia, 289
Aurobindo, Sri, 351
autism
   seeing auras, 289
   telepathy, 265–68
   theory of mind and, 265–67
Bandyopadhyay, Anirban, 279
Baron-Cohen, Simon, 266–67
Barušs, Imants (*Transcendent Mind*), 39–40, 326
Bealer, George (*The Waning of Materialism*), 41
Beauregard, Mario (*Expanding Science*), 136
Beischel, Julie, 152
Beitman, Bernard
   Coincidence Science, 334, 343
   meaningful coincidences, 339, 343
   personal experiences with serial coincidences, 344–46
   website, 345
   Weird Coincidence Survey, 339–46
beliefs changed
   belief in God, 256–57
   community of believers, 16–18, 193, 327–30
   convergence of evidence, 3–5
   direct personal experience, 18–22
   evidence interpretation, 2–3
   evidence scientific, 14–16
   FACT analysis. *See* five additive criteria test
   hard truth as heart of science, 3
   humans' attitude toward Earth, 325
   mainstream acceptance of postmaterialism, 39–42
   neuroscientists, 160–63, 189, 244–45
   nonlocal event emotional wallop, 324
   ostrich vs. eagle science, 8–9
   personal stories of, 1–3, 4–5, 160–63, 178, 189, 244–45, 350–52
   reason and theory, 9–16
   skepticism considered, 22–24
Bell's Theorem of inequality, 54, 117
Berger, Hans, 271
Bergson, Henri, 157, 183
Big Bang theory, 107–9
biofeedback, 296, 297
biophotons, 277–78, 280
Blake, William ("Augeries of Innocence"), 323
blind children with savant skills, 268
blind spots in reality construction, 277
Bohm, David
   consciousness of mankind is one, 305
   meaning is being, 297
   pilot waves of double-slit experiment, 367
   unbroken wholeness, 306, 325
Bohr, Niels
   complementarity, 305
   EPR Paradox, 53
   physics about what we can say, 95
   quantum mechanics development, 53
Borowski, Brian, 268
brain
   angular gyrus for psi, 289–90
   brain is not mind quote, 293
   brain-brain nonlocal communication, 309, 313–14
   brain-machine prosthesis control, 281
   brain-mind models, 14
   consciousness created by, 10–14, 154, 156–58
   cybernetics, 261
   electromagnetic nature of, 268–73
   filtering by, 157, 182–87, 188–89, 260
   glial cells, 262–65, 276, 287–88
   GPS within, 273–76
   holograms and reality construction, 276–80

hydrocephalus and abilities, 259, 275–76
light and brain function, 280
mapping by neurosurgeons, 255
materialism persisting, 253–55, 256
meditation's effects on, 164–67
mental activity shaping, 139
microtubules, 279–80
mind's power to influence, 144–46, 155
NDE EEG flat-lined yet perceptions, 14, 171, 175
neuroscience focus on neurons, 246
perception differences, 248
processing power of, 261–65
receiver of consciousness, 10–16
repair via astrocytes, 263
reverse engineering, 268–73
sea squirt reabsorbing, 268
seat of consciousness, 254
sensory input deluge, 248
space-time navigation, 289
thinking styles, 249–50
transcendent experiences, 157
trauma and savant syndrome, 259–60, 275
ventricular system, 275–76
Brandin, Vladimir, 49
Brandt, Jason, 264
Broadbent, Daniel, 184
Brown, G. Spencer (*Laws of Form*), 62
Bruyere, Rosalyn, 239
Bullard, Edward, 329
Calculus of Dimensional Distinctions (CoDD)
about, 62
consciousness in Quantum Calculus, 63–64
Dimensional Extrapolation, 63, 77
gimmel for unification. *See* gimmel
publication of, 49
quantum equivalence unit basis, 64–68
quantum equivalence unit derivation, 68–74
quantum equivalence units of elementary particles, 74–114

Triadic Dimensional Distinction Vortical Paradigm, 91–92
triadic logic of, 64
triadic nature of reality, 90–91
Triadic Rotational Units of Equivalence, 85–86, 90
unification via. *See* unification of consciousness and reality
Capote, Truman, 209
cardiac arrest and near-death experiences, 148–50
Carpenter, Edward, 188
Castaneda, Carlos, 227
causality
scientific worldview, 29, 30
synchronicity, 338
Cayce, Edgar, 211–16
books on, 214
pineal gland, 276
Cayce, Edgar Evans, 215
Cayce, Hugh Lynn, 215, 218, 219, 220–23
cellular microtubules, 278–80, 288
cerebrospinal fluid, 275–76
Chalmers, David
awareness in all matter, 172–73, 187
consciousness fundamental, 326
hard problem of consciousness, 187, 245
organism complexity and consciousness, 155, 173
Chopra, Deepak, 267
Cicoria, Anthony, 260
claustrum as seat of consciousness, 254
climate change
collective mind concentrated by, 325
nonlocal consciousness, 241, 243
One-Mind perspective, 306–7
Close, Edward R.
Infinite Continuity, 49
Reality Begins with Consciousness, 49
Transcendental Physics, 49
Cohen, Jerry, 18
Coincidence Science, 334, 343
coincidences
accuracy of mathematical predictions, 36

coincidence or higher power, 349–50
coincidence science website, 339–46
   definitions of, 342
   meaningful coincidences of Beitman, 339, 343
   micro- and macroscopic ratios, 112–16
   number 11 coincidences, 345–48
   personal experiences, 344–50
   scientific evidence, 353–68
   subset not "just coincidences," 343
   super-synchronicities. *See* supersynchronicity science
   synchronicity. *See* synchronicity
   twin nonlocal communication, 317
   underlying unity manifested by, 331
   Universal Coincidence Creator, 343
   Weird Coincidence Survey, 339–46
   Western astronomy, 142
   word frequency analysis, 359–61
Coleridge, Samuel Taylor, 323
communication
   after-death communications, 14
   bad news travels, 318
   coincidence or higher power, 349–50
   distant mental interactions with living systems, 309–14
   dreams acted on, 210–14, 320
   images for, 229
   nonlocal. *See* nonlocal communication
   signs and symbols as, 334–37
   spirit communication personal experience, 18–22
   spirit communication technology, 15, 18–22
   telepathy. *See* telepathy
   vague gut feeling, 321
community of believers, 16–18, 193, 327–30, 367–70
complementarity
   about, 103
   Conscious Universe, 121–27

Copenhagen Interpretation, 53, 108, 117
corporate world and quantum mechanics, 130–31
generalized complementarity framework, 117
One Mind and individuality, 305
relationships and quantum mechanics, 131–33
universal diagrams revealing, 120
Concept Analysis Protocol, 228
Conscious Universe, The (Radin), 28
consciousness
   brain as receiver of, 10–16
   brain creating, 10–14, 154, 156–58
   definition attempts, 248
   electromagnetic, 268–73
   esoteric literature commonalities, 31
   force-field actions by, 246
   fundamental physical force, 284–87
   gimmel as atomic-level. *See* gimmel
   inside-mind vs. outside-matter, 34–42
   meditation and, 182–88
   mind as matrix of all matter, ii
   models of, 14, 170–74, 188–91
   NDEs and, 182–88
   nonlocal. *See* nonlocal consciousness
   ontologic framework, 104
   physics as parallel concept, 32–34
   science of. *See* science of Consciousness
   science when consciousness primary, 389
   seat of consciousness in claustrum, 254
   unification with reality. *See* unification of consciousness and reality
   unitary equivalence of measure, 67–68
   Universal Intelligent. *See* Universal Intelligent Consciousness
   waking consciousness only, 248

Consciousness Beyond Life (van Lommel), 14
constants of mathematics not constant, 112, 114–16
convergence of evidence, 3–5
   five additive criteria test (FACT), 6–8
Copenhagen Interpretation of quantum mechanics, 53, 108
Copernicus, Nicolaus, 25, 142, 143
Correspondence. *See* Recursion
cosmology, 107–13
Creative Interactivity, 104
Crichton, Michael, 239
Crick, Francis, 254
Cummiskey, Barbara, 291–92, 294
Dalai Lama, 159
Damasio, Antonio, 327
dark matter, 94–96, 108, 111
Darwin, Charles, 323
Davids, Paul J.
   An Atheist in Heaven, 14, 15
   Life After Death Project, The, 357
Davies, Paul, 37
Davis, Gladys, 214–15
death and Eternity vs. Temporal Medicine, 303–5
deathbed communications (DBCs), 153–54
deceased individuals
   after-death communications, 14
   bringing deceased to mediums, 2
   mediums' information accuracy, 15, 152–53
Decoding Reality (Vedral), 39
Decoding the Universe (Siefe), 39
Deep Quest remote viewing archaeology, 229–30
delayed-choice slit experiment, 55, 117–19
Dennis, Kingsley L., 325
Deuterium quantum equivalence units, 74–114
Dimensional Extrapolation, 63, 77
Dirac, P. A. M., 112, 113
direct experience. *See* experiences; personal experiences; subjective experience
dissociative identity disorder (DID), 282
distant cursing, 304

distant healing
   healing with intention, 311, 312
   love and compassion through nonlocal mind, 304
distant mental interactions with living systems (DMILS), 309–14
   visualization avoiding amputation, 280
distant viewing. *See* remote viewing
Dossey, Larry
   Healing Words, 292
   One Mind, 4, 305–6, 351
   prayer as medical tool, 281
double-slit experiment
   act of measuring and distributions, 366
   delayed-choice experiment, 55, 117–19
   focused attention and, 283
   measurement and nature of light, 54, 252
   single photon "randomness," 366–67
down-quarks. *See* quarks
dreams acted on, 210–14, 320
Dyson, Freeman, 155, 329
eagle vs. ostrich science, 8–9
Earth
   climate change, 241, 243, 306–7, 325
   crossroads of sacredness or annihilation, 333
   geomagnetic field, 242
   One-Mind perspective, 306–7
Eccles, John, 251, 273, 294
Eddington, Arthur, 305
EEG (encephalogram)
   brain-to-brain communication, 314
   consciousness as electromagnetic, 271
   glial cells reflected, 264
   NDE flat-lined yet perceptions, 14, 171, 175
Eiffel Tower–giraffe synchronicities, 349, 354–68
Einstein, Albert
   belief in telepathy, 251
   cosmological constant, 111
   electron–photon equivalence, 91

energy and mass interchangeable, 52, 53, 60, 64–68, 91, 252
EPR Paradox, 53–54, 61, 117
God clever but not malicious, 83
God does not play dice, 53
gravity via space-time curvature, 284
light speed constant, 51–52
no such thing as empty space, 65, 66
photoelectric effect, 260
relativity and quantum mechanics, 53–54
simple as possible, not simpler, 61
space-time does not exist on its own, 56, 65, 86
electrical engineering receiver analogy for brain, 11–13
electromagnetism
consciousness as, 268–73
GPS in brain, 273–76
magnetite in body, 274–75, 290
microtubules in cells, 279
pineal gland sensitivity, 276
psi as, 225–28, 229–30, 270, 273
electrons
dual nature of, 283
mass as inertia from spin, 88–89
mass via colliders, 74–75
photon equivalence, 91
quantum equivalence units, 74–114
triadic nature of reality, 90–91
Triadic Rotational Units of Equivalence, 85–86
unification of quantum physics and relativity, 89–90
elementary mind
evidence challenging scientific materialism, 144–58
failure of materialist science, 140–42
personal neuroscience journey, 138–40
personal spiritual experiences, 136–38
power of mind to influence, 144–46, 155
scientific revolutions, 142–44

Theory of Psychelementarity, 154–58
eleven. *See* number 11 coincidences
ELF (extremely low frequency)
brain detecting, 275
organ for sensing, 290
psi and, 225–28, 229–30, 270–71
embodied cognition, 281
emotional self-regulation and power of mind, 139, 144
empathic resonance, 316
energy–matter continuum model, 14, 173
Entangled Minds (Radin), 28
EPR Paradox (Einstein, Podolsky, Rosen), 53–54, 61, 117
esoteric literature
reality image, 32–34
similarities among, 30–31
ESP (extrasensory perception)
materialism challenged by, 146–48
savant skill, 265
scientific acceptance of, 250–51
scientific method to study, 383, 384
telepathy. *See* telepathy
ESP Enigma, The (Powell), 246, 250, 287
essential science, 375–77
psychical research applying, 383
essential spirituality, 379–80, 391
Evans, Donald (*Spirituality and Human Nature*), 324
evidence of postmaterialism
after-death communications, 14
brain as receiver of consciousness, 10–16
brain creating consciousness, 10–14
consciousness shaping reality, 54, 55
convergence of information, 3–5
datasets unexplainable under materialism, 195
deathbed communications, 153–54
five additive criteria test (FACT), 4–5
mediums providing, 2–3, 15, 151–53

mind shaping brain and body, 139, 144–46
near-death experiences, 14, 148–50
prevailing, 329
psychic (psi) phenomena, 50, 146–48
reincarnation, 14, 150–51
remote viewing, 224
remote viewing, Alexandria Project, 231–40
scientific research, 14–16, 195
serial coincidences, 334–37
spirit communication technology, 15, 18–22
supersynchronicity, 353–68
Universal Intelligent Consciousness, 334–37, 373–74

Expanding Science (Beauregard), 136
experiences
consciousness framework via mathematics, 121–27
cultural influence on, 186
essential spirituality, 379–80
five additive criteria test (FACT), 4–5, 18–22
generalizing own to everyone, 249
materialist beliefs affecting, 190–91
mind is primordial, 154
models of consciousness, 188–89
panpsychic model of consciousness, 172–73
personal. *See* personal experiences
qualia of subjective experience, 34, 105–7, 121, 125
Spirit, 378
subjective. *See* subjective experience
transpersonal, 378–80
extracerebral consciousness, 186
extrasensory perception. *See* ESP
extremely low frequency. *See* ELF
Eysenck, Hans, 250
FACT. *See* five additive criteria test
Fakharani, Fawzi, 231, 234, 236
Faticoni, Theodore G. (*The Mathematics of Infinity*), 331
Ferlinghetti, Lawrence, 305

fiber-optic system of microtubules, 280
five additive criteria test (FACT)
about, 4–5
accuracy of, 24–26
community of credible believers criterion, 16–18, 367–70
direct personal experiences criterion, 18–22, 370
reason and theory criterion, 9–16, 363–67
scientific evidence criterion, 14–16, 353–68
Seven S people, 16–18, 368–69
skepticism criterion, 22–24, 370–73
supersynchronicities, 352–80
top-down and bottom-up nature of, 9
flow
corporate world and quantum mechanics, 130–31
relationships and quantum mechanics, 131–33
focused intentioned consciousness. *See* intentioned consciousness
Fodor, Jerry A., 329
Foundational Questions Institute, 35
Freud, Sigmund, 251
fugue state, 254
functional magnetic resonance imaging (fMRI)
brain imaging, 139, 327
brain to brain nonlocal communication, 309, 314
distant intentionality, 320
future history of postmaterialism, 193–200
G.O.D. Experiments, The (G. E. Schwartz), 333
geomagnetic field (GMF) of earth, 242
Geschwind, Norman, 289
gimmel in quantum equivalence unit, 68, 85–86
Hydrogen atom, 86–94
Triadic Dimensional Distinction Vortical Paradigm, 91–92
unification via, 89–90, 91–96
giraffe-Paris synchronicities, 349, 354–68

glial cells in brain, 262–65, 276, 287–88
Global Consciousness Project, 241
gluons, 61, 94–96
Gödel's Incompleteness Theorem, 37, 58
Goldberg, Philip (*American Veda*), 323, 325
Goodman, Maurice, 284
GPS in brain, 273–76
Greater Reality Living (Pitstick and G. E. Schwartz), 333
Greyson, Bruce, 180
Grosso, Michael, 325
Guggenheim, Bill and Judy (*Hello from Heaven*), 14
Gurwitsch, Alexander, 278
Haisch, Bernard, 190
Haldane, J. B. S., 294
Hameroff, Stuart, 262, 279, 288
Hammid, Hella, 231–40
Haraldsson, Erlendur, 150
Hauck, Jack, 239
Haun, Jolie, 19
healing
  intentioned consciousness, 240, 309–14, 321
  love and compassion through nonlocal mind, 304
  medical. *See* medicine
  nonlocal communication of healers, 319–20
  prayer power, 281, 291–93, 321
  shamanic ritual, 219–23
  sickness as, 297
  Therapeutic Touch, 309
  wholeness of, 330
Healing Words (Dossey), 292
Heisenberg Uncertainty Principle, 53
Heisenberg Cut, 103
Heisenberg, Werner, 53
Hello from Heaven (Guggenheims), 14
Henry, Richard, 32
Herbert, Nick, 328
hierarchies of knowledge, 34–37
Hiley, Basil J., 306, 325
Hobson, Allan, 327
Hoffman, Donald D., 328

holograms and reality construction, 276–80
Holy Science, The (Yukteswar), 48
Humanity in a Creative Universe (Kauffman), 40
Huxley, Aldus, 30, 184
Hydrogen
  consciousness, 88
  quantum equivalence units, 74–114
  triadic nature of reality, 90–91
  Triadic Rotational Units of Equivalence, 86–94
Hypothesized Harry (HH) spirit communication, 18–22
idealism, 31–32
  Idealist Theories, 9
  panpsychic idealism, 186
identity
  dissociative identity disorder, 282
  One Mind and individuality, 305
immune response influenced by mind, 145
Incompleteness Theorem (Gödel), 37, 58
Infinite Awareness (Woollacott), 159, 163, 178, 351
Infinite Continuity (Close), 49
information
  astrocytes in brain, 263–64, 265, 274, 288
  convergence as evidence, 3–5
  encoding of mental events, 155
  holograms and reality construction, 276–80
  intentioned consciousness creating informational architectures, 242
  mental and physical world interconnectedness, 156
  neurons encoding, 262
  nonlocal information via consciousness, 212–28, 245
  panpsychic model of consciousness, 172–73
  psi phenomena, 28, 455, 245, 258
  reality as, 35–39, 243
  reality as intentioned consciousness, 240
  savants, 258–60

savants as nonlocal information, 265–68
Instrumental Trans-Communication (ITC), 15
Integrated Polarity. *See* complementarity
intentioned consciousness
  ability to attain and sustain key, 216, 240, 242
  across cultures, 215–17
  distant intentionality, 319–20
  distant mental interactions with living systems, 309–14
  double slit experiment, 283
  focused attention by many people, 241–42, 283
  good intentions focused on wine, 224
  healing with intentions, 240, 309–14, 321
  informational architectures from, 242
  intentions influencing matter, 196, 224, 240, 242
  medical personnel telecebo effects, 299–300, 308
  meditation for, 216, 297
  physiological effects of, 298
  prayer power, 281, 291–93, 321
  reality as, 240, 283
  visualization avoiding amputation, 280
Interactivity, Creative, 104
interconnected consciousness of meditation, 171–72
intuition
  coincidences and, 342
  psychiatry minimizing, 250
IONS (Institute of Noetic Sciences), 307
iridology as holographic information, 277
ITC (Instrumental Trans-Communication), 15
James, William
  brain as filter theory, 157, 183–84, 188
  meditation mystical characteristics, 181
  mediumship research, 151
  One Mind and individuality, 306
  reality plus The More, 381
  Varieties of Religious Experience, 217
Jeans, James, 169
Jefferson, Thomas, 211–14
Johnson, Samuel, 325
Jones, Ernest, 251
Jones, Tamara, 292
Jung, Carl
  quote on synchronicity, 331, 367, 370
  synchronicity definition, 338
Kaballah number 11 meaning, 347
Kafatos, Menas C.
  capitalization of key concepts, 332
  "coincidences" as underlying unity, 331
  corporations and quantum mechanics, 130–31
  cosmos derived from awareness, 40
  crossroads of sacredness or annihilation, 333
  Living the Living Presence, 126–28
  mind befriended for awareness, 129–30
  relationships and quantum mechanics, 131–33
  science and spirituality converging, 333
  Universal Intelligent Consciousness as Living Presence, 332, 334, 351
Kashmir Shaivism, 126
Kastrup, Bernardo (*Why Materialism Is Baloney*), 32
Kauffman, Stuart, A.
  consciousness unknown, 328
  Humanity in a Creative Universe, 40
Kelly, Ed, 187
Kelly, Emily, 152
Kepler, Johannes, 3
Ketch, Don, 229
Kirkpatrick, Sidney (*An American Prophet*), 214
knowledge hierarchies, 34–37
Koch, Christof
  consciousness in everything, 172

consciousness within science, 38–39
cosmos suffused with sentience, 189
physics from the inside, 33
primacy of consciousness, 195, 326
seat of consciousness, 254
Koestler, Arthur (The Roots of Coincidence), 250–51
Kolbaba, Scott J. (*Physicians' Untold Stories*), 292
Koons, Robert (*The Waning of Materialism*), 41
Kramer, Peter (*Listening to Prozac*), 246
Krippner, Stanley, 218
Kuhn, Thomas (*The Structure of Scientific Revolutions*), 142–43, 377, 390
Kundalini awakening, 180–87
Large Hadron Collider (LHC), 58
Lashley, Karl, 272
Lawrence, D. H., 325
Laws of Form (Brown), 62
Leibniz, Gottfried Wilhelm, 78, 322
Letters to a Young Poet (Rilke), 297
Life After Death Project, The (Davids and G. E. Schwartz), 357
Life After Life (Moody), 14
light
  Being of Light in near-death experience, 137, 148, 177, 379
  biophotons, 277–78, 280
  brain functioning and, 280
  connecting everything in universe, 114–16
  double-slit experiment, 54, 252, 283, 366–67
  double-slit experiment delayed-choice, 55, 117–19
  dual nature of, 54–55, 283
  photoelectric effect, 260
  photoreception in retina, 261
  pineal gland sensitivity, 276
  speed as agent of change, 115
  speed constant, 51–52
lightning strike and savant syndrome, 260, 275
Listening to Prozac (Kramer), 246

Living Energy Universe, The (G. E. Schwartz and Russek), 333
Living the Living Presence (Kafatos), 126–28, 126–28
  corporations and quantum mechanics, 130–31
  mind befriended for awareness, 129–30
  relationships and quantum mechanics, 131–33
  Universal Intelligent Consciousness as Living Presence, 332, 334, 351
local consciousness models, 14, 173
locality in scientific worldview, 29, 30
Lommel, Pim van, 14, 175
Long, Joseph, 227
Lorber, John, 259, 275
Lorimer, David (*Whole in One*), 315
love
  Being of Light in NDE, 137, 148, 177, 379
  distant healing, 304
  information not love as building block, 39
  Living the Living Presence, 133
  meditation experience, 161, 168, 179
  mother's love blocking healing, 223
  "My brain loves you," 294
  One Mind connectedness, 307
  quote by Alice Walker, 307
  Reverence for Life, 326
Macy, Mark, 15
Maddox, John R., 329
magnetism and human GPS, 274
magnetite in body, 274–75, 290
Marshall, Paul, 185–87
Marshall, Thomas E., 292
materialist science
  about, 294
  anomalous experiences and, 244–47
  belief in affecting experiences, 190–91
  bottom-up nature of, 9
  brain creating consciousness, 10–14, 249

brain-consciousness models, 14, 173, 188–89
everything is matter and energy, 94
evidence challenging. *See* evidence
failure of, 140–42, 246, 260
future history of, 193–200
gluons and dark matter, 94–96
idealism versus, 31–32
materialism in scientific worldview, 29
medical model of consciousness, 170–71
medicine, 293, 294–95, 300
neuroscience focus on neurons, 246–47
neuroscience materialism persisting, 253–55, 256
neuroscientists defending, 159–60
physicalism in scientific worldview, 29
postmaterialist paradigm and, 9–10
pragmatic materialist, 382, 391
promising consciousness explanations, 293–95, 327–30
receding as postmaterialism accepted, 39–42, 192, 326, 329–30
reductionism as dogma, 140–42
reductive materialism, 27, 29, 31–32, 41, 58–60
reductive mathematics, 60–62
religious belief, 294
supersynchronicity explanations, 346–48
Total Materialism, 381, 384–85, 392
materialist/Newtonian brain–consciousness model, 14, 173
mathematics
 bridge between science and consciousness, 121–27
 CoDD. *See* Calculus of Dimensional Distinctions
 constants not constant, 112, 114–16
 Conveyance Expression, 76, 77
 Dimensional Extrapolation, 63, 77
 Pythagorean Theorem, 77–78
 qualia in most refined form, 105
 Quantum Calculus, 63–64
 quantum equivalence unit basis, 64–68
 quantum equivalence unit derivation, 68–74
 quantum equivalence units of elementary particles, 74–114
 quantum mechanics mathematics, 59–62
 reality via, 32–34, 90–91
 Standard Model of particle physics, 59–62
 triadic nature of reality, 90–91
 unifying consciousness and reality. *See* unification of consciousness and reality
 units for quantum mechanics, 60–62, 64–68
 universe as mathematics, 34–42
Mathematics of Infinity, The (Faticoni), 331
Matthews, B. H. C., 271
McDaniel, Stan V., 327
McMullen, George, 231–40
meaning therapy, 295–97
 naming what happened, 308–9
mechanism in scientific worldview, 29
medicine
 biofeedback, 296, 297
 distant mental interactions with living systems, 309–14
 eras of, 300–302
 Eternity vs. Temporal Medicine, 303–5
 healing as. *See* healing
 materialism lacking wholeness, 322–27
 materialist modern medicine, 293, 294–95, 298
 meaning therapy, 296–97, 308–9
 medical model of consciousness, 170–71
 medical personnel telecebo effect, 298–300, 308
 medical professionals as parents, 204–7
 migraines and meaning, 295–97
 nonlocal medicine, 301–2
 One Mind, 4, 305–7

postmaterial clinical applications, 308–9
postmaterial medical school curricula, 298
postmaterial personal story, 295–98
postmaterial preventive medicine, 320–21
prayer power, 281, 291–93, 294, 321
Therapeutic Touch, 309
meditation
 biophotons, 277
 culture and meditative states, 186
 EEG flat-lined, 171
 expanded consciousness of, 171–72
 expanded consciousness of NDE and, 179, 180–87
 intentioned focused awareness via, 216, 297
 intentions influencing matter, 196, 224
 medical model of consciousness, 170–71
 mind as friend, 129–30
 models of consciousness, 170–74, 188–91
 nature of consciousness and, 182–88
 neuroscientists protesting, 159
 panpsychic model of consciousness, 172–73
 personal experience, 161–63, 167–69, 171
 scientific integration of, 169–70
 scientific research on, 164–67
 Self-Realization Fellowship, 48
 spiritual awakening via, 161–63, 168–69
mediums
 deceased bringing deceased to, 2
 evidence for supersynchronicity, 353–61, 358
 information accuracy as evidence, 15, 152–53
 pre-reading communications, 2
 researchers of, 151–52
memory
 brain excision experiment, 272
 brain mapping eliciting, 255
 cardiac arrest survivors, 149, 175
 consciousness-inclusive time travel, 198
 GPS in brain, 274
 near-death experiences, 148
 previous lives, 150–51
 white matter of savant, 264
Mental Radio (Sinclair), 217
metaphysics. *See* science of Consciousness
microtubules in cells, 278–80, 288
migraines meaning shift, 295–97
Miller, Lisa, 354
mind
 befriending for awareness, 129–30
 brain is not mind quote, 293
 co-evolution of mind and matter, 187
 consciousness. *See* consciousness
 elementary mind neuroscience. *See* elementary mind
 idealism, 31–32
 inside-mind vs. outside-matter, 34–42
 matrix of all matter, ii
 mental activity beyond space and time, 146–48
 mental activity shaping brain and body, 139, 144–46, 155
 mind-body connection in AEs, 280–83
 mind-body medicine history, 301
 mind-brain models, 14, 173
 observer shaping physical events, 54–56, 95, 99, 141, 252, 283, 366
 One Mind, 4, 305–6
 scientists changing their minds. *See* beliefs changed
 Super Mind, 351
 Theory of Psychelementarity, 154–58
Mind and Cosmos (Nagel), 41
Mind to Mind (Warcollier), 217
Miracles in the Storm (Macy), 15
Mitchell, Edgar, 307
mitogenic rays, 278–79
Mobius Consensus Protocol, 217, 227, 228, 239

Moody, Raymond (*Life After Life*), 14
Moser, Edvard, 274
Moser, May-Britt, 274
Moses, Ben, 239
Mossbridge, Julia (*Transcendent Mind*), 39–40, 326
Muldoon, Sylvan, 386
music
 at one with instrument, 281
 heightened sensory awareness, 47
 mathematical precision, 49, 121
 savant syndrome, 260, 265, 268
 sensory input individualized, 184
mystical scientist, 136
Nagel, Thomas (*Mind and Cosmos*), 41
near-death experiences (NDEs)
 Being of Light, 137, 148, 177, 379
 climate change causing mass, 325
 consciousness remaining after death, 174–79
 culture and experiences, 186
 description, 148
 EEG flat-lined yet perceptions, 14, 171, 175
 essential spirituality, 379
 evidence, 14, 148–50
 experience of Dr. Bettina Peyton, 175–79
 fear of death gone, 179
 interconnected consciousness, 171
 meditation and NDE expanded consciousness, 179, 180–87
 nature of consciousness and, 182–88
 personal experience, 137, 175–79
 unconsciousness similar, 257
Nelson, Roger, 241
Neppe, Vernon
 collaboration with Close, 44, 49, 57
 consciousness as fundamental, 55
 Reality Begins with Consciousness, 49
 Triadic Dimensional Distinction Vortical Paradigm, 91
 Triadic Rotational Unit of Equivalence (TRUE), 85
neuroscience
 anomalous experiences and materialist model, 244–47
 brain creating consciousness belief, 159–60
 brain creating consciousness evidence, 10–14
 consciousness as waking only, 248
 electromagnetic nature of consciousness, 268–73
 elementary mind. *See* elementary mind
 explanations of consciousness, 293–95, 327–30
 future history of postmaterialism, 193–200
 materialism defended by, 159–60
 materialism persisting, 253–55
 materialist history, 246–47
 meditation. *See* meditation
 microtubules directing neuron development, 279
 mind's power to influence brain and body, 144–46
 near-death experiences. *See* near-death experiences
 neurobiology of spiritual experiences, 139
 neuron to neuron nonlocal communication, 309, 313
 neurons encoding information, 262
 neuroscientists' beliefs changed, 160–63, 189, 244–45
 neurotransmitters, 246–47, 273
 personal experiences as neuroscientists, 138–40, 160–61, 194, 255–58
 quantum neuroscience, 260–65
 Type I postmaterialist theories, 252, 260–65
 Type II postmaterialist theories, 252, 265–68
 Type III postmaterialist theories, 252, 280–87
neutral monism, 31
neutrons
 mass as inertia from spin, 88–89
 mass via colliders, 74–75
 quantum equivalence units, 74–114
 quarks constituting, 84

triadic nature of reality, 90–91
nonlocal communication
  brain to brain, 309, 313–14
  cell to cell, 309, 313
  DMILS (distant mental interactions with living systems), 309–14
  dreams acted on, 210–14, 320
  person to person, 309
  person to person, healers, 319–20
  person to person, telesomatic events, 308–9, 315–19
  person to person, twins, 316–19
  telepathy as, 309
  vague gut feeling, 321
nonlocal consciousness
  archaeology sites via remote viewing, 227–40, 228
  assumption of authoritative language, 215
  becoming a researcher, 214–28
  brain-consciousness models, 14, 173
  climate change intentions, 241
  creativity and insight, 242
  Decline Effect in laboratory access, 217
  distant cursing, 304
  distant healing, 304
  distant viewing, 224, 226
  dreams acted on, 210–14, 320
  holograms and reality construction, 276–80
  intentioned focused awareness. *See* intentioned consciousness
  nonlocal information of savant syndrome, 265–68
  nonlocal information via consciousness, 212–28, 245
  nonlocal medicine, 301–2
  personal path to research, 203–14
  research design, 216–28
  research Mobius Consensus Protocol, 217
  shamanic healing ritual, 219–23
  spiritual awakening via meditation, 168–69
  Theory of Psychelementarity, 155
  understanding, 242–43

nonlocal perception. *See* remote viewing
nonlocal universe, 116–19
  universal diagrams revealing, 120
normal science, 377, 390
number 11 coincidences
  explanations possible, 346–48
  number 11 and Kaballah, 347
  personal experiences, 345–46
observation science
  essential science, 375–77, 383
  essential spirituality, 379–80, 391
  laboratory versus, 337–38, 353
  personal experiences beyond the material, 386–87
  postmaterialist personal importance, 382–87, 390
  scientific method applied to spirituality, 383, 384
  Society for Psychical Research applying, 383
Occam's razor, 83
O'Keefe, John, 274
One Mind, 4, 305–6
  supersynchronicity explanation, 351
  undivided universe, 306–7
O'Neill, Ann, 292–93
Opening to the Infinite (S. A. Schwartz), 324
oracular rituals. *See* shamanism
Ordered to Return (Ritchie), 225
Orloff, Judith, 239
ostrich vs. eagle science, 8–9
Our Mathematical Universe (Tegmark), 35–36, 37
out-of-body experiences (OBEs)
  angular gyrus in brain, 290
  essential spirituality, 379
  holographic sensory perception, 277
  inducing, 386
  mind not produced by brain, 156
  near-death experiences, 148
  surgical patient, 204–7
owl synchronicity, 286
Padgett, Jason, 259
panpsychism
  model of consciousness, 172–73
  panpsychic idealism, 186–87

perennial philosophy, 31
Theory of Psychelementarity, 155
paradigmatic science, 377, 390
paradigms
   bridging science and spirituality, 133–34
   can and should change, 142–44, 378, 390
   definition, 142
   postmaterialist paradigm, 9–10
   Triadic Dimensional Distinction Vortical Paradigm, 91–92
   unifying relativity and quantum physics, 91–96
parapsychology. *See* psychic (psi) phenomena
Paris-giraffe synchronicities, 349, 354–68
past life research, 150–51
Peek, Kim, 259, 275
Penfield, Wilder, 293
Penrose, Roger, 36, 262, 279, 288
perception
   brain differences, 248
   out-of-body experiences, 277
   psi and thresholds of perception, 184
   sensory input vs. processing, 248
perennial philosophy, 30–32
Persinger, Michael, 226
personal domain of consciousness, 186
personal experiences
   anecdote label, 308
   belief and direct personal experience, 18–22
   beliefs changed, 1–3, 4–5
   beyond the material, 386–87
   books as path to consciousness research, 203–4
   consciousness melting into surroundings, 44
   five additive criteria test (FACT), 4–5, 7, 18–22, 370
   general, nonpersonal. *See* experiences
   generalizing own to everyone, 249
   identical twin, 316
   mathematical modeler and engineer, 43

medical professionals as parents, 204–7
meditation expanded consciousness, 171
meditation spiritual awakening, 161–63, 168–69
merging with Ultimate Reality, 138
near death experience, 137, 175–79
neuroscientists, 138–40, 160–61, 194
nonlocal event emotional wallop, 324
psychiatrist meeting psychic, 245
psychic phenomena, 28–29, 45, 136–38, 207–14, 245, 258, 387
science pursuit, 98, 100, 107
synchronicity, 286–87, 344–50
Weird Coincidence Survey, 339–46
Peyton, Bettina, 175–79
Philosophy of Inductive Sciences (Whewell), 1, 4
philosophy rejecting materialism, 41
photons
   biophotons, 277–78, 280
   double-slit experiment. *See* double-slit experiment
   dual nature of, 54–55, 283
   electron equivalence, 91
   light. *See* light
   photoelectric effect, 260
physicalism. *See* materialist science
Physicians' Untold Stories (Kolbaba), 292
physics
   about, 56
   anomalous experiences supported, 252
   atom smashing, 58–62
   consciousness as fundamental force, 284–87
   consciousness as parallel concept, 32–34
   consciousness missing, 56–58
   consciousness represented by gimmel, 91–96
   cosmological constraints, 109–13
   mathematics of quantum phenomena, 59–62, 64–68

observer shaping, 54–56, 95, 99, 141, 252, 283, 366
quantum mechanics. *See* quantum mechanics
pineal gland, 276
Pinker, Steven A., 328
Pitstick, Mark R. (*Greater Reality Living*), 333
placebo effect, 145, 282
  animals exhibiting, 312
  medical personnel telecebo effect, 298–300, 308
Planck units, 65
Planck, Max
  cannot speak of matter or energy alone, 66
  consciousness is fundamental, 242, 326
  Einstein's theory, 52
  matter as derivative of consciousness, 51, 56
  mind as matrix of matter, ii
  quantization of energy, 52
  smallest unit of measurement, 62
Playfair, Guy Lyon (*Twin Telepathy*), 316–19
Podolsky, Boris, 53–54, 61, 117
poets capturing wholeness, 323
Popper, Karl, 273
postmaterialist science
  belief in affecting experiences, 190–91
  beliefs changed. *See* beliefs changed
  brain as receiver of consciousness, 10–16
  community of believers, 16–18
  consciousness framework via mathematics, 121–27
  evidence supporting. *See* evidence
  future history of, 193–200
  idealism, 31–32
  mainstream acceptance of, 39–42, 194, 326, 328–30
  medical school curricula, 298
  medicine, 320–21
  observation science. *See* observation science
  paradigm, 9–10, 252–53, 260–68, 280–87
  personal importance of, 382–87, 390
  quantum neuroscience, 260–65
  researchers listed, 101
  supersynchronicity explanations, 346–48
  Theory of Psychelementarity, 154–58
  top-down nature of, 9
  Type I theories, 9, 11, 252, 260–65
  Type II theories, 9, 11, 252, 265–68
  Type III theories, 5, 9, 11, 252, 280–87
  wholeness of, 330
Powell, Diane Hennacy (*The ESP Enigma*), 246, 250, 287
prayer power
  healing with intentions, 240, 309–14, 321
  materialistic modern medicine, 293, 294–95
  medical tool, 281
  story of Ann O'Neill, 292–93
  story of Barbara Cummiskey, 291–92
Protium. *See* Hydrogen
protons
  Hydrogen TRUE, 86–94
  mass as inertia from spin, 88–89
  mass via colliders, 74–75
  quantum equivalence units, 74–114
  quarks constituting, 61
  triadic nature of reality, 90–91
psi. *See* psychic (psi) phenomena
PSI-Q mass studies, 240
psyche. *See* mind
Psychelementarity Theory, 154–58
psychiatry
  dissociative identity disorder, 282
  EEG inventor, 271
  focus on neurons and neurotransmitters, 246–47
  Freud's belief in telepathy, 251
  intuition and psychotherapy minimized, 250
  skepticism about anomalous experiences, 244–46

synchronicity studies, 351
psychic (psi) phenomena
   angular gyrus in brain, 289–90
   anomalous experiences. *See* anomalous experiences
   brain as filter and psi abilities, 184, 260
   consciousness permeating world, 38
   electromagnetic nature of psi, 225–28, 229–30, 270, 273
   ESP. *See* ESP
   evidence of, 50, 146–48
   identifying viewers via psychological profiles, 240–42
   magnetite lining of skulls and, 275
   mind and physical world interconnection, 156
   parapsychology, 28, 225, 383
   perennial philosophy, 30–32
   personal experiences, 27–29, 45, 136–38, 207–14, 245, 258, 387
   pineal gland and, 276
   popular culture knowing before scientists, 194
   psi (Ψ) symbol, 28
   psychic reading of psychiatrist, 245
   readings by Edgar Cayce, 212–15
   scientific acceptance of, 250–53
   scientific method to study, 383, 384
   scientific worldview, 29–30
   sheep-goat effect in research, 282
   space and time not constraining, 146–48
   telepathy. *See* telepathy
psychokinesis (PK), 146, 147–48
psychological profile of remote viewers, 240–42
Puthoff, Hal, 228
Pythagorean Theorem, 77–78
   Pythagorean triples, 77
qualia of subjective experience, 34, 105–7, 121, 125
quantum mechanics (QM)
   about, 98, 260
   anomalous experiences supported, 252
   biological quantum effects, 261
   brain quantum processing, 260–65
   Conscious Universe, 121–27
   Copenhagen Interpretation, 53, 108
   corporate world and, 130–31
   double-slit experiment. *See* double-slit experiment
   formulation of, 53
   Laws behind the Laws, 102–7
   locality vs. action at a distance, 30
   materialist assumptions refuted, 141
   mathematics of, 59–62
   observer shaping, 54–56, 95, 99, 141, 252, 283, 366
   paradigm shift, 143
   Quantum Calculus with consciousness. *See* Calculus of Dimensional Distinctions
   quantum equivalence unit basis, 64–68
   quantum equivalence unit derivation, 68–74
   quantum equivalence units of elementary particles, 74–114
   quantum neuroscience, 260–65
   Quantum Synchronicity Theory, 367
   realism incompatible with, 32
   relationships and, 131–33
   relativity and, 51–56, 89–90, 91–92
   subconscious as parallel concept, 32–34
   Triadic Dimensional Distinction Vortical Paradigm, 91–92
   Triadic Rotational Units of Equivalence, 85–86
   world reflects conscious activity, 298
   Zeno effect on radioactive decay, 283, 284
quarks
   gluons and, 61
   masses via colliders, 74–75
   masses via geometry of particles, 88–89
   neutron constituents, 84
   proton constituents, 61
   quantum equivalence units, 74–114
   triadic nature of reality, 90–91

Triadic Rotational Units of
Equivalence, 85–86
Radin, Dean
Conscious Universe, The, 28
Entangled Minds, 28
Real Magic, 27, 28
remote focus same as direct
observation, 283
Supernormal, 28
Ramon y Cajal, Santiago, 246
random number generators, 147–48,
241, 283, 366
randomness fallacy in
supersynchronicity, 363–67
Quantum Synchronicity Theory,
367
raven synchronicities, 286–87
Real Magic (Radin), 27, 28
reality
consciousness fundamental, 32–
34, 51, 121, 127
holograms and reality
construction, 276–80
idealism, 31–32
inside-mind vs. outside-matter,
34–37
intentioned consciousness, 240,
283
large scales of, 107–9
materialist science failures, 140–
42
mental and physical world
interconnection, 156
merging with Ultimate Reality
experience, 138
observer shaping, 54–56, 95, 99,
141, 252, 283, 366
One-Mind perspective, 306–7
realism incompatible with
quantum theory, 32
reality as information, 35–39, 243
scientific worldview of, 29, 30
symbolic reality, 36, 37–42
Total Materialism totally
explaining, 381
triadic nature of, 90–91
unconscious shaping of, 248
unification of consciousness and.
See unification of
consciousness and reality

Reality Begins with Consciousness
(Neppe and Close), 49
recursion
about, 104
Conscious Universe, 121–27
corporate world and quantum
mechanics, 130–31
relationships and quantum
mechanics, 131–33
universal guiding Law, 119–21
reductionism
cosmology and, 109
reductive materialism, 27
reductive mathematics, 60–62
scientific dogma, 140–42
scientific worldview, 29, 31–32,
41, 58–60
reflexology as holographic
information, 277
reincarnation
evidence, 14, 150–51
readings of Edgar Cayce, 212–16
Thomas Jefferson, 211–14
relationships and quantum
mechanics, 131–33
relativity and quantum physics, 51–
56, 89–90
Triadic Dimensional Distinction
Vortical Paradigm, 91–92
religion defined, 381
remote viewing
archaeology sites, 227–40
archaeology sites, Alexandria
Project, 231–40
Deep Quest, 229–30
deep sea shielding of psi, 226,
227–30
grid experiment, 224
identifying viewers via
psychological profiles, 240–42
numinous sites increase success,
239, 242
participating viewers, 239
Stanford Research Institute
literature, 245
research. *See* scientific validity, *See*
evidence
Return to Life (Tucker), 14
Rhine, J. B., 45, 227, 384

Rhine-Swanton Parapsychology and Anthropology Seminar, 227
Rickover, Hyman, 226
Rilke, Rainer Maria (*Letters to a Young Poet*), 297
Ritchie, George (*Ordered to Return*), 225
rituals
  protocols of empirical science, 216, 228
  water associated with, 240
Rolling Thunder, 219–23
Roots of Coincidence, The (Koestler), 250–51
Rosen, Nathan, 53–54, 61, 117
Ross, Terry, 239
Ruskin, John, 315
Russek, Linda G. S. (*Living Energy Universe*), 333
Rutherford, Ernest, 58
Sacks, Milton, 292–93, 294
Sacks, Oliver, 258
Sacred Promise, The (G. E. Schwartz), 15, 18
Sagan, Carl, 3, 23
savant syndrome, 258–60
  holograms and reality construction, 276–80, 288
  materialism failing with, 246, 260
  nonlocal information of, 265–68
  trauma and, 259–60, 275
Schrödinger, Erwin
  consciousness fundamental, 136, 326
  one mind, 305
  qualia not material, 105
  science pretends to answer, 322
Schulberg, Bud, 209
Schwartz, Gary E.
  Afterlife Experiments, The, 15
  Atheist in Heaven, An, 14, 15
  G.O.D. Experiments, The, 333
  Greater Reality Living, 333
  Life After Death Project, The, 357
  Living Energy Universe, The, 333
  raven synchronicities, 287
  researcher, 152
  Sacred Promise, The, 15, 18
  Super Synchronicity, 333, 339, 344, 351
  Truth About Medium, The, 15

Schwartz, Stephan A.
  Alexandria Project, The, 238
  Opening to the Infinite, 324
  Secret Vaults of Time, The, 228
Schwarz, Berthold E., 315
Schweitzer, Albert, 326
science of Consciousness
  constants not constant, 114–16
  cosmology, 107–9
  cosmology constraints, 109–13
  introduction, 97–102
  Laws behind the Laws, 102–7
  light connecting everything in universe, 114–16
  Living the Living Presence, 126–30
  mathematics as bridge, 121–27
  micro- and macroscopic ratios, 112–16
  mind befriended for awareness, 129–30
  non-local universe, 116–19, 120
  objectivity in science, 105
  ontologic framework of Consciousness, 104
  paradigm bridging science and spirituality, 133–34
  qualia of subjective experience, 105–7
  quantum mechanics and corporate world, 130–31
  quantum mechanics and relationships, 131–33
  recursion, 104, 119–21
  spirituality and science converging, 127–28, 383, 384
  time deriving from consciousness, 114–16
  universal diagrams and recursion, 119–21
scientific materialism. *See* materialist science
scientific method, 377
  applied to religion and spirituality, 383, 384
scientific validity
  beliefs changed, 1–3, 4–5, 160–63, 178, 189, 244–45, 350–52
  Consciousness as science. *See* science of Consciousness
  convergence of information, 3–5

Decline Effect in accessing nonlocal consciousness, 217
essential science, 375–77
evidence interpretation, 2–3
evidence scientific, 14–16, 195
FACT analysis. *See* five additive criteria test
gimmel as atomic-level consciousness, 94–96
hard truth as heart of, 3
healing with intentions, 309–14
hierarchies of knowledge, 34–42
intentionality effects on physiology, 280, 298
laboratory versus observation science, 337–38, 353
meditation research, 164–67
Mobius Consensus Protocol, 217
nature as frugal and resourceful, 247
nonlocal communication, 309–22
objectivity in science, 105
observation science. *See* observation science
ostrich vs. eagle science, 8–9
paradigmatic science, 377, 390
paradigms can and should change, 142–44, 378, 390
psi phenomena scientifically accepted, 250–53
reason and theory, 9–16
reductionism, 29, 31–32, 411, 58–60
reductive mathematics, 60–62
research design, 216–28
research environment important, 318
scientific worldview, 29–30
scientism, 378, 390
sheep-goat effect in psi research, 282
skepticism required, 22–24
spirituality of consciousness study, 332–34
supersynchronicity, 353–68
wholeness lacking, 322–27, 329–30
scientism, 378, 390
sea squirt reabsorbing brain, 268
Searle, John R., 329

Secret Vaults of Time, The (S. A. Schwartz), 228
Serrell, Orlando, 259
Seven S people, 16–18, 368–69
Severn, Arthur, 315
shamanism
  healing ritual, 219–23
  lightning strike initiation, 260
  rituals as protocols of empirical science, 216, 228
Sheldrake, Rupert, 268
Shelley, Percy Bysshe ("Adonais"), 323
Sherman, Harold (*Thoughts Through Space*), 217
Shermer, Michael, 4
Siefe, Charles (*Decoding the Universe*), 39
signs and symbols as communication, 334–37
silicon photomultiplier system, 18–22
Sinclair, Upton (*Mental Radio*), 217
skepticism
  Seven S people, 17, 368
  five additive criteria test (FACT), 4–5, 22–24, 370–73
  trained into psychiatrists, 244
Sleeping Prophet, The (Stern), 214, 218
Smith, Susy, 218
Sobleski, Barbara, 239
Society for Anthropology of Consciousness, 227
Society for Psychical Research (SPR), 383
Sperry, Roger W., 328
spirit communication
  direct personal experience of, 18–22
  technology for, 15, 18–22
spirituality
  consciousness science, 332–34
  essential spirituality, 379–80, 391
  personal scientific focus, 383
  religion defined, 381
  science converging with, 127–28, 383, 384
Spirit, 378
Spirituality and Human Nature (Evans), 324

Spirituality in Clinical Practice journal, 351
Stapp, Henry P., 102, 103, 189
"States of consciousness and state-specific sciences" (Tart), 226
Stek, Robert, 21
Stern, Jess (*The Sleeping Prophet*), 214, 218
Stevenson, Ian
  reincarnation research, 14, 150, 225
  telesomatic events, 316
  Twenty Cases Suggestive of Reincarnation, 225
Stokes, Douglas, 315
Structure of Scientific Revolutions, The (Kuhn), 142–43, 377
subconscious manifesting consciousness, 32–34
subjective experience
  Conscious Universe, 121–27
  object-subject separation, 106, 124
  placebo effect, 145
  qualia as, 34, 105–7, 121, 125
  synchronicity ever-present, 331, 367, 370
submarine test of psi shielding, 226–27, 229–30
Sugrue, Thomas (*There a River*), 214
Super Synchronicity (G. E. Schwartz), 333, 339, 344, 351
Supernormal (Radin), 28
supersynchronicity science
  coincidence or higher power, 349–50
  coincidence science website, 339–46
  evidence for Universal Intelligent Consciousness, 334–37, 373–74
  explanations that are possible, 346–50, 351
  FACT analysis, 352–80
  FACT criterion 1: reason and scientific theory, 363–67
  FACT criterion 2: scientific evidence, 353–68
  FACT criterion 3: community of believers, 367–70
  FACT criterion 4: direct personal experience, 370
  FACT criterion 5: skepticism, 370–73
  giraffe-Paris pairs, 349, 354–68
  history, 338–39
  introduction to Universal Intelligence Consiousness, 331–34
  laboratory versus observation science, 337–38, 353
  number 11 coincidences, 345–48
  One Mind, 4
  personal experiences, 286–87, 344–50
  Quantum Synchronicity Theory, 367
  randomness fallacy, 363–67
  supersynchronicity definition, 339
  synchronicity categories, 338–39
  synchronicity definition, 338
  Type III postmaterialism evidence, 284–87
  Weird Coincidence Survey, 339–46
  word frequency analysis, 359–61
Swann, Ingo, 239
Swanton, John Reed, 227
symbolic reality, 36, 37–42
symbols as communication, 334–37
synchronicity
  categorization of, 338–39
  definition from Jung, 338
  giraffe-Paris pairs, 349, 354–68
  Guiding-Organizing-Designing Process, 212–14
  Jung quote as ever-present reality, 331, 367, 370
  personal experiences, 286–87, 344–50
  Quantum Synchronicity Theory, 367
  selection of reading by Edgar Cayce, 212–14
  supersynchronicities. *See* supersynchronicity science
  word frequency analysis, 359–61
synesthesia, 258
  seeing auras as, 289
Tammet, Daniel, 258
Targ, Russell, 228
Tart, Charles T.
  books by, 385, 388

"States of consciousness and state-specific sciences," 226
Total Materialism exercise, 392
Tegmark, Max (*Our Mathematical Universe*), 35–36, 37
telecebo effect, 298–300, 308
telepathy
    autistic savants, 265–68
    EEG inventor, 271
    electromagnetic nature of, 270, 273
    interplanetary communication, 197
    materialism challenged by, 146–47
    nonlocal communication. *See* nonlocal communication
    scientists' belief in, 251
telesomatic events, 308–9, 315–19
television receiver analogy for brain, 11–13, 157
temporo-parietal junction for space-time navigation, 289
terminal lucidity, 254
Tesla, Nikola, 43
Theise, Neil, 40
theory of mind and autism, 265–67
Theory of Psychelementarity (TOP), 154–58
Therapeutic Touch (TT), 309
There a River (Sugrue), 214
Thoreau, Henry David, 295
Thoughts Through Space (Wilkins and Sherman), 217
time
    deriving from consciousness, 114–16
    Eternity vs. Temporal Medicine, 303–5
    mental activity not constrained by, 146–48
    precognition and, 245
    time travel event manipulation, 198
"Tintern Abbey" (Wordsworth), 323
Tononi, Giulio, 38–39, 195
Total Materialism, 381
    effects on spiritual belief, 392
    evidence for perspective beyond, 384–85

Transcendent Mind (Baruss and Mossbridge), 39–40, 326
Transcendental Physics (Close), 49
transpersonal domain of consciousness, 186
transpersonal experiences, 378–80
trauma and savant syndrome, 259–60, 275
Treffert, Darold, 267
Triadic Dimensional Distinction Vortical Paradigm (TDVP), 91–92
Triadic Rotational Units of Equivalence (TRUE), 85–86
    Hydrogen atom, 86–94
    triadic nature of reality, 90–91
TRUE. *See* Triadic Rotational Units of Equivalence
Truth About Medium, The (G. E. Schwartz), 15
Tucker, James
    past life research, 150
    Return to Life, 14
    Twenty Cases Suggestive of Reincarnation (Stevenson), 225
Twin Telepathy (Playfair), 316–19
twins
    brain-to-brain connections, 313–14
    personal experience, 316
    person-to-person connections, 316–19
    research environment important, 318
    synchronicities, 285
unconscious shaping of reality, 248
unification of consciousness and reality
    background, 43–48
    Calculus of Dimensional Distinctions, 49, 62–63
    consciousness as fundamental, 51
    consciousness component, 85
    consciousness in Quantum Calculus, 63–64
    evidence for psychic (psi) phenomena, 50
    gimmel for unification, 89–90, 91–96
    Gödel's Incompleteness Theorem, 58

particle mass as inertia from spin, 88–89
particle mass via colliders, 74–75
quantum equivalence unit basis, 64–68
quantum equivalence unit derivation, 68–74
quantum equivalence units of elementary particles, 74–114
relativity and quantum mechanics, 51–56, 89–90
Standard Model mathematics, 60–62
Triadic Dimensional Distinction Vortical Paradigm, 91–92
triadic nature of reality, 90–91
Triadic Rotational Units of Equivalence, 85–94
Universal Intelligent Consciousness
beliefs changed, 350–52
coincidence or higher power, 349–50
evidence via serial coincidences, 334–37, 373–74
explanations for supersynchronicities, 346–48, 351
FACT analysis, 352–80
FACT criterion 1: reason and scientific theory, 363–67
FACT criterion 2: scientific evidence, 353–68
FACT criterion 3: community of believers, 367–70
FACT criterion 4: direct personal experience, 370
FACT criterion 5: skepticism, 370–73
introduction to, 332–34
Living Presence as, 332, 334, 351
questions to answer, 331–32
spirituality of, 332–34
Universal Coincidence Creator, 343
universality. *See* recursion
universe
cosmological constraints, 109–13
entirely mental, 32–34
light connecting everything, 114–16

micro- and macroscopic ratios, 112–14
nonlocal universe, 116–19, 120
ontologic framework of Consciousness, 104
participants in co-creating universe, 283
Pure Consciousness, 93
qualia science manifesting, 106
unbroken wholeness, 306–7
universal consciousness, 121–27
universal diagrams and recursion, 119–21
up-quarks. *See* quarks
Vaillancourt, Andre, 239
van Lommel, Pim, 14, 175
Varieties of Religious Experience (James), 217
Vasiliev, Leonard, 225
Vaughan, Alan, 239
Vedral, Vlatko (*Decoding Reality*), 39
ventricular system of brain, 275–76
Vincent van Gogh: A New Way of Seeing (movie), 362
visual blind spots in reality construction, 277
visualization to avoid amputation, 280
waking consciousness as consciousness, 248
Walker, Alice, 307
Walker, Sara, 37
Walsh, Don, 229
Waning of Materialism, The (Koons and Bealer), 41
Warcollier, R. (*Mind to Mind*), 217
Warhol, Andy, 209
Weird Coincidence Survey, 339–46
Wheeler, John
delayed-choice experiment, 55, 117–19
It From Bit or Bit From It?, 35
observer shaping phenomena, 99
participants in co-creating universe, 283
Whewell, William, 1, 4
Whole in One (Lorimer), 315
Why Materialism Is Baloney (Kastrup), 32
Wiener, Norbert, 45

Wigner, Eugene, 36, 328
Williamsburg spirit, 207–9
wine affected by consciousness, 224
Wittgenstein, Ludwig, 95
Woollacott, Marjorie
    giraffe-Paris pairing coincidence, 362–63
    Infinite Awareness, 159, 163, 178, 351
word frequency analysis, 359–61
Wordsworth, William ("Tintern Abbey"), 323
Yukteswar, Sri, 48
Zeilinger, Anton, 39
Zeno effect on radioactive decay, 283, 284

Made in the USA
Las Vegas, NV
22 February 2021